# Perspectives on Turkey's Multi-Regional Role in the 21st Century

# Perspectives on Turkey's Multi-Regional Role in the 21st Century

*Edited by*

Mujib Alam

KNOWLEDGE WORLD

KW Publishers Pvt Ltd
New Delhi

ISBN 978-93-83649-55-6

Published in India by Kalpana Shukla

KNOWLEDGE WORLD

KW Publishers Pvt Ltd
4676/21, First Floor, Ansari Road, Daryaganj, New Delhi 110002
Phone: +91 11 23263498/43528107
Email: knowledgeworld@vsnl.net • www.kwpub.com

2011 FPBA BEST PUBLISHERS AWARD (ENGLISH)

Printed and Bound in India

# Contents

# List of Abbreviation

| | |
|---|---|
| ACQ | Annual Contact Quantity |
| ACU | Asian Clearing Union |
| AIHRC | Afghanistan Independent Human Rights Commission |
| AKP | Justice and Development Party (*Adalet ve Kalkinma Partisi*) |
| ANA | Afghan National Army |
| ANCA | Armenian National Committee of America |
| ANP | Afghan National Police |
| ANSF | Afghan National Security Forces |
| BBP | Nationalist Great Union Party |
| BDP | *Barış ve Demokrasi Partisi* (Peace and Democracy Party) |
| BDP | Peace and Democratic Party |
| BMZ | Economic Cooperation and Development |
| BOTAS | Turkish State-Owned Petroleum Pipeline Corporation |
| BRICS | Brazil, Russia, India, China and South Africa |
| BRSA-BDDK | Turkish Central Bank and Banking Regulation and Supervision Agency |
| BTC | *Baku-Tbilisi-Ceyhan* |
| CARs | Central Asian Republics |
| CCP | Chinese Communist Party |
| CEEC | Central and Eastern European Countries |
| CENTO | Central Treaty Organisation |
| CHP | *Cumhuriyet Halk Partisi* (Republican People's Party) |
| CIDA | Canadian International Development Agency |
| CIS | Commonwealth of Independent States |

| | |
|---|---|
| CISADA | Comprehensive Iran Sanctions, Accountability, and Divestment Act |
| CLJ | Constitutional *Loya Jirga* |
| CSIS | Centre for Strategic and International Studies |
| CTP | Republican Turkish Party |
| DAC | Development Assistance Committee |
| DEIK | Turkish Foreign Economic Relation Board |
| DFID | Department of International Development |
| DP | Democratic Party |
| ECO | Economic Cooperation Organisation |
| ECOTA | Economic Cooperation Organisation Trade Agreement |
| EEC | European Economic Community |
| EOKA | *Ethniki Organosis Kyprion Agoniston* (National Organisation of Cypriot Fighters) |
| EU | European Union |
| FDI | Foreign Direct Investment |
| FEBA | Federation of Balkan American Associations |
| FRP | Free Republican Party |
| FSA | Free Syrian Army |
| G-20 | Group of Twenty |
| GDP | Gross Domestic Product |
| GTZ | Deutsche Gesellschaft fur Technische Zusammenarbeit |
| HSYK | Supreme Board Prosecutors and Judges |
| IAF | Israel Air Force |
| IARCSC | Independent Administrative Reform and Civil Service Commission |
| IDF | Israeli Defence Forces |
| IDP | Internally Displaced People |
| IEA | International Energy Agency |
| IMU | Islamic Movement of Uzbekistan |
| IOTGD | Turkish Association for Development and Trade with Iran and Middle East |
| IRGC | Iran's Revolutionary Guard Corps |
| ISAF | International Security Assistance Force |
| ISID | Iranian Industrialists' and Businesspersons' Association |

| | |
|---|---|
| ISIS | Islamic State of Iraq and al-Sham |
| IT | Information Technology |
| ITC | International Trade Centre |
| ITSTA | Iran–Turkey Strategic Trade Association |
| JEC | Joint Economic Commission |
| JICA | Japan International Cooperation Agency |
| KCK | Kurdish Communities' Union |
| KRG | Kurdish Regional Government |
| LDCs | Least Developed Countries |
| MHP | National Action Party |
| MHP | Nationalist Action Party |
| MoU | Memorandum of Understanding |
| MUSAID | Independent Industrialists' and Businesspersons' Association |
| NATO | North Atlantic Treaty Organization |
| NDAA | National Defence Authorization Act |
| NID | Nice Implementation Document |
| NSC | National Security Council |
| ODA | Official Development Assistance |
| OECD | Economic Cooperation and Development |
| OECD | Organisation for Economic Cooperation and Development |
| OIC | Organisation of the Islamic Conference |
| OIC-IRCICA | Research Centre for Islamic History, Art, and Culture |
| OXEN | Orthodox Christian Youth Association |
| PEON | Pancyprian Youth Organization (of Cyprus) |
| PKK | Kurdistan Workers' Party |
| PRT | Provincial Reconstruction Team |
| PTA | Preferential Trade Agreement |
| PYD | *Partiya Yekîtiya Demokrat* (Democratic Union Party) |
| RCD | Regional Cooperation for Development |
| RPP | Republican People's Party (*Cumhuriyet Halk Partisi*) |
| SAM | Surface-to-Air Missile |
| SCO | Shanghai Cooperation Organisation |
| SEDEF | Sarajevo Education Development Foundation |

| | |
|---|---|
| SNC | Syrian National Council |
| SPA | Strategic Partnership Agreement |
| SPO | State Planning Organisation (of Turkey) |
| SUV | Sports Utility Vehicle |
| TAV | Turkish–American Consortium |
| TFP | Turkish Foreign Policy |
| TIBC | Turkish–Iranian Business Council |
| TIKA | Turkish International Cooperation and Development Agency |
| T-LORAMIDS | Long-Range Air and Missile Defence System |
| TNC | Transitional National Council |
| TPAO | Turkish Petroleum Corporation |
| TRNC | Turkish Republic of Northern Cyprus |
| TSAFED | Turkish–Slovak Alliance for Education and Development |
| TUGAID | Turkish Young Businesspersons' Association |
| TUSKON | Confederation of Businessmen and Industrialists of Turkey |
| UAE | United Arab Emirates |
| UNAMA | United Nations Assistance Mission in Afghanistan |
| UNAOC | United Nations Alliance of Civilizations |
| UNDP | United Nations Development Programme |
| UNFICYP | United Nations Peacekeeping Force in Cyprus |
| UNIDO | United Nations Industrial Development Organization |
| UNIFIL | United Nations Interim Force in Lebanon |
| UNSC | United Nations Security Council |
| USAID | United States Agency for International Development |
| USD | United States Dollar |
| USSR | Union of Soviet Socialist Republics |
| WEU | Western European Union |
| WFP | World Food Programme |
| WHO | World Health organisation |

# Acknowledgements

I am grateful to all the contributors to this volume and to other scholars who first assembled to deliberate upon the theme during a two-day International Conference on the 'Perspectives on Turkey's Emerging Multi-regional Role,' and also painstakingly provided their views on the same on paper. I acknowledge the financial support of the Indian Council of Social Science Research (ICSSR) and Jamia Millia Islamia (JMI) in organising this Conference, without which this book would not have seen the light of the day. I also acknowledge the support of the administrative staff of the Academy of International Studies (AIS), JMI, who took care of all the logistical issues during the Conference, leaving me free to concentrate on the academic deliberations. I am indebted to a lot of friends, colleagues, teachers and students of mine who have provided support—whenever needed—in this effort. My wife and colleague, Sujata Ashwarya, has been a steady support in this endeavour, as has my daughter, Brinda, whose constant enquiries about the progress of this book, helped me to keep the schedules on track. I would be failing in my duty if I do not thank the members of my extended family for their constant encouragement to my work. Last but not the least, I am thankful to Mr Jose Mathew and Ms Kalpana Shukla of KW Publishers, for accepting the proposal for this book and going through the rigours of publishing.

# Contributors

---

**Arshi Khan** teaches Political Science and International Relations at Aligarh Muslim University. He completed his MPhil and PhD from Jawaharlal Nehru University, New Delhi. He has worked previously at the Centre for Federal Studies, New Delhi. He has published extensively on Turkey, West Asia and various international issues. He has edited the book, *Federalism, Democracy and Conflict Resolution* (New Delhi: Macmillan, 2012) and is accredited with 4 monographs, over 18 research articles in refereed and indexed national and international journals, over 33 comprehensive articles in the *Mainstream*, over 180 articles/analyses in *The Telegraph*, *The Pioneer*, *The Hindu*, *The Indian Express* and *Jordan Times* (Amman). His papers have been published in over 14 books edited in India and in over 14 books edited in USA, UK, Switzerland, Italy, Germany, Cyprus, Turkey, UAE and Iraq. He has presented over 16 papers in conferences in India and 17 papers abroad and has delivered over 90 lectures in India and over 15 lectures in Switzerland, UAE, Iraq, Thailand and Malaysia. He has visited Turkey under the Cultural Exchange Programme of the UGC, and the US as a short-term Fulbright Fellow. He has visited more than 20 countries.

**Nitish Kumar** is Assistant Professor, Department of Political Science, Kamala Nehru College, University of Delhi, New Delhi. He obtained his MA, MPhil and PhD degrees from the Jawaharlal Nehru University. He was conferred the Doctoral degree in the year 2012 on the topic of *Turkish Foreign Policy in West Asia, 1990-2006*. He has also been awarded the Junior Research Fellowship (JRF) of the University Grant Commission (UGC) and has contributed articles in books. His fields of specialisation are politics, international relations, comparative politics and West Asian studies. Dr. Kumar has also presented papers in national and international seminars.

**Özden Zeynep Oktav** is Professor at the Department of Political Science and International Relations, Yildiz Technical University. She obtained her MA and PhD degrees from Bosphorus University, Istanbul. She is the author of two books: *Basra Körfezinin Değişen Dinamikleri* (Changing Dynamics of the Persian Gulf) (Istanbul: Beta, 2011) and *Limits of Relations with the West: Turkey, Syria and Iran* (Istanbul: Beta, 2008). She has also written articles and chapters for a number of books. She is the editor of the book, *Turkey in the 21st Century: Quest for a New Turkish Foreign Policy* (Aldershot, Burlington: Ashgate, 2011). She was awarded the Government of Turkey, Council of Higher Education scholarship in 2011 and the Scientific and Technological Research Council of Turkey scholarship in 2013. She was a Visiting Researcher at the Cambridge University, UK and St. Andrews University, Scotland, UK in 2011 and 2013 respectively.

**Sujata Ashwarya Cheema** is Assistant Professor at the Centre for West Asian Studies, Jamia Millia Islamia, New Delhi. She studied for an honours degree in Political Science at the Lady Shri Ram College in Delhi University. She then did an MA in International Politics at the School of International Studies in the Jawaharlal Nehru University, New Delhi, and later received MPhil and PhD degrees from the same university. She was awarded the Government of Israel Graduate Fellowship and Visiting Research Fellowship to do research at the Rothberg International School, Hebrew University of Jerusalem, Israel. She was also awarded the Hermes Post-Doctoral Fellowship at Maison des Sciences de l'Homme (MSH) and Centre d'Etudes et des Recherches Internationales (CERI), Paris. She was a Visiting Fellow at the MSH under the Indo-French Cultural Exchange Programme and a Visiting Researcher at the Faculty of World Studies, University of Tehran. Her research interests include India's West Asia policy, politics and foreign policy of Iran, Iraq and Israel, and issues relating to democratisation in the region. She is the author of numerous research articles and book chapters. Her books, *Civil*

*Society, Democracy and State in West Asia* (edited) and *Essays on Iran and Israel: An Indian Perspective*, were published in 2010 and 2014 respectively.

**Anita Sengupta** is Fellow at the Maulana Abul Kalam Azad Institute of Asian Studies (MAKAIAS), Kolkata, India. She is an area studies specialist and her work has focused on the Eurasian region with Uzbekistan being her area of special interest. She has also worked extensively on Turkish politics. Her book *Heartlands of Eurasia: The Geopolitics of Political Space* published in 2009 (Lanham, Boulder, New York, Toronto, Oxford: Lexington Books) was selected by the Oxford Bibliographies Online in 2011 as a must-read on the section *Geopolitics and Geostrategy*. She is also the author of *Russia, China and Multilateralism in Central Asia* (New Delhi: Shipra Publications, 2005); *The Formation of the Uzbek Nation-State: A Study in Transition* (Lanham, Boulder, New York, Toronto, Oxford: Lexington Books, 2003) and *Frontiers into Borders: The Transformation of Identities in Central Asia* (Delhi and London: Hope India Publications and Greenwich Millennium Press Ltd, 2002). She has also edited a number of volumes on Eurasian politics. Her latest publication is *Myth and Rhetoric of the Turkish Model: Exploring Developmental Alternatives* (New Delhi, Heidelberg, New York, Dordrecht, London: Springer 2014).

**Priya Singh** is a Fellow at the Maulana Abul Kalam Azad Institute of Asian Studies, Kolkata, India. Her area of interest and specialisation is West Asia/Middle East in general and Israel in particular. Her research areas include the Arab–Israeli conflict, Israeli society and politics, comparative ethnic relations in the region, nationalism and post-nationalism and comparative politics and democracy. She has authored, edited and co-edited publications on Israel and the Middle East. She is currently working on a project entitled *Expressions of Resistance: the Language of the Arab Spring.* She can be contacted at priyasingh70@gmail.com

**Davood Kiani** is Assistant Professor at the Islamic Azad University (Qom Branch), Iran. He obtained PhD in International Relations from the Faculty of Law and Political Science, Islamic Azad University. His areas of interest include foreign aspects of Iran, Russia and the European Union. He has several publications including research articles, books, etc. to his credit. His publications include *National Interest of the Islamic Republic of Iran* (edited) (Tehran: 2007), *Politics, Identity and Security in European Union*, co-edited (Tehran: 2010) and *Islamism in the West following 11 Sep. 2001* (Tehran: 2013).

**Emirhan Göral** is an Assistant Professor at the Department of EU Politics and International Relations, EU Institute, the Marmara University, Istanbul, Turkey. He received his BA degree in Political Science and International Relations from the Marmara University and his MA and PhD degrees from its EU Institute. In 2006, he joined the EU Institute as a research assistant and in 2012 he became a lecturer. His current research interests include the political system of the EU, the international political system and energy security. He currently works as vice-director in the EU Institute at Marmara University and is the vice-editor of the Marmara Journal of European Studies as well as the Journal of Turkish-German Studies published by the same University.

**Indrani Talukdar** is a Research Fellow at the Indian Council of World Affairs (ICWA), New Delhi. She obtained her Doctoral degree from the Jawaharlal Nehru University, New Delhi. She has worked as a Research Associate in the Center for Air Power Studies, New Delhi. Her areas of interest include international relation studies, security studies, conflict resolution and peace studies along with area studies with a specialisation in Turkey, Russia, Cyprus and the European Union.

**Gabriel Pirický** is a Senior Research Fellow at the Institute of Oriental Studies of the Slovak Academy of Sciences and lecturer at the Faculty of Philosophy of the Comenius University in Bratislava, Slovakia. After graduating from Charles University, Prague and the School of Oriental and African Studies at the University of London, his main fields of activity included Islamic, Turkish and Arabic studies, with special emphasis on Islam, nationalism and secularism in modern Turkey. He has published and lectured extensively at various universities both in Slovakia and the Czech Republic. His monographs include *Turkey: A Short History* (2006, in Czech) and *Islam in Turkey* (2004, in Slovak). Gabriel Pirický is also the Chairman of the Slovak Oriental Society.

**Zeynep Didem Akinoğlu** is a Research Scholar at the Centre for West Asian Studies, School of International Studies, Jawaharlal Nehru University, New Delhi. After completing her BA programme from the Department of International Relations, Gazi University, Ankara, Turkey (2007–2011), she was granted the ICCR Scholarship within the framework of the Indo-Turkish Cultural Exchange Programme and joined the MA in Politics at the School of International Studies (SIS), JNU (2011–2013). Recently, she participated in the "International Conference on Changing Contours of Indo-US Relations: Perceptions, Continuity& Change" ( October 31–November 2, 2014) at BITS Pilani, Goa and the First West Asian Studies National Convention (November 12–14, 2014) at Centre for West Asian Studies, SIS, JNU, New Delhi. Her research interests include Turkish foreign policy, Turkey–South Asia relations and foreign policy of India.

**Mahesh Ranjan Debata** is currently working as an Assistant Professor in the Centre for Inner Asian Studies, School of International Studies, Jawaharlal Nehru University, New Delhi, India. His main research interests include studies on China's Xinjiang region, Chinese neighbourhood policies and Chinese nationality policies, Silk Road studies and Central Asia. Dr. Mahesh has done his PhD in Xinjiang Studies. Dr. Debata is the author of a book *China's Minorities: Ethnic-Religious Separatism in Xinjiang*, besides two dozens of scholarly papers published at national and international levels. He is a member of the Editorial Board of a prestigious journal *International Journal of Business Anthropology*. He was awarded with the Distinguished Speaker Award by the Advanced Forum of Applied Anthropology, Jishou University, 2013. He has travelled extensively in USA, China, Central Asia, Turkey and Europe in connection with his research work.

**Mohammad Monir Alam** is former Director, Department of Strategic and Regional Studies, University of Jammu, Jammu and Kashmir, India. After completing his Doctorate from the School of International Studies, Jawaharlal Nehru University, New Delhi, he served as a Fellow at the Maulana Azad Institute of Asian Studies, Kolkata. After joining the University of Jammu in 2002, he has been actively engaged in teaching and research. Besides co-editing a book *Central Asia: Present Challenges and Future Prospects,* he has authored four books namely—*Russia and Tajikistan: Political and Security Relationship; Pakistan-Occupied Kashmir: Constitutional Status and Political Reality; Revival of the Silk Route: Growing Role of India; Pakistan-Occupied Kashmir: Internal Dynamics and Externalities* and one monograph as the Brig. Rajinder Singh Paper on "Origin, Evolution and Development of Security Studies". The author has published many research papers in journals and books of national and international repute on diverse themes like geopolitics of Central Asia, Iran, Afghanistan, Pakistan-Occupied Kashmir, strategic and security Studies and India's energy security. He is also the editor of a bi-annual international refereed journal *Security and Society* as well as *ACROSS LOC,* a quarterly digest on developments in Pakistan-Occupied Kashmir.

**Md. Rahat Hasan** is working as a Guest Teacher in the Department of Political Science at the Aligarh Muslim University (AMU), Aligarh, UP (India). He obtained his BA, MA, and PhD degrees in Political Science from the AMU. The topic of his Doctorial thesis was "American Think Tanks' Formulation of US Foreign Policy since World War II" which was financially assisted by the ICSSR (2006–07) and UGC (2007–08). He has also cleared UGC National Eligibility Test (NET) for Lectureship. Prior to joining the AMU, he worked as a Research Associate at the Academy of International Studies, Jamia Millia Islamia, New Delhi and completed a one-year internship at the Lok Sabha Secretariat, Parliament of India. His main areas of research interest include politics and security of South Asia; US foreign policy towards South Asia with focus on India, Afghanistan and Pakistan; Indo-US strategic partnership in South Asia; India and South Asia. He has contributed a number of research papers on the abovementiond themes in international and national academic journals like the *India Quarterly*, *South Asian Diplomacy* and the *Indian Journal of Public Administration*. He also regularly presents papers at national and international conferences/seminars.

**Ahmed Raza** is a Research Scholar at the Academy of International Studies, Jamia Millia Islamia, New Delhi. He has worked previously as a Project Coordinator during 2011–12 for the Qatar Unified Imaging Project (QUIP), funded by the Qatar Foundation. He has also worked as Visiting Faculty (Political Science) at the Department of Islamic Studies, Hamdard University, New Delhi. His research work focuses on public administration in India and Turkey, public policy, foreign policy, Arab politics, etc. He has a number of published works in reputed journals to his credit. He has also presented numerous research papers at national and international conferences.

# Introduction

*Mujib Alam*

During the past nine decades of its republican history, Turkey has undergone several phases of striking transformations either on the domestic front and/or in its external sphere. The contemporary world is witnessing the impact of one such transformation in Turkey that has taken place simultaneously in the country's internal as well as external realms. With the start of the twenty-first century, several phenomenal changes have occurred in different aspects of the Turkish state and society. Especially, Turkey's economic rise has led to its rising ambition and assertion for a more significant role in international affairs. These transformations, particularly those having ramifications on Turkey's external environment, began a decade ago when the present ruling party, *Adalet ve Kalkınma Partisi* (AKP) or the Justice and Development Party (JDP), came to power in late 2002—and which has been at the helm of affairs since then—began reorienting the country's foreign policy in line with the concept of 'Strategic Depth'.[1] The concept as well as the 'new' foreign policy direction have been envisaged by Ahmet Davutoğlu, the current Prime Minister of the country, who served as chief advisor (2002–2009) to the then PM and present President Recep Tayyip Erdoğan and later as Foreign Minister during the period between 2009 and 2014.

As envisioned by Davutoğlu, the AKP projected Turkey as a 'central' country in its foreign policy domain on the basis of the strength deriving from the country's geography, history and identity.[2] The new foreign policy thinking discarded the labels attached earlier to Turkey such as being a "flank country (of NATO)" during the heydays of the Cold War or a "bridge country" between West Asia/Muslim world and the Western world. As part of the concept of 'strategic depth,' Turkey attempted to follow a policy of 'zero problems with neighbours' and this policy was very successful until recently when it was upset by the developments mainly in Syria, its southern neighbourhood. Following this principle, Turkey under the AKP developed close relations with almost all its neighbouring countries during the first decade of the present century.

Another key principle of the doctrine has been the emphasis on multidimensionality in foreign policy. Accordingly, the AKP government diversified Turkey's foreign relations and endeavoured to reach out to other regions, which had not been important to the country previously. Besides the West Asian region, Turkey's policy became active in Central Asia, the Caucasus, southern Mediterranean and the Balkans.[3] It has also shown a noticeable interest in Africa, Latin America and other parts of Asia—particularly South Asia and Southeast Asia, in forging and developing relations in economic, political, strategic and cultural fields. The AKP's foreign policy activism particularly in the West Asian and Balkan regions was dubbed by many as "Neo-Ottomanism"—by hinting at Turkey's growing attraction and emphasis on developing close relations with the Muslim countries of the former Ottoman territories. However, many scholars, including this author, refute this tag for Turkey's activism and assertive role because of the fact that during this period Turkey developed close relations with almost all the neighbouring countries. Due to the multidimensional policy of AKP, many in the West even put question marks on Turkey's Western/European-oriented foreign policy approach and pointed towards the country's "axis-shift" or deviation from the previously followed foreign policy. However, according to the decision-makers at Ankara, Turkey's 'new' engagements with West Asia and other non-Western areas are not in contravention to its traditional policy; rather, it is complementary to its ties with the West.[4] It is to be noted here that the focus on foreign policy diversification was not a novel scheme of the AKP; rather, it had been emphasised by several preceding governments during the post-Cold War period.

Apart from the above two principles, the AKP's foreign policy emphasised Turkey's active diplomacy and mediation role in various regional and global conflicts. During the first decade of the twenty-first century, Turkey actively undertook several such initiatives. The 'Strategic Depth' concept of the AKP also downplayed the primacy of hard power and took initiatives for the de-securitisation of Turkey's foreign policy. The AKP's foreign policy orientation was to project the country's soft power and rely on economic engagements in bilateral and multilateral relations. In my opinion, because of these transformations in the foreign policy front, Turkey has emerged as a regional player or rather a multi-regional player having clout in West Asia, Central Asia, the Caucasus, southern Mediterranean, the Balkans, Asia, Africa and Latin America. Moreover, Turkey is vying to play an important role in conflict resolution in some of these regions. It has been aiming to play an important role in almost all political and economic issues at the regional and global levels and its role is visible in many of these areas.

We can enumerate several developments at the international/regional and domestic levels that have provided a context to the transformation in the twenty-first century Turkey in general and in the country's external realm in particular.[5] By the beginning of the 2000s, Turkey's regional security environment continued to be the same one it had inherited a decade ago with the end of the Cold War. The aftermath of the 9/11 incident and the subsequent "War on Terror" and the increasing overemphasis on the "clash of civilisations" thesis, complicated the state of affairs at the international level. Turkey being a Muslim-majority country and having close ties with the West was well-placed in refuting this discourse. Hence, Turkey's attempts under the AKP rule to invoke the discourse of an "alliance of civilisation" instead of a clash should be seen in this context.[6] Turkey's participation in the NATO-led ISAF security mission and reconstruction efforts in Afghanistan provided an opportunity for the AKP government to amplify the country's importance in the regional and global affairs. Besides, in the post-Helsinki summit (1999) decision, the EU factor became an enabler and prime motivation for a number of reforms at the domestic level; particularly, in the early years of the first decade.

Several factors at the domestic level can also be cited which led to the transformations in the twenty-first century Turkey. First, the AKP's ascendance to power with an overwhelming majority ended the spree of political instability caused by the coalition governments of the preceding decade and brought much needed political stability to the country. The

AKP government thus became a vehicle for political and economic reforms. Secondly, the role of the military in politics or for that matter in the country's foreign policy was drastically curtailed which in turn led to the desecuritisation of the Turkish foreign policy in the current century.[7] This was a clear departure from the decades of a securitised foreign policy. Thirdly, a newly emerging class of small and medium-ranked entrepreneurs and businessmen, the so-called "Anatolian Tigers"—who are equally interested in expanding Turkey's relations with the countries of Asia, Africa, Latin America along with Europe and other Western countries—have made major contributions in transforming Turkey into a leading "trading state" in the region and beyond from a state that was hitherto oriented towards the West.[8] Turkey's growth has been consistent during the past decade and its GDP has tripled during the same period. The country is currently the world's seventeenth[th] largest economy and one of the fastest-growing economies in the world for which it has been categorised as "New Tiger" of the global economy. Fourthly, the AKP's championing of a 'conservative democracy' and its revamped ideology backed by maverick leaders such as Erdoğan, Davutoğlu and others became attractive for a vast majority of the Turkish population. As a corollary to the political and economic reforms, Turkey has embarked upon a fast-paced liberalisation which in turn has led to an immense macro-economic performance in the country. Hence, several reforms undertaken domestically during the past decade, have become catalysts for the growing clout of Turkey at the external front.

However, it is not suggested here that everything has been buoyant for Turkey all these years. The occurrences of democratic Arab uprisings, popularly known as the Arab Spring, in Turkey's vicinity and its supposed areas of (growing) influence, though initially provided leverage to it in many aspects, of late has caused the country several challenges.[9] The 'Turkish Model' which was considered to be attractive to the West Asian countries in the early years of the AKP rule, seems to have lost its charm in the post-Spring period. Lately, the validity of AKP's policy of 'zero problems with neighbours' has also come under question. The most recent and grievous challenges to Turkey's foreign policy relates to the situation that emanated in its next-door Syria due to the ongoing civil war and also due to the emergence of the so-called 'Islamic State' in some parts of Syrian and Iraqi territories.

The contributors to this volume have analysed the different aspects of Turkey's foreign policy towards the neighbouring regions and beyond. The chapter writers have offered their own perspectives, while examining the implications of Turkey's changing foreign policy behaviour at political, strategic and economic spheres, and its bilateral and multilateral relations with several players as well as its role in various international organisations.

The present volume is the outcome of a two-day International Conference, bearing the same title as this volume, which was convened by the editor of this book under the auspices of the Academy of International Studies, Jamia Millia Islamia, New Delhi. The Conference was held on November 21–22, 2013, and was sponsored by the Indian Council of Social Science Research (ICSSR) and the University. The contributors to this volume are scholars having expertise in different disciplines and area studies. By bringing together scholars to deliberate and offer their perspectives on Turkey's foreign policy, this volume aims to understand the various aspects of Turkey's multi-regional role in the contemporary period.

## Organisation of the Volume

In Chapter 1, Arshi Khan discusses the domestic transformations of Turkey and also their reflections on the external interactions of the country by providing a trajectory of developments from the Ottoman Empire to the contemporary period. He compares and analyses the political and socio-economic initiatives and imperatives to understand the nature of the state and society of the Ottoman Empire as well as of the Turkish Republic. He underlines that Turkey under the AKP has entered into a new phase of politics mainly driven by people's power. He further argues that the AKP has succeeded in proving its credibility as a strong supporter of democracy, freedom, security, human rights and economic freedom. The AKP's policies have propelled the country on a rapid growth track among the emerging economies. Khan identifies some examples of the AKP's achievements during its decade-long rule such as its attempt at a full membership of the EU, its emergence as a peace actor in the West Asian region and a friendly partner in the Mediterranean, Aegean and the Caspian Seas as well as its support of peace projects in Afghanistan and North Africa.

In Chapter 2, Nurullah Ardıç analyses the conceptual framework of the AKP's foreign policy by highlighting the discourse of the 'alliance of civilisation'. He argues that the AKP's general foreign policy approach has been based, at least partly, on a civilisational discourse as manifested in the speeches of Turkey's 'new' political elites. He accentuates that this discourse consists of three main layers or concentric circles—national, regional and universal—which respectively invoke the Turkish history and culture (national), Islamic history and Middle Eastern geography (regional) and the destiny of the entire humanity (universal). He argues that the AKP's discourse of "alliance/dialogue/meeting of civilisations" might be better understood if located within the universal layer. He enumerates several factors that have contributed to the crystallisation of the civilisational discourse and its use in Turkey's foreign policy during the AKP rule. The scholar further asserts that the civilisational discourse is a useful tool for the AKP government for expanding its foreign policy options in order to become a "central country/power" and play a diplomatic role in different regions simultaneously.

In Chapter 3, Nitish Kumar examines the "Strategic Depth Doctrine" which has broadly guided Turkey's foreign policy during the AKP rule and the scholar tests the applicability of this concept in the West Asian region. He identifies the two main factors which motivated the AKP to pursue this doctrine: (i) Turkey's sudden economic rise (ii) the country's disenchantment with the EU membership pursuit. He highlights the relative success of this doctrine, particularly the 'zero-problem policy with neighbours', which was successfully and smoothly pursued till the Arab Spring phenomenon appeared in the region. On the basis of the Strategic Depth doctrine, Turkey developed good relations with almost all the neighbours and tried to play an active mediatory role in many inter-state conflicts in the region. Even during the early phase of the Arab Spring, the AKP could reap benefits by pursuing this doctrine. However, as Kumar points out, with the escalation of crisis in Syria, there appeared several deficiencies in the implementation of this doctrine. The Syrian crisis has hugely overshadowed the AKP's foreign policy activism of the initial years and put several question marks on at least two of the important components of the doctrine i.e. 'zero-problem with neighbours' and 'balance between security and freedom'. He concludes by saying that though Turkey's standing and influence in the region have increased over the years, it would encounter numerous challenges in the post-crisis regional order with most having a sectarian flavour. Kumar further concludes that a pragmatic calculation rather than any ideological conviction should be the guiding principle for the foreign policy makers in Ankara.

In Chapter 4, Ozden Zeynep Oktav examines Turkey's relationship with two of its important West Asian neighbours—Syria and Iran—during the AKP period and the changing nature of these relationships in the context of the Syrian crisis. She underlines the transformation process and the foreign policy activism that Turkey has witnessed post-9/11, and, especially during the current century. Turkey transformed itself from a "frontier", "pivot", "bridge" country into a "central" country. Quoting Fontain and Kliman,[10] the author underscores Turkey's growing alleviation as a "global-swing state" and its growing influence in the regional and international order. Turkey's activism on issues important for the global order has mainly been intended to bring stability and peace to the Middle Eastern region. She characterises the changing nature of Turkey's relations with Syria as strategic where the former had been playing an active role on the principle of 'zero-problems with neighbours'.

In Chapter 5, Sujata Ashwarya Cheema discusses Turkey's relations with Iran with an emphasis the trade and economic aspects since the year the AKP came to power in 2002. After providing an incisive overview of the Turkey–Iran relations, she highlights the fact that over the last decade, their economic relations have grown exponentially and she attributes this to their mutually complementary interests. One important reason among others, she underlines, has been Turkey's foreign policy reorientation and emphasis on better relations with neighbours. Expansion of trade links with Iran as well as the Arab states became one of the many significant outcomes of this policy shift. Cheema enumerates several geopolitical developments that have brought the two countries closer, and serve as the main driving force: (i) Turkey's refusal to support the US invasion of Iraq in 2003 (ii) its willingness to re-evaluate its close relationship with Israel that had continued since the early 1990s and (iii) its agreement with Iraq to preserve the latter's integrity especially with respect to the Kurdish separatist movement. As highlighted by the scholar, the energy sector is the strongest as far as Turkey's trade with Iran is concerned; as the former is substantially dependent on the latter for its energy imports. In addition, Iran's international isolation due to sanctions has deepened economic engagements between the two countries. Despite the prevalence of positive trends in the Turkey–Iran trade relations, the economic relations have not been immune from issues arising out of sanctions and developments in the region. The AKP's tough balancing act between the US and Iran has been testing the Turkish government's resolve for conducting a multi-pronged foreign policy. Cheema asserts that despite the external challenges posed by Western sanctions, Turkey and Iran are likely to continue their economic cooperation in the future.

In Chapter 6, Anita Sengupta puts into perspective the debate whether Turkey could be a 'model' for those countries that have embraced democracy post-Arab Spring. She argues that the projection of the Turkish model as an alternative in the West Asia and North Africa (WANA) region in the wake of the Arab Uprisings has made the debate relevant both from the historical and contemporary perspectives. Sengupta further emphasises that there are at least two divergent shades of the Turkish model which are on display in the region; the model epitomised by the AKP, rather than the traditional classical model based on state modernisation led by secular elites, has caught the imagination of large segments of the Arab society. The AKP's ability to strike a balance between Islam and Western democracy could be projected as a potential model for the Arab societies. Though the 'new' Turkish model as embodied by the AKP seems to be very attractive to the Arab street, the author argues that it cannot be readily replicated by the post-Arab Spring states. She further adds that the AKP model can be replicated only by the countries that have already switched to a functioning and legitimate democratic system. By looking at the present scenario in the Arab Spring states, Sengupta argues, the Arab leaders should begin looking iat the Kemalist model rather than at the one as projected by the AKP.

In Chapter 7, Priya Singh examines the contours of the Turkey–Israel relations from Israel's perspective. She provides an in-depth description of their relations during the past six decades or so by focusing on the dynamics of the ongoing relationship. Recognition of the establishment of Israel (Turkey was the first Muslim country to recognise and establish diplomatic ties with Israel), establishment of the diplomatic relations thereafter, formalisation of the 'periphery alliance' between Turkey and Israel (along with Iran and Ethiopia) were some of the points that the scholar wants to emphasise as manifestations of positive relations between Turkey and Israel during the initial phase. In the changed strategic milieu of the post-Cold War period and with an assertive foreign policy posture, Turkey's relations with Israel entered into a new era. Singh highlights that in the early 1990s, the focus areas of their bilateral relations were multifarious and including military intelligence and defence. However, the aspects of the relations that flourished were largely economic, technical and cultural. In the twenty-first century, however, Israeli–Turkish relations clearly lack the intimacy and vibrancy that had characterised those relations during the 1990s. Turkey's reorientation towards Israel, however, conforms to its 'Strategic Depth doctrine' and can be explained in many ways, such as the advent of the proto-Islamic AKP; procrastination of Turkey's EU membership and Ankara's energy-related considerations. Despite all these, Singh emphasises, there exists a tremendous scope for cooperation in the future.

In Chapter 8, Davood Kiani deals with Turkey's role in West Asia and analyses the European Union's approach towards this aspect. He stresses that in the twenty-first century Turkey has been able to establish itself as a significant player not only in West Asia but also in the Islamic world. On the other hand, it has also projected itself as a European and development-oriented Muslim country by taking active initiatives in regional and international affairs. Turkey is the only Muslim state in West Asia that has managed to have balanced relation with the West, Israel and the regional states. Turkey under the AKP has played mediating roles in many inter-state conflicts in the region and sought to play such a role between Europe and the regional states. Kiani argues that the EU, however, is not enthusiastic about Turkey's regional activism. There is competition and cooperation between Turkey and the EU in West Asia. He further stresses thatTurkey can be a conduit for EU's own multi-dimensional policies in West Asia. However, the EU is worried about a proactive behaviour of Turkey towards West Asia as it would lead to the former's greater influence in the region just like its predecessor, the Ottoman Empire, had enjoyed in the past.

In Chapter 9, Emirhan Göral examines Turkey–EU relations from a structural neorealist perspective. He stresses the importance of the world order as a fundamental factor in shaping the Turkey–EU relations and asserts that the future relations will be determined by the emerging world order. He argues that during the previous century, the main concerns for Turkey's membership issue were the country's underdeveloped economy as compared to the European Economic Community (the predecessor of EU) as well as the potential for a huge wave of immigration from Turkey into Europe. However, with Turkey's economic rise during the past decade, the focus has shifted more towards Turkey's potential power in the EU decision-making, cultural and religious differences, lacunae in the political aspects of the Copenhagen criteria, and gaps in implementing *acquis communautaire*. Göral underlines that the structure of international relations may force both Turkey and the European countries either to develop a close alliance or to become rivals; depending on other actors' decision-making imperatives. Both the parties require defining their foreign policy strategies keeping in mind the nature of the evolving world order. He further suggests that the accession process will be mostly shaped by the shift from a unipolar world to a 'new world order'.

In Chapter 10, Indrani Talukdar explores Turkey's European vocation and the protracted hurdles to its EU membership mainly from a constructivist approach. She emphasises that Turkey and Europe share centuries-old engagement. Even Turkey's EEC/EU membership issue is intertwined in their engagement history and covers a multitude of issues. Despite the massive reforms undertaken by Turkey during the AKP rule and even prior to it, Turkey's membership issue is still confronting several hurdles. Talukdar points out that the EU's changing position from time to time with regard to Turkey's membership has complicated the issue in Turkey especially for the section of the population which identifies itself with Europe. She highlights the recent instances of Turkey's deviation from its reformist path, distancing itself from the EU membership bid and the AKP's drive to move Turkey towards West Asia and the assertion of Muslim identity which might place further hurdles to Turkey's EU membership.

In Chapter 11, Gabriel Piricky examines the Gulen/Hizmet community's role as a foreign policy actor in two ex-communist countries of the Balkans (Bosnia and Herzegovina) and Central Europe (Slovakia) respectively. He dilates upon the issue of Turkish political Islam and its transformation in the past few decades, which in turn has effected significant changes in various socio-religious groups. His focus on the Hizmet movement stems from the fact that even though AKP's efforts to inject Islam-based morality into Turkish politics was appreciated by various religious communities, it helped Turkish transnational movements to have a good amount of freedom in their activities. Hizmet rose from a mere movement to an important source of political and economic support to the AKP government during the first two terms and eventually became a major foreign policy actor. He concludes by emphasising how the Hizmet community had been playing the role of an international bridge between Turkey and the outside world.

In Chapter 12, Zeynep Didem Akınoğlu sheds light on the change and continuity in Turkey's policy towards the Cyprus conflict under the AKP rule. She first explicates different phases of this long-standing and intractable ethno-territorial conflict and the policy of Turkey—one of the international parties to the conflict—towards the same. She cites a series of developments in recent times that have led to changes in Turkey's Cyprus policy: (i) the EU's decision in 1999 to accept Turkey's candidacy for membership (ii) the rise of the AKP and its new foreign policy doctrine that de-emphasised the aspect of security in the country's foreign policy. The AKP emphasised on conflict resolution under the Annan Plan. However, after the failure of the Annan Plan in 2004 the

AKP gradually adopted a less-compromising attitude on the dispute, by giving precedence to the domestic interests rather than its consideration of the EU membership. Akinoğlu concludes with the note that the change in policy towards Cyprus was a reflection of th etransformation of Turkey's foreign policy as a whole.

In Chapter 13, Mahesh Ranjan Debata, examines Turkey's relationship with China—the most populous and the second largest economy of the world—and puts into perspective the Uyghur factor in their relationship. Due to the presence of a substantially large Uyghur diaspora in Turkey (numbering 50,000), mostly in Istanbul and their close ethnic and linguistic ties with the Turkish people, this factor comes up periodically in the Sino-Turkish relationship. During the early years of 1990s, amidst the pan-Turkic sentiments in Turkey, the country had a pro-Uyghur attitude and accorded state patronage to its Istanbul-based leader Isa Yusuf Alptekin in internationalising the Uyghur cause. However, with growing trade and military collaborations with China, especially during the AKP era, the Uyghur factor has been sidelined or at least has not been taken into consideration in Turkey's bilateral relations with China. Debata underlines that amidst 'sometimes strong' and 'sometimes strained' relations between Turkey and China, Uyghur pleas for greater recognition are likely to remain a major cause of concern for the Sino-Turkish relationship. He further asserts that since the Uyghur problem in Xinjiang is a political issue, and in the present-day world, economic issues outflank political issues, Turkey does not want to sacrifice its economic interests with China for the sake of the Uyghurs.

In Chapter 14, Mohammad Monir Alam explores Turkey's changing role in Central Asia, a complex geopolitical region that emerged at the end of the Cold War. He stresses the strategic significance of Central Asia due to its large hydrocarbon resources which has attracted many regional and external players besides Turkey and Iran, the two most important regional players wanting to employ their historical and social inter-linkages to have greater access. Turkey, which tried to assume the role of a state-bridge as well as the representative of the Western powers in the Central Asian region, failed to achieve its objectives during the 1990s primarily because of its internal economic and political constraints.

Alam underlines that although in recent times Turkey wanted to reassert its importance as a regional power after a gap of many years, Ankara could not sustain its political–economic interests in Central Asia in the changing dynamics of the regional countries.

In Chapter 15, Md. Rahat Hasan dwells upon Turkey's peacemaking role in Afghanistan post-2002 NATO intervention. He explains the various dimensions of the peace-building efforts in Afghanistan and asserts that Turkey being a member of the NATO has made both military and non-military contributions to Afghanistan. He further highlights that Turkey's role in the reconstruction of Afghanistan with both its hard and soft-power assets and its eagerness to be seen as a significant actor cannot be underestimated. The historical and cultural ties between these two countries have made it easier for Turkey to establish credibility among the people of Afghanistan. In accordance with Turkey's new proactive foreign policy, it took several diplomatic initiatives such as the Trilateral Summit process (between Turkey-Afghanistan-Pakistan) and the Istanbul Summit for Friendship and Cooperation in the Heart of Asia, which contributed immensely and effectively for bringing peace, security and stability in Afghanistan. Besides, Turkey took an active role in training the Afghan military and police, and by taking on economic reconstruction projects through its Provincial Reconstruction Teams (PRTs) in Wardak and Jowzjan provinces, by developing infrastructure and by supporting projects such as health and education aimed at raising the quality of life of the locals.

In Chapter 16, Ahmed Raza examines Turkey's foreign policy activism in Africa especially through its aid programmes. His assertion is that Turkey's experience in foreign-aid programmes has been reflective of the broader transformations in the country's economy and foreign policy activism. Within a span of the last six decades, Turkey emerged from an aid recipient to a donor country. While the Turkish Cooperation and Coordination Agency (TIKA) oversees foreign aid policy and funds there are many NGOs that have been disbursing technical assistance. He further notes that Turkey has used its foreign-aid programmes as a new instrument with the purpose of supporting its foreign policy activism in Africa and elsewhere.

## Notes

1. Ahmet Davutoglu, *Stratejik Derinlik: Türkiye□nin Uluslararasi Konumu* (*Strategic Depth: Turkey's International Position* ) (Istanbul: Küre Publications, 2001); Detailed analysis in English in one of the earliest articles can be found in Alexander Murinson, "The Strategic Depth Doctrine of Turkish Foreign Policy", *Middle Eastern Studies*, vol. 42, no. 6, 2006, pp. 945-64.
2. Murat Yeşiltaş and Ali Balcı, "A Dictionary of Turkish Foreign Policy in the AK Party Era: A Conceptual Map", SAM (Centre for Strategic Research: Ankara), Paper, No.7, May 2013, p.8.
3. Suat Kınıklıoğlu, "Turkey's Neighbourhood and Beyond: Tectonic Transformation at Work?" *The International Spectator: Italian Journal of International Affairs*, vol. 45, no. 4, 2010, pp. 93-100
4. Mesut Özcan and Ali Resul Usul, "Understanding the "New" Turkish Foreign Policy: Changes within Continuity, Is Turkey Departing From The West?" *Uluslararasi Hukuk ve Politika*, vol. 6, no. 21, 2010, pp.109-133.
5. For a general understanding of the context of Turkish foreign policy under the AKP rule, a few select articles are suggested here: Muhittin Ataman, "Interdependence and Diversification: A New Framework for Turkish Foreign Policy", *Bilgi*, vol. 18, no. 1, 2009, pp. 38-57; Ahmet Sözen, "A Paradigm Shift in Turkish Foreign Policy: Transition and Challenges", *Turkish Studies*, vol. 11, no. 1, 2010, pp. 103-123; Ziya Öniş, "Multiple Faces of the "New" Turkish Foreign Policy: Underlying Dynamics and a Critique", *Insight Turkey,* vol. 13, no. 1, 2011, pp. 47-65; Kemal Kirişci, "Turkey's Engagement with Its Neighborhood: A "Synthetic" and Multidimensional Look at Turkey's Foreign Policy Transformation", *Turkish Studies*, vol. 13, no.3, 2012, pp. 319-341; Murat Yeşiltaş, "The Transformation of the Geopolitical Vision in Turkish Foreign Policy", *Turkish Studies*, vol. 14, no. 4, 2013, pp. 661-687.
6. A. Balci and N. Mis, "Turkey's Role in the Alliance of Civilizations: A New Perspective in Turkish Foreign Policy?" *Turkish Studies*, vol. 9, no. 3, 2008, pp. 387-406.
7. Gencer Özcan, "The Changing Role of Turkey's Military in Foreign Policy Making", *UNISCI Discussion Papers*, no.23, May 2010, pp. 23-46.
8. Kemal Kirişci, "The Transformation of Turkish Foreign Policy: The Rise of the Trading State", *New Perspectives on Turkey*, no. 40, 2009, pp. 29-57. By utilising the conceptual framework based on Richard Rosecrance's notion of the "trading state" the scholar explores the impact of economic considerations on the Turkish foreign policy.
9. Bilgin Ayata, "Turkish Foreign Policy in a Changing Arab World: Rise and Fall of a Regional Actor?" *Journal of European Integration*, vol. 37, no. 1, 2015; Bulent Aras, "Davutoğlu Era in Turkish Foreign Policy Revisited", *Journal of Balkan and Near Eastern Studies*, vol. 16, no. 4, 2014, pp. 404-18.
10. Richard Fontain and Daniel M. Kliman, "International Order and Global Swing States", *The Washington Quarterly*, vol. 36, no.1, pp. 93-109.

# 1
# Titanic Shift in the Republic of Turkey from *Stasis* to *Homonoia*

*Arshi Khan*

Every country is a living political entity in its own consciousness. The nature of consciousness depends upon the historical roots, experiences, goals, policies and the symbiotic community of a nation or country. Each political community as a national state or a political unit in the matrix of the world system continues to grow and interact with many actors at different levels for achieving its national aspirations, interests and goals in addition to playing regional and international roles. The Ottoman territory was called 'Turkey' in 1921 and it became a 'Republic' in 1923 after the signing of the Lausanne Treaty in which conditions were imposed by external powers. In the midst of a political quandary created by an artificial divide between the people associated with tradition, culture, values, religion, script, attire, manners and history, and 'the new citizens' of a new political entity called the 'Republic' that was not democratic but Kemalist in every aspect, *Kemalism* emerged as the guiding principle of governance and social reconstruction with the dominance of one political party—Republican People's Party. The new political players known as Kemalists dominating the structures of power began to translate national and international life of the country and the people according to their own canon.

Development and growth of the community largely depend upon its 'nature' (as reflected in Aristotle's theory of nature and Hegel's approach to Idea) which manifested in some parts of the world including the emergence of a strong State. Non-Western epistemological framework of the understanding of development looks into Plato's approach to wisdom, rationalism and the Idea of Good. Here material temptations and self-interests are considered as the main cause of ignorance. Turks are credited with maintaining the legacy of humanism both during their administration in overseas territories and when they were reduced to being the nation-state. The theory of nature[1] is quite applicable for understanding both the Ottoman *Devlet* and the present *Milli Devlet* which have in their respective capacities shown their unfolding institutions, policies and actions.

Political developments are intrinsically connected with the community which seeks higher goals and objectives through advancing its nature in the form of a vibrant State and polity. This certainly requires the availability of basic physical conditions for the adequate growth of the State reflecting the Aristotelian conception of the 'nature' located in some of the human groupings. The logical outcome of the 'nature' in terms of transition from the primitive form to highest form was more reflexive and dialectical, based on certain conditionalities. The statesman is supposed to assess the potentialities of the physical conditions and their efficaciousness for creating a functional and practical polity. These were some of the theorising principles of Aristotle who subscribed to the redefinition of 'nature' in the art of politics.[2] However, his priority to the promotion of morality and virtue of the individual—Platonic indoctrination—was instrumental in avoiding the dominance of economic and coercive factors commonly associated with the concept of the State.

Aristotle found the merit of the meteoric rise of the *Polis* in the nature of the state which had already existed prior to the time of the actual growth. Similarly, the Turks whose primitive stage began with a kind of tribal formation, emerged into *Devlet-e-Aaliyye Osmanliye*[3] after reaching the higher state of development. The *Osmanli Devlet* also proved to be capable of a sustainable maintenance of freedom, justice, prosperity and creativity for several centuries. This planetary State provided opportunities to minorities and other nationalities safety, security, dignity and rights including representation in development and governance. The 'nature-inspired' *Devlet* driven by the duty of justice relied heavily on moral principles despite being one of the mightiest powers in the world. It neither used force against the people (who were subjects) nor used it as a means of revenge against the people of enemy territories. It showed its major interests in serving the communities of different faiths as its duty to do justice.

Turkey has a very rich historical legacy of being the most powerful seat in three continents—Europe, Asia and Africa. The Ottoman Sultans can be considered as the followers of the ruling principles of the *Umawis* (661–750), *Abbasids* (750–1258), *Great Seljuqs* (1038–1157) *and Anatolian Seljuqs* (1075–1308) whose reigns are known for many contributions in the field of science, medicine, astronomy, artillery, architectures and cultural and economic rights to structured socio-cultural diversities. Mehmet Maksudoglu finds that the *Osmanli Devlet* (which the Western scholars call Ottoman Empire) was founded in 1289 and not in 1299 as generally assumed. Having no sons, the Seljuqi sovereign sent in 1289 the *menshur*, a big drum, sword and a flag to Osman Gazi whom he perceived as his son. The latter had in fact planned to go to Qonya, the Seljuqi capital, with precious gifts in the hope that he would become the *veliahad* (successor) to the Seljuqi Sultan, but he could not because of the Sultan's death.[4]

Maksudoglu's[5] book whose research works are based on the use of original and primary sources, has noted that non-Muslims were holding many important posts like *Vezir* and a strong position in trade and commerce activities. The Ottomans Empire (*Devlet-i-Aliyye-i Osmaniyye or Devlet-i Seniyye* from the *Osmanli* original sources) are known for their incomparable hospitality extended to over 12000 Jews facing expulsion in Spain after the decline of the Muslim rule. Similarly their administration in the West Asian region was providing a strong defence and resistance against the advancement and expansion of European colonial forces in and around the regions. They did not allow the Zionist Jews to illegally occupy the lands of Palestinians and the Arabs and Persians were free from such confrontations till 1918 when the Palestinian territories were placed under the British Mandate system ratified by the League of Nations. The so-called first Arab Spring (known as Arab Nationalism) was engineered by the colonial agents in collaboration with some Arab revolutionaries whose rebellion weakened the *Osmanli* power and opened the gates for British and French hegemony. This resulted in creating colonial vassals in West Asia and the artificial creation of Israel with the involvement of the British, Americans and the Zionists.

Turkey is strategically located within the main frontier of southeastern Europe from its western side and forms its geographical contiguity with Asia by its elongated Anatolian reach out to the area bordering Azerbaijan, Armenia, Iran, Syria and Iraq. Its geographic canvas includes natural fences and very important sea routes proving energy supplies to the European continent. Turkey has full control over the Bosphorus which makes it an inevitable actor in the Mediterranean region. The Black Sea and the Caspian Sea have energised Turkish regional capacity for cooperation, commerce and wider interactions. Its historical, social and cultural convergence and confluence in the Balkans and the presence of strong *Osmanli* communities along with friendly ties with their governments indicate that Turkey is a subsidiary force in this region. The Balkan States also need Turkey for more democracy, peace and development. Turkey seems to be more Western and modern in its political formation, policy decisions, regional associations and foreign policy. On the other hand, its historical, religious, social and cultural matrix provides and evolves multiple opportunities and connectivity within non-Western panorama. This rational-natural fabric of blend creates Turkish dynamism for accessibilities to different traditions and experiences keeping it always engaged with regional and international activism.

In other words, this *Devlet* reflected the natural consequences of the natural growth of the Turkish community into the grand State. The history of the Ottoman Empire can be remembered in many ways. Some have taken it as a 600-year old hostility to Europe which seems to be a kind of appeasement. In reality, the Ottomans offered opportunities for peace and cohabitation to different nationalities in three continents at socio-cultural and economic levels through the *Millet* system, modernisation, and inclusive constitution of 1876. As a result, minorities were also treated as nationalities which prospered economically and were empowered politically. A decree dated May 7, 1572 issued by Sultan Selim II upon the conquest of Cyprus:[6]

> Treat native people with justice and affection. Protect them in court collection of taxes and all kinds of state affairs in order to develop within a short time and to achieve prosperity and happiness. They are entrusted to us by the protector God. It is appropriate to protect and support them for the honour of the state. Let them all live in comfort being sure about their chastity, life and property and concentrate on their economic gains. My justice requires this. Each one of you should be attentive and careful to fulfil this order of mine. Do not show any heedlessness by knowing that I would never accept any excuse whatsoever if I hear you have done otherwise.

After the First World War was over, political forces of the union of economic and military powers built a larger coalition against the new political forces in Turkey which were confused and bewildered over the wasteful expression of Arab rebellion in the name of 'nationalism'. This rebellion weakened both the Arabs and the Turks. The coalition was trying to redefine and reset the Arab world which in general got territorially fragmented and politically subjugated by the forces of colonialism. The Arab community largely failed to acquire those physical conditions which could make its natural development unfold. However, this change and consequential events brought Turks to the playing field of 'political realism' which advocated the view of understanding and realising goals and interests through power-politics. Power became the essence of the existence of human beings, national politics and international relations. National interests became the motivating force behind the policies and actions of the Turkish State. On the other hand, Turks, later, wanted to create a balanced centre within the anarchic world. For this they also appreciated liberal institutionalism by showing their interests in the European Union and other international institutions.

The Turks saw the rise of nationalist forces in Europe turning into imperialist powers which were compressing Ottoman/Turkish *Devlet* by helping the Arab rebellion from one side and capturing Turkish territories by their armies on the other. Moreover, the same forces on the Western front were framing their terms and conditions for Turks to have their own political formation. Under the external pressures, Turks were in the reverse gear to translate their political future into a nation-state after having the long experience of administering tri-continental territories and different nationalities. Turkey as a newborn State was the earliest state confronting the advances of the British, French, Italian and Greek forces which were more interested in imposing conditions than facilitating the growth of the Turkish State. This was the age of great political trial and turmoil of the community into accepting the terms and conditions of victorious empire-states. Imposed conditionalities were mostly intended to create a subjugated political community with lost territories but they certainly provided space for the establishment of the State in turbulent situation. This was certainly a political development more in terms of structure than in substance.

There always exists a discourse in understanding and theorising political growth and development which seeks legitimacy in the corporate will of the society to be a decisive and determining factor in preparing the future road-map of a new Nation-State. Such a will is generally reflected in the form of law-makers/representatives in the law-making body which signifies the stakes and shares of citizens in national political formation. It is this body, having the legitimacy of the electorates, national and local governing institutions, which constitutionalises the rights of the governmental agencies, people and the citizens, in addition to their respective roles within and outside the national boundaries.

There were times when the imperialist forces were determining the future of dependent peoples and threatened nations. The West European powers were engaged in making unlawful and unreasonable political, territorial and economic gains by capturing others' territories as mandate territories and in some cases, they were using the instrument of treaties to nullify the legitimate rights of the rival powers. Similarly, the Communist power in the East was engaged in universalising its ideological gains based on force by annexing others' territories.

In all such affairs, the worst sufferers were the Ottoman subjects who had already lost a lot during the disastrous Balkan wars. After making the biggest physical and economic sacrifices in numerous battles against invading forces following the First World War, the Turks faced the decisive phase of human losses and unfair treaties against the Allies which somehow linked the approval and agreement over the Lausanne Treaty (1923) with the making of the Turkish Republic. This treaty seems to be a kind of Allies' Constitution for the becoming of the young Republic and to oblige her to re-frame laws, rules, national policies and institutions and to follow the major guidelines mentioned therein.

In pursuit of political existence and survival, the new leadership of Turkey under Ghazi Mustafa Kemal Pasha resorted to a new social and cultural engineering to adapt Western values, culture, language, laws and institutions. This created a great political and social upheaval in Turkey, taking a new turn towards accepting Western culture and values and shelving own history, memories and cultural values. On the one hand, this brought about severe internal conflicts between the new government and culturally conscious people while on the other such drastic changes driven by the new State indicated political aspirations of the ruling institutions to negotiate and adjust with Europe. In fact, such changes seemed to have been directed at the final goal of being the organic part of the European social whole. This was most probably the long term national interest of Turkish President to slowly enter into the European club. Acceptance of the Lausanne Treaty was some of the preliminary steps towards re-building her national identity.

Embracing the principle of friendly relations with the West, Turkish representatives accepted in good faith even the stringent Articles and Clauses with the main purpose of securing the Turkish share and space in the European rim. The Turkish approval of the Lausanne was in fact inherently conditional to the extent of seeking political merger in terms of today's membership of the European Union. This was a kind of a social contract between the Contracting Parties under which the institutions, values, rights and powers would be re-designed for the purpose of securing equality, liberty and dignity at the end. The kind of 'General Will' (which was never endorsed by the Contractualists and the Idealists) decided by the Western Powers and Turkish leaders ultimately resulted in substituting one institution by another without looking into the purpose of their basic transformation.

There are numerous Articles in the category of political rights mentioned within the Lausanne Treaty where the sovereign rights of the Turkish Republic were constrained by the choices of the Western Powers particularly in the sphere of Ottoman Territories, Nationality question and the protection of minorities. Political writings in the name of the Treaty resemble the "Melian Dialogue" mentioned in Thucydides' *History of the Peloponnesian War.* Kemalist conformity vis-à-vis the Western political interests is one of the political subjects of study by scholars which indicates the sacrifice of sovereign interests for the cause of peace. There is a need to look into the purpose of introducing such punitive measures in the form of a Treaty and they need to be re-examined in the context of the emerging needs and prospects of the Republic which has thrived for nine decades mostly on its vibrant will and action to live in peace and dignity. Things have changed in the last nine decades opening many opportunities and avenues before Turkey which necessitate a Turkish course of political developments.

Certain changes have been categorised as reforms and developments in social sciences but they need to be examined in the interest of strengthening the domain of knowledge. The Western epistemological paradigm would not be sufficient to decide the merits of the case in a society where the concept of knowledge is rooted in a different cultural and logical context. Long ago, the father of Political Science who categorised this subject as practical science, Aristotle, saw certain changes as sedition which is generally catalogued as 'revolution'. He took the course of radical changes or the existence of radical party in power as anti-thesis to the established rules and norms of governance causing instability and widening the rift between the groups which make conflicting claims. Aristotle seems to have favoured a compromise formula to avoid the exclusion of the representative characters of the meaningful section of society.[7]

For centuries, particularly since 500 B.C., philosophy of the Greek thinkers, Socrates and Plato onwards is generally considered by the Western scholars as a decisive turn in the history of human kind for rational generalisation and systematic study of political aspects of human beings. Plato's Republic generally referred as the Ideal State is both a moral–ethical institution as well as the reflection of a rational thought particularly in the context of the basic purpose of the formation and continuation of the state system. His 'parallelism' between the 'Individual' and the 'State', is mainly based on the kind of relationship between them not as a 'giver and taker', or 'governor' and 'governed' or a hostile camp of factions but as partners, stakeholders and necessary 'good' for one another.

Meaningful dialogues of Plato in the *Republic* basically educate us about the main purpose of the state and society particularly in terms of its actions and objectives. In other words, the purpose of political management is to benefit all individuals and groups. This is based on the understanding that every social unit and political institutions are reciprocal, cooperative, friendly and beneficial for one another. In the eyes of Plato, the wealth of a ruler is neither is his/her material possessions nor empowerment but selfless service to the people in the interest of humanity. This is the purpose of human wisdom to elevate above the self. Thus, it can be understood that the purpose of state is the well-being of people.

Plato's Ideal State is mostly indicative and suggestive of the fact of pragmatism, legitimacy and civilisational legacy which expect both the people and the ruling institution to promote better opportunities and grounds for unity, harmony, security, justice and peace within the state. This is not an anecdote but the evidence of the efforts of humanity at large in different parts of the world to pursue this agenda on the part of the state. Almost all kinds of states existing today and in history, all the constitutions and governing philosophies as well as the all the governing institutions in different societies have unanimously claimed for the objective of unity, justice, security and peace in the interest of the people and national interest. Ionians and Sophists and Greek City-States had made such claims. Similarly the Roman Empire, the Teutonic tribes, Medieval Europe,

Renaissance, Absolute monarchy, political revolutions in America, France, Russia and Turkey and post-1945 Western democracies, including other political formations in different parts of the world have made such claims for national unity, peace and security. However, all such claims can be tested and investigated on dialectics and performance.

It is quite relevant in the case of Turkey which experienced an unthinkable change in its political history where a particular group of society imposed itself as 'winners-all-the-time' and 'real representatives of the people' without creating institutions for its legitimacy vis-à-vis the large section of powerless society. A large number of people were not only confronted with the Kemalist elite accumulating power, position, privileges and rights but they were faced with the threats to their identity, religion and cultures as they are construed as the fundamental base of understanding, expression and performance. The turbulent period (1923–1946) is viewed by Ilter Turan as an era of the consolidation of the Turkish Nation-State by completing two phases of political development—consolidation among the elites (urban educated segments and population) and consolidation of the Nation-State[8] (in terms of *Kemalising* Turks).

This emerging cleft within the society, emanating from the standardised rules of qualification for sharing power and position, was a gigantic challenge to the notion of the 'republic' itself in terms of reality/falsehood of State–Society relationships, accessibility of citizens to various levels of the government, democratic decentralisation, representative government and the main question of constitution-making aimed at the peaceful process of nation-building. Post-Ottoman Turkey was faced with the question of settling democratic rights of the people who were otherwise disappointed with authoritarian experiences within the domain of the republic. It is said that a large number of *Ulema* and respectable members of the community were eliminated for their protests against the new political order. The fear of the State in the mind of the people was supplemented by a number of steps during the Kemalist regime to either create a type of proxy political parties or to deny the rise of independent political parties.

In February–March 1925, Said Nursi revolted against the state which manifested the alienation of one such group—the Kurds. Moreover, even moderate opposition to the Kemalist campaign was turned down. For example, the Progressive Republican Party, the only opposition to the Republican People's Party of Kemal Ataturk, was closed down soon after outlawing the Sufi orders in November 1925. Another opposition—the Free Republican Party, founded by the close associate of Kemal Ataturk, was dissolved within three months of its existence (November 1930). This party was critical of Kemalist reforms. After the end of the one-party rule in the Turkish Republic in 1946, its democratisation encouraged Turkish citizens and leaders to critically examine the working of democratic state.

On May 19, 1945, President Ismet Inonu in his famous speech, mentioned the need for new steps in the direction of democracy. On January 7, 1946, four Deputies of the Grand national Assembly—Celal Bayar, Adnan Menderes, Refik Koraltan and Fuad Koprulu, formed the Democratic Party to experiment with democracy. Turkey adopted the direct election system in June 1946 with the freedom of press and the autonomy of the universities. Elections, held on July 21 were manipulated but did not prevent many Democrats to enter the Assembly. This experiment certainly indicated a major shift in Turkish politics which occurred from time to time interrupted by military takeovers in 1960, 1971, 1980 and 1997.

Consequential changes were taking place both within Turkey and in world affairs. By 1947, it was not merely an agricultural economy. Its literacy rate had increased by the end of the Second World War to thirty percent and twice that amount in the cities. By 1930s, a new class of industrialists had emerged and the number of factory workers had increased from 25000 in 1923 to 300,000 in 1946 and at least twice that number were employed in agriculture and small industries. This nature of development necessitated a responsive and representative government with the existence of a strong political party to strengthen the democratic culture in the country.[9]

During 1946–1947, these developments were also instrumental in party level reforms within the Kemalist circle and softened the posture vis-à-vis the principle of 'revolutionism' and state-controlled economy. On the other hand, dissents also brew within the Democratic Party which was alleged to be the B-team of Ismet Inonu of the RPP. In March 1948, five expelled Deputies of the DP in the Assembly announced themselves as Independent Democrats. Another group founded a new party—the Nation Party on May 10, 1948 with which Independent Democrats merged in 1949. Turkey entered into a new era of competitive politics after the death of Mustafa Kemal and more particularly after the beginning of the Cold War era. Turkish neutrality was challenged by those from whom Kemalist elite borrowed the legal codes, values and modernity. The West had a design to act decisively under the environment of 'Iron Curtain' and the policy 'Containment' which required a strategically located Turkey to be the part of the Western bloc on south-west of the erstwhile Soviet Union. Turkish compliance with the American aid under the Truman Doctrine and its membership of the North Atlantic Treaty Organization in 1952 was an astonishing shift in Turkish foreign policy. This affected the national political struggle within the Turkish society which was a short-lived political development. However, it is important to note that this shift was caused by the political change brought by the Democrats in Turkey in the general elections on 14 May 1950. The Democrats got fifty percent of the rural votes with the rise in the numbers of the elected members of the Assembly belonging to legal and business sectors with the setback to the candidates with official backgrounds like bureaucracy and military.[10]

Adnan Menderes was the first democratically elected Prime Minister of Turkey in 1950 who began to change Turkey's direction in May 1950. He was born in 1899 in the West-Anatolian province of Aydın. Menderes graduated as a jurist from the Law School of Ankara University in 1935 and was able to speak fluent English and Greek. Apart from his political experience as a member of the short-lived Free Republican Party (FRP) which was closed down by the regime after four months in 1930, Menderes entered into politics as a member of the only party in the country, the Republican People's Party (CHP) on the eve of President Mustafa Kemal's (who was also the head of the CHP) visit to Aydın. Later, Menderes even became a deputy in the Turkish Parliament until his expulsion in 1945, at which time the Democrat Party was established. With superior rhetorical skills and his ability to understand Turkish citizens, Menderes's popularity increased during the opposition years (1945–50).[11]

It is known that during its initial phases, the DP had become the most serious candidate for power because of its role as spokesman of all social groups in Turkey who had old and new grievances against the 27 year-old CHP government. Interestingly, the DP promulgated, despite its famous devotion to "change," its loyalty to the entrenched state ideology, Kemalism. Apart from the fact that the Menderes government changed fundamental radical secularist policies implemented by the CHP, such as the re-introduction of the original Arabic version of the prayer's call (*ezan*) which was required to be recited in Turkish from 1932 to 1950 as a part of nationalist-secularist CHP policies. However, the DP also passed the so-called "Law No: 5816" "concerning criminal acts against Atatürk"—A globally unique case which prevented many post-Menderes scholars even to make appropriate researches about the Kemalist era.[12]

In the first "controversial" democratic election in 1946, for which the DP did not have the necessary time to mobilise and organise itself, the DP won 62 seats in the Parliament. The DP remained in the opposition until May 14, 1950 when it ultimately won the election, receiving 53 percent of all votes. The 1950 elections constituted a watershed in the history of Turkish and Middle Eastern democracy. Until that time parliamentary politics were perceived merely as an extension of the state bureaucracy and administration led by the single-party regime. The CHP, which henceforth represented the opposition, could not come close to challenging and bringing about the fall of the DP government in three subsequent elections until the 1960 coup d'état: In these three assemblies—1950, 1954, and 1957—the CHP, the largest opposition party, had 69, 31 and 178 seats, respectively, as compared to 408, 503 and 424 seats held by the DP. Even the famous socialist politician and writer, Şevket Süreyya Aydemir, who can be counted as an ideological counterpart of Menderes, had honestly admitted that Menderes was a man that represented the people's voice. Consequently, he became the people's beloved one which is very much an exception in Turkish history.[13]

When the Democrats came to power in 1950, the party wanted to change things as soon as possible. Their famous motto, "Enough! It is the Nation's Turn to Speak," which is also a famous slogan today, was a fundamental symbol for the era of change. Furthermore, the DP represented a more tolerant and respectful position toward religion and religious lifestyles, and, was more lenient to the Kurdish minorities while being more supportive of free-market capitalism. Subsequent to the deposing of the government by the military on May 27, 1960, Menderes was arrested along with various leading party members charged with violating the constitution. One interesting argument regarding the reasons for the military coup is the alleged support by the U.S. and some Western countries, which according to some accounts backed the military coup as a reaction to Menderes' ambitions to seek better relations with the Soviet Union and even ask for loans.[14] When Menderes was put on trial until September 17, 1961 he and two of his ministers were ultimately hung at the gallows; measures which were implemented by the DP governments in the 1950s that were allegedly contradictory to the "Atatürk reforms" were cancelled by the military junta. Secularism and nationalism, after an alleviation period of 10 years between 1950 and 1960 again gained importance as was the case from 1923 to 1950. In addition, many economic projects initiated by the DP were also abandoned during this military period.[15]

The nature of the government began to change after the first free elections with Celal Bayar and Adnan Menderes as the President and the Prime Minister of the country. Factions were being reconstructed as responsive agencies to translate the interests of the people into national policies. Candidates connected with masses and the constituencies replaced a good number of Kemalist elites associated with the principles of 'six arrows' and the political criteria imposed under the Lausanne Treaty of 1923. The Democrats had promised many things: redressal of 27 years of accumulated grievances against local administration, religious freedom, better roads, protection from excesses committed in the villages by gendarmes, easier farm credits and greater liberalism. They promised maximum participation of the private sector in economy and also stressed on agricultural development. Turkish economy grew at the rate of five percent annually and they established *Imam-Hatip* schools in 1951 for education in religious values.

For the first time in its Republican history, Turkish society demonstrated its 'general will', in a limited sense, to switch over to a non-Republican political party to govern the entire country. The Kemalist forces particularly the army overthrew the elected government in 1960 and hanged the first independent Prime Minister of Turkey. This military takeover continued for over three more times with the practice of closing down political parties. In fact, closure of political parties and imposition of many restrictions upon some indicted deputies and political leaders has put many democrats and scholars of Turkish polity in a difficult situation for legitimising the politics of closure. Closure of political parties was justified particularly on the pretext of threats to secularism and constitution but in reality this was more for the purpose of continuing the political claim of the armed forces over and above the political rights of the citizens in a democratic polity. In fact, the main problem of Turkey was to secure 'reconciliation' between the Constitution-Government and the Turkish society whose values and culture could not be accommodated within the governing system. The State needs to reflect the nature, need and choice of the society as one can find in the case of Swiss polity, Canada and the United Kingdom. In these countries, people are directly connected with the layers of governments (Swiss case), greater autonomy to the French speaking area (Canada) and the maintenance of the conservative royal system of a monarchical head (UK).

Till 2002, Turkish elites seem to be over-concerned with 'the security paradigm' but not at the broader level. Beyond the borders, they remained NATO-centric and valued Turkish association with the West as a lifeline type of thing. This created a kind of dependency syndrome. Most of the time, they prioritised West-centric policies over the ground realities within Turkey. The West was mostly interested to use Turkey in its own interests but its policy changed after Turkish policy made a big stride towards representative and cohesive polity creating more opportunities for the symbionts. At the domestic level, the pre-2002 Turkish State distrusted its own people as a threat to Kemalist secularism. These eight decades of internal divide began to dwindle under the forces of the merging Turkish general will.

After the conservative members of the Turkish political community began democratic mobilisation, particularly after 1996, external forces became active in creating cleavages within the largest segment of society which finally appeared in mid-2010 when Fethullah Gulen, living in the United States criticised Turkey over the Freedom Flotilla tragedy in May 2010.[16] It became more evident when he became instrumental in the Gezi Park protests in mid-2013 and in an anti-government campaign over the issue of corruption. This is to be noted that in the declining age of unilateralism, efforts were selectively made to denounce and finally remove certain political actors from power in different countries on the pretext of the 'corruption' issue by misusing media and social media. This happened in the case of Palestinian National Authority, China, Russia, Turkey, India, Egypt and Iraq. The corruption issue resulted in the downfall of recognised political actors and parties who were perceived as threats to the monopolisers of economy, political power, arms industry and the politics of security.

In the long transition phase of political developments and evolution of democratic institutions, democratic forces began to assert themselves as the covenantal guardians of the Republic based on the periodic verification of the consent of the people in local and general elections. In the last one and a half decade, old foundations were shaken to be replaced by the new ones ensuring *Homonoia* in Turkey. The new forces created alternatives to resolve conflicting interests by endorsing major policy changes and re-determining and re-shaping the natural goal of the country. The new leadership under the Justice and Development Party in power and the reformed Republican People's Party in opposition seem to consciously or unconsciously adhere to the Aristotle's theory of nature, Locke's theory of the government as a trust and Kant's theory of democratic peace.

The largest political party today in Turkey—Justice and Development Party (*Adalet ve Kalkınma Partisi*) seems to be replacing focus and priority from the 'privileged' to the 'public' and from the 'state' to the 'society' but at the same time it has not fully departed from the Kemalist attributes of 'Statism'. Most of the newly elected Deputies and the new government have widened the societal base of the democratisation process in 'the military-monitored-controlled administration'. This can be called a kind of Turkish dialectical advance towards the 'civilianisation' of polity. It is also important to point out that the electoral verdict is perceived 'read as a kind of civilian coup against the two branches of the government'— military and judiciary.

On April 23, 2014, Turkish Prime Minister Recep Tayyip Erdoğan published a written statement offering his condolences to Ottoman citizens of all ethnic and religious backgrounds who endured, in his words, what was a difficult period for the empire's entire population. The statement on the Prime Ministry's official website rightfully maintained that it was one's human duty to remember the victims while calling upon all groups involved not to exploit "our shared pain" to promote hostility against the Turkish government. Another important gesture was that Erdoğan's office simultaneously released translations of the original text in a number of foreign languages including Eastern and Western Armenian.[17]

Mr. Erdoğan's latest outreach efforts received mixed reactions. Archbishop Aram Ateşyan, in his official capacity as Patriarchal Vicar of the Armenian Patriarchate of Istanbul, welcomed the Prime Minister's "exciting" statement and argued that the initiative represented a solid response to all of Turkey's opponents. Similarly, Orhan Dink, brother of the late Hrant Dink who was assassinated in January 2007, maintained that the Prime Minister's condolences would serve as a cornerstone of the kind of democracy that the country will establish. Speaking at a vigil commemorating Ottoman Armenians, President Serzh Sargsyan emphasised that his country did not view the Turks as its enemies. Despite the overall positive feedback from Turkey's Armenian community and the Armenian government, lobbyists including Aram Hamparian, who heads the Armenian National Committee of America (ANCA), failed to acknowledge this historic event and dismissed the Turkish government's reconciliation effort as "genocide denial repackaged." Similarly, Mr. Erdoğan's domestic opponents sought to downplay the significance of a Turkish Prime Minister offering his government's condolences by claiming that the country's political leadership did not act in good faith and was not motivated by genuine sentiments.[18] Furthermore, the statement embodied a new thinking within the Turkish government, which has grown considerably more confident and courageous over the past decade.

The AKP passed constitutional amendments to legalise the voluntary use of headscarf. When Kemal Ataturk founded Turkey as a secular republic after World War I, he looked to Europe, and especially France, for his inspiration. While American secularism provides freedom of religion, the French version that Ataturk adopted emphasises freedom from religion—that is, keeping religion and its symbols out of government and education. Turkey's secular courts have considered the turban a political religious symbol.[19] The headscarf is a political wedge that bitterly divides Turkish society. Conservative women in Turkey have always covered their heads as a sign of modesty. There are a variety of styles to choose from: the *esarp*, an eastern and southern European-style handkerchief, worn by urban women. According to a poll (2008), almost half (49 percent) of Turkish women used these traditional head coverings, while 37 percent did not cover at all. The turban, however, is a specific, nontraditional type of headwear that arose in Turkey during the early 1980s after first appearing in other Muslim countries.[20]

In full conformity with its "democratic" understanding, the AKP, has unveiled its 26-article—three of them provisional articles—constitutional amendment package calling for amendments in articles 10, 20, 23, 41, 53, 69, 74, 84, 94, 125, 128, 129, 144, 145, 146, 147, 148, 149, 156 and 159 and the Provisional Article 15—all together 21 articles—of the 1982 military-scissored constitution of the country. The package calls for the abolition of the Provisional Article 15, which granted full judicial immunity to the 1980 coup leaders, administration and the Consultative Assembly members for their actions, decisions and undertakings during the military coup period. Indeed there is a full consensus in Parliament and by and large in the nation that the Provisional Article 15 must be scrapped.[21]

Recently, tendencies of "intellectual deformation" have become prominent in Turkey whereby renowned authors, academics and intellectuals systematically resort to distortions in conceptual or analytical frameworks to interfere in the tense political conjuncture. There were also frequent cases of "intellectual neocolonialism" aimed at stigmatising the government and the wider political establishment through accusations of authoritarianism, dictatorship and economic mismanagement, which were deemed to take the country into systemic failure. Soma mining disaster (2014), Gezi Park Protest and violence (2013) and corruption (2013 onwards) are some of the headlines which have characterised the nature of democracy in Turkey in which the leadership of the Turkish Prime Minister Recep Tayyip Erdoğan heading the AK Party has been at the centre-stage of criticisms. The opposition forces were boosted by the entry of the former AKP ally Fethullah Gulen and his syndicate which were more interested in a kind of Turkish Spring. The issue of corruption was raised in China, Russia, Iraq, Palestine, Pakistan, India and Ukraine to make a type of civilian coup in the name of democratic rights.[22]

Erdoğan said that Gezi Park incidents (May 2013) inflicted heavy economic losses afterwards on Turkey's hardworking people. He said "In spite of all the attacks, Turkey is walking towards its 2023 target." He praised the 5.8 percent rise in exports in May—the highest in Turkey's history. He said: "Over the decades Turkey faced many challenges, mostly negative. While coups provided benefits to certain elites, the country was severely damaged. Gangs and media organizations provided great opportunities for elitist groups."[23]

Erdoğan's government is criticised by different forces within and outside the country. Its once-upon-a-time fellows belonging to Fethullah Gulen group including their media and intellectuals call the Premier as upholding corruption and authoritarianism in Turkey in addition to doing business with Iran. The closest friends have turned into fierce enemies resulting in the Turkish request to the US government to extradite Gulen from Pennsylvania. National Action Party (MHP) has protested against him for concessions to the Kurdish community in the country. Moreover, Republican People's Party (CHP) has accused Erdoğan of weakening the secular credentials of the country. On the other hand, the US Embassy in Ankara is currently involved in encouraging the use of social media and the corruption issue in Turkey. Earlier, the US in collaboration with some internal forces manufactured anti-national and anti-government charges against the Army known as Ergenkon and Sledgehammer.

This resulted in several judicial verdicts against high officers and many of them resigned. After the Erdoğan–Gulen divide, various cases of manipulations appeared on the scene related to terror charges against the Army. It is also interesting to note that the US and Israel succeeded in separating both from each other in order to weaken the combined strength of the political unity of the community in Turkey. This divide has benefited anti-Turkish elements in the country, in the region and in Europe. The April 2014 local elections' results have shown the citizens' will towards *homonoia* from *stasis*.

Since it came to power in 2002, the Justice and Development Party (AK Party) has been under the pressure of many institutions including opposition parties, mainstream media, legal elites, the old bureaucracy and Istanbul's nobility. Furthermore, the Gulen Movement, which has infiltrated the deepest network of the state, has been recently added to this camarilla. Despite all this, the AK Party continues to increase its votes as higher in each and every election and overcome the hardest times successfully with the support of its social grassroots. This is such an astonishing picture that it may confuse a political scientist who does not know that Turkey's "civic political culture" developed in the 20th century. The above observations were made by Haşmet Babaoğlu in the *Daily Sabah* of May 16, 2014.[24]

Since the coup d'état of 27 May 1960—its ill effects still continuing today—the majority of the public has expected a political party that is completely independent from the status quo, i.e. the state of the elites. It should be remembered that the military coup was an overwhelming defeat for the public and the system was once again turned into a "sovereignty of the elites for the benefit of the public." Despite the heavy frustration, nobody gave up going to the polls. But, they were aware that they elected "the lesser evil" at every return, and they could not vanquish the status quo. Throughout the 1960s and 1970s, German political scientist Frederick W. Frey carried out a series of field studies and found out that the perspectives of the electorate and Turkey's political elites towards democracy and political parties were totally in contrast with one another. Frey stated that Turkish political elites always viewed people with the discrimination of "we and others," and this prevented the development of a legitimate political competitive environment. Haşmet argues that 2002 is a milestone in Turkish politics. People found what they politically desired in the AK Party and Erdoğan, and they launched a "second democratic initiative." People have experiences, memories and a civic culture that are handed down from one generation to another. And they do not want this process to be crippled through illegal means once again.[25]

AKP's consecutive victory in three elections (2002, 2007, 2011) is the reflection of its policies towards strengthening civilian power, major constitutional reforms, economic growth and development and a pro-active role in international affairs, in terms of balancing excessiveness of Israel and cooperation with the US and the EU. The main opposition—Republican People's Party (*Cumhuriyet Halk Partisi*) is weak in its foreign policy objectives and open economic system in the country. Its allegiance to Kemalism failed to create a wealthy country. The CHP leader Kemal Kilichdaroglu has said to cooperate with the government and anyone else who wants to be involved in the drafting of a new constitution, although it does have some red lines that it will not allow to be crossed. On June 17, 2011, he said his party was positive about overhauling the current constitution, which is highly problematic in many areas such as press freedoms and freedom of expression because it was adopted two years after a 1980 coup d'etat.[26]

The most important consequence of the 2014 local elections in Turkey is the increase in votes for both the AK Party and BDP (Kurdish). This may raise hopes for the continuation of the reconciliation process. The anti-government campaign which utilised wiretapped conversations also targeted the AK Party's policy for a solution to the decades-long Kurdish question in Turkey. For example, a leaked conversation aimed to increase suspicion among the Kurds that the Turkish state was involved in the killing of three Kurdish activists in Paris at the beginning of 2013. More importantly, leaked recordings of PKK imprisoned leader Abdullah Öcalan's conversations with other prisoners aimed to imply that the AK Party government had reached an agreement with Öcalan on certain matters such as regional autonomy. The Peace and Democratic Party (BDP) and some Kurdish organisations close to the PKK said during their campaigns that the 2014 local elections would be a referendum on regional autonomy for the Kurdish-majority region in Turkey. For example, the Kurdish Communities Union (KCK) stressed that local elections would be the most important stage of the autonomy project. Similarly, Gülten Kışanak, the BDP's mayoral candidate for Diyarbakır, said: "If we emerge stronger, we don't have to wait for the government to have our share of power." The call of pro-Kurdish actors for regional autonomy and the leaked records of Öcalan popularised the question "Did Erdoğan promise Kurdish autonomy?" as part of the reconciliation process. After the elections, pro-Kurdish dailies interpreted the election results as an approval of regional autonomy by Kurds.[27]

When we look at Kurdish-majority provinces (Adıyaman, Ağrı, Batman, Bingöl, Bitlis, Diyarbakır, Hakkari, Iğdır, Kars, Mardin, Muş, Siirt, Şırnak, Tunceli, Hakkari, and Van) a number of important conclusions seem plausible. First, the Kurdish-majority region is dominated by two parties (the BDP and AK Party) as in the last two previous elections. Second, the BDP increased the number of cities where it won the elections from eight to 11, taking the provinces of Mardin, Bitlis and Ağrı from the AK Party. Third, compared with the 2009 local elections, it is easy to realise that both parties increased their votes considerably. Fourth, the AK Party's votes decreased remarkably when compared with the 2011 general elections. The main success of the BDP is, of course, the takeover of the religiously conservative provinces from the AK Party. For example, the BDP increased its votes in Bitlis from 27 percent in 2009 local elections to 38 percent in 2014. In Ağrı and Mardin, however, the BDP took municipalities from the AK Party although pro-Kurdish votes did not drastically change. When results from 2014 are compared with the previous local elections in 2009, the BDP increased its share of the vote in 10 cities while its votes decreased in six, including Diyarbakır, the most populated Kurdish city in the region. Importantly, in three cities (Iğdır, Bitlis, and Şırnak) the BDP increased its share of the vote by more than 10 percent and more than 5 percent in five other cities (Ağrı, Muş, Tunceli, Urfa, and Mardin).[28]

Kurdish-majority provinces in which the BDP won more than 50 percent of the popular votes number six, including Hakkari, Van, Şırnak,

Batman, Mardin and Diyarbakır. However, pro-Kurdish parties' vote shares in these cities were already more than 50 percent in two previous elections with the exception of Mardin (44 in the 2009 local elections). On the other hand, the BDP decreased its votes in both Diyarbakır and Hakkari considerably. In four cities (Siirt, Muş, Ağrı, and Iğdır) the BDP took more than 40 percent of the popular vote by increasing its share in a relatively high ratio. The AK Party increased its votes in the region too in comparison with the 2009 local elections. However, votes for the AK Party decreased compared to 2011. When compared to the 2009 local elections, the AK Party increased its vote in 11 provinces. Of them, Muş, Bitlis, Bingöl, and Urfa witnessed an increase of more than 10 percent in the AK Party's votes. In other cities except Tunceli, the decrease in AK Party's votes is minor. Only in Tunceli and Iğdır, were the AK Party's votes below 20 percent. However, this inferior percentage is unrelated with Kurdish consciousness in these cities. In cities where the BDP took more than 50 percent of the vote, except Şırnak and Hakkari, the AK Party received nearly more than 35 percent. There are three possible explanations for the increase in the AK Party's share of the vote. First, the Kurdish people voted for the reconciliation process. Second, small parties lost their voters to the AK Party. Third, turning the local elections into a referendum for the AK Party had an effect on Kurdish voters. Whatever the reason, it is clear that the AK Party continued its competitive power in provinces in which BDP gained less than 50 percent of the vote.[29]

The 2014 elections also showed that Kurdish votes continue to be flexible while the BDP's unrivalled status is certain in Diyarbakır, Şırnak and Hakkari provinces and it is clear that in the Kurdish-majority provinces support for the Kurdish parties is gradually rising. More importantly, the AK Party proved that it is able to increase or secure its vote in the region. However, in my opinion, the most important consequence of the 2014 elections is the increase of both parties' votes. This may raise hopes for the continuation of the reconciliation process. For example, pro-Kurdish parties' sense of failure in the 2007 general elections in which votes for Kurdish parties decreased from 6.2 percent in the 2002 elections to 3.8 percent resulted in the rise of PKK activities. Though, it should be kept in mind that the PKK is not disarmed yet and its members are in northern Iraq, which makes the reconciliation process brittle.[30]

At the beginning of its reign, AK Party governments had to rehabilitate a fragile macroeconomic structure devastated by recurrent financial crises in 1989, 1994, 1999 and 2001 as a result of acute institutional inability to regulate financial liberalisation. But in the aftermath of the twin crises in 2000–2001 the pursuit of fiscal discipline and prudence in macroeconomic management gradually became the norm, while political stability and policy coordination advantages of successive single-party governments improved the effectiveness of structural reforms. In the early 2000s, substantial reforms were accomplished in critical areas such as the regulation of banking and financial markets; management of public debt and expenditure regimes for increased fiscal discipline; reinforcement of the independence of the central bank and autonomy of regulatory agencies; and streamlining the subsidies for agricultural producers and state economic enterprises. Over time, crucial institutions holding the pulse of stability, such as the Turkish central bank and Banking Regulation and Supervision Agency (BRSA-BDDK) developed substantial human and governance capacities to the extent that they became innovative models for the developing world before, during and after the global economic crisis in 2008.[31]

Taking due advantage of favourable global liquidity conditions, Turkey displayed a shining economic performance associated with high economic growth, fiscal discipline, single-digit inflation and record inflows of foreign direct investment (FDI). Particularly important among these was the issue of FDI as with the impetus provided by the start of EU accession negotiations; the country managed to attract unprecedented amounts of inward investment. The annual FDI figure for the critical year of 2007 just before the global crisis was around $20 billion which represented a record in the Republic's history and exceeded the total FDI inflows between 1980 and 2000 as a whole. In this period, some of the massive privatisation projects in critical sectors such as energy (Tüpraş), petrochemicals (Petkim) and telecommunications (Türk Telekom) were successfully completed at globally competitive prices. Attainment of high primary surpluses in the existence of high economic growth brought the ratio of public debt to GDP to manageable levels and the single-digit inflation target was accomplished.[32]

In other words, the transformation of Turkey's political economy in the new millennium produced a new structural pattern that approximated the "post-Washington consensus" principles of the Bretton Woods institutions with market-friendly yet robust regulatory mechanisms, fiscal discipline and prudence in macroeconomic management. From a different vantage point, the close coordination between the conduct of foreign policy and macroeconomic governance precipitated new openings in the international trade strategy which supported Turkey's nascent institutional reflexes as a BRICS-like "trading state." In this context, visa-free travel arrangements, preferential trade agreements (PTAs), and "high-level strategic cooperation councils" applied to numerous countries in the Middle East, Africa, Latin America and East Asia intensified the cross-border mobility of goods, services and people to support the ongoing international trade dynamism.[33]

Erdoğan said in his electoral campaign in 2011 that his government will embrace everyone, whether they voted for the AKP or not. He said the following words after his victory: "The lifestyles, faiths and values of 74 million people are entrusted to us. Freedoms will broaden and everyone will be able to express themselves even better. Our responsibility has grown. We have also been given the authority to make the new constitution. We have been given the chance to make the new constitution with consensus". On the question of constitutional changes, he said to sit and to talk, and he would have dialogue with the political parties outside the Parliament, nongovernmental organisations and associations. Together he will make a liberal constitution altogether. The east, the west, the north and the south will find themselves in this constitution. This new constitution will be addressed to every single individual in Turkey. In the new constitution, every citizen will be the first. This constitution will focus on peace. This constitution will be the constitution of the Kurd, of Turkmen people, of Alevis, of all minorities; which means all 74 million people. This constitution will be for fraternity, for sharing, for unity and solidarity.[34]

## Conclusion

Turkish elections with a high percentage of voters' participation since 2002 and a clear mandate in favour of the AKP in April 2014 local elections clearly show not only the liberal interests of citizens but also manifest the vibrant image and appreciation of democracy in Turkey. Voters have been the backbone for the 'change' in the country where new but democratic experiments are being made in pursuit of both 'security' and 'conveniences' which are the two major concerns of the State. The AKP has mitigated ethnic tension by taking some measures and promising more initiatives in south-eastern Turkey. It is trying to give a new lesson to the key agencies of the privileged categories to give up 'self-driven guardianship' of the country as they are no more the Platonic 'ruling class'. On the other hand, both the CHP and its supporters in the army, judiciary and others are also thinking of not resisting 'change' as they have already played their cards on the board.

The recent election and policies of the government has signalled a new civilian assertion over the 'self-authorised' role of some of the members of the army who were probed and sentenced by the judiciary. This probe is basically not meant to dismantle the heritage of the army but to make it a more barrack-based defence unit. The AKP later came in defence of the accused army officers against whom cases were found fabricated by some internal and external forces. This happened when some conspiracies were exposed after the Erdoğan–Gulen divide recently. The AKP gave a strong indication of keeping the army under civilian control. The ruling party has also indicated entry into the grand process of consultations for making the new constitution with more civilian attributes. AKP's move for change is not isolated by the main opposition as the CHP has also disagreed with old pattern of Kemalism. The CHP is trying to build new bridges with the masses which manifests its approval for a post-modern coup.

Resignation of the top-ranking commanders over the order of the trial court seems to give a serious note about the future path of compulsive cooperation between the elected government and the military agency. Tayyip Erdoğan and the President Abdullah Gul have managed to down play this unprecedented resignation of military guardians. The government has been said to follow the law whereas the tradition of the overarching role of the army is certainly damaged.

The AKP has succeeded in proving its political credentials for being the strong supporter of democracy, freedom, security, reforms, human rights and open economy. In all its three terms of heading the national government, it pursued the Turkish case as a friendly, peaceful, democratic and prosperous polity and society both at the domestic and international levels. Its policies have also shown results in enhancing the graph of Turkey as the fastest growing economy of Europe. The AKP has also removed the fear of being a reactionary force by mainstreaming itself in democratic governance. Its developmental agenda, voice for democratic pursuits, attempts for the full membership of the EU, its emergence as a peace-actor in the Middle Eastern region and friendly partner in the Mediterranean, Aegean and the Caspian Seas, supporter of peace projects of EU, NATO and other bodies in Afghanistan and North Africa and power-balancer vis-à-vis Israel in the Middle East and so on are some of the examples of the AKP.

Thus, Turkey has entered into a new phase of politics mainly driven by people's power in real terms and it should not be equated with an upsurge in as in other parts of West Asia. This new phase of politics is quite peaceful in nature, democratic in process, and forward looking in developmental achievements and goals. As a result, most of the Turkish citizens seem to be more conscious and concerned over the secular matters of development. This election also shows the approval of the role of the Turkish government beyond its borders. Over the years, Turkish overtures over Israeli crimes against humanity, war crimes, crimes of aggression and crimes against peace in Occupied Palestinian Territories, nuclear swap deal over Iran and other peace-building roles in the turbulent region cannot be ignored. Turkey is already burdened with heavy expenditures incurred on its forces in Afghanistan and Northern Cyprus. Moreover, the Western drive against Turkey over recognising Armenian genocides has been disturbing and painful to Turkey. It is in this quagmire that the Turkish voters have preferred a strong government to meet various challenges in the time to come. However, it can be said that considerable changes have taken place in the country where people seem to be more free, transparent, accommodative and open than in the past decades. It is also a fact that the AKP has been instrumental in this democratic drive but it is also assigned with the complex task of harmonising conflicting interests within the country.

## Notes

1. George H Sabine and Thomas L Thorson, *A History of Political Theory* (New Delhi: Oxford and IBH Publishing Co. Pvt. Ltd., 1973), pp. 121-123.
2. Ibid.
3. Mehmet Maksudoglu, *Osmanli History and Institutions* (Istanbul: Ensar Nesriyat Tic. A.S, 2011), pp. XXXV.
4. Ibid., p. XXXVI.
5. Ibid., pp. V-675.
6. Menter Sahinler, *Cyprus Policy 1974 of Turkey* (Istanbul: Rumelia Culture and Solidarity Association, 1979), p.103.
7. George H Sabine and Thomas L Thorson, *A History of Political Theory*, pp. 115-117.
8 Ilter Turan, "Stages of Political Development in the Turkish Republic", *Social and Economic History of Turkey* (Princeton University, 24-26 August 1983), pp. 382-383.
9. Arshi Khan, "Democracy and Party Politics in Turkey: 1960-1990", *Ph.D Thesis*, Jawaharlal Nehru University, 1994, pp. 18-19.
10. Ibid., p. 25.
11. Erkut Ayvazoğlu, "Adnan Menderes and the Transition to Democracy", *Daily Sabah*, 14 May 2014. http://www.dailysabah.com/opinion/2014/05/13/adnan-menderes-and-the-transition-to-democracy
12. Ibid.
13. Ibid.
14. Ibid.
15. Ibid.
16. http://www.dailysabah.com/opinion/2014/04/28/armenians-should-not-reject-turkish-initiative
17. Ibid.
18. Soner Cagaptay, "After Headscarves, What's Next", *Turkish Daily News*, 9 February 2008.
19. Ibid.
20. Yusuf Kanli, "The package (I)", *Hurriyet Daily News*, 23 March 2010. http://www.hurriyetdailynews.com/n.php?n=the-package-i--2010-03-23
21. Sadik Unay, "Rentierism: Distorted Representations of Turkey", *Daily Sabah*, 24 May 2014. http://www.dailysabah.com/columns/sadik_unay/2014/05/24/rentierism-distorted-representations-of-turkey
22. Prime Minister Recep Tayyip Erdoğan's Speech at the Turkish Exporters Assembly General Council, reported in *Daily Sabah*, 7 June 2014.
23. http://www.dailysabah.com/columns/hasmet-babaoglu/2014/05/16/how-did-the-ak-party-change-turkish-politics

24. Ibid.
25. *Hurriyet Daily News*, 18 June 2011.
26. Ali Balcı, "The 2014 Local Elections and the Kurdish Question in Turkey", *Daily Sabah*, 9 April 2014. http://www.dailysabah.com/opinion/2014/04/09/the-2014-local-elections-and-the-kurdish-question-in-turkey
27. Ibid.
28. Ibid.
29. Ali Balcı, "The 2014 Local Elections and the Kurdish Question in Turkey", *Daily Sabah*, 9 April 2014. http://www.dailysabah.com/opinion/2014/04/09/the-2014-local-elections-and-the-kurdish-question-in-turkey
30. Ibid.
31. Sadik Unay, "Turkish Economy: Taking Stock of the Last Decade", *Daily Sabah*, 14 March 2014. http://www.dailysabah.com/opinion/2014/03/14/turkish-economy-taking-stock-of-the-last-decade
32. Ibid.
33. Ibid.
34. "AKP will Embrace All, Erdogan Says", *Hurriyet Daily News*, 12 June 2011.

# 2
# The 'Alliance of Civilizations' and Turkish Foreign Policy

*Nurullah Ardıç*

## Introduction

The concept of 'civilisation' was not very popular among most Western social scientists in the 20th century, though it had been somewhat influential in 19th century scientific thought. More recently, 'civilisation' has been re-discovered by some social scientists in the West after it was inserted into politics through the 'clash of civilisations' thesis and September 11 attacks as well as with the rise of what is known as the 'Asian tigers' with their different 'civilisational' roots on the one hand, and the increasing migrations to the industrial, Western countries from different parts of the world, on the other. In Turkey, too, the concept has increasingly been used in foreign policy discourses as well as in popular political debates. Prime Minister R. Tayyip Erdoğan and Foreign Minister Ahmet Davutoğlu, in particular, frequently make references to 'civilisation'. This chapter argues that these references (and the AKP's civilisational discourse in general) are heavily influenced by Davutoğlu's philosophical perspective, and constitute one of the areas in which Davutoğlu's vision has been shaping the Turkish Foreign Policy (TFP). This vision is systematically delineated in his influential work, *Strategic Depth*, published in Turkish in 2001.[1]

Based on a Foucaultian "discourse analysis" method, which conceives "discourse" as both reflecting 'actual' socio-political developments and practices formed within a historical context, *and* constitutive of these social relations (and social reality in general),[2] the chapter mainly argues that the AK Party government's general FP approach has been based—at least partly—on a "civilisational discourse" that is somewhat ambiguous but also very flexible. It tries to demonstrate that the concept of civilisation in the TFP's discourse has a vague meaning, entailing at least three different layers, including 'national', 'regional' and 'universal' dimensions. Thus, the Turkish political actors often refer to 'our civilisation' implying a vague Turkish civilisational tradition; they sometimes mean by this Islamic civilisation and/or the Muslim people and cultures of the Middle East and the Balkans. But they also often invoke 'universal' humanitarian values and 'common legacy of the humanity', including such elements as justice and freedom. It is not only the case that the exact boundaries among these layers of civilisation are not clear, but also that these actors also often switch between them in a pragmatic and skilful manner. Furthermore, this ambiguity adds dynamism to TFP and is useful within the pragmatic discourse of the AKP leadership.

Third, the chapter demonstrates that the 'Alliance of Civilizations' is located, both as a concept and institution, within the third, universal, dimension of the TFP's discourse, particularly in relation to Turkey's EU membership process. Thus, on the one hand, the 'Alliance of Civilizations' is discursively constructed as a concept that brings Turkey (as the representative of the 'East') and Europe (as that of the West) together on the common ground of the 'common legacy of the humanity'; on the other hand, it is presented as a socio-political project and institution that will end current divisions and clashes among different regions and countries on a global scale. This double utilisation of the 'Alliance of Civilizations' (as a concept and institution) proves useful in TFP's self-presentation and as an element of Turkish diplomacy. The chapter explores how the concept of civilisation is variously utilised within this framework. Finally, the chapter ends with a discussion on why the AK Party leadership finds the civilisational discourse useful for Turkey's assertive FP performance and the party itself.

## "Civilisation" and the AK Party

During the first several years of its rule, the AK Party government had adopted a Western-oriented foreign policy discourse with the impact of the existing (domestic and international) political and ideological conditions, which were largely unfavourable for a government party with "Islamic roots," including particularly the hostile atmosphere of the post-September 11 events and the Turkish military's harsh stance against previous Islamic political movements, of which the AKP was an offspring. After all, Turkish politics had just come out of the highly polarised and contentious ideological environment caused by the "February 28" coup d'état in 1997; and international politics was ideologically occupied by the "clash of civilizations" thesis, which mainly posed Islam and the West as two archenemies, and was put into practice by the Bush administration's "war on terror" campaign that resulted in two wars in Afghanistan and Iraq, as well as a more targeted military campaigns against the al-Qaida etc.

Despite all these unfavourable conditions, the AKP leadership gradually adopted a more "civilisational" FP discourse, particularly with Prime Minister Erdoğan's personal efforts, which intensified after the appointment of Ahmet Davutoğlu as Foreign Minister in 2009. However, as we shall see below, this new discourse is not exclusive of the Western orientation that the Turkish government had previously adopted. For the AKP government has on the whole improved its relations with the Western countries, and cultivated and moved forward its EU accession process, particularly during its first two terms. However, the existing political, military, economic and cultural relations with Western countries are often framed as "civilisational alliance" or "meeting of civilisations" within this new discourse.

On the other hand, there has also emerged a discursive emphasis on the "Islamic civilisation" and the significance of the neighbouring "region" that has increasingly been visible in the TFP in parallel to the recent intensification of sectarian conflicts in the Middle East, which is also sometimes used in an attempt to prevent these conflicts. In addition to these, we also observe an increase in the discursive references to Turkish history in both domestic politics and foreign policy.[3] All these developments could be read as signs of a significant, albeit partial, transformation at the discursive level in TFP under the AKP rule.

This discursive change was made clear by the party leadership during the 4th Grand Congress of the AK Party on September 30, 2012. In his long speech at the Congress, Prime Minister Erdoğan mentioned the term "civilisation" 14 times whereas he used the term "conservative democrat," which is the AK Party's official ideological position, only two times.[4] Moreover, while the Party previously emphasised such themes as "service" and "development" as its main goals, this speech and the booklet prepared for this Congress by the Party emphasised its mission through various historical references and themes like the "2023 and 2071 vision."[5] Furthermore, by emphasising the inclusive aspects of this civilisational discourse, the AKP constructs it on a transnational scale going beyond the Turkish national identity and borders; by discursively positioning the other peoples in the Middle East, particularly the Kurds and the Arabs, within the framework of "brotherhood." The party leadership is also careful to frame this discourse so as not to harm the existing institutional (political and military) cooperation with the "West."

## TFP's "Civilisational" Discourse

The main feature of the AK Party Government's civilisational discourse is that it is multi-layered (or multi-dimensional) and vague, but at the same time it has a very dynamic character. For this discourse simultaneously accommodates the national identity, history and values on the one hand and the membership in the Muslim World and the Middle East on the other. At the same time, it often makes references to the common values and heritage of "the humanity." Let us now discuss each of these three layers in more detail.[6]

### *The National Dimension*

The first, "national," dimension of this flexible discourse contains a number of significant discursive elements, including (i) frequent references to the glorious episodes of Turkish history, particularly an emphasis on the "opening of the gates of Anatolia" by the (Muslim) Turks with the Battle of Manzikert in 1071, and on the epic "War of Independence" against the West that resulted in the establishment of the Republic in 1923; (ii) the related significance of the two dates, 2023 and 2071, as the turning points in the future of modern Turkey (see also note 6); (iii) a stress on Turkey's territorial integrity as a fundamental condition to be protected at any cost and the crucial significance of the "brotherhood" between Turks and Kurds for this integrity; (iv) an emphasis on Turkey's regional leadership as a "pivotal country"(or "central power") and on (v) the significance of its mediation roles to solve the inter-state problems among the neighbouring countries through such FP instruments as "rhythmic diplomacy" and, consequently, its rising profile as a "wise country" in the region; and finally, (vi) the promotion of the so-called "Turkish schools" controlled by the Gülen movement through proprietary and facilitating policies.

One might take the historical references that the AK Party leadership often makes as evidence of the significance of this first dimension. In his above-mentioned Congress address, for instance, PM Erdoğan not only invoked the glorious episodes of Turkish history but also presented them in a quite comprehensive manner:

> [The Seljuk] Sultan Alparslan sowed the seeds of a 'civilization of love' that would last for centuries. This civilization burgeoned at the hands of Osman Gazi [the founder of the Ottoman Empire] turning into an offshoot and then a sapling, which in turn transformed into a large plant tree that branched out to heavens and covered seas, from the Caucasus Mountains to the Alps, from the Euphrates and the Tigris to the fiery Danube...There is no blood in the shadow of this large plant tree—the Seljuk, Ottoman and Republican tree. There is no discrimination in the shadow of this plant tree. There is no oppression, repression, and otherization in the shadow of this tree... Now, as the AK Party, we are one of the branches of this large plant tree. The path we follow has been forged by [Seljuk sultans] Alparslan, Melikşah and Kılıçarslan. The path we follow is the same as that of Osman Gazi, Fatih Sultan Mehmet, Sultan Süleyman, Yavuz Sultan Selim.[7]

This "national" layer of the TFP's civilisational discourse is supported and solidified by concrete policies designed and pursued according to the interests of Turkey as a nation-state. Constituting the non-discursive bases of the first dimension of the TFP's civilisational discourse, these policies include, among others, the increasingly expanding and globalising humanitarian efforts through the TİKA (Turkish International Cooperation and Development Agency); the renovation and reconstruction of historic buildings, such as mosques, tombs, madrasas and cemeteries in the former Ottoman territories; efforts to revitalise and promote the traditional Turkish culture through the Yunus Emre Centers (that function like the British Councils) in most part of the world; the foundation of Turkish universities abroad, particularly in Central Asia and the Balkans and attempts at greater role in international politics, such as the Chairmanship of the Committee of Ministers of the Council of Europe in 2011, hosting the 2016 World Humanitarian Summit and moving UNDP's regional bureau for Europe and the Commonwealth of Independent States to Istanbul.[8] Furthermore, we observe that the most intensive activities at the level of non-discursive practices take place, both quantitatively and qualitatively, within this national dimension of the TFP.

### *The Regional Dimension*

The second, "regional," dimension of the civilisational discourse essentially entails two elements: the Middle East as a geographical identity/membership on the one hand, and the wider Muslim World as a cultural identity, on the other. It is often the case that the AKP leadership, particularly Prime Minister R. Tayyip Erdoğan and Foreign Minister Ahmet Davutoğlu, frequently make references in their speeches to these two elements in a relatively ambiguous manner, sometimes emphasising the geographical dimension and at other times the cultural one, which also brings certain flexibility to their discourse. The second layer of this civilisational discourse entails a number of discursive practices, including (i) a rather possessive and protectionist approach to the Palestinian cause and the related critical attitude towards Israel, manifested with continuous, sometimes harsh, but always coherent criticisms; (ii) efforts to support the living conditions, and to defend the humanitarian, economic and political rights of Muslim peoples in a vast geography, from Somalia to Myanmar, and from the Balkans to Syria and South Africa;[9] (iii) a concern for, and a diplomatic affinity with, some Islamic political movements, such as Palestine's Hamas and Tunisia's Ennahda; (iv) discussions on (and Turkey's self-promotion as) a "model country" for the region during the process of the "Arab Spring;" and, underlining all these elements; and (v) Turkey's "zero problems with neighbours" and economic and cultural integration approaches, which are among the essential elements of the Strategic Depth doctrine.[10]

Davutoğlu's recent comments on the hostage crisis where two Turkish pilots and nine Lebanese pilgrims were rescued with the help of the Qatari government on October 19, 2013 may also serve as a representative example:

> … We have also paid close attention to the Lebanese pilgrims. From the very beginning, we have approached the issue from a humanitarian perspective and put all the efforts we could, even though it wasn't part of our responsibility… Whoever feels the pain of separation in our region, we feel the same. It doesn't matter which sect or ethnic group they belong to. We work hard for them all.[11]

Likewise, PM Erdoğan's speech in a recent visit to Kosovo, where he enthusiastically declared that Kosovars and Turks are part of the same history and civilisation, further demonstrates that the second layer of the AK Party's civilisational discourse is not confined to the Middle East only. In his address to a large crowd in a public gathering in Prizren, Erdoğan said:

> Turkey is Kosovo, and Kosovo is Turkey. Languages can be different, religions, sects, faces can be different, but we are all children of the same country… My family, I, and ministers of my delegation feel at home here. Today I greet all Albanians, Bosnians, Turks and Gorans… We will build our future together, just like our grandfathers, our ancestors did. We have lived here as brothers for centuries and we will continue to do so.[12]

Moreover, as with the first dimension, these discursive practices have been supported by a number of concrete policies designed to improve relations with the Middle Eastern and Islamic countries. Constituting the non-discursive bases of the second dimension of the TFP's civilisational discourse, these policies include, for example, undertaking the General Secretariat of the OIC (Organization of Islamic Cooperation) and its revitalisation and intense diplomatic efforts particularly in crisis areas such as Bosnia, Iraq and Syria (e.g. the trilateral consultation mechanisms among Bosnia and Herzegovina, Serbia and Croatia initiated by Turkey in 2009, the Conference of the Interior Ministers of the Neighboring Countries of Iraq started by Turkey in 2004, and the Group of Friends of the Syrian People launched in 2011). Furthermore, some of the "national" policies mentioned above (such as the TİKA's activities) are often integrated, and presented as part of the regional policies and those addressing the Muslim World, at the level of discourse.

Apparently quite different from the traditional TFP, which was mainly Kemalist-oriented and parochial,[13] this new discourse and the practices associated with it are usually perceived as successful, playing a positive role in terms of increasing Turkey's regional influence and prestige. For instance, Turkey's Israel policy, which initially took the form of controlled tension followed by open and harsh criticisms as well as political and military isolation (e.g. cancelling a collectively planned military manoeuvre in October 2009), reached its peak with the "Mavi Marmara crisis" that eventually resulted in an official apology by the Israeli government (The Israelis also seem to have agreed on paying compensation money to the families of the Mavi Marmara victims killed by Israeli soldiers). Turkey has also played a role in the resolution of various regional conflicts, such as between Hamas and al-Fatah, between Syria and Israel (which was not successfully concluded due to Israel's withdrawal), between Iran and the P5+1 group, and most recently between the Syrian opposition forces on the one hand and the Iranian and Lebanese governments on the other, in the hostage crisis during September–October 2013, which also resulted in the freeing of two Turkish airline pilots on October 19, 2013. These success stories may contribute to Turkey's possible leadership in the region. Thus, for example, the leader of Tunisia's Ennahda movement, Rashid al-Ghannuchi, is reported to have said that "the AK Party has moved Turkey to the heart of the [Islamic] *ummah* after living in the margins of history for more than hundred years."[14] Similarly, Michael Rubin, a member of the American Enterprise Institute, the famous 'neo-con' and pro-Israeli think tank, and a harsh critic of the AK Party (and Davutoğlu), has criticised the TFP for the same reason:

> There has been a profound shift in Turkish foreign policy. The ruling *Adalet ve Kalkinma Partisi* [AKP] has sought to reorient Turkish policy away from the United States, toward both Europe and the Islamic world. Turkey's press, much of which makes the BBC look level-headed and unbiased, happily cooperated. The first victim of Turkey's shifting diplomacy has been Israel.[15]

Though these statements are quite partisan and exaggerated, the stress in TFP's civilisational discourse on the Muslim World is unmistakable. This orientation often takes the form of either emphasising the peaceful and cooperative aspects of Islamic culture and history, or drawing attention to the current Muslim suffering and invoking the historical and recent injustices done to Muslims causing their present problems. However, it does not always involve blaming Westerners for Muslims' political and economic backwardness. For instance, in his address at a conference organised by the OIC's IRCICA on the significance of the Qur'an (a discursive act which is itself telling), PM Erdoğan put the blame for the current crisis of the Muslim World squarely on Muslims themselves; still invoking Islamic sources and history and maintaining the perfection of Islam, however:

...Unfortunately, in my visits to Islamic countries I have seen ... extreme poverty, increasing gap in income distribution, widespread intolerance, wars, conflicts and terror... No doubt, this picture is not a product of the doctrines that inform our very existence. No doubt, this picture cannot be the destination to which the sources that constitute the foundations of our civilization would lead us. On the contrary, this picture is a product of an estrangement, a wide gap between theory and practice. Upon witnessing these scenes, I wondered why today's Muslims are so far away from building the monuments that people will admire and constructing glorious cities, despite the fact that they [Muslims] established countless virtuous cities, and magnificent states and great empires based on the Qur'anic message throughout history... I know very well that civilizations, countries and nations have their own days and nights. Our profound civilization, which has greatly contributed to humanity, and to the common cultural and scientific legacy of the mankind in the history, will one day revert to type and reclaim its well-deserved status on the globe.[16]

On the other hand, the emphasis on "democratisation" and "common destiny" with the Muslim World present since 2003 has been intensified with the process of the "Arab Awakening." This intensification might, together with the economic and cultural integration policies that have been in place for the last decade (such as the increase in trade volumes, visa exceptions and cultural exchanges with Muslim countries) strengthen the second dimension of the AKP's civilisational discourse.

### *The Universal Dimension*

The third, "universal," dimension of this discourse entails an emphasis on "universal" values of mankind and its common legacy. Within this framework, the leadership of the AKP government, Prime Minister Erdoğan and Foreign Minister Davutoğlu in particular, frequently refer to the "family of mankind" that shares the "common legacy of humanity" as a basis of their argument for the necessity of a global expansion of peace and cooperation between civilisations as well as national countries. This emphasis on the "common destiny of humanity" becomes visible in their discourses on two particular themes: justice and environmental concerns. Thus, for example, Davutoğlu said in his address at the 2010 UN Climate Change Conference in Cancun, Mexico (and at the preceding Preparatory Meeting of Foreign Ministers in New York) that the Ministers present in the Conference should "act as the Interior Minister of the entire humanity, rather than as Foreign Ministers of individual nation-states" for the protection of natural environment.[17]

The Turkish government also supports this inclusive discourse with a dynamic diplomacy often taking leading initiatives in many international organisations and projects, such as the 5$^{th}$ World Water Forum (Istanbul

2009); Istanbul European Capital of Culture (2010); Summit of the Heads of States of South East Europe (Istanbul 2011); and the United Nations Least Developed Countries Conference (Istanbul 2011). Ankara often presents these initiatives as part of its efforts to promote global peace and cooperation as well as inter-cultural and inter-civilisational dialogue. Moreover, these initiatives discursively function, like the ones mentioned above, as manifestations of Turkey's increasing role in regional politics and its rising profile in international relations. Thus, in terms of the internal dynamics of the TFP's civilisational discourse, they also operate as the connection points that link the three dimensions of this discourse.

A significant feature of the "universalist" dimension of this discourse is its critical tone, which centres particularly on the concept of justice. Criticisms addressed toward the governments of advanced Western countries based on this universal notion thus constitute an important element of this civilisational discourse. This is particularly evident in the Turkish leaders' criticisms of the double standards applied by Western governments, especially by the members of the UN Security Council, in the face of humanitarian crises that emerge in different (mostly Muslim) countries (e.g. Myanmar, Somalia, Iraq and Syria): AKP's leaders openly (and sometimes harshly) criticise these powerful states' attitudes, which often take the form of either ignorance or active support as in the case of Syria most recently on the basis of such universal concepts as "justice" and "shared humanitarian responsibility." Thus, Foreign Minister Davutoğlu has recently criticised the UN and the Western governments for failing to act properly in the Syrian crisis, emphasising the need for acting, as in the case of environmental protection, like the "Interior Minister of Humanity" instead of relying on parochial national interests and callous geostrategic calculations.[18]

Still, TFP's discourse is not entirely critical toward the West; for this third dimension also involves the Turkish Government's concerns (and desires) to improve the relationships with the Western world in general, and the European Union (EU) in particular. In this connection, the most frequently emphasised discursive elements include the *historical relations and cultural exchanges* with the West, whose roots are said to be going back to the classical Ottoman period starting from the 15$^{th}$ century, as well as the idea of *mutual economic interdependence*, which is often emphasised in the context of trade and natural gas. On the other hand, this non-critical aspect of Turkey's universalist civilisational discourse is crystallised in the case of the "alliance of civilizations."

**"Alliance of Civilizations"**

The concept of "alliance of civilizations" also represents the discursive layer where the operationalisation of "civilisation" is most clearly visible in the third dimension of the TFP's discourse. However, parallel with the general characteristics of this discourse, the utilisation of this concept entails flexibility and plurality as well. For, on the one hand, the "alliance of civilizations" refers in a more restricted sense to an institution (UNAOC), which was launched in 2005 as a United Nations initiative under the leadership of Turkey's Prime Minister Erdoğan and the former Prime Minister of Spain, José Luis Rodriguez Zapatero. On the other hand, as a broader and more abstract concept, the "alliance of civilizations" is discursively constructed by the Turkish government as the main framework of Turkey's relationships with the European Union and its EU membership process. Moreover, in both aspects of the concept of "alliance [or dialogue] of civilizations," one may observe some important connections among the three dimensions of TFP's general civilisational discourse.

First of all, the "Alliance of Civilizations initiative" (UNAOC) that is co-chaired by Prime Minister Erdoğan, is an institution that aims "to prevent potential tensions and conflicts among cultures and civilizations, to promote understanding, tolerance and peace, and to secure cooperation among countries and international and non-governmental organizations."[19] Organised under the auspices of the UN Secretary-General and supported by the "Alliance of Civilizations Group of Friends" consisting of over 130 UN member countries, the initiative is particularly concerned for the "tensions that have emerged between Muslim and Western societies," and openly opposes the Islamophobia that has been increasingly intensified in the Western popular culture since the September 11 attacks and to the infamous "clash of civilizations" thesis proposed by Samuel Huntington.[20]

The initiative has organised many projects and activities, such as "Istanbul Conferences," where leading academics and politicians have been invited to deliver talks on intercultural understanding and youth projects to promote dialogue among different youth groups. Moreover, the Institute of the Alliance of Civilizations was established at Fatih Sultan Mehmet Waqf University in Istanbul in 2010 to "provide graduate studies in the area of culture and civilization, and to carry out activities in accordance with the objectives of the Alliance."[21] Turkey has also organised the "Alliance of Civilizations International Traditional Sports Festival" in Denizli in 2012. The fact that Turkey has been actively involved in this initiative since its inception in 2005, trying to play a leading role in various organisations and projects within this framework and committing resources for this purpose, shows that this institution constitutes the most concrete element of the universal dimension of TFP's civilisational discourse, which entails an emphasis on global cooperation and universal values. For instance, in his address to the Second Forum of Alliance of Civilizations, PM Erdoğan located Turkey's efforts for UNAOC within the larger discursive field of inter-civilisational understanding and cooperation:

> We have wholeheartedly believed that Christian, Islamic and Jewish worlds can understand one another. We have also believed that prejudices can be very dangerous in a globalizing world… We have declared against those who push forward the clash of civilizations that alliance of civilizations is possible… Mutual fears and alienation have emerged with the impact of deep historical political and cultural dynamics…We need to foster an understanding that will overcome the 'us and them' dichotomy, which has become the symbol of polarization. The first step toward this is to enhance tolerance, improve dialogue and bring forth solidarity.[22]

Yet, the significance of this element is not confined to the third dimension of this discourse, For the Turkish government members often present the UNAOC as a manifestation of Turkey's (and the AK Party's) desire to further improve their relationships with the West. They also often refer to this initiative (and Turkey's position as a co-founder in its inception) as one of the steps they have taken in order to make Turkey a "global actor" that is efficient in the international arena, as well as a "pivotal country" that assumes a regional leadership in inter-civilisational relations. In other words, the new TFP discourse frames the UNAOC's function in connection with the increasing power of Turkey as a nation-state within the first dimension, and with its "leadership roles" in the Middle East and Muslim world within the second. For instance, in a recent comment of the "unjust" structure and inefficiency of the UN, Erdoğan inserted "alliance of civilizations" as a significant discourse particle into his criticism:

> As Alliance of Civilizations I'd like to ask: Does the United Nations Security Council represent the entire world? ... Do its members represent all religious groups in the world? No, they don't! ... If the United Nations exists for world peace, then it urgently needs reform.[23]

On the other hand, as mentioned above, the AK Party government also presents, in a stark contradistinction to previous periods, the concept of "alliance/dialogue/meeting of civilizations" as the main framework of Turkey's EU accession perspective. This framework entails as a fundamental assumption the idea of a non-hierarchical inter-subjectivity and a negotiation-centred relationship between two parties on an equal ground. The subjects/parties of this relationship (Europe and Turkey) are thus discursively constructed as—actual and potential—partners who must respect each other's civilisational identity and cultural specificity and nourish a non-asymmetrical and cooperative relationship, which would provide mutual benefits for both, on the basis of equality. A reflection of the increasing self-confidence in the TFP, this concept implies that far from being a Third World country hopelessly waiting at the "gates" of Europe, an image that was common in previous periods, Turkey is now a strong candidate country that desires a partnership ("meeting") with the EU as an equal subject with its increasingly stronger economy and its "pivotal country" position that makes it a viable candidate for regional leadership. The manifestations of such a FP perspective are abundant in the discourses of the AKP leadership, particularly that of Prime Minister Erdoğan, on Turkey's relations with the EU. For instance, Erdoğan thus explained his government's EU perspective in an interview with the *Independent* in 2004:

> [Samuel] Huntington declares that there might be a conflict of civilisations. Turkey is a catalyst to make sure we have harmony of civilisations. It is a bridge between the Islamic world and the rest of the world ... [To have] a country like Turkey, where the cultures of Islam and democracy have merged together, taking part in such an institution as the EU, will bring harmony of civilisations. That is why we think it is the project of the century. We are there as a guarantee of an entente between the civilisations.[24]

Likewise, in 2006 Erdoğan said:

> We have put forward our most significant mission as alliance of civilizations. We have also argued that otherwise the EU will remain as a Christian club. When Turkey joins the EU, the EU will no longer be remembered as a Christian club. Conversely, it will become a locus of the alliance of civilizations.[25]

What we see here, particularly in the first quote, is an intertwining of the two elements of the concept of "alliance of civilizations" (the UN initiative and Turkey's EU membership perspective): the phrase "the project of the century" is an official slogan of the UNAOC co-chaired by Erdoğan. The fact that he inserts both meanings simultaneously into one single sentence implies that he constructs a subject position for Turkey (and himself) as a representative of a different civilisation[26] at an equal status with Turkey's/his European counterparts at the negotiation table.

Therefore, it is safe to argue that one of the essential elements of Erdoğan's (and the AKP government's)—critical—approach to the EU is a civilisational discourse whose historical, geographical and cultural dimensions are often emphasised by the Turkish political elites. In fact, this discursive framework might also help explain the increasingly bold claim by the members of the Turkish government that Turkey's EU membership will be more beneficial for EU countries—many of which are in financial crisis—than Turkey itself, which is accompanied by their discursive emphasis on Turkey's economic and demographic dynamism in this context.

On the other hand, the concept of "alliance/dialogue of civilizations" also refers to the interlocking of the universal(ist) discursive layer in which it is located with the two other layers. For, on the one hand, it assumes a conceptual ground on which universal human values and the "common legacy of the humanity" are of paramount importance; on the other hand, this concept implies the existence not only of a multi-civilisational world order, both historically and today, but also of an authentic Turkish–Islamic civilisation, which is different (and independent) from the Western one. The concept of "alliance of civilizations" further implies that Turkey is the most important representative of this authentic civilisation that the Westerners may (and should) talk to as a main interlocutor. Therefore, this concept refers not only to civilisational pluralism and differences, but at the same time to the idea that these differences are not to be understood as reasons for a civilisational clash, but they may (and should) instead live together through the methods of "dialogue" and "cooperation," and even "alliance."

Within this framework, a specific element included in the discourse of the "alliance of civilizations" is that these dialogues and alliance are to be established primarily between the Islamic and Western civilisations, and that their philosophical/ideational foundation is to involve the notions of the "family of humanity" and "common destiny," as often emphasised by FM Davutoğlu. In this sense, "alliance/dialogue of civilizations" as a concept contains the apparent traces of Davutoğlu's own discourse in his academic studies, particularly in *Strategic Depth* and *Civilisational Transformation and the Muslim World.*[27]

On the other hand, the three concentric circles of this flexible civilisational discourse bear similarities, in both content and form, with the three intellectual perspectives that were dominant in the late-Ottoman Turkey in the early 20$^{th}$ century: Ottomanism (the idea of the unification of all Ottoman peoples, regardless of religious and ethnic differences, under the Ottoman flag), Islamism (the idea of the unification of Muslims under Turkey's leadership), and "Westernism"(the idea of a full integration with the "European civilization") (Soon, however, Turkish nationalism would hold sway and become dominant, in alliance with Westernism, in Kemalist Turkey.) Though different and rival, these ideologies existed simultaneously and sometimes intermingled with one another; their traces are manifested in the AKP leadership's discursive strategies, such as various historical references, emphasising national values and/or the "common legacy of the humanity," thereby producing a hybrid discourse, which is not, naturally, without its internal 'contradictions'. For example, we often observe the juxtaposition of a strong emphasis on identity with an authentic Islamic civilisation on the one hand, and the desire to expand such originally Western values as democracy and human rights etc. to the entire Muslim World. These 'foreign' elements that surface in their speeches from time to time are tried to be dissolved within this hybrid discourse.

Finally, discourse cannot, of course, exist in a vacuum; nor can it live without any 'actual' basis formed by political, ideological, economic and military power sources.[28] In the case of Turkey's civilisational FP discourse, these power sources are crystallised in the three main non-discursive factors that help this hybrid discourse to survive: Turkey's economic dynamism and continuing growth, Prime Minister Erdoğan's charismatic leadership and Davutoğlu's foreign policy activism and ideological guidance.[29] Turkey's increasingly strong economy facilitates its supportive (and even possessive) attitude toward the problems of particular Turkish and Islamic peoples, thereby enhancing Turkey's standing on international platforms. Likewise, Erdoğan's strong leadership and charismatic personality help maintain people's trust in TFP, in both Turkey and the Middle East, thereby strengthening the legitimacy of the steps taken by TFP. Finally, the new, "hyper-active" TFP paradigm formed around Davutoğlu's strong academic background as well as his personal leadership and persuasive diplomatic skills, makes it easier to constantly expand its horizon to new areas (both geographically and methodologically) and create new syntheses with its continuous dynamism and "rhythmic diplomacy" style. When banded together, these three factors help either reconcile the potential contradictory elements within the hybrid TFP discourse or cover them by emphasising some of these elements on certain occasions and at the same time ignoring or de-emphasising others. Consequently, the internal coherence and relative efficacy of the TFP's civilisational discourse are improved through such an accommodation, or what we may call a "meta-discursive strategy."[30] Clearly, however, the ultimate success of this discourse depends on concrete developments and practical results: for any discourse needs to be supported by relevant action in order to be effective. On the other hand, as Michel Foucault emphasises, discourse is not merely a reflection of "real life;" it is at the same time one of the essential elements that constitute and shape social reality.[31] Thus, to the extent that it is effective, the new TFP's civilisational discourse also exemplifies a case of such constitutive character.

**Conclusion: Why Civilisational Discourse?**

I have argued throughout the chapter that the AK Party government's general FP approach has been based—at least partly—on a civilisational discourse that is ambiguous but also very flexible; which has been increasingly visible in the speeches of Turkish political elites, including particularly Prime Minister R. Tayyip Erdoğan and Foreign Minister Ahmet Davutoğlu, for the last decade. I have tried to demonstrate that this discourse consists of three main 'layers' or concentric circles, including national, regional and universal ones, which respectively invoke Turkish history and culture, Islamic history and Middle Eastern geography, and the common legacy and destiny of entire humanity. I have tried to examine them by analytically separating them from each other, though in reality they are closely connected and even often mixed with one another, which is what makes this discourse both vague and flexible—and also effective. I have also argued that the AKP's discourse of "alliance/dialogue/meeting of civilizations" might be better understood if located within the third ("universal") layer. Employed by the AKP leadership both as a main conceptual framework of Turkey's EU membership process and as a mechanism of inter-cultural rapprochement through the "Alliance of Civilizations" (UNAOC) initiative founded and co-chaired by Prime

Minister Erdoğan under the auspices of the UN, this discourse and the policies associated with it simultaneously facilitate Turkey's claim for regional leadership and as representative of the Muslim World, as well as increasing its standing in international relations and enhancing its relations with the Western world. We have also observed that the Turkish leadership often backs this discourse with concrete policies and activism through a very dynamic diplomacy in order to increase the efficiency of this multi-faceted civilisational discourse.

At this point, it might be useful to briefly discuss the possible factors, in addition to Davutoğlu's obvious ideological and academic influences, that have led the AK Party leadership to adopt such a civilisational discourse. First of all, one observes, from a historical perspective, that processes of globalisation and democratisation have facilitated the ascendance of the AK Party (and the previous National Outlook tradition), whose members were already familiar with the concept of "civilisation." For debates on civilisation have been present in Turkey (and the wider Muslim World) since the mid-19th century: intellectuals and statesmen from the "Young Ottomans" (e.g. Namık Kemal) to Ziya Gökalp and Prince Sabahattin, from Jamaluddin al-Afghani to Rashid Rida and Maududi etc. have extensively debated the past, present and future of "Islamic civilization" vis-à-vis the "Western" one. These debates continued among the Islamic intellectuals during the second half of the 20th century as well.[32] On the other hand, the religious middle classes in Turkey have become stronger and more assertive politically and economically with the help of the process of globalisation in general, and the liberal economic policies and the relatively free environment for political competition in particular; all of which have been increasingly developing in Turkey since the early 1980s. In the 1990s, the members of this new middle class started seeing themselves as beneficiaries of globalisation, instead of its victims. Equipped with a newly found but increasingly stronger self-confidence, these religious people, who also constitute the main base of the AK Party, began to regard primarily with sympathy—rather than fear and enmity—the 'requirements' of globalisation (cultural, as well as economic and political), including Turkey's EU membership, during the 2000s.[33] As Kösebalaban points out, for Turkey's religious middle classes Europe (or the EU) turned from a Hobbesian "other" (enemy) into a Lockean "other" (rival), in Alexander Wendt's classification.[34]

On the other hand, parallel to the globalisation process, Turkey's democratisation that began in the 1950s and intensified during the 1980s has been advantageous for religious-conservative groups in Turkish politics. For the relative relaxation and free environment experienced in the public sphere in the last three decades have enhanced their status and political power, eventually opening the way for their coming to power—first with the Welfare Party (1996), and then the AK Party (2002) following the "February 28" coup d'état. Kept under constant pressure politically, economically and culturally by the Kemalist elites in the name of secularism for a long time, these religious-conservative groups have made use of the "opportunity windows" (in the form of enhanced opportunities for higher education, trade and business, and political participation) offered by a relative democratisation process beginning from the transition to the multi-party system in 1950, which culminated in their coming to power. For the last decade, moreover, they have been transforming the Turkish political system, which had been under the tight control of the military and Kemalist ideology, from within. The AK Party opted for an intensely Western-oriented FP discourse and practice during the first years of its rule due to the legitimacy problem that its leaders experienced in the eyes of both Western powers and the local bureaucratic and economic elites. However, with the aid of the self-confidence that they developed as a result of their victory over the existing military-bureaucratic tutelage system through various politico-legal battles (particularly the Ergenekon and Balyoz court cases) since 2009, AK Party leaders have had the opportunity to bring the question of "civilization," which has been debated in Turkey since the late-Ottoman era, to the fore more loudly and comfortably. Furthermore, under the guidance of Davutoğlu's profound intellectual background, this concept has increasingly been turned into a "discourse"—a series of systematic, integrated and coherent statements.

However, there is also a third, external, factor that has contributed to the crystallisation of this concept: the regional security context of the Middle East, which has been transformed as a result of the September

11 attacks and the 2003 Iraq War. The Middle East turned into a most critical region for the US and other global powers following the changes in international political-military conditions after September 11, 2011. With the further impact of the Iraq War, the "region" has become one of the two most important dossiers (the other being the EU membership process) in TFP. This situation has been further solidified by the "Arab Spring" that started in late 2010, and especially by the Syrian civil war. As a result, the 'Middle East' has probably gained a more prominent status than the EU membership in TFP: Both Erdoğan and Davutoğlu on the one hand, and the FM bureaucracy (and consequently the Turkish media) on the other, have started spending more time and energy on the "region" than on the EU. For this reason, the above-mentioned change in the international politico-military context forced the TFP to be more focused on the Middle East, thereby making it an issue that the AK Party (that has "Islamic references") had to deal with for geopolitical reasons—and not seem to be paying special attention to for cultural-religious reasons. Consequently, this requirement has expanded the AK Party government's manoeuvring capacity and enhanced its discursive transformation in relation to the Middle East, thereby contributing—as *an unintended consequence*—to the strengthening of the "regional dimension" of Turkey's FP discourse. It is thus with the help of this external factor that the TFP has, after a long hiatus caused by the Kemalist ideology and institutions, returned to the Middle East.[35]

Fourt, this vague civilisational discourse is fairly rational and quite useful for the AK Party government, for it expands its FP options. Simultaneously invoking both the "Eastern" and "Western" cultures, this discourse helps Turkey claim its membership in both Islamic/Middle Eastern and Western worlds, but at the same time allows for an emphasis on the Turkish national identity. Furthermore, it forges a discursive ground for one of Davutoğlu's (and increasingly the government's) central assertions—that Turkey is a "central country/power" within the Afro-Eurasian geopolitical continent, rather than a "bridge" or a "frontier country" (or Huntington's "torn country" for that matter) between the East and the West. It is on this ground that the AK Party leadership bases Turkey's claim for being a "regional and global actor."

A fifth advantage of this civilisational discourse for Turkey is observed in both domestic and international politics. The first two layers of the discourse emphasise the peaceful co-existence and cooperation, both historically and today, of different ethnic and religious groups within Turkey and the wider Middle East (particularly the Arabs, Kurds, the Shia and Alevis as well as Sunnis and Turks) on the one hand, and justify and re-claim Turkey's territorial integrity and historical depth by invoking the glorious epochs of Turkish history (particularly the Ottoman and Seljuk periods), on the other. On a more practical ground, the discursive synthesis of Turkish, Middle Eastern, Islamic and Western identities and values plays a mitigating function that softens up the potential criticisms by both domestic and global power actors. Therefore, this inclusive discourse carries quite a positive function for both the legitimacy of the AK Party government and the desired integrity of Turkey and the Middle East.[36]

Finally, we observe that the AK Party leadership, and PM Erdoğan in particular, also make an effective use of historical references as part of this multi-faceted discourse. The primary implication of the above-mentioned references to such historical turning points as 1071, 1453, and 1923 is that they simultaneously invoke both domestic politics (particularly the issue of territorial and cultural integrity in the context of the Kurdish question) and the new direction of the TFP with its more inclusive and cosmopolitan identity.[37] Moreover, this discourse makes it possible to establish parallels between historical co-existence ("brotherhood") of particularly Turks, Kurds and Arabs in both Turkey and the Middle East on the one hand, and TFP's civilisational orientation, on the other. Thus, Erdoğan clearly states that Turkey should play "a leading role" in the construction of "a new civilisational consciousness" in the Muslim World.[38] Hence the AK Party government's ambiguous, but quite flexible, dynamic and pragmatically useful civilisational discourse.

## Notes

1. The impact of the "Davutoğlu vision" on TFP may be seen in his various interviews with the Turkish and international media since 2002, when he was appointed as the Chief Advisor to Prime Minister. See Davutoğlu 2004a, 2004b, 2004c, 2006, 2007, 2008; see also Davutoğlu 2013: 14-15.For an examination of Davutoğlu's discourse of civilisation in his academic work, particularly in *Strategic Depth*, see Ardiç 2014 (forthcoming).

2. Foucault 1972: 64 ff.
3. Duran 2013: 94.
4. For the text of Erdoğan's speech, see http://www.akparti.org.tr/site/haberler/basbakan-erdoganin-ak-parti-4.-olagan-buyuk-kongresi-konusmasinin-tam-metni/31771; see also Duran 2013: 93.
5. See *AK Parti 2023 Siyasi Vizyonu: Siyaset, Toplum, Dünya* (30 Eylül 2012), http://www.akparti.org.tr/upload/documents/akparti2023siyasivizyonuturkce.pdf, accessed January 4, 2013. Here 2023 refers to the centenary of the establishment of the Republic of Turkey, and 2071 to the millenary of the arrival of the Turks in Anatolia/Asia Minor.
6. Duran (2013) is the first to pay attention to these three layers in the AK Party's civilisational discourse. His examination focuses, however, more on domestic politics than the TFP discourse, primarily on Prime Minister Erdoğan's statements, and on the last few years of the AKP rule. Furthermore, the second layer in Duran's classification entails the Middle East only, rather than the entire Muslim World. Moreover, his study is based on a brief textual examination of Erdoğan's statements in connection with the AK Party's political struggles with domestic and foreign power actors, rather than a thorough discourse analysis, which the present chapter aims to do. Finally, Duran's analysis does not involve the concept (and institution) of "Alliance of Civilizations" that is an integral part of the AK Party's civilisational discourse. Despite these limitations, however, his examination is inspirational and quite useful in understanding the AK Party government's current policies.
7. See http://www.akparti.org.tr/site/haberler/basbakan-erdoganin-ak-parti-4.-olagan-buyuk-kongresi-konusmasinin-tam-metni/31771, accessed January 4, 2013.
8. See e.g. http://www.tccb.gov.tr/news/397/87256/president-gul-evaluates-his-visit-to-new-york.html accessed September 29, 2013.
9. Duran correctly calls these efforts "Islamic solidarity politics." See Duran 2013: 94.
10. See Davutoğlu (2013) for a detailed discussion on the principles guiding the new TFP.
11. "Ahmet Davutoğlu'ndan pilotların son durumlarıyla ilgili açıklama" http://www.turkiyegazetesi.com.tr/editorunsectikleri/91265.aspx, accessed October 20, 2013.
12. "PM Erdogan: Turkey is Kosovo and Kosovo is Turkey" 24.10.2013, http://www.worldbulletin.net/?aType=haber&ArticleID=121375, accessed October 25, 2013. The Turkish leadership is also careful to stress that Turkey's interest in the Balkans does not stem from any "neo-Ottomanist ambitions" but Turkey's "historical and cultural depth" in the region. (See e.g. Davutoğlu's statements in an interview with a Bosnian journalist: "Davutoglu: 'I'm Not a Neo-Ottoman'" 26.04.2011, http://www.balkaninsight.com/en/article/davutoglu-i-m-not-a-neo-ottoman, accessed October 25, 2013.) The Balkan case further complicates the TFP's civilisational discourse because it is quite inclusive and accommodative as it reserves room for non-Muslim, as well as Muslim, peoples of the region, including Serbs, Croatians and Bulgarians, by invoking common history and "cultural depth." The Balkans as an object of TFP's discourse thus represents the limits of this discourse—by simultaneously signifying these limits and blurring them.
13. See Balci 2013 for an overview of the traditional TFP. The short period during 1996–1997 under the Erbakan government may be said to be different from the traditional, Kemalist- and Western-oriented TFP; however, the AKP's FP vision and practices are also different (and vastly more successful) than Erbakan's "National

Outlook" vision, which essentially aimed to make Turkey a "leader country" in the Muslim World by severing relations with the West and focusing on the former only. Unlike the AKP, it also failed to integrate FP with domestic politics (political and economic structures and relations with the military). For a detailed account of the FP preferences and vision of Erbakan's Refah (Welfare) Party government, see Dağı 1998.

14. "Gannuşi: Türkiye, İslam aleminin tam kalbinde" 30.12.2012, http://www.dunyabulteni.net/?aType=haber&ArticleID=229047, accessed March 14,2013.
15. M. Rubin, "Shifting Sides? The Problems of Neo-Ottomanism," *National Review*, August 10, 2004http://www.meforum.org/628/shifting-sides,accessed September 15,2013.
16. "Başbakan: Suçlu biziz Kur'an'ı anlamadık" 05.09.2010, http://www.haber7.com/siyaset/haber/600047-basbakan-suclu-biziz-kuran-i-anlamadik, accessed September 15, 2013. Note also that the term "virtuous city" is a central theme in the political philosophy of the famous 10th-century Islamic philosopher al-Farabi and the title of his well-known book. The glorification of Islamic civilisation with reference to the historical achievements of Muslims in science and arts (and urban development) at an academic conference mostly attended by Islamic scholars is quite significant in terms of manifesting Erdoğan's inspirations. Though probably not directly connected to this, Davutoğlu too makes references to al-Farabi (and other Muslim scholars) quite frequently in his earlier, more philosophical, works (e.g. Davutoğlu 1994a).
17. "Dışişleri Bakanı Sayın Ahmet Davutoğlu'nun Dünya Kadınlar Haftası Vesilesiyle Türkiye İş Kadınları Derneği Tarafından Düzenlenen Toplantıda Yaptıkları Konuşma, 9 Mart 2013, İstanbul" http://www.mfa.gov.tr/disisleri-bakani-sayin-ahmet-davutoglu_nun-dunya-kadinlar-haftasi-vesilesiyle-turkiye-is-kadinlari-dernegi-tarafindan-duzenlenen.tr.mfa, accessed March 14, 2013.
18. "Davutoğlu: Tarih hepimizi yargılayacak" 08.03.2013. http://www.radikal.com.tr/radikal.aspx?atype=radikaldetayv3&articleid=1124295&categoryid=78, accessed March 14, 2013.
19. *Alliance of Civilizations Second National Implementation Plan Turkey*, nd., p. 8.See also http://www.medeniyetlerittifaki.org.tr/index.php?option=com_content&view=article&id=1&Itemid=32, accessed March 15, 2013.
20. *Ibid.* See also http://www.medeniyetlerittifaki.org.tr/index.php?option=com_content&view=article&id=25&Itemid=11, accessed March 15, 2013. For the "clash of civilizations" thesis, see Huntington 1993.
21. *Alliance of Civilizations Second National Implementation Plan Turkey*, nd., p. 9.
22. "Erdoğan, dünyaya Mevlana dizeleriyle mesaj verdi" 06.04.2009, http://www.zaman.com.tr/gundem_erdogan-dunyaya-mevlana-dizeleriyle-mesaj-verdi_834332.html, accessed March 16, 2013.
23. "Başbakandan BM'ye kritik soru"http://www.haberturk.com/dunya/haber/823641-basbakandan-bmye-kritik-soru, February 27 2013, accessed July 11, 2013. Note the ambiguous use of the term "alliance of civilizations" here.
24. "The Monday Interview: Prime Minister of Turkey" *Independent*, December 13, 2004. http://www.independent.co.uk/news/people/profiles/recep-tayyip-erdogan-taking-part-in-the-eu-will-bring-harmony-of-civilisations--it-is-the-project-of-the-century-24489.html.

25. "Kadına karşı ayrımcılık ırkçılık kadar tehlikeli" *Yeni Şafak*, 29.01.2006. http://yenisafak.com.tr/arsiv/2006/Ocak/29/p01.html, accessed March 16, 2013.
26. Whether this 'different civilization' refers to an "Eastern" or specifically a "Turkish–Islamic" one is left unclear, of course, in line with the intrinsic vagueness of this discourse.
27. See Davutoğlu 1994b, 2001. See also note 2 above.
28. For a sophisticated theorisation of these four sources of power, see Mann 1986, particularly ch. 1.
29. Turkey's military muscle might also help this discourse be effective, but a full analysis of this factor is beyond the scope of this article.
30. I use the concept of "meta-discursive strategy" to refer to a general discursive strategy that connects and/or brings together all specific discursive strategies (in the Foucaultian sense) within a general framework. See Ardiç (2012: 35-36) for an explication of the concept of "meta-discursive strategy."
31. Foucault 1972: 64 ff.
32. For a useful discussion on these debates see Kara 1986 (Türkiye'de İslamcılık Düşüncesi, Istanbul: Dergah, 1986) and Aydin 2007.
33. See Ardiç 2009 for an account of globalisation and its effects on Turkey; see Ardiç and Özcan (eds.) 2012 for a collection of articles that examine this issue from different angles.
34. Kösebalaban 2009: 5.
35. See also Kösebalaban 2009: 8.
36. Duran (2013: 93, 95) argues that this discourse primarily allows the AK Party to accommodate the three challenges that it has been facing since the beginning: the "Islamic past," "Kemalism's legacy" and the "regional power balances."
37. Furthermore, as Duran (2013: 94) points out, these historical references are also functional in terms of forging an identity for the AK Party itself.
38. Erdoğan 2012: 23.

# 3
# Strategic Depth Doctrine and Turkish Engagement in West Asia

*Nitish Kumar*

## Introduction

Over the course of the rise to power of the Justice and Development Party (AKP) since 2002, Turkey has emerged as a major actor in the West Asian region. Under the leadership of Recep Tayyip Erdoğan, the Turkish government embarked upon some of the issues which were unthinkable earlier. Turkey, while following a foreign policy known as 'Strategic Depth Doctrine', not only initiated several mediating missions such as a peace deal between Israel and the Palestinians and indirect talks between Israel and Syria, but even improved the relationship with some of its own traditional rivals such as Syria and Iran. Emphasising mainly on the component of 'zero problem with neighbours', of the 'new foreign policy', Turkey signed multilevel cooperation agreements with Bashar al-Assad's government in Syria and adopted a reconciliatory approach on the issue of the Iranian nuclear programme. Moreover, policy makers in Ankara justified this new orientation even despite the fact that Turkey's relations with its traditional allies, such as Israel and United States, witnessed a relative coolness under this new initiative. The new approach was regarded successful as it was helpful in raising the popularity of Turkey's leadership in the Arab World and was also seen as an attempt to strike an 'independent' foreign policy from the United States, besides as a reaction to the delayed process of European Union membership.

But with the onset of the 'Arab Spring', Turkey's ambitious foreign policy came under serious constraint. Brutal crackdowns of the protesters by the authoritarian rulers of the West Asian countries forced Turkey to adopt a tough stance against those regimes with whom it had built a good relationship in the preceding years via its new orientation known in some quarters as 'neo-Ottomanism'. Similarly, by showing Turkish limitations in its failed attempt to pursue the belligerent regimes to give up their power in course of peaceful resolution of the crisis, the 'Arab Spring' also altered the delicate balance of power in the region which has its crucial ramifications over the Kurdish demand of autonomy; an anathema for the Turkish establishment. As the ethnic factors are gaining currency and many regional and international players are increasingly pursing their interest in the Syrian quagmire, it is obvious that Turkish policy makers will face new challenges and risks in the coming future. Therefore, this chapter, while discussing the basic principle and aim of the 'Strategic Depth Doctrine' tries to look into the question of how Turkey's foreign policy will be affected by these new challenges, manifested mainly in the intra-state conflict in Syria. Also, an attempt has been made in this chapter to establish the point that besides being influenced by the idea of Foreign Minister Ahmet Davutoğlu, changes in Turkish foreign policy are also determined by the structural changes in the region and strategic consideration in Ankara.

## Strategic Depth Doctrine and West Asia before 'Arab Spring'

When the newly formed and Islamic-oriented AKP came into power in Ankara in 2002, Turkey confronted a new set of problems such as rising violence of Kurdish terrorism, slowing down of booming economy, and deepening divide between the East and the West. Therefore, to confront the new challenges, Turkish foreign relations strategists re-mapped the region and adopted a new foreign policy approach. Turkey which has largely followed the Kemalist vision of foreign policy during the 1990s and established itself as a 'coercive regional power' by giving prominence to 'national security considerations', tried the alternative of 'neo-Ottomanism' in the new millennium and projected itself as a 'benign regional power' with less prominence of the 'securitisation consideration'.[1] Although the 'neo-Ottamanism' has its roots in the vision and policy of the former Prime Minister and President Turgut Ozal, it took a concrete form, a moderate stance and a new name in the idea of Ahmet Davutoğlu, an academician and Foreign Minister of Turkey since 2009. Giving a new name of 'Strategic Depth Doctrine', in place of 'neo-Ottomanism', professor Davutoğlu reformulated the various aspects of not only Turkish engagements with the outside world but even its approach towards solving the domestic problems.

Under the doctrine of 'Strategic Depth', Davutoğlu, advocated five basic principles of Turkey's foreign policy, helpful in achieving an active engagement in a regional political system and moving away from its previous 'threat assessment approach'.[2] According to the first principle, to establish an area of influence in the region it is necessary for Turkey to have a 'balance between security and democracy' within. The second prerequisite for the successful implementation of 'Strategic Depth Doctrine' is the principle of 'Zero Problem' policy towards Turkey's neighbours', which implies good relations with the countries bordering Turkey. The third principle of the doctrine is the extension of the second one and is focused on the neighbouring region rather than country. According to this principle Turkey should attempt to 'play an active role in resolving regional disputes'. More broadly, Turkey should act as a leader in its attempts to overcome the supposed clash between the West and the Muslim world. The fourth principle is the adherence to a 'multi-dimensional foreign policy', where Turkey's relations with other countries are seen in complementarities rather than in competition. The fifth and the last principle in this framework is 'rhythmic diplomacy' which means pushing for sustained pro-activism in the field of diplomacy, trying to achieve a more active role in international organisations and opening up to new areas where Turkish contacts have been limited in the past.[3]

Based on these principles, the AKP-led government in Turkey initiated a number of structural and substantive changes in the domain of foreign policy formulation. Foremost among them were the attempts to redefine the thinking related with the concept of 'national security' in Ankara besides a conscious effort to weaken Turkey's infamous

'Sèvres-phobia'.[4] Secondly, the growing role of civil society in foreign policy-making or broader civilianisation of Turkish politics especially in 'high politics' issues, has also been recognised. Apart from these two changes, willingness to be proactive and take risks has also been added as the third characteristic of Turkey's new foreign policy under the new government of AKP. Finally, it has also been decided that in an attempt to resolve bilateral problems and actively develop closer relations with the neighbouring countries Turkey would follow a new approach of 'win–win' rather than 'win–lose'.[5]

Under the whole idea of 'Strategic Depth Doctrine', some specific policy prescription regarding Turkey's engagement with its south-eastern neighbours has been given. For Davutoğlu, any engagement with the West Asian countries or West Asianisation of Turkish foreign policy should be based on four principles. First of all, common security for the entire region or in other words security for everyone instead of one particular group or country has been upheld. Secondly, it has been said that priority must be given to dialogue rather than conflict as a means to solve crises. Third principle is the economic interdependence where it was assumed that for lasting peace and order in the region, an end of the atmosphere of isolated economies is an essential prerequisite. And lastly, taking into account of the fact that none of the West Asian countries or cities has been composed of a homogenous ethnic and sectarian fabric, Davutoğlu, advanced the principle of cultural coexistence and plurality for the governments of the region.[6]

Following the above principle, the AKP government adopted a foreign policy which was full with a sense of self-confidence. Although Turkey's renewed approach in the foreign policy domain witnessed significant changes in almost all spheres, it was Ankara's perception and strategy towards the West Asian region and the southeastern neighbours that was unprecedented and most visible. Turkey's eagerness to play third party roles in the management and, if possible, the resolution of regional conflicts could be regarded as the first step in the employment of its soft power in the immediate neighbourhood.[7] Utilising its main asset i.e. having good relations with the parties of different conflicts, Turkey attempted to restart negotiations between Israel and Syria and the mediation process between Israel and Palestine. By sending its own forces to UNIFIL II, and by attempting to mediate, albeit unsuccessfully, the political crisis in Lebanon, Turkey also tried to relate itself to larger regional geopolitical struggles which was earlier a no-go area for the Turkish policy makers.[8]

Taking the specific case of Turkey's engagement with the southeastern neighbours, AKP's new approach in the region manifested firstly during the 2003 Iraq war when the Turkish Parliament (Grand National Assembly) refused to allow the deployment of 62,000 US soldiers in Turkey in order to open a second front in northern Iraq.[9] Turkey's unprecedented move in Iraq continued even during the post-war period as Turkey changed its policy toward the Kurdish Regional Government (KRG) in Northern Iraq from containment to engagement, and recognised the legitimacy of KRG as a federal entity within Iraq.[10] Similarly, Ankara also appeared willing to engage in more direct relations with Iran and it was Turkey's policy towards the Iranian nuclear programme, that indicated a clear drift from Turkey's old perception regarding its role and policies in the West Asian region. Turkey, in a bid to solve the standoff, assumed a key mediating role and distanced itself from the US and the EU stance. In 2010, Turkey along with Brazil tried hard to broker a deal on the issue of Iranian uranium enrichment, so that the UN Security Council would not impose additional sanctions on Iran.[11] Although, Turkey could not succeed in a compromise solution between Iran and the Western alliance, but its policy on this matter demonstrated another example of autonomous foreign policy actions, and attracted criticism from US and EU officials.[12]

Similarly, Ankara's relations with Damascus also witnessed a dramatic upward shift in such a way that it was presented by the AKP's leader as the model of the 'zero problem with neighbours' policy. The very first sign of improvement was the Turkish decision to raise the flow of water to above 900 cubic metres to Syria even though Turkey guaranteed a water flow of 500 cubic metres per second in a protocol signed in 1987.[13] This rapprochement was underscored by an unprecedented level of bilateral visits and by the collaboration in political, strategic and economic fields. On the political side, Syria's claim for the province of

Alexandretta/Hatay was effectively shelved. It is also noteworthy that Syria, a traditional Turkey-skeptic country in the Arab world, did not object to the election of a Turkish head of the OIC.[14] On the economic front one can see a phenomenal growth in trade between the two countries from $729 million in 2000 to $1,174 million in 2007, when a free trade agreement was signed. Between 2005 and 2007, Syrian authorities also approved more than 30 Turkish investment projects in the country and the number of Turkish tourists to Syria increased nineteen fold between 2000 and 2005.[15]

Contrary to this, Turkey's relations with Israel witnessed a significant downturn as Prime Minister Erdoğan, reacting over the Israeli policy, described it as "State-sponsored terrorism", called for an end of violence, and hosted in Ankara a high-ranking Hamas delegation led by Khaled Mashaal.[16] Tension escalated further since Turkey harshly criticised Israel following the latter's invasion of the Gaza strip in December 2008 known as 'Operation Cast Lead' and Prime Minister Erdoğan's outburst at Israel's President Shimon Peres in a panel at the World Economic Forum in Davos in January 2009.[17] The fall-out of the Gaza war continues to plague ties between Israel and Turkey as Ankara abruptly cancelled Israel's participation in the multinational 'Anatolian Eagle' air exercise in October 2009. The bottom point in the Turkey–Israel–relations was reached with the crisis of *Mavi Marmara*, in which ships comprising the aid flotilla arrived from Britain, Ireland, Algeria, Kuwait, Greece and Turkey and coordinated by a Turkish NGO namely *Insani Yardim Vakfi* to Gaza were attacked by Israeli commandos, killing up to 19 people—mostly Turkish nationals.

Although Davutoğlu's 'Strategic Depth Doctrine' has its implementational rationale in the changing structural setting at the regional and domestic level, AKP's pursuit of 'Zero Problem with Neighbours' policy with the West Asian countries was also aimed to achieve certain dividends. In other words, with the US invasion of Iraq in 2003, EU's 'yes but no' approach regarding Turkey's membership and the spectacular development of the Turkish economy with special reference to its Anatolian hinterland, provided the ground for the Turkish opening or implementing Davutoğlu's vision to the West Asian region and the rest of the world, one can also explain Erdoğan's attempt to alter Turkey's relational pattern with West Asian neighbours with the reference to specific issues. AKP's out-of-war decision in Iraq in 2003 and subsequently its willingness to establish close relations with KRG could also be explained from the realist perspective rather than from the point of view of the Strategic Depth Doctrine. As Turkey's previous experience with the Iraqi crisis was less than ideal and Turkey had to suffer from considerable economic loss and terrorist strikes from Kurdish groups, it was very difficult for the policy makers in Ankara to give assent to another adventure in Iraq.[18] Moreover, in the post-Saddam era, it was again a meticulous conclusion by the policy makers in Ankara that made Turkey drift towards establishing a close relation with the KRG. For the AKP government, better relations with the KRG contained the tantalising chance of improving its checkered relations with its own Kurdish minority as the KRG leadership were widely respected by the Turkish Kurds and also exercised a significant influence over them.[19]

Kurdish consideration also played a crucial role in improving relations between Turkey, Iran, and Syria as all three were interested in a stable and a territorially unified Iraq and they rejected the formation of an independent Kurdish state.[20] Moreover it is also a fact that in the new millennium, Iran's importance as an energy supplier of Turkey has increased and some Turkish companies engage themselves in the development of Iranian hydrocarbon fields as well, and the Turkish government desired to transit Iranian gas to the West through Turkey as it has the potential of great economic benefit.[21] However, all these economic dividends were based on the precondition that the Iranian and Western relations get on a stable and peaceful track whose possibilities were being increasingly shadowed by the deadlock on the nuclear issue. Therefore, Turkey fearing that the resulting chaos would have certainly undermined Turkish economic gains and domestic prosperity—which have been AKP's most important accomplishment and source of domestic support—attempted reconciliation and mediation.[22]

Although, Syria was considered as 'the poster child for Zero Problem policy', Davutoğlu's approach alone could not explain Turkey's improved ties with Damascus. Besides the possibility of an independent

Kurdish state, which has automatically pushed Ankara to adopt more cooperative and closer relations with Syria, the Turkish perspective of having good bilateral relations was also grounded on the assumptions that better trade ties with Syria would open up the Arab markets for Turkish traders.[23] Moreover, there was also an argument that a good relation with Damascus could have been helpful in 'peeling away' Syria from its strategic relationship with Iran, which would have been a strategic gain not only for Turkey but even for the US.[24] Similarly, it has been also thought that improvement in Turkish–Syrian relations would be helpful in enhancing Ankara's soft power in the region, as good relations with Assad's regime was an important prerequisite for any successful mediation efforts regarding the Israeli–Syrian track.

Turkey's deteriorating relations with Israel was also a result of the AKP's quest to consolidate their domestic support and regional popularity as the relations between Israel and Turkey were only supported by a very small segment of population and it has been believed that the more the Turks appeared to be at odds with the US and its allies, the higher Erdoğan's popularity would rise in the region.[25] Moreover, some analysts have also argued that it is the improvement in Turkey's strategic environment, which is most helpful in locating the change in Ankara's relations with Israel, rather than the 'Strategic Depth Doctrine'.[26] For them, a dramatic decline in Turkey's threat perception since the mid-1990s: the fear of a war with Greece ended, bilateral relationship with Syria improved, threat regarding Nicosia stationing S-300 SAM (Surface to Air Missile) on its soil minimised, and the challenge of Saddam Hussein's Iraq was made ineffective, resulted into a drastically less hostile environment for Turkey. In such a situation a decrease in Turkey's reliance on the West and Israel was affordable.[27]

Through the above discussion it becomes clear that the perceived reorientation in the Turkish engagement with the West Asian countries before the 'Arab Spring' was not the sole result of Davutoğlu's vision. The basic objective of the assertive foreign policy in the region during the AKP rule was to attain a two-pronged and essentially a pragmatic goal. Ankara firstly wanted to stabilise its volatile strategic environment to make sure that the negative developments in the dangerously combustible region did not affect its domestic stability. Secondly, for Ankara, a stabilised southeastern neighbourhood was a valuable market for Turkish goods and services particularly at the time of the contraction of the European demand.[28]

Even in their efforts regarding the reorientation of relations with the West Asian neighbours, Turkish policy makers were fully aware of the contradictions and limitations as the most substantial challenge to the viability of the zero problem approach prior to the 'Arab Spring' has been the deteriorating relation of Turkey with Israel. The disruption of the Turkish–Israeli alliance, coupled with faltering relations with the US, significantly undermined the coherence of the zero problem approach. Acrimonious relations with Israel inevitably affected Turkey's relations with the US; thus both the Western and Eastern dimensions of Turkey's foreign policy faced an apparent setback.[29] Similarly, Ankara's efforts to establish good relations with KRG were in clear contradiction to its harmonious relations with Baghdad. In sum, one can conclude that the 'zero problem policy' has not been a strictly adhered principle of Turkish foreign policy prior to the 'Arab Spring' and was not a constantly active component of the Strategic Depth Doctrine.

## Arab Spring and 'Strategic Depth Doctrine'

When the 'Arab Spring' unfolded from Tunisia and spread to other countries, it created new challenges for Turkey's foreign policy including a failure of the 'zero problems policy'.[30] Before the popular uprising, the government in Ankara was getting along with the authoritarian regimes of Tunisia, Libya, Egypt, and Syria.[31] But once the revolt started on the streets of Tunisia and reached Egypt, Turkish policy makers considered this situation as an opportunity to adopt a 'pro-democracy' approach.[32] Thus, Prime Minister Erdoğan claimed that the inspiration for popular uprisings in the Arab world was Turkey and its 'advanced democracy'.[33] Similarly, emphasising on the idea that countries need to have the right balance between freedom and security, Foreign Minister Davutoğlu argued that the West Asian region is just being normalised by adjusting to the Post-Cold War environment, as 'throughout the Cold War, because of the Israeli–Arab war, and because of the Soviet type of governance, there was an absence of...the legitimacy link between the leaders and the people'.[34] Therefore, taking the side of the streets against the authoritarian regimes, Ankara, in case of Tunisia, declared its support for the Tunisian people's demand for a more democratic and free society and in case of Egypt, called on Hosni Mubarak to resign voluntarily.[35] However, when the protest movements engulfed Libya and Syria, Turkey found itself in a serious dilemma and struggled in its role as the promoter of democracy. Losing its clarity of vision it shifted its position on nearly a daily basis from supporting the Gaddafi and Assad regimes to backing the protesters.[36] Turkey's initial reactions to the revolts in Tunisia and Egypt on the one hand, and Libya and Syria on the other appear to be different from each other.[37]

In the case of Egypt, Turkey's call for 'democratisation' and regime change and therefore a halt to the 'policy of no problem' was in agreement with the Turkish desire of spreading 'soft power' across the region. Although, Egypt in 2010 absorbed some two percent of Turkish exports, Ankara could afford the temporary setback in economic relations with Cairo that a regime change would bring about.[38] Similarly, although relatively cooperative, both states considered each other as probable rivals for regional influence and Egypt never welcomed a Turkey deeply involved in Arab affairs. The collapse of the Mubarak regime might, therefore, bring to power a new group, which would be, according to Turkish calculation, much more enthusiastic in developing more cordial relations with Turkey.[39] Furthermore, and more importantly perhaps, the possibility of bringing to light Turkey as a model to be emulated in post-Mubarak Egypt, and then in the rest of the Arab world, also encouraged Ankara to support the Egyptian people and call for a change. Therefore, in regard to the above calculation the departure from 'Zero-Problems' was seen consistent with 'Strategic Depth'.[40]

A relatively easy walk for the policy makers in Ankara ended soon when the 'Arab spring' reached Libya and Syria. In the case of these two countries the situation became complicated not only because the leaders were not succumbing to the protesters, as had happened in Tunisia or Egypt, and were willing to resort to violence if necessary[41] but also due to the deepening of economic links with Libya, and improved bilateral relations with Syria. As reported by the Turkish Ministry of Economy, Libya was the "most significant market for Turkish contractors in Africa" until 2011. Economic imperatives to keep good relations were clear, and therefore, Erdoğan found it difficult to cut ties with Muammar al-Qaddafi abruptly. When the civil war broke out in Libya and the international community called for deposing the Libyan autocrat and bringing him to trial, Turkey took Gaddafi's side by encouraging him to take steps toward reforms, and opposing the idea of international intervention.[42] Rather, Erdoğan and his foreign policy team saw in this situation another opportunity to polish Turkey's image in the Arab world and gave priority to the trade and investment benefits the country enjoyed from its relationship with Libya's leadership. Therefore, Ankara objected to the prospect of a no-fly zone, which was being discussed by NATO members in February 2011.[43]

However, as the humanitarian costs of the attacks perpetrated by Qaddafi's henchmen increased, and Ankara found itself isolated and surprised by the anti-Turkish demonstrations in the rebel capital Benghazi, Turkey decided, in a series of quick policy shifts, to support NATO's intervention in Libya. On May 3, 2011, Erdoğan, therefore, declared to a gathering of journalists in Istanbul that Turkey "wishes to see Libya's leader step down immediately and leave Libya immediately for his own sake and for the sake of his country's future."[44] Moreover, the Turkish leadership severed their diplomatic ties with Qaddafi's Libyan government and recalled its ambassador besides pledging $200 million in aid to the NATO-backed rebel, Transitional National Council (TNC).[45]

In the above context one can say that Libya presented the first major test for Turkey's new foreign policy as the developments in the North African state was unfolding towards a situation in which Ankara was not only risking its regional influence by becoming an apologiser for the new Libyan regime, but was also threatening already fragile relations with own traditional Western partners. Turkey's shift in behaviour with Libya could be explained as a combined response to international pressure and regional opinion as Ankara's early response to the crisis was bound to endanger regional and global prospects of Turkey's influence. Seeking to preserve its carefully built regional influence, Turkey calculated that engaging with authoritarian regimes amid crackdowns would seriously undermine the Strategic Depth it has sought to achieve via the zero problems approach. By participating in the subsequent international action in Libya, Turkey balanced its regional aspirations with its wider commitments, supporting its Western allies' intervention, yet limiting its visibility in the Western-dominated operation by agreeing only to provide humanitarian aid and overseeing implementation of the economic and military embargo put on Qaddafi's forces. In this case, adherence to Zero Problems proved incompatible, even actively obstructive to the pursuit of Strategic Depth.[46]

The zero problems policy, however faced its most serious challenges from the unpredicted and the on-going unpredictable Syrian crisis as Turkey's policy has undergone several dramatic shifts in relation to Damascus. Utilising a similar but advanced formula of its approach in Libya, leaders in Ankara initially called for a positive engagement with the beleaguered Assad regime. Turkey hoped that its labourious efforts in crafting positive relations with Syria would provide a sufficient influence to ease the crackdown and persuade Assad to implement political reforms.[47] Turkey's policy of such 'prudent optimism' was based on several assumptions and calculations. Turkey's early reactions appear to have been shaped by the following assumptions: First, Ankara assumed that Assad has a chance for a peaceful transformation at the initial stage. Second, Ankara held that Assad had some liberal instincts and would be able to steer his country out of its authoritarian character. Third, Turkish rulers seem to have believed that the close personal relations they had developed with Assad over the years would give them a psychological advantage as they counselled him to set in motion a reform process to heed the people's demands.[48] Similarly, Turkey wished to avoid any deterioration in its relationship with Syria simply because this relationship was important in several ways. First of all, Syria occupied a central position in the new Turkish policy toward West Asia, based on the principle of 'zero problems' with its neighbours, allowing Turkey to project itself as a regional power. Secondly, there were economic motives in the quest for good relations with Syria. In addition to the importance of trade between the countries, for the Turkish economy, Syria was the door leading to other countries in the region, notably Egypt, Jordan and the Gulf States. Thirdly, and most importantly, Ankara did not wish to jeopardise its cooperation with Damascus in the fight against the terrorism of the PKK.[49]

However, the obstinacy of the Assad regime in implementing reforms and the intensification of violence within Syria which in turn created an influx of asylum seekers at the Syro-Turkish border compelled Turkey to take a harsher line, and a breaking away from its previous Zero Problem compatible stance.[50] At present, and especially since a Turkish reconnaissance aircraft that violated Syrian air space was brought down by Syria, Turkey has been at the forefront of a support extended to the opposition against the regime in Damascus. In effect, it was in Turkey and with help from Ankara that the principal Syrian opposition movement, the Syrian National Council (SNC), saw daylight and established its headquarters. Turkey is also the major receiver of Syrian refugees continuing to flee hostilities between the loyalist army and rebel forces. Finally, it is by harbouring in its territory of the principal leaders of the Free Syrian Army (FSA) that Turkey has most clearly been expressing its commitment in favour of a regime change in Damascus.[51]

Turkey's decisively altered role in Syria from an interested mediator to a determined antagonist has certainly brought a challenge for the Turkish leadership and their commitment to the 'zero problems' approach.[52] Policy makers in Ankara have to strike an appropriate balance between the *Realpolitik* foreign policy stance and the *moral-politics* foreign policy vision in explaining Turkey's involvement in the crisis.[53] Normatively, one can argue that the intensification of Turkey's liberal democratic transformation at home since the late 1990s seems to have increasingly led Turkish leaders to pay more attention to democracy and human rights promotion in Syria.[54] Moreover, Turkey's desires to see a democratic transformation in Syria can also be linked to Ankara's naïve assessment that in the midst of the democratic wave the demonstrative impact of Turkey which can boast of having a functioning democracy would be a source of inspiration for post-conflict Syria.[55] A renewed emphasis on democracy instead of 'zero problem' can also be endorsed even on the ground of 'Strategic Depth Doctrine' as Davutoglu in his vision has clearly mentioned that there should be a balance between security and freedom at all levels as cardinal goals of the Turkish new foreign policy. [56] However, Turkey's adoption of democratic instance is not immune from criticism. The fact of the matter is that in reality, Ankara has never made democracy a priority in its relations. For instance, following the contested June 2009 elections and the violent suppression of the opposition in Iran, Turkey was among the first countries congratulating President Ahmedinejad for his victory.[57] Similarly, even during the 'Arab Spring' Turkey supported the military intervention in Bahrain to suppress Shiite popular protests, presumably backed by Iran.[58]

In that way one can argue that behind the democracy-promotion stance, Turkey in its policy formulation regarding the Syrian crisis was mainly guided by the certain pragmatic concerns and calculations. The most imminent and obvious factor appears to have been the continuing influx of Syrian people into Turkey and the kind of tragedy this has engendered. Accepting numerous Syrians has been a risky move on Turkey's part, given Assad's view of those refugees as insurgents.[59] Another pragmatic concern was the possibility of Syria's Kurds, who live alongside the border with Turkey, getting an autonomous status like their Iraqi counterpart and thus putting additional pressure on Turkey's own Kurdish problem.[60] Besides having a clear chance of bolstering its hard and soft power capabilities in the West Asian region, Turkey's anti-Assad approach should also be seen as an effort to reconcile its widening gap with the Euro-Atlantic countries in the sense that Turkey's current position on Syria is nearly identical with those of the United States and the European Union.[61] Finally, to preserve its claims to be a regional leader, escalation was a necessary move for Turkey for if it could not influence Damascus despite having a significant diplomatic clout in the Assad regime, support to the opposition group was the only alternative to have an influence on the development in Syria.[62]

## Challenges Ahead

The implications of the 'Arab Spring' in general and Syrian crisis in particular are quite significant for Ankara in the sense that despite its limited contribution to democratisation, recent developments in the West

Asian region have altered the dynamics and priorities of both the external and regional players along with many non-state actors. The first and most important challenge for Turkey is the possibility of the Syrian conflict progressively taking on a sectarian nature.[63] The fact that the Assad clan, which has ruled Syria for four decades, belongs to the religious minority of Alawites, an offshoot of the Shia,[64] and the SNC, the main opposition group backed by Turkey and recognised as a sole representative of the Syrian people by countries such as Saudi Arabia, Qatar, Bahrain, UAE, Kuwait and Oman, is largely a Sunni group, certainly enhanced the prospect of a Shia–Sunni rivalry in the region. At the regional level, this sectarian conflict has captured the imagination of Turkish leaders in their uneasiness towards the prospective rise of the Shiite axis in West Asia. Shi'a Islam, which was politically influential in countries like Iran, Iraq and Lebanon, has come further to the forefront of West Asian politics after the 'Arab Spring'.[65] The Shiite–Sunni split becomes a critical issue for Turkey and coerces it into pursuing alternative strategies other than the 'Zero Problem' policy—as seen in Iraq, Bahrain and Syria—especially when the sectarian demographic balance is sensitive and different sectarian groups compete for power.[66] At the domestic level, although the Syrian crisis has not had much impact on the relations between the different religious communities in Turkey, it has the potential to divide the Turkish political elite on sectarian lines.[67] Yet, while the crisis in Syria worsens, growing into a sectarian war pitting Alawites against Sunni, the question of the position that the Alevis and Nusairis of Turkey will adopt may arise. [68]

The irony related with the quagmire of the possible sectarian conflict between Shia and Sunni gets more complicated and transformed into intra-Sunni conflict when Arabs vs. non-Arabs dynamic is added. In other words, although Turkey's emerging regional leadership role and the positioning of itself as a role model offered to the Arab Islamists as a 'Sunni alternative' to Iran, this perception also put Turkey into an intra-Sunni conflict with the Saudis, who for many decades have claimed the position of the leader of the Sunnis.[69] The inevitability of this conflict becomes apparent when one looks towards the fact that beneath a shallow collaboration of Sunni countries against the Alawi (and Shia) regime of

Assad, Turkey supports political forces and parties affiliated with the Muslim Brotherhood, while the Saudis back the Salafis.[70] Even in a country like Egypt, where Muslim Brotherhood has gained considerable political clout in the post-uprising arrangements, the ruling elite and especially military cannot tolerate Turkey replacing Egypt as the leader of the Muslim world.[71] A clear manifestation of the Arab apprehension regarding 'Turkey's neo-Ottomanist meddling' into intra-Arab affairs was the exclusion of Turkey from the Baghdad meeting of the Arab League in March 2012.[72] Speaking on this occasion the Iraqi foreign minister clearly said that "This summit will enhance our (Arabs) position to stand on our feet vis-à-vis these regional powers (Turkey and Iran)."[73]

However, the most serious challenge for the Turkish leadership related to the ethno-national conflict in Syria manifested itself in the re-emergence of Turkey's Kurdish problem as Turkey is facing radicalised Kurdish masses inspired by the successful model of the Kurdish autonomy of the KRG in Iraq and prospect of the same in Syria.[74] As the 'Arab Spring' has a strong inner 'Kurdish Spring' effect and if the Kurds become able to secure the ability to have two regional governments, the traditional Turkish strategy of 'solution within the nation-state' may fall forever.[75] So far the Kurds have adopted a very prudent strategy regarding the Syrian crisis where on one hand they are part of the Arab dynamic aiming to overthrow the Assad regime and on the other, they have an independent agenda to secure a more structured political setting for themselves.[76] In short, the Kurds are not making the overthrow of the Assad regime their sole aim. They are also positioning themselves to create a better environment for themselves in Syria.[77] Traditionally, Turkey along with other Kurdish inhabited states has put aside their differences and was united on the issue of opposing the prospect of Kurdish autonomy. Since such a coalition is not possible, as neither Iraq nor Syria have a strong central authority and political stability, Ankara in its bid to curtail the 'more autonomy' demand of Kurds in the region, has developed a new strategy of coexistence with autonomous Kurdish regions in countries like Iraq and Syria.[78] However, it can be speculated whether Turkey's strategy might bring a miscalculated outcome, resulting in secession of Turkish Kurdish regions from Turkey and the formation of an independent and sovereign Kurdistan consisting of Kurds from around the region or not. In effect, by supporting the Syrian opposition forces, who are striving to topple the Assad regime in Damascus, the highest Turkish political echelons are likely to trigger the dissolution of the unitary Turkish state.[79]

The sectarian dimension of the Syrian crisis in terms of the Shia–Sunni divide and the rising prospect of the Kurdish nation-state have their clear brunt on Turkey's relations with an almost bicephalous Iraq. The rising complication in the bilateral relations can be ascertained from the fact that Ankara has to negotiate as much with Baghdad as with Erbil, the capital of the Kurdish autonomous region.[80] Whereas, Turkey, for the sake of economic benefit and out of immediate political pragmatism, has established steady and solid relations with the Kurds of Iraq and has ignored the prospect of Kurdish autonomy at home, it has also invited the wrath of the Baghdad government accusing Ankara of meddling into the internal affair of Iraq and deliberately poisoning relations between the Sunnis and Shiites of Iraq.[81] As far as the Syrian crisis is concerned, Shiite solidarity has led the Baghdad government along with Iran to not to oppose the Alawite government of Assad, for which Turkey is a determined antagonist.[82] Moreover, on more than one occasion the Iraqi Prime Minister Nuri al Maliki has expressed his apprehensions regarding Turkey's 'sectarian' support for the Sunnis in Syria based on its privileged relations with the SNC, in which the Muslim Brotherhood, which is close to Turkey, has a strong position.[83] However, the irony for Turkey in its relations with Iraq is that the same Syrian crisis which has poisoned its relations with the government in Baghdad on sectarian lines has stimulated it to improve its relations with the Kurdish Regional Government of Iraq out of pragmatic concern related to the need of containing the Kurdish demand for autonomy. Turkey's realisation that Erbil is the only political actor capable of influencing the Kurds of Syria, including and, above all, the PYD, which seems to be a black sheep for Ankara because of its ties to the PKK, has manifested in establishing good terms with leaders of the autonomous Kurdish region.[84] In other words, the Kurds of Iraq have become more important for Turkey than ever before in their capacity of preferred mediators for any future talks with the PKK.[85] However, by talking on an equal footing with the autonomous region, Ankara has increased the autonomy of this quasi-state of the Kurds, which does not necessarily coincide with its interests. Inevitably, the Syrian conflict is pushing Turkey into a new Kurdish dilemma and forcing it to seek external levers that it lends strength to, but can, in the long run, put it in a difficult situation.[86]

If there is one country with whom Ankara's interests are completely colliding in Syria and which has clearly manifested in its sectarian antagonism undermining Davutoğlu's 'zero problem policy' is Iran. While Iran's Revolutionary Guards participated in suppressing the opposition to Assad's regime, Turkey provides bases and financial support to Syria's opposing political body, the National Council.[87] Moreover, Iran which has four decades of strategic partnership with Syria and its client Hezbollah in Lebanon has continued to back the Assad regime, has been worried about the possibility of the establishment of a pro-American, pro-Saudi regime in Syria and that its links to Hezbollah in Lebanon would be severed after the fall of Assad.[88] In other words, for Tehran events unfolding in Syria are the result of a conspiracy of the West and Turkey in line with this is the Trojan horse of the West in the region.[89] Turkey, on the other hand, after openly supporting the opposition forces in Syria, is well aware that if Assad manages to survive politically with Iranian help, Ankara might find itself confronting a Shia axis extending from Tehran through Baghdad and Damascus to Hezbollah in Beirut determined to curb the exercise of Turkish influence in the West Asian region.[90] Although, views have been expressed that neither Turkey nor Iran would be aided by an Israeli-style break and Saudi-style antagonism in their respective relations, and development of the situation, particularly on the issue of granting of autonomy to the Kurds in the new Syria, may push them towards cooperation[91] it is clear that there is real danger for the first time in a decade of a fundamental split between the two because of Syria.[92] Even if the two countries immunise their relationship from the corrosive effects of the Syrian bloodbath, Ankara has to consider the implications of a Turkey–Iran relationship for the US–Turkey partnership, as it contends with all the other changes in the region.[93]

As the above discussion has shown, if the persistence of the Syrian crisis has sharpened the Kurdish question and has put Turkish regional policy and leadership in jeopardy, then the question regarding Turkey's prospective role in post-conflict reconstruction or Turkish leverage in post-Assad government in Syria assumes upmost importance for Ankara.[94] To the extent that the outcome of the crisis is hardly foreseeable and the orientation of the future regime is unknown, one can be sure that the Turkish trump card in this regard is the SNC, with whom Turkish government has maintained very good relations. Although, the Turkish bond with SNC could be solidified through the fact that the Muslim Brotherhood, one of the important constituents of the SNC is quit sensitive to the Islamic rhetoric of the AKP, it is also a fact of the matter that the Islamic element in the Syrian revolution may not necessarily be tied to the Brotherhood. Within the country, Salafist cells and others affiliated with Hizb ut-Tahrir are also active and their views are different from those of the Brotherhood.[95] Certain religious dissidents, such as Mahmut Osman, who has lived in Turkey for several decades, are in the SNC without being affiliated with the Brotherhood. Finally, another Syrian Islamist party in exile in London, the Justice and Construction Party whose members are more dynamic and younger, is beginning to shadow the greying historic leadership of the Brotherhood in Syria.[96] Thus, Turkish policy makers have to be ready for more complicated and uncertain challenges in the region emanating largely from the Syrian quagmire and which have the potential to undermine the gains made by Ankara.

## Conclusion

The 'Arab Spring' in general and the Syrian crisis in particular has drastically changed Turkey's active foreign policy based on the principal of 'Strategic Depth Doctrine' as at least two important components of the doctrine i.e. 'zero problem with neighbours' and 'balance between security and freedom' or the quest of democratisation have been seriously undermined and used selectively. As argued above, 'Strategic Depth Doctrine' was not only the result of Davutoglu's vision, but was the response to changing domestic and regional changes that

Turkey witnessed at the beginning of the new millennium. Aimed for enhancing Turkey's influence in and around the West Asian region through establishing privileged relations with existing power structures and maximised economic linkages, leaders in Ankara preferred to project the 'zero problems with Neighbours' component in place of 'democratisation' of Strategic Depth Doctrine and therefore decided to get along with Assad, Qaddafi, and Mubarak, while refrained from pushing hard on democracy and human rights before the beginning of 'Arab Spring'. Even the 'zero problem policy', has not been fully adhered to and it encountered significant problems as analysts have identified the most substantial challenge to the viability of this approach prior to the 'Arab Spring' in the deteriorating relations with Israel. When the Arab rebellion happened, it upended Ankara's calculation as Turkey became aware of the limitation of its influence in the neighbouring countries and prepared itself for alternative contingencies by upholding the voice of democracy and human rights. However, even in this regard Turkey's approach was selective, and after doing meticulous calculations the authorities in Ankara decided to support the US and Saudi efforts to suppress the peoples' uprising in Bahrain while deciding to go along with the opposition forces in Syria. So far, Ankara's handling of the crises has not been bad in general as Turkey's standing and influence in the region have increased significantly and in any post-crisis settlement its participation has been regarded as very important; it is also a fact of the matter that in the post-crisis regional order Turkey has to encounter many new challenges, most of them having a sectarian flavour. The way by which Turkish policy makers will confront these challenges is an open-ended question; however taking a clue from Ankara's early approach in this regard one can tentatively conclude that pragmatic calculations rather than any ideological convictions would be the guiding principle.

## Notes

1. Ziya Onis, "Turkey and the Middle East After September 11: The Importance of the EU Dimension", *Turkish Policy Quarterly* II, No. 4, (Winter 2003).
2. William Hale and Ergun Ozbudun, *Islamism, Democracy and Liberalism in Turkey the Case of the AKP* (London: Routledge, 2010), 120.
3. Ahmet Davutoglu, "Turkey's Foreign Policy Vision: An Assessment of 2007",

*Insight Turkey* 10, no. 1, (2008): 77-79; Alexander Murison, 'The Strategic Depth Doctrine of Turkish Foreign Policy, *Middle Eastern Studies*. XXXXII, no. 6 (2006): 945-55.

4. Kemal Kirisci, *Turkey's Foreign Policy in Turbulent Times*, (Institute for Security Studies, Chaillot Paper No. 2, September 2006): 32.
5. Ibid. pp. 32-52.
6. Davutoglu, "Turkey's Foreign Policy Vision", pp: 84-85.
7. Meliha Benli Altunisk, "The Possibilities and Limits of Turkey's Soft Power in the Middle East", *Insight Turkey* X, no. 2 (2008): 50.
8. Ibid. p. 52.
9. Ramazan Gozen, "Causes and Consequences of Turkey's Out-of-War Position in the Iraq War of 2003", *The Turkish Yearbook* XXXVI (2005): 74; Joshua W. Walker, "Reexamining the US-Turkish Alliance", *The Washington Quarterly*, (winter 2007-08): 98.
10. Ioannis N. Grigoriadis, "The Davutoğlu Doctrine and Turkish Foreign Policy", Hellenic Foundation for European and Foreign Policy Working Paper No:8/2010: 7
11. Fahrettin Sumer, "Turkey's Changing Foreign Policy and Arab Spring", *The Innovation Journal: The Public Sector Innovation Journal* XVIII, no.1 (2013): 17.
12. Ziya Öniş, "Multiple Faces of the "New" Turkish Foreign Policy: Underlying Dynamics and a Critique" *GLODEM Working Paper Series 04/2010*. Istanbul: Center for Globalization and Democratic Governance. Koç University.
13. Bulent Aras, "Turkey Between Syria and Israel: Turkey's Rising Soft Power", *SETA Policy Brief* No. 15 May 2008.
14. William Hale and Ergun Ozbudun, *Islamism, Democracy and Liberalism in Turkey the Case of the AKP* (London: Routledge, 2010): 142.; Tarik Oguzlu, "Soft Power in Turkish Foreign Policy", *Australian Journal of International Affairs*, XXXXXI, no. 1, (March 2007): 93.
15. Hale and Ozbudun, *Islamism, Democracy and Liberalism:* p. 142; Omer Taspinar, "Turkey's Middle East Policies Between Neo-Ottomanism and Kemalism", Carnegie Paper number 10, September 2008, p: 24.
16. Bulent Aras, "Turkey and the Palestinian Question since al-Aqsa Intifada" *Alternatives* I, no. 3 (fall 2002): 4; Steven A. Cook and Elizabeth Sherwood-Randall, *Generating Momentum for a New Era in US Turkey Relations*, (USA: Council on Foreign Relations, 2006), 21.
17. Ibid.
18. Walker, "Reexamining the US-Turkish Alliance", p. 97.
19. Henery J. Barkey, "Turkish Foreign Policy and the Middle East" CERI Strategy Paper: No 10, June 2011: 1-9; Sumer, "Turkey's Changing Foreign Policy", p: 17.
20. A. Öztürk, "The Domestic Context of Turkey's Changing Foreign Policy toward the Middle East and the Caspian Region" German Development Institute Discussion Paper 10, 2009: 22-23.
21. I Grigoriadis, "The Davutoğlu Doctrine and Turkish Foreign Policy", Hellenic Foundation for European and Foreign Policy Working Paper No 8 2010: 7.
22. Sumer, "Turkey's Changing Foreign Policy"; Barkey, "Turkish Foreign Policy and the Middle East": 1-9.
23. Ibid; Philips Robins, "Turkish Foreign Policy Since 2002: Between a 'Post-Islamist' Government and a Kemalist State", *International Affairs*, 83, no. 1 (2007): 296.
24. Ibid; F. Stephen Larrabee, "Turkey Rediscovers the Middle East", *Foreign Affairs*,

86, no. 4 (July/August 2007).

25. Barkey, "Turkish Foreign Policy and the Middle East": 1-9; Sumer, "Turkey's Changing Foreign Policy".
26. Efrain Inbar, "Israeli-Turkish Tensions and Beyond", *Turkish Policy Quarterly* VIII, no. 3: 44.
27. Ibid.
28. Igor Torbakov and Hanna Ojanen, "Looking for a New Strategic Identity: Is Turkey Emerging as an Independent Regional Power?", The Finnish Institute of International Affairs, Briefing Paper 30, 2009: 06.
29. David Murdo Ian Macdonald, "Turkey and the Arab Spring, the End of Zero-Problems?" http://archive.atlantic-community.org/index/Open_Think_Tank_Article/Turkey_and_the_Arab_Spring,_the_End_of_Zero-Problems%3F
30. Alexander Murinson, "Turkish Foreign Policy in the Twenty-First Century", The Begin-Sadat Center for Strategic Studies, Bar-Ilan University Mideast Security and Policy Studies, No. 97:16.
31. Sumer, "Turkey's Changing Foreign Policy and Arab Spring": 19.
32. Tank Oguzlu, "The 'Arab Spring' and the Rise of the 2.0 Version of Turkey's 'Zero Problem with Neighbors Policy'", SAM P42. Sumer, "Turkey's Changing Foreign Policy": 20; Murinson, SAM Paper, center for strategic research: 5.
33. Murinson, "Turkish Foreign Policy in the Twenty-First Century": 16.
34. A Davutoğlu, "Turkey's Foreign Policy Objectives in a Changing World", His Speech on February 10, 2012. Washington, D.C.: Center for Strategic and International Studies (CSIS).
35. Sumer, "Turkey's Changing Foreign Policy and Arab Spring": 20.
36. Soli Özel and Gencer Özcan, "Turkey's Dilemmas." *Journal of Democracy* XXII, no. 4 (2011): 124-138.
37. Oguzlu, "The 'Arab Spring'": 5.
38. Sumer, "Turkey's Changing Foreign Policy": 20; Barkey, "Turkish Foreign Policy and the Middle East": 9-10.
39. Birol Baskan, "Ankara Torn Apart: Arab Spring Turns into Turkish Autumn", *The Turkish Yearbook of International Relations* XXXXII, (2011): 1-2; Benjamin Harvey, "Erdoğan Tells Egypt's Mubarak He Should Listen to His People," *Bloomberg*, February 1, 2011 (http://www.bloomberg.com/news/2011-02-01/Erdoğan-tells-egypt-s-mubarak-he-should-listen-to-his-people.html ); Nick Baumann and Siddhartha Mahanta, "What's Happening in Egypt Explained," *Mother Jones*, February 23, 2011.
40. David Murdo Ian Macdonald, "Turkey and the Arab Spring, the End of Zero Problems", http://archive.atlantic-community.org/index/Open_Think_Tank_Article/Turkey_and_the_Arab_Spring,_the_End_of_Zero-Problems%3F.
41. Oguzlu, "The 'Arab Spring'": 5.
42. Sumer, "Turkey's Changing Foreign Policy": 20: Murinson, "Turkish Foreign Policy in the Twenty-First Century": 20.
43. Sumer, "Turkey's Changing Foreign Policy": 20; Murinson, "Turkish Foreign Policy in the Twenty-First Century": 20; Macdonald, "Turkey and the Arab Spring".
44. S. Cook, "Arab Spring, Turkish Fall", *Foreign Policy*, (May 5, 2011). Retrieved June 22, 2012 p:2 at: http://www.foreignpolicy.com/articles/2011/05/05/arab_spring_turkish_fall?print=yes&hid
45. "Turkey Throws Weight behind Libyan Opposition," *Zaman*, July 4, 2011.

46. Macdonald, "Turkey and the Arab Spring".
47. Ibid.; Murinson, "Turkish Foreign Policy in the Twenty-First Century": 21-22. "Syria Crisis: Aleppo and Homs Clashes amid Prison Revolts," *BBC World News*, 24 July 2012 (http://www.bbc.co.uk/news/world-middle-east-18964998
48. Oguzlu, "The 'Arab Spring'": 5-6.
49. Bayram Balci, "Does the Syrian Crisis Imply the End of the Turkish Dream in the Middle East, Perspectives: Political Analysis and Commentary from Turkey", p:9.
50. Macdonald, "Turkey and the Arab Spring".
51. Balcı, "Does the Syrian Crisis": 9.
52. Macdonald, "Turkey and the Arab Spring".
53. Oguzlu, "The 'Arab Spring'": 11.
54. Şaban Kardaş, "Turkey and the Arab Spring: Coming to Terms with Democracy Promotion", *German Marshall Fund Policy Brief*, (October 2011).
55. Oguzlu, "The 'Arab Spring'": 9.
56. Barkey, "Turkish Foreign Policy and the Middle East": 10-11.
57. Ibid.
58. Murinson, "Turkish Foreign Policy in the Twenty-First Century": 17.
59. Oguzlu, "The 'Arab Spring'": 7.
60. "Syria Challenges Turkey's 'Neighborly' Relations", *The Daily Star*, 13 June 2011.
61. Emiliano Alessandri, "Turkey and the West Address the Arab Spring", *German Marshall Fund Analysis*, (8 June 2011); Tarık Oğuzlu, "Turkey and Europeanization of Foreign Policy", *Political Science Quarterly*, Vol. 125, no. 4 (Winter 2010-2011): 657-683.
62. Macdonald, "Turkey and the Arab Spring".
63. Balci, "Does the Syrian crisis": 10.
64. Heinz Halm, "The Shi'ites: A Short History" (Wien, Markus Pub, 2007).
65. Gokhan Bacik, "Turkey and the New Middle East" Commentary, European Policy Centre, 27 July 2012.
66. Ibid.
67. Balcı, "Does the Syrian Crisis": 11.
68. "TURKEY: Hundreds of People in Border town of Antakya Demonstrate in Support of Syrian President Bashar al-Assad", February 20, 2012, URL: http://www.itnsource.com/shotlist/RTV/2012/02/20/RTV555612/?v=0&a=1.
69 Hassan Mneimneh, "The Turkish Model in Arab Islamism: Rejection or Emulation", *Current Trends in Islamist Ideology*, *11*, 2011, p.18.; Murinson, Alexander, 2012, "Turkish Foreign Policy in the Twenty-First Century", The Begin-Sadat Center for Strategic Studies, Bar-Ilan University Mideast Security and Policy Studies, No. 97. p: 18.
70. Murinson, "Turkish Foreign Policy in the Twenty-First Century": 18: Meliha Benli Altunisik, "The Not-Quite-Alliance Between Saudi Arabia and Turkey", *Foreign Affairs*, May 15, 2012 (http://turkishcentralnews.com/archives/14075 )
71. Murinson, "Turkish Foreign Policy in the Twenty-First Century": 18.
72. See Egyptian editorial "Ottomans and Persians in Iraq," *Al-Ahram*, January 25, 2012. ; Ali Nader, Taha Ozhan, Steve Larrabee, and Muhittin Ataman, "Arab Spring and its Effect on Turkey's Regional Policy," SETADC, Ankara Hall, Public Panel, Washington, October 24, 2011 (http://setadc.org/pdfs/SETA_Policy_Debate_Arab_Spring_and_its_Effect_on_Turkeys_Regional_Policy.pdf )
73. Serkan Demirtaş, "Arab League Shuns Turkey, Iran on Syria", *Hurriyet*, March 29,

2012.

74. Murinson, "Turkish Foreign Policy in the Twenty-First Century": 22; Christophe Ayad, "Kurdistan Conflict Threatens to Bring New Violence to Iraq," *Guardian Weekly*, August 14, 2012.
75. Bacik, "Turkey and the".
76. Ibid.
77. Ibid.
78. Ibid.
79. Murinson, "Turkish foreign policy in the Twenty-First Century": 23.
80. Balcı, "Does the Syrian crisis": 12.
81. Gönul Tol, "Turkey Cozies Up to the KRG", *National Interest*, May 29, 2012, URL: http://nationalinterest.org/commentary/turkey-cozies-thekrg-6975.; Nick Ottens, "Diplomatic Crisis Between Iraq, Turkey Deepening", *Atlantic Sentinel*, April 29, 2012, URL: http://atlanticsentinel.com/2012/04/diplomatic-crisis-between-iraq-turkey-deepening.
82. Balcı, "Does the Syrian crisis": 12.
83. Ibid.
84. Ibid.: 13.
85. Ibid.
86. Ibid.
87. Murinson, "Turkish Foreign Policy in the Twenty-First Century": 22.
88. J. Pack and M. Van Creveld, "In the Arab Spring, Watch Turkey". *The New York Times*, the Opinion Pages, January 5, 2012; A. Miller, "Everything in Syria Is Going to Plan: It Just Depends on Whose Plan You're Talking About", *Foreign Policy* (June 12). Retrieved June 5, 2012 at: http://www.foreignpolicy.com/articles/2012/06/13/everything_in_syria_is_going_to_plan?; A. Paul, "Syria, Russia and Iran", *Today's Zaman* (19 June).
89. Alex Vatanka, "Syria Drives a Wedge between Turkey and Iran", Middle East Institute, http://www.mei.edu/content/syria-drives-wedge-betweenturkey-and-iran
90. Bulent Aliriza and Stephen Flanagan, "The End of Zero Problems? Turkey and Shifting Regional Dynamics", *Global Forecast*, Center for Strategic and International Studies. April 12, 2012.
91. Balcı, "Does the Syrian crisis": 12.
92. Aliriza, "The End of Zero Problems?"
93. Ibid.
94. Balci, "Does the Syrian crisis": 13.
95. Balci, "Does the Syrian crisis": 14.
96. Abdulrahman Alhaj, "Political Islam and the Syrian Revolution", Al Jazeera Center for Studies, http://studies.aljazeera.net/ResourceGallery/media/Documents/2012/6/10/20126109615611734Political%20Islam%20and%20the%20Syrian%20Revolution.pdf.; Interview with Mohammad Farouk Tayfour, deputy comptroller general of the Syrian Muslim Brotherhood and representative in the Syrian National Council, Istanbul, June 19, 2012. Quoted in Balci, "Does the Syrian crisis": 13.

# 4
# The Syrian Uprising and Turkey-Syria-Iran Relations

*Özden Zeynep Oktav*

Within the last decade, Turkish foreign policy underwent a dramatic change so as to raise some question marks in its Western allies' mind concerning whether Turkey has ceased to be a part of the West and international society. Beginning with the 2000s, Turkish foreign policy makers started to change the Cold War mentality which urged Turkey to have a "*faith*" in the West without questioning its norms, values, policies and conducts. In doing this, Ankara adopted a different language; for example, it started to address the masses on the Arab streets giving the message that it was on the side of the oppressed masses. This became most evident after Turkish PM Recep Tayyip Erdoğan walked out and shouted "You Israelis know how to kill" at the Davos World Economic Forum.

However, with the outburst of the Arab Spring in the Middle East, Turkey was caught off guard and the mass demonstrations on the Arab streets forced Ankara to reshape its foreign policy calculations in the Arab world. Put differently, the Arab Spring became a litmus test for Ankara's policies playing to the Arab streets. While it lent quick support to popular movements in Tunisia and Egypt, where Turkish investments were relatively limited, Ankara's first reaction to the uprisings in Syria was more cautious and it prioritised stability and gradual reform towards the uprisings in Syria, where Turkish investments were substantial. In a similar vein, Ankara preferred the status quo in Libya because of its economic interests in the country.

In the first part of this chapter, the changing dynamics of Turkish foreign policy which became crystallised after the beginning of the

Syrian uprising will be discussed in detail with a special emphasis on current relations with Iran. Apart from the analysis on relations with Syria, understanding whether Turkey is still a part of the West in a changing international order will be another concern of the study. Put differently, the article will investigate the reasons why Turkey, despite the abundant diverging interests, still keeps its relations with Iran on a stable level while on the other hand it cut its links with Damascus totally, with a special focus on changing international order.

## Ups and Downs in Turkey's Relations with Syria and Iran

With the AKP's coming to power in 2002, some drastic changes took place in the Turkish foreign policy such as focusing on regional alliances as an alternative to relations with the global actors, principally the United States and the European Union. In the first half of the 2000s Turkey adopted a bridge-country role between East and West so as to balance its relations between the West/Israel on one hand and Syria/Iran on the other. However, with the renewed hostilities in Gaza at the end of 2008, Erdoğan who felt a 'sense of betrayal' after his mediating efforts between Israel and Syria adopted a very harsh rhetoric towards Israel. This marked a new era in Turkish foreign policy because Ankara made it evident that it had dropped its previous balancing policy between the East and the West.

By March 2010, Ankara had signed 51 protocols with Syria.[1] This was a groundbreaking event in bilateral relations because those protocols which are based on the slogan of "common destiny, history and future" (*"Al-qadar al-mushtarak, Ettarikh al-mushtarak, Al-mustaqbal al-mushtarak")* aimed at economic integration and at the same time inflamed a hot debate concerning Turkey's shift of axis. Erdoğan, "referring to the ongoing debates whether Turkey was shifting its axis in foreign policy, said: "the focus is not shifting but rather the focus of Turkish foreign policy is normalizing."[2]

Turkish officials emphasised that it was trade rather than politics which determined the new contours of Turkish foreign policy. For example, Davutoğlu commented lifting of visas with Syria as "the first step of turning economic cooperation into economic unity."[3] In a similar vein, Turkey tried to create a common free trade area by negotiating High Level Strategic Cooperation Councils with Jordan, Iraq and Lebanon apart from Syria. In parallel with increasing efforts to enhance trade relations with Syria, Ankara also increased its trade volume with Iran to $10 billion annually. Not only have Turkey's exports to Iran doubled, but also Turkey has become quite dependent on Iranian oil and gas.[4] Exports to Iran rose more than seven-fold, from $300 million to $2 billion, between 2002–2009.[5] Turkey's great efforts together with Brazil to prevent the application of UN sanctions on Iran in 2010, should be read against this background.

Ankara's increasing trade relations with Iran have become completely incompatible with the US policy of bringing Iran to heel. The mutual distrust between Ankara and Washington crystallised better as US pressurised Turkey to put the sanctions into effect. Washington has been increasingly uneasy about the probability that Turkey could emerge as a new safety net for Iranian business as the Turkish government insisted that it will abide by UN sanctions but not the more sweeping restrictions imposed on Tehran by the US and the European Union.[6] Ankara's reluctance to guarantee its obedience to apply the sanctions of individual countries and Turkish official circles' suspicions concerning the application of sanctions by EU and American companies depict best Turkey's distrust in the West and its enthusiasm to be an independent regional actor.

Towards the end of 2010, the two developments clarified the limits of Turkey's capability of continuing its good neighbourhood policy and being an independent actor in the international system whose patron is the United States. One is the deployment of the missile defence system under NATO's command on entire Turkish territory and of the early warning radar system in Malatya.[7] Turkey's consent to participate in a defence mechanism which was believed by many to be against Iran was perceived as an example of the JDP Government's difficulty of following good neighbourhood relations at the expense of its relations with the global actors, especially the United States.[8] Although Ankara declared that the system did not target Iranian nuclear sites, US Defense Secretary Leon Panetta's statement that the purpose of the

US radar system to be installed in eastern Turkey was to defend against Iranian missiles, became a collateral damage to Turkey–Iran relations.[9] In addition, the arguments concerning the share of knowledge between Turkey and Israel owing to the US radar system in Turkey which is similar to the one at Negev Desert, Israel, strained the Iranian–Turkish relations further.[10] Iranian Chief of General Staff's threatening words[11] were noteworthy with respect to understanding how Ankara's big efforts to reinstate mutual trust and cooperative relations with Iran came to a halt in a very short period of time.

The second development that crystallised the unsustainability of Turkey's policy of being nice to everyone was the outburst of the Arab Spring at the end of 2010. Especially the Libyan rebellion became a litmus test for Turkey's institutional relations with the West. At first, Turkey, a NATO member, objected to a military interference in Libya, mainly because it would curtail lucrative construction contracts in Libya and its large investments in the country. Turkish president Abdullah Gül openly stated Ankara's suspicions concerning the hidden agenda of the coalition forces whose main partners were the United States and EU.[12] However, in the face of the increasing support given to the Libyan rebels by the Western countries, Ankara recalled its ambassador from Tripoli and recognised the rebel Transnational National Council.[13]

With the outburst of Syrian uprisings and Assad regime's indifference to Turkey's warnings to stop crackdown on opposition protests, Ankara became beware of making a similar mistake it had made in the Libyan case (of following an anti-Western policy). For the first time in the history of Turkish foreign policy, Ankara officially declared that it would interfere in what was happening in Syria so as to shift from its traditional principle of non-interference in internal affairs of a neighbouring country. Erdoğan openly stated that what was happening in Syria was an internal Turkish matter and he had run out of patience.[14]

There were three motives behind Ankara's shift from a non-interference policy after the outburst of Syrian uprisings: one was to show that Ankara was no more out of the orbit of the West, the second one was the enthusiasm to continue its policy of order instituting and to be on the table in the post-Assad period assuming that Assad would be deposed by the Western allies in a short period of time as it happened to Qaddafi. Thirdly, the most important of all, because the Syrian civil war would lead to a flood of Syrian refugees so as to endanger the Turkish–Syrian border, Ankara wanted to prevent its frontier from becoming a backdoor for Kurdish terrorism.

## The Syrian Uprising and Turkey

Ankara firmly believed that the overthrow of the Assad regime was essential to resolving the conflict. Turkey, hoping to bring the regime to the negotiating table, empowered Syrian opposition elements, allowing them to organise and convene in Turkey, as well as hosting defectors from the Syrian military and reportedly allowing the Free Syrian Army (FSA) to set up their headquarters in the southeast of the country.[15] In addition, Ankara, aiming to strangle Syria's economy and severely diminish the power of the Assad government, decided to freeze assets of officials involved in the government's crackdown on the uprising, suspended its ties with the nation's central bank and banned all military sales.[16] All efforts of Turkey such as forging an international "Friends of Syria" coalition to secure regime change, however, remained useless and moreover deepened Turkey's mistrust in its Western allies, EU and the United States who had followed low-profile policies towards Syria.

First of all, Ankara understood that Washington was not so willing to shoulder responsibility and take bold initiatives such as setting up a "buffer zone" inside Syria to protect—Syria is underlined and colour is differentrefugees fleeing President Bashar al-Assad's forces, raising the prospect of foreign intervention in the year-long revolt.[17] Second, that the UN and Washington would not favour a military solution became evident towards the end of the 1st anniversary of the Syrian uprising. Turkey was disappointed by "the negligent U.S. attitude toward the Syrian regime, and the fact that Washington has not offered diplomatic, political, financial, or logistical support to the revolution in equal measure to what Russia has given to the Syrian regime."[18]

Thus, a hot debate was inflamed in the Turkish media whether Turkey was left alone by the international society in its struggle against the Syrian regime, which has committed crimes against civilians.[19] The lack of international consensus[20] and Russia's standing by Assad "to rebuff what it sees as Western plots to induce regime change in countries friendly to Russia had a negative impact on Turkey's efforts to realize a regime change in Syria."[21]

Partly due to the increasing critiques in Turkish media that Turkey was left alone and pushed to initiate a military intervention by the United States against Syria,[22] top Turkish officials have made statements that Turkey would not interfere in the Syrian uprising militarily; instead they would seek a solution based on diplomacy so as to include Iran, China and Russia.[23]

In parallel to the increasing disappointment regarding Washington's passive role towards Syria, NATO's inactivity[24] and Moscow's blocking of United Nations moves, Ankara made serious modifications of its Syria policy and initiated the "triple negotiation system"[25] which would bring together Turkey, Egypt and Iran; Turkey, Russia and Iran; and Turkey, Egypt and Saudi Arabia to work separately towards a solution in Syria. The involvement of Russia and Iran not only clarified that Assad's regime, if not Assad, would have a place at the negotiating table but also made it evident that Turkey was seeking alliances alternative to the Western one so as to find a diplomatic solution to the war.

One reason for Ankara's efforts to start the "triple negotiation system" including Iran and Russia was that Ankara was disappointed by the inactivity of the West, UN and NATO to stop the crackdown of Assad. Secondly, because Ankara has been aware of the fact that a unilateral Turkish military intervention in Syria would be costly since Assad had dual Russo-Iranian support it has been cautious to take any initiative for a military intervention in Syria so far. Instead, Ankara sought the alliance of Russia and Iran to be able to ensure its border security in the face of increasing border violations. Last but not the least, a probable military intervention could lead to internationalisation of Turkey's Kurdish issue.[26]

As the border violations and explosions on its borders such as Ceylanpınar, Akçakalc and Reyhanlı increased in number and severity, Ankara took further measures and declared new engagement rules. According to those rules, "any military instruments or troops approaching to the Turkish borders from the Syrian side in the form of a threat would be perceived as military threats and would be shot down."[27] However, Turkey whose ultimate aim was to ensure stability as well as toppling the regime, could not achieve its goal; on the contrary, it was accused of pursuing a sectarian policy on international platforms. Moreover, Ankara has had new neighbours along its 900 km border with Syria—for one there were the jihadist groups such as Al Nusra and the Islamic State of Iraq and al-Sham (ISIS), and the other one was the PYD, the Syrian branch of the PKK.

## New Neighbours, New Threat Perceptions

With the emergence of the PYD, the Syrian branch of the PKK, and al-Qaeda-inspired fighters who take advantage of a power vacuum to fight for control of key northern towns, Ankara has been exposed to new threats and new accusations. It was alleged that Ankara was providing members of radical groups medical care in Turkish hospitals and supplying them with arms and ammunition, because those groups have been fighting against the PYD[28] whom Assad had promised to give autonomy in an area covering six districts in the region, including Haseki, Ras al- Ain, Afrin, Darbasiyya, Ainal-Arab and and Kamishli.[29]" From Ankara's perspective, at a time when Turkey has been in an effort to make peace with its own Kurds in Turkey, PYD's aspirations to gain autonomy so as to lead to a probable foundation of an independent Kurdish state which would have a way out to the Mediterranean was unacceptable. In a region under PYD control, the PKK would have the ability to establish a strong foothold so as to lead to a serious border security issue for Turkey.

In this context, Ankara has been accused of turning a blind eye to the presence of jihadist groups on Turkish territories and using those groups to suppress the Syrian Kurds' aspirations not only by leaders of PYD but also by Washington. While the Obama administration has encouraged a broad Syrian opposition coalition, in which the influence of Islamists would be circumscribed, from Washington's perspective, the Turkish government has continued to throw its weight behind the Muslim Brotherhood. The Brotherhood dominated the Syrian National Council (SNC), which is headquartered in Istanbul, and has succeeded in eclipsing other groups within the new opposition coalition, effectively thwarting the American effort to empower non-Islamists. [30]

In a nutshell, the war in Syria has gained a totally different dimension because it has become evident that the prevailing war is no longer one against a brutal dictator for the sake of democracy. The war is now over whether Syria will be run according to the Sunni Shariah—Sunni is is underlined and colour is differentor remain a secular country even if it is not a democratic one. [31] Most important of all, Assad has become tremendously successful in giving the impression that he has been standing against the radical groups in the region. The arrival of jihadists not only strengthened Assad's hand on international platforms but also has provided one of the incentives for Washington and Tehran to start searching for common ground. Tehran is concerned about the al-Qaida-affiliated groups in Syria as much as the United States is.

Ankara's current approach to international politics in the Middle East is increasingly making Turkey lonely on international platforms; this has become most evident when Erdoğan got furious with both the West and Arab nations over the military coup that ousted Egypt's first democratically elected president, Mohammed Morsi, in early July 2013.[32] According to some analysts, because Turkish foreign policy is "purely ethics-based" rather than "the interest based" one, it should be defined as a "precious loneliness/worthy solitude." This precious loneliness[33] of Turkey became more visible when the Russian Foreign Minister Sergei Lavrov and US Secretary of State John Kerry reached an agreement to secure and eliminate Syria's chemical weapons although Obama had clearly declared that the United States would apply force if chemical weapons were used.[34]

Turkey has welcomed the UNSC resolution adopted in New York and the US–Russian agreement on the destruction of chemical weapons; however, that Assad was not obliged to quit his position immediately although approximately 1300 Syrian people were gassed in August 2013 came as a shock for Ankara.[35] Thus, Bashar al-Assad not only won his war by managing to stay in power but also achieved to avert the US-led coalition forces with the help of the Russian inspired diplomatic efforts.

In addition, the lack of any reference to refugees or the humanitarian situation in the neighbouring countries in the UN resolution deepened Turkey's existing uneasiness about the negligent attitude of the international community towards Turkey's refugee problem.[36] As the number of Syrian refugees which Turkey hosts in 21 refugee camps and the cost of those refugees as a result of Turkey's open door policy increase on each passing day, Ankara demands that the international community—and especially the European Union and the United States— be much more forthcoming in funding humanitarian assistance programmes and live up to pledges made in the context of the UN's Syria Regional Response Plan.[37]

In sum, Ankara made a lot of miscalculations while formulating its policies towards Syria by putting all its chips in a 'non-Assad scenario'. For example, Turkey did not foresee that Washington would not favour a more Islamised Syria and would not consent to Assad's replacement by the Muslim Brotherhood, *Ikhwan*, especially after Mohammed Morsi came to power in Egypt since Israel would be sandwiched between two Ikhwan-ruled countries, Egypt and Syria. Assad's fall and his replacement by an Islamist rule would not only endanger the security of Israel but also lead to radical groups' control of chemical weapons existing in Syria. In addition, in the post-Iraq war period, the Obama Administration did not want to go into another war in the Middle East after the Iraqi quagmire while struggling with its own economic problems in inner politics.

Another important miscalculation of Turkey was concerned with the power of anti-Ikhwan regional countries such as Saudi Arabia, Jordan and United Arab Emirates. Erdoğan, while voicing the allegations that it was Israel which had organised and supported the military coup in Egypt, disregarded the fact that it might be Saudi Arabia which supported the army against the Ikhwan rule.[38] Lastly, Ankara did not take into account that Russia would not give up supporting Syria, for several reasons. First, Syria is the only country for Moscow to have an outlet to the Mediterranean. Russia currently has a naval installation in Tartus which is strategically important and Russia's last foreign military base outside the former Soviet Union. Second, the Syrian uprising has clearly shown that Russia still acts according to the Cold War mentality and spends great effort in preventing Syria from being under Western control.

Most important of all, Ankara did not want to foresee that Iran would double down in Syria in an attempt to keep the Shiite crescent, to support a valuable ally in the Arab world, and a convenient conduit to Hezbollah in Lebanon. The main divergence between Turkey and Iran has come out on the basis of sectarian division. Tehran has achieved to show the rebellion against the Assad regime as a Sunni uprising against minority Alawites, an outlier sect of Shiism, whereas Ankara played to a Sunni party, the Muslim Brotherhood. When looking closely, however, Ankara and Tehran have become pragmatic enough to manage the relationship and maintain amity rather than enmity whenever a crisis has come out.

## Syrian Uprising and Turkey–Iran Relations

The Syrian civil war has become a severe test for the sustainability of Turkey–Iran relations which have become interdependent on the basis of trade, security and politics to some extent, mainly due to expanding relations throughout the 2000s. Erdoğan and Ahmedinejad openly stated that they would seek ways of cooperation over the Syrian issue in October 2012 during a meeting in Azerbaijan. While Tehran demanded that Ankara provide negotiations between moderates from the opposition groups and the Assad regime,[39] Ankara wanted Iran to take its place in two different negotiating groups; Turkey–Egypt and Iran, Turkey–Iran and Russia and openly stated its positive view about Iran's cooperation in finding out a solution to the Syrian issue.[40]

From Tehran's perspective, the sense of being encircled by neighbouring countries is the main motive behind its policy of maintaining its relation with Ankara so as to secure its frontier with Turkey. Apart from the Patriots deployed on Turkish territories that Washington strengthened its military presence in Qatar having long range missiles, set alarm bells in Tehran. Besides, the expanded American military influence in the Gulf, for example, after selling F15 war planes of $30 billion in 2011 to Saudi Arabia exacerbated Iranian security concerns. Some developments such as the bilateral visits between the Turkish and Saudi Chief of General Staff in November 2012 and the signing of a military agreement between

Turkey and Qatar in July 2012 also made Tehran think that a new Sunni axis was being realised by neighbouring countries.[41] In order to cope with this feeling of being surrounded, Tehran wanted not only to maintain a cordial relationship with Turkey but also favoured mending the relations with Egypt under Ikhwan rule after Morsi came to power. Ahmedinejad became the first Iranian president who visited Egypt, an important ally of USA, since the Islamic revolution.[42]

Secondly, Iranians cannot afford to lose the Turkish gas market which has become increasingly important at a time when the Iranian economy has been weakened by the severest sanctions ever applied in its history. Because both sides have developed relatively interdependent trade and energy relations throughout the 2000s, the officials from Iran and Turkey insistently state that they were determined to develop trade relations despite diverging interests in Syria and Iraq. For example, in October 2012, Erdoğan stated at a meeting with the Iranian vice-president, Mohammed Reza Rahimi that the volume of Iranian–Turkish trade would increase from $16.5 billion to $30 billion.[43] This statement of Erdoğan has been noteworthy with respect to understanding Ankara's uneasiness about the sanctions applied on Iran by the UN since 2010 which has obstructed mostly Turkey's purchase of Iranian natural gas which consists of 20 percent of Turkey's natural gas need. In addition, Ankara as well as Turkish business circles have been increasingly uneasy about the double standards applied by the United States which bypassed the sanctions and covertly exported its goods to Iran.[44]

"At the insistence of the Obama administration, in 2012 Turkey reduced its imports of oil from Iran; at the same time, however, it began selling gold to the country to circumvent the difficulties associated with payments in dollars."[45] The tension between Turkey and the United States was heightened with Obama's Executive order 13622 prohibiting the export of gold and "other precious metals" to the Islamic Republic.[46] However, currently, the Obama Administration has declined to issue any sanctions pursuant to the order in the face of growing tension between Turkey and the United States. Ankara is still Tehran's largest export market for natural gas.[47]

From Turkey's perspective, the most important reason for maintaining bilateral relations with Iran is related to Turkey's escalating security concerns especially after the spillover effect of the Syrian civil war became evident with the attacks on Akçakale, Cilvegözü and Reyhanlı.[48] Put differently, at a time when the NATO general secretary Rasmussen openly stated that "NATO cannot act like the policeman of the world,"[49] Ankara, whose economy and on the board security has been increasingly under threat because of the refugee flood and bomb attacks, favoured to retain cordial relations with Iran. Despite occasional outbreaks of crisis, both sides quickly contained and ameliorated bilateral relations through diplomatic channels. For example, in the face of the Iranian Chief of General Staff's threats concerning the Patriots deployed on Turkish territories, Davutoğlu "reassured his Iranian counterpart Ali-Akbar Salehi during a joint news conference in Tehran in January 2012 that Turkey "would never take any step that could negatively affect our relations with our neighbour ... We would never accept any attack on any of our neighbours from our soil. We don't want such a perception of threat to exist, especially against Iran." In return, Salehi put the remarks of the IRGC general in context underlining that "some people, knowingly or not, express views without much knowledge and by stepping beyond their responsibilities, and it causes misunderstandings."[50]

The existence of some reasons for the two neighbouring countries not to cut their links completely does not mean that there is no problem in bilateral relations. On the contrary, leaving aside the war by proxy in Syria, especially the rivalry over filling the gap in Iraq after US troops' removal has influenced the current relations in a negative way. While Turkey's relations with Iraqi Kurdistan improved especially on the basis of energy and trade so as to strengthen Iraqi Kurdistan's capacity to act freely from the Baghdad Administration, Iran tried to have a sphere of influence especially in the south of Iraq.

The existing Shiite-based Maliki government is of crucial importance for Iran to keep its sphere of influence in Syria for the Iranian arms flow to Syria via Iraq. In addition, the Maliki government supports the Assad regime by hosting official visits by Syrians, signing pacts to expand business ties and offering political support so as to help the Assad regime to cope with the problem of being excluded by the Arab League members. Currently, Turkey has been labelled as "a hostile state" and accused by the Maliki government of interfering in the internal affairs of Iraq. Turkey's rapprochement with Iraqi Kurdistan has been perceived as a Turkish plot against the unity of Iraq. For example, Turkey and Iraqi Kurdistan have signed a pipeline agreement[51] which would transfer one million barrel crude oil via Kirkuk. The Yumurtalık pipeline came as a shock to the Baghdad government since this agreement was perceived by Maliki as Erbil's breaking away with the central government.[52]

Another area of competition between Iran and Turkey has also become more visible after the outburst of the Arab Spring. For example, Erdoğan's travels to Egypt, Tunisia and Libya five days before the opening of Iran's Islamic Awakening conference and his message of secular democracy were perceived by Tehran as an attempt of Erdoğan to pull the carpet from under Iran's regional ambitions with his growing popularity on the Arab street.[53] Erdoğan's messages were harshly criticised by Tehran on the grounds that Turkey's model of "secular Islam" was a version of Western liberal democracy and unacceptable for countries that are going through "Islamic awakening."[54] From a different angle, Erdoğan's Arab tour and his words encouraging the Arab street to be more democratised automatically touched the sensitive chords of Iranian political elite whose biggest concern is about the survival of their regime which was endangered by big mass protests only a couple of years ago.[55]

The beginning of Rouhani's moderate Iranian diplomacy, however, offers a good opportunity for a new beginning with Turkey so as to reduce the existing tension stemming from the black cat, Syria. Although the deal on chemical weapons averting the prospect of a military strike was seen as a development which weakened Turkey's position, and strengthened Tehran's hand, there was no doubt that Ankara could hardly afford to continue its current policy of putting all chips in a non-Assad scenario due to some reasons. First of all, the possibility that the al-Qaeda-linked Jabhat al-Nusra and the Islamic State of Iraq and al-Sham could eventually grow too strong to control and threaten Turkey urged Ankara to seek more cooperative relations with Iran. The international conflict based on sectarian divisions on its longest border has been threatening and might stoke a dangerous escalation on Turkey's inner politics issue—the Sunni–Alawite divide. In a similar vein, Tehran, which has been increasingly concerned with a probable emergence of a de facto Kurdish autonomy emerging in northern Syria under the leadership of the Democratic Union Party, linked to the Kurdistan Workers' Party along at least 400 km of the Turkish border, has no choice but to ally with Turkey.[56]

In a nutshell, Turkey, weary about the "Pakistanisation" prospect in its border provinces, and Tehran, pressurised on its nuclear efforts and its economy by the international community are currently willing to turn a new page. They do not want to jeopardise their bilateral relations, even over the civil war in Syria that has crystallised the urgency of cooperation of the two countries despite many obstacles.

## Conclusion

The Syrian civil war has not only crystallised the limits of "new activism" in Turkish foreign policy formulated by a newly emerging Turkey but also inflamed a hot debate about its role in an extending global order whose web of norms, institutions, rules, and relationships are under a heavy criticism of Ankara.

Put differently, Ankara's stance towards the Arab spring as well as the Syrian uprising made it evident that Turkey's various labels such as "frontier", "pivot", "bridge" country have been transformed into another one that is "central country." This new label which Ankara adopted during the transformation process including 9/11 brought about an unprecedented activism in Turkish foreign policy parallel to the renewal of international order on many areas such as trade, finance, non-proliferation and human rights.[57]

According to Fontain and Kliman, Turkey is one of the four rising democracies that might be termed "global swing states" which has been defined in the American political context as the countries which "desire changes to international order, and whose choices will, in aggregate, decisively influence the trajectory of today's world. Although the two analysts note that Turkey, and the other swing states, Brazil, Indonesia and India have neither the power nor ambition to construct a rival system"[58] it is apparent that the general belief in Washington, that 'only through a *pax-Americana* the anarchic world can be saved' has no more validity with the emergence of drastic changes in the international order and the rise of China as a global power.

Parallel to this, Turkey has maintained a sustained criticism of the international order. However, this does not mean that Turkey challenges the existing US-led global order, mainly due to two reasons. One is that Turkey still benefits from the existing international order, the second reason is that as Kardaş notes, Ankara's priority is to "bolster the country's regional standing rather than to establish itself as a global player."[59] The issue is that to what extent Turkey's regional interests will be compatible with those of the global powers, especially the West. The ultimate aim of Turkey's global activism, on the other hand, is to bring stability and peace to the region, the Middle East, by emphasising a fair order rather than a strategic restoration. That is why Ankara, on many platforms, questions and calls for the change of decision-making mechanism of the UN Security Council on the ground that justice cannot be achieved through decisions made by only five countries, meaning the five permanent members of the Council.[60]

The Turkish top officials' statements or some policies of Ankara, from Washington's perspective, indicate Turkey's enthusiasm or potential to act in ways that would undermine the order.[61] In this context, Turkey's no vote toward sanctions applied on Iran by the United Nations, or its position on navigation in Eastern Mediterranean,[62] its controversial decision to select a Chinese company for its long-range air and missile defence system[63] are regarded in a negative way by Washington. The US top officials who have been accustomed to a Turkey having a "*faith*" in the West without questioning its norms, values, policies and conducts under the Cold War mentality are quite reluctant to understand the "New Turkey" in a changing international order.

The policies of Ankara towards Syria and Iran throughout the Arab Spring process should be evaluated by taking into consideration Turkey's uniqueness on geographical/ regional as well as its Western and liberal identity level rather than debating whether it is a "neo-third-worldist" country.[64]

In a nutshell, the Syrian uprising has clarified that the Middle East is a sub-region whose dynamics are shaped around the interests of the global powers; therefore, Syria has emerged as a country where the global politics is reproduced by means of a war by proxy. Turkey currently has no choice but of following a good neighbourhood policy especially with the countries such as Iran and Kurdish Regional Government/Iraq at a time when Washington,[65] whose sole objective is to maintain a stalemate in Syria, prefers to be a mere spectator in the face of crimes committed by both the Assad regime and other radical groups.

## Notes

1. With the September 16, 2009 Treaty, visa requirements were lifted and the first ministerial meeting of the Turkey–Syria High Level Strategic Cooperation Council which was held with the participation of ten ministers on October 13, 2009 aimed exchange on trade, development and education (Ayhan 2009, 30; Turkish NY 2009).
2. (Tur 2010).
3. (Gürcanli 2009).
4. "Turkey receives 18 million cubic meters per day from Iran, making Iran the second largest supplier of gas to Turkey after Russia" (Associated Press 2009).
5. (TSIDICG 2010, 6).
6. (Khalaf and Strauss 2010).
7. Gürsel, K. (2010, November 21). "AKP Dış Politikası Lizbon'da İflas Etti", *Milliyet*, (Kürecik 19-20 November 2010)
8. (Özalp 2010).
9. *China Daily*, "Panetta to Visit Turkey Over Shield Plan," 14 December 2011, http://www.chinadaily.com.cn/world/2011-12/14/content_14266117.htm ; Kadri Gürsel, "Füze Kalkanının Eğrisi Doğrusu," *Milliyet*, October9, 2011.
10. Metin Münir, "İran'ın Erdoğan'a Sunduğu Fırsat", *Milliyet*, 18 October 2012.
11. "Turkey will be next in line for violence after Syria if it continues to work on behalf of Western interests," İran "Genel Kurmay Başkanı Hasan Firuzabadi: Sıra Türkiye'ye gelir", *Star*, August 28, 2012.
12. Turkish President Abdullah Gül stated on a TV channel: "some coalition governments have ulterior motives and Libya could be "looted" as Iraq had been. Because the aim (of coalition forces) is not the liberation of the Libyan people. There are hidden agendas and differing interests", 2011, *TV 24*. 23 March. *Gül: Libya'yla ilgili bazı ülkeler fırsatçılık içinde.* Retrieved May 14, 2011, from *TV 24*: viewed 22 December 2012, <http://www.yirmidort.tv/dunya/gul-libya-yla-ilgili-bazi-ulkeler-firsatcilik-icinde-haber-27719.htm>
13. Habibi N. and W. Walker, J. 2011, 'Turkey's Grand Miscalculation on Libya', 6 March, *Boston.com*, viewed 18 December 2012, <http://www.boston.com/bostonglobe/editorial_opinion/blogs/the_angle/2011/03/turkeys_grand_m.html>
14. (Bugün 2011).
15. Nuh Yılmaz, "Syria: The View from Turkey", European Council on Foreign

Relations, June 19, 2013, http://www.ecfr.eu/content/entry/commentary_syria_the_view_from_turkey139

16.
17. Asli Aydintasbas, "Davutoğlu'ndan ABD'ye: Humus Sarajevo Olmasin", *Milliyet*, February 13, 2012.
18. Zagros Osman, "Syrian revolution and Washington's Miscalculations", *Fıkra Forum*, May 17, 2012, accessible at http://fikraforum.org/?p=2241
19. Semih Idiz, "Turkiye Suriye'de Yalniz Kalmamali", *Milliyet*, March 31, 2012. "Türkiye Stratejisinde Yollar Ayriliyor, Turkiye'nin Planina Veto", *Milliyet*, March 25, 2012.
20. "Ankara accused the United Nations Security Council (UNSC) of indirectly supporting the oppression of the Syrian people by failing to unite on Syria." Semih Idiz, "Ankara BM'nin Suriye Surecine Karsi Soguk", *Milliyet*, March 26, 2012.
21. Erol Cebeci and Kadir Üstün, "The Syrian Quagmire: What is Holding Turkey Back?", *Insight Turkey*, Vol. 14, No.2, 2012, p. 20.
22. Can Dundar, "Sam Amca Seni Iteliyor", *Milliyet*, April 12, 2012. For example, Hilary Clinton declared 'we expect the regime change process in Syria will be realized without violence under the leadership of the Arab League and Turkey' (*Hürriyet*, November 20, 2011).
23. "For example, Turkish President, Gul stated that Turkey favoured a solution based on diplomacy and opposed any foreign intervention in Syria,""BM'nin Son Kararını Tasvip Etmiyoruz", *Hurriyet*, March 25, 2012 and Semih Idiz, "Ankara'nin Kafasi Suriye Konusunda Karisikk Gorunuyor", *Milliyet*, March 10, 2012.
24. "NATO to Stay out of Syria Even If UN Mandate Emerges", *Reuters*, February 17, 2012, http://www.reuters.com/article/2012/02/17/us-syria-nato-idUSTRE81G0ZF20120217 accessed Oct. 12, 2013. "Rasmussen said the Western alliance had no intention of intervening in Syria even in the event of a U.N. mandate to protect civilians, and urged Middle East countries to find a way to end the spiraling violence."
25. Semih İdiz, "Turkey's New Strategy could Broker Force", *Al-monitor*, October 20, 2012, http://www.al-monitor.com/pulse/ar/contents/articles/politics/2012/10/vision-and-imagination-required-over-syria.html accessed October 12, 2013.
26. Unver, H. A., 'Turkey's Syria Calculations: Kurdish Dimension', *Foreign Policy Association*, March 22, 2012.
27. Kareem Fahim and Sebnem Arsu, "Turkey Says It Shot Down Syrian Military Helicopter Flying in Its Airspace", *The New York Times*, September 16, 2013, http://www.nytimes.com/2013/09/17/world/europe/turkey-syria.html?_r=0 accessed October 13, 2013.
28. Amberin Zaman, "Syrian Kurdish Leader Urges Turkey To End Support for Salafists", *Al-Monitor*, October 9, 2013, http://www.al-monitor.com/pulse/originals/2013/10/syrian-kurdish-leader-calls-turkey-shut-down-salafists.html accessed October 13, 2013.
29. "Turkey warns Syrian PYD against seeking autonomy", *Today's Zaman.*
30. Halil M. Karaveli, "Turkey, the Unelpful Ally", *The New York Times*, February 27, 2013, http://www.nytimes.com/2013/02/27/opinion/turkey-the-unhelpful-ally.html?_r=0 accessed Oct. 14, 2013.
31. Semih Idiz, "Jihadists Alter the Syrian Equation," October 3, 2013, http://www.hurriyetdailynews.com/jihadists-alter-the-syrian-equation.

aspx?pageID=449&nID=55566&NewsCatID=416

32. Erdoğan was puzzled at the Saudi officials' support for the Egyptian coup and said: "How could a country claiming to uphold Islam and Sharia support the overthrow of an elected Islamist president who came to power after fair elections?" Al-Rasheed, M. 2013, "Saudi Arabia and Turkey Falter Over Egypt", *Al-Monitor*, 20 August, viewed 14 September 2013, <http://www.al-monitor.com/pulse/originals/2013/08/saudi-arabia-turkey-strained-relations.html>
33. Adilgazi, L. 2013, "Zero Problems' Policy Supplanted by 'Precious Loneliness' Approach", *Today's Zaman,* 25 August, viewed September 14, 2013, <http://www.todayszaman.com/news-324415-zero-problems-policy-supplanted-by-precious-loneliness-approach.html>
34. Chris Good, "President Obama's Red Line; What He Actually Said about Syria and Chemical Weapons", *ABC News*, August 26, 2013, http://abcnews.go.com/blogs/politics/2013/08/president-obamas-red-line-what-he-actually-said-about-syria-and-chemical-weapons/ accessed Oct. 15, 2013.
35. Dominic Evans and Khaled Yacoub Oweis, "Syria Gas Kills Hundreds Security Council Meets", Reuters, August 21, 2013, http://www.reuters.com/article/2013/08/21/us-syria-crisis-idUSBRE97K0EL20130821 accessed Oct 15, 2013.
36. Davutoğlu Disappointed by UN Security Council Resolution", *Today's Zaman*, September 30, 2013, http://www.todayszaman.com/news-327814-davutoglu-disappointed-by-un-security-council-resolution.html accessed Oct 19, 2013.
37. Kemal Kirişçi, "Syrian Refugees in Turkey: The Limits of an Open Door Policy", *Brookings*, June 27, 2013, http://www.brookings.edu/blogs/up-front/posts/2013/06/27-syrian-refugees-in-turkey-kirisci accessed Oct. 19, 2013.
38. Serpil Çevikcan, "Suriye, Mısır, Görünen Köy", *Milliyet*, August 24, 2013.
39. "İran Dışişleri Bakan Yardımcısı, Abdullahiyan, Suriye'deki sorunun çözümüne ilişkin Türkiye ile istişare halinde olduklarını, iki ülkenin önerilerinin yüzde 70'inin birbiriyle uyumlu olduğunu açıklamıştır." "İran: Suriye Konusunda Türkiye'yle Uyumluyuz," *Milliyet*, January 8, 2013.
40. "Esad'a Karşı İran'ı İşbirliğine Çağırdı," *Milliyet*, October 17, 2012.
41. Semih İdiz, "Turkey's Sectarian War over Syria and Iraq," *Al-Monitor Turkey*, January 4, 2013.
42. "Mısır Dışişleri Bakanı Kemal Amr, ziyaret esnasında Körfez ülkelerinin güvenliği Mısır'ın kırmızı çizgisi olduğunu söyleyerek İran'la yakınlaşma olmadığı sinyalini vermiştir." İran Lideri İlk Kez Mısır'da, *Milliyet*, February 6, 2013.
43. Seda Kırdar, ABD'nin İran'a Uyguladığı Altın Yaptırımı ve Olası Sonuçları, Türkiye Ekonomi Politikaları Araştırma Vakfı (TEPAV), April 2013, p. 2.
44. "Asıl ABD İran'la Ticareti Kessin," *Sabah*, December 1, 2012.
45. In fact, Turkey's gold exports to Iran significantly reduced its balance of payments deficits in the first six months of 2012. See Guliyeva and Pak, 'What's Iran doing with Turkish Gold?'; and "Gold Sales to Iran and Economic Slowdown Curb Turkey Trade Deficit", *The Daily Star*, August 1, 2012 in Barkey, p. 146.
46. Serkan Demirtaş, Türkiye-ABD Arasında Altın Gerginliği, BBC Türkçe, December 5, 2012, http://www.bbc.co.uk/turkce/haberler/2012/12/121205_us_turkey_gold.shtml
47. Robert Zarate, Patrick Christy, FPI Bulletein, "Obama and Congress must Max Out Iran Sanctions Now", *The Foreign Policy Initiative*, May 14, 2013, http://www.

foreignpolicyi.org/content/fpi-bulletin-obama-and-congress-must-max-out-iran-sanctions%E2%80%94now accessed 24 Oct.
48. Reyhanlı'da Katliam: 43 Ölü, *Milliyet*, 12 Mayıs 2013. Murat yetkin, Suriye Savaşı kapımıza Dayandı, *Radikal*, July 18, 2013.
49. *Reuters*, "NATO to Stay out of Syria Even If UN Mandate Emerges", February 17, 2012, http://www.reuters.com/article/2012/02/17/us-syria-nato-idUSTRE81G0ZF20120217
50. Arshin Adib-Moghaddam, "Turkey & Iran: Islamic Brotherhood or Regional Rivalry?", *Al Jazeera*, June 4, 2013, http://studies.aljazeera.net/en/reports/2013/05/20135139554264452.htm.
51. "Iraqi Kurdistan Poised to Pipe Oil to World via Turkey," *El Arabiya*, April 17, 2013, http://english.alarabiya.net/en/business/energy/2013/04/17/Iraqi-Kurdistan-poised-to-pipe-oil-to-world-via-Turkey.html
52. Denge Azad, Cengiz Çandar: Kürdistan petrolü, Türkiye, *Ortadoğu jeopolitiği* April 24, 2013.
53. *Hürriyet Daily News*, "Erdoğan Offers "Arab Spring" neo-Laicism," September 15, 2011, http://www.hurriyetdailynews.com/default.aspx?pageid=438&n=erdogan-offers-8216arab-spring8217-neo-laicism-2011-09-15 accessed 23 Oct.
54. Henry J. Barkey, "Turkish-Iranian Competition after the Arab Spring", *Survival: Global Politics and Strategy*, vol. 54, no.6, December 2012- January 2013, p. 154. Iran which was caught off guard with the outburst of the mass protests in the Arab world and sought to find and develop commonalities between the raison d'être of the Iranian state and the protests, therefore described the mass protests as 'Islamic Awakening' (*Bidari-ye Eslami*)," Mahan Abedin, "Khamanei Throws the Gauntlet at the West," *Asia Times Online*, September 21, 2011. http://www.lse.ac.uk/IDEAS/publications/reports/pdf/SR011/FINAL_LSE_IDEAS__IranAndArabSpring_Rafati.pdf
55. "Iran Says Turkey's Secular System Not Suitable for Arab Spring Nations," *Today's Zaman*, December 13, 2011, http://www.todayszaman.com/news-265659-iran-says-turkeys-secular-system-not-suitable-for-arab-spring-nations.html accessed Oct 23, 2013.
56. Fehim Taştekin, "Rouhani Offers Chance to Turkey, Too," *Al Monitor*, September 26, 2013, http://www.al-monitor.com/pulse/originals/2013/09/rouhani-turkey-opportunity-iran-relations.html accessed 23 Oct.
57. Murat Yeşiltaş, "Global Swing and Turkey", *The New Turkey*, February 7, 2013, http://www.thenewturkey.org/global-swing-and-turkey/new-turkey/205
58. Richard Fontain, Daniel M. Kliman, "International Order and Global Swing States", *The Washington Quarterly*, 36:1, pp. 93_109.
59. Şaban Kardaş, "Global Swing States and International Order: A Turkish View", *The German Murshall Fund of the United States*, December 21, 2012, p. 3.
60. "Erdoğan Says UN Security Council is Paralyzed," *Sunday's Zaman*, October 2, 2013, http://www.todayszaman.com/news-327961-erdogan-says-un-security-council-is-paralyzed.html accessed 27 October
61. Yeşiltaş, "Global Swing and Turkey," *The New Turkey*, February 7, 2013.
62. After the discovery of abundant natural gas resources in Eastern Mediterranean, the problem of sovereignty of Cyprus came to the forefront and Turkey objected to the Greek Cypriot-controlled government's sovereignty to have explorative and drilling rights in Cyprus' EEZ (Exclusive Economic Zone) unless there is a solution

to the Cyprus problem. Alper Ali Rıza, "The Law of the Sea: Turkey vs. Cyprus," *Sunday's Zaman*, December 13, 2011, http://www.todayszaman.com/news-265640-the-law-of-the-sea-turkey-vs-cyprus-by-alper-ali-riza*.html

63. Fulya Ozerkan, "US Seriously Concerned about Turkey's Chinese Missile Choice," *Defense News*, October 24, 2013, http://www.defensenews.com/article/20131024/DEFREG01/310240021/US-Seriously-Concerned-About-Turkey-s-Chinese-Missile-Choice
64. Jean Marcou, "Turkey's Foreign Policy: Shifting Back to the West after a Drift to the East?" *TEPAV*, 2013, Eighth edition, p.3.
65. U.S. Secretary of State John Kerry praised Syrian President Bashar al-Assad saying that Assad deserved credit for honoring the terms of a deal reached last month to secure and destroy the regime's weapons. "Kerry Said Asad Deserves Credit for Honoring Weapons Agreement," *Fox News*, October 7, 2013.

# 5

# Turkey–Iran Economic Ties Post-2002

*Sujata Ashwarya Cheema*

Bilateral economic relations between Turkey and Iran have grown exponentially since 2002, driven by complementary trade interests, of which, energy trade is the most significant. For over a decade, Turkey has cultivated ties with its neighbours, under the rubric of the popularly known 'zero-problem' foreign policy, advocated and implemented by the moderate Islamist *Adalet ve Kalkınma Partisi* (AKP) or Justice and Development Party that swept to power in 2002. Turkey under the government of Prime Minster Erdoğan opened borders and trade routes with all its neighbours, sought to resolve political issues with them, including brokering political deals and talks on their behalf, and more controversially, promoted the idea that Turkish democracy could serve as a model for political organisation in the region notorious for resilient authoritarianism.

Ankara's reengagement with the regional Middle Eastern countries also reflected the change in the composition of the ruling elite in the country. Members of the AKP came from conservative, religious background, as opposed to the West-oriented and secular Kemalist elite, that had dominated Turkish politics for more than seven decades. The AKP emphasised that the cultural affinity of Turkish society with the Middle Eastern countries could be harnessed for better political and economic relations. Turkey claimed that the zero problem policy logically followed the country's rich cultural and historical ties with the region. However, this did not mean giving up traditionally good relations with the West or betraying Western values and commitments, assiduously cultivated by the state since 1923, although misgivings of this nature emanated from some Western quarters.

The 'zero-problem' policy was an ambitious attempt by Turkey's new elites to predicate their country's global supremacy on regional pre-eminence. Ahmet Davutoğlu—Erdoğan's foreign policy advisor, foreign minister (2009–2014) and the chief architect of the new strategy—wrote a hugely popular book, *Strategic Depth*, in which he elaborated his strategic vision for Turkey. He believed that Ankara had made a mistake for decades by disengaging itself from the Middle Eastern region, which constituted the country's 'strategic depth.' Self-imposed isolation under Kemalism had inhibited Turkey's emergence as a powerful regional actor and, indeed, a dominant global power. Its strategic depth could be secured along a fourfold direction: a) by strengthening economic and diplomatic relations with its neighbours; b) by promoting greater regional integration and cooperation; c) by repositioning Turkey as an important mediator of regional conflict; and d) by becoming an indispensible interlocutor between the Middle East and the West.

Davutoğlu argued that Turkey's ascent to the global power status could be enabled if all its outstanding bilateral problems with its neighbours were resolved. Such disputes with neighbouring states had constrained Turkey into inertia, which could only be broken with active diplomacy. Echoing the view that 'zero-problem-based' relations could be achieved by 'maximal mutual-interest-based' ones, Turkey's new elites sought to better trade and commercial ties with Turkey's neighbours and indeed with all the Middle Eastern countries. What followed for the next ten years was "a slow build-up of pragmatic diplomatic engagement with all parties, economic integration and people-to-people outreach,"[1] which laid the groundwork for the emergence of Turkey as a leading economic player in the region, whose growth remained stable despite the world economic crisis. An increase in trade ties, reciprocal investments and joint projects with neighbouring countries provided the blueprint for promoting regional cooperation based on the *soft-power* approach.

## Turkey and Iran: The Evolution of Diplomatic and Economic Relations

The common goal of secular modernisation brought Turkey under Mustafa Kemal Atatürk and Iran under Reza Shah Pahlavi in close contact and the two countries remained so up until the Iranian Revolution of 1979, which brought an Islamist regime to power in Tehran.[2] On April 22, 1926, Iran and Turkey signed a 'friendship treaty' in Tehran, pledging neutrality and nonaggression. Reza Shah visited Turkey in 1934 at the invitation of Ataturk and was reportedly impressed by the accomplishments of Ankara's modernisation reforms. The Shah of Iran saw Turkey's development as a template for advances in his own country. At that time Turkey and Iran along with Pakistan, Iraq and Britain became a part of the CENTO, a mutual security pact designed to contain the Soviet Union from penetrating into the West Asian region. As both Ankara and Tehran were wary of Soviet expansion southwards, the pact thrust the two countries together on a common security issue. The first regional organisation for economic cooperation in this part of the world, the Regional Cooperation for Development (RCD), aimed at joint projects between Turkey, Iran and Pakistan was established in 1964.[3] In effect, Turkey and Iran, by circumstances and resolve, were close allies during the period of the monarchy in Tehran.

The Iranian Revolution of 1979 soured relations between the two countries, as Turkey felt threatened by Iran's ambitions to 'export the revolution' and change the regional order. Tehran in turn saw Ankara as a close ally of the West and therefore potentially opposed to its interests. Further, ideological tensions introduced by the Islamic Revolution of 1979 disrupted ties between the two friendly West Asian neighbours. Iran's Islamist regime was a clear anti-thesis of constitutionally secular Turkey. Whereas *sharia* and clerics played decisive roles, including control over the military in Iran, Turkey's secularism was protected by the military, its self-appointed guardian. In the immediate aftermath of the revolution in Iran, mistrust and tension ran high, primarily because the military establishment of the Kemalist elites suspected Iran of lending support to the Islamists in Turkey. For Turkey, Iran had regressed into backwardness and political indifference to Islamist Iran was the best possible way to deal with it. Nonetheless, there were people less circumspect of Ankara's relations with post-revolutionary Tehran. The more moderate Kemalists took a more nuanced view of Iran, including a less alarmist view of its ideological threat, and they favoured a balanced and realist approach to relations with the Islamic Republic.[4] As a consequence of these varied perceptions within the ruling elite, Turkey kept a distance from Iran, politically, but tried to develop economic relations. The two governments cooperated tactically on energy and Kurdish issues.

By 1984–85, a gradual but steady relationship began to develop. The change was attributed to the government of Turgut Özal, Turkey's first democratically elected Prime Minister after the 1980 coup. Once he took over the government as PM, Özal liberalised the state-dominated and heavily protected economy with policies designed to encourage exports, rationalize the tax system and encourage foreign investment.[5] These structural changes set off Turkey's stagnating economy on a high-growth path and gradual globalisation. Turkey could no longer remain shielded from regional market and resources, both natural and capital. With economic considerations as priority, Turkey's foreign policy horizons broadened as Ankara reached out to the hitherto removed Middle Eastern region. Export to the regional Muslim countries touched 40 percent of Turkey's export, higher than that to the traditional Western markets. The lead was taken by the Turkish construction sector, which dramatically increased its projects in the Middle East.[6]

Turgut Özal's pragmatism as well as his comfort with Turkey's 'Islamic' identity in order to develop political and economic relations with the West Asian countries "contributed greatly to the maintenance of reasonable relations between Turkey and Iran, largely because, unlike the generals (who were ultra-Kemalist), Özal did not see Iran's Islamic ideology as an immediate threat to Turkey."[7] Turkey's isolation from Europe following the 1980 military coup d'état enabled Özal to develop economic linkages to Turkey's east. He also gradually empowered the devout Muslims of inner Anatolia, who, with their small capital were eager to trade with their Muslim counterparts in West Asia.[8] Likewise, Iran showed a clear preference for Turkey as an economic partner, though the Islamic regime resented the fact that Turkey allowed fugitive Iranians to enter the country and would not hand them over to Tehran.[9] The Turkish security authorities, however, did not lose sight of the ideological difference that separated governments of Turkey and Iran and remained convinced of Iranian attempts to undermine the secular order in Turkey. In reality, Iran never seriously attempted to export Islamist ideology to Turkey.

During his tenure as the Prime Minister (1983–1989), Özal used the economy as a new foreign policy tool,[10] paving the way for transformation of Turkey from a "security state" to a "trading state."[11] He made a substantial push towards Iran, believing that close economic relations with Tehran were important for Turkish interests, even as the United States and the European Community strongly opposed the Islamic regime.[12] The Özal government strongly "believed that good relations with Muslim countries would help improve the economic and security concerns of Turkey. In fact, Turkey saw in Iran an important trade partner and Anatolia soon became the trade route for movement of goods travelling by truck between Iran and Europe."[13]

During the Iran–Iraq War (1980–88), Turkey maintained a neutral policy, and acted as a conduit for the supply of basic commodities to the two warring countries. Iraq and Iran also offered new markets for the Turkish economy. Özal used this opportunity very well, and took representatives of the newly emerging class of Turkish businessmen on all his foreign visits that opened up new horizons for them. As far as Iran was concerned, tourism leaped from a marginal industry to a major earner of foreign currency. Özal's policies paid off financially and economically, evidenced in the rise of the number of Iranian firms operating in Turkey, from 1 in 1984 to 22 in 1986.

Western backing for Baghdad in the Iran–Iraq War did not impact on Ankara's declared neutrality and economic ties with Tehran. Nonetheless, the economic dimensions of the relationship had to increasingly compete with security considerations towards the latter half of the 1980s as the Kurdish issue began to dominate Turkish foreign policy. Turkey became increasingly concerned regarding how to combat the Kurdistan Workers' Party (PKK) challenge across the border. On October 15, 1984, Turkey signed a security protocol with Iraq that allowed the two countries to enter each other's territory for 5 km without prior consent.[14] For the sake of neutrality, Ankara also sought a similar arrangement with Tehran.

However, Prime Minister Mir Hossein Mousavi rejected the Turkish request on the ground that it would amount to infringement of Iran's sovereignty.[15]

Turkey became increasingly bitter in the early 1990s over Iranian aid to the PKK insurgents, which operated from bases deep inside the Iranian territory. In 1991, Turkey intercepted an Iranian-flagged vessel on suspicion that it was carrying weapons for the PKK. Conversely, mirroring Turkey's concerns, Tehran complained that Ankara was not doing enough to control Iranian dissidents freely operating on Turkish soil. Iran also claimed that Turkey was interfering in its northern Azeri province and stoking linguistic ties in order to weaken the Islamic Republic. However, Iran's wariness of Turkey had more to do with the latter's NATO membership, which brought the world's sole and strongest military alliance close to their common border in the post-Cold War period in the context of Tehran's adversarial relations with Washington.[16]

Simultaneously, the same period saw changes in Turkey's domestic scene, particularly the changing political fortunes of its various interest groups that effected changes in Turkish–Iranian relations. Particularly important was the rise of new political and Islamic elite, which challenged the exclusive hold of the Kemalist elite on power, thus leading to secular–Islamist tensions in Turkey during the 1990s. It adversely effected relations between Ankara and Tehran, as Turkey's secularists blamed Iran for this occurrence. The Turkish government in January 2000 accused Iran, especially the Quds brigade of the Revolutionary Guards of training the Hezbollah, an Islamist group in the Kurdish region of Turkey. Prime Minister Bulent Ecevit and President Ahmet Necdet Sezer criticised Iran for 'exporting' its revolution and destabilising Turkey by helping the PKK. The only two years in which Turkey–Iran relations saw stability was when Necmettin Erbakan, the leader the Islamic Refah (Welfare) Party became the Prime Minister. With ascension to power, he tried to expand Turkey's relations with Muslim countries in general, including Iran.

Turgut Özal's export-oriented economic reforms in 1980s had created a new set of business and trading interests that emerged from the conservative/religious periphery and began to erode the economic power from the hands of the Kemalist bureaucracy and state-sponsored businessmen. They continued to gain traction in the 1990s, as they pushed for Turkey's entry into newer markets and good relations with the Muslim and the Turkic worlds, which perceptibly shared common values.[17]Therefore, the chief driving factor in Turkey's rapprochement with Iran was the interests of the new economic elite nurtured on religious values, who sought the Iranian market for trade and investment.

The rise to power of the moderate Islamist AKP in Turkey at the turn of the millennium brought a renewed vigour to Turkish–Iranian relations. The AKP's 'neo-Ottomanist' proclivities, embracing the Ottoman 'great power legacy' led to a more 'activist foreign policy' on the part of the new government. Ankara sought to exert, according to Ömer Taşpinar, "soft power—political, economic, diplomatic, and cultural influence—in formerly Ottoman territories such as Middle East, North Africa, and Balkans, as well as in other reasons where Turkey has strategic and national interests."[18] Quite logically, then, this approach led Turkey to gravitate towards Iran, an immediate neighbour and a major regional player. Iran represented an important market with immense potential for export and investment. Iran on its part also slowly shifted its stance on the sensitive Kurdish issue, first, by preventing the PKK from having a free run in its territory, and, second, by launching a military strike against the Kurdish insurgents' hideouts in the northern Iraq in response to PJAK's (Free Life Party of Kurdistan, a PKK affiliate) attack on Iranian security forces. This was followed by Turkish–Iranian intelligence cooperation.[19]

## Trade and Economic Ties

After the 'lost decade' of the 1990s, during which the Turkish economy was saddled with all round problems—deep recession, skyrocketing inflation (77 percent), high public debt, financial crises in which the nation's currency collapsed, the banks had to be rescued, and recurring political instability—the AKP introduced structural reforms that ushered in a decade of growth. Turkish economy grew at an average of 6.8 percent during 2002–2008, compared to an annual average of 4 percent in the 1990s; it touched 9.2 percent in 2010 and 8.7 percent in 2011.[20] Trade relations with Iran contributed significantly to that growth.[21] In fact, some argue that 'Turkey handled the global financial crisis by structurally altering its strategic economic opening towards the Middle East, especially Iran.'[22]

Expansion in Turkish–Iranian trade took place in the context of the AKP's overall policy to increase trade and economic relations with all the Middle Eastern countries and especially its neighbours. Economic ties between the two countries grew rapidly over the ten-year period from 2003, underpinned by Turkey's large energy import from Iran. By 2012, Iran had become Turkey's largest supplier of crude oil and the second largest supplier of natural gas. Several economic agreements have been signed between Turkey and Iran with the ascension of the AKP to power in 2002 (Table 1) that have facilitated trade and commerce between the two countries.

At the institutional level, the Turkey Iran Joint Economic Commission (JEC) meets on a regular basis to discuss means of improving economic relations and resolve impediments to bilateral trade. In addition to governmental channels, the private sector of the two countries has facilitated business contacts, by organising meetings and reciprocal visits by business delegations. These include: the Turkish–Iranian Business Council (TIBC), established on November 6, 2001 by Turkish Foreign Economic Relations Board (DEIK); the Turkish Association for Development of Trade with Iran and the Middle East (IOTGD); the Iran–Turkey Strategic Trade Association (ITSTA), the Iranian Industrialists' and Businesspersons' Association (ISID) and the Independent Industrialists' and Businesspersons' Association (MUSAID). What deserves a mention here is that a significant number of private sector contacts between Turkish and Iranian businesses/companies are those owned by Iran's Turkic-speaking Azeri minority. Both MUSAID and Turkish Young Businesspersons' Association (TUGAID) have opened branch offices in Tabriz.

**Table 1: Economic Agreements between Iran and Turkey since 1995**

| Date | Economic Agreements |
|---|---|
| August 1996 | Iran and Turkey signed a $20 billion natural gas sales agreement that includes the construction of a 1,600-mile gas pipeline between Tabriz and Ankara. The deal became hugely controversial due to the America's Iran Sanctions Act (1997), which prohibits investment of more than $20 million annually in Iran's energy sector. However, sanctions did not affect Turkey, as each was to construct the pipeline on its side of border. This pipeline was completed in July 2001, whereupon gas delivery began immediately. |
| March 2003 | The Turkish government issued a decree on March 25, 2003 (effective from April 10, 2003) providing for 40 percent reductions in customs duties on agricultural products and 100 percent on industrial products imported from Iran, Iraq and Syria. |
| July 2003 | Within the framework of the ECO, Turkey, Iran and other members signed the Economic Cooperation Organization Trade Agreement (ECOTA) on July 17, 2003, under which they pledged to reduce customs tariffs and minimise all other obstacles to trade between ECO states. |
| October 2003 | Turkish State Minister Kursad Tuzmen visited Tehran with 300 businessmen, who managed to sign a $200 million worth of contracts with their Iranian counterparts. |
| December 2003 | Iran and a consortium of Turkish firms sign a $193 million construction project for phase two of the Imam Khomeini International Airport in Central Iran. Under political pressure from conservative political factions, the Iranian government cancelled the Turkish firm's contract and paid $15 million in damages. |
| February 2005 | An agreement on the Encouragement and Protection of Mutual Investments was signed on December 21, 1996 which came into effect on February 25, 2005. |
| March 2005 | Agreement on the Prevention of Double Taxation was first signed on June 17, 2002, which was formally implemented on March 7, 2005. |

| | |
|---|---|
| July 2007 | Iran and Turkey signed a Memorandum of Understanding (MoU) to transfer 30 billion cubic meters of Iranian and Turkmen natural gas to Europe via Turkey. A MoU was signed between Turkey and Iran on July 14, 2007, in which state-owned Turkish Petroleum Corporation (TPAO) received a licence from Iran for the exploration and development of three sections (22, 23 & 24) of the South Pars natural gas field. It also included buy-back contracts between Turkey and Iran. TPAO independently provided $3.5 billion and began the construction of facilities in the South pars field in 2008. Later on Turkey shelved the agreement under US pressure. |
| February 2008 | A Consortium of four Turkish firms purchased the Razi Petrochemical Company (located in southwestern Iran) for $650 million. |
| March 2009 | AKP passed a decree lifting the last restrictions on the use of Iranian Rial by Turkish banks. On April 8, 2009, Iranian officials declared that Iranian financial institutions were now permitted to handle transactions in Turkish Lira. Besides, Iran and Turkey signed an MoU for cooperation in air, land, and sea transportation. |
| April 2009 | Iran, Iraq, and Turkey signed an agreement to link their electric power grids. |
| June 2009 | Iran and Turkey signed a telecommunications agreement, which gives them access to each other's telecommunications network. |
| February 2010 | The Central Bank of Iran approved the establishment and operation of a Turkish-owned bank in Iran's Qeshm Island free zone.<br>Iran signed a customs an MoU with Turkey that opened up the Bazergan, Khoy, Saro, and Maku border points for trade. This agreement has also mandated the revival of the joint border markets in Kuzrosh and Salmas. |
| March 2010 | Iran and Turkey agreed to build a prototype joint industrial park in border areas near the Iranian city of Makou. |
| February 2011 | Iran's largest automaker, Iran Khodro, and the Turkish firm Hema Endustri signed a $200 million agreement to jointly produce a car in Turkey. |

| | |
|---|---|
| May 2011 | The energy ministers of Iran and Turkey signed an agreement to expand bilateral investments in the energy sector. |
| July 2011 | Iran, Iraq, and Turkey agreed to establish a joint investment bank to facilitate trade and investment among them. The initial capital is $200 million, and the main office of this bank will be in Tehran. |
| October 2011 | Iran and Turkey signed an agreement to cooperate on human resource development and exchange expertise in public administration. |
| January 2012 | Iran and Turkey signed a comprehensive economic cooperation agreement covering trade, transportation and investment. Besides, the Turkish Parliament approved health cooperation 2012 agreement with Iran. |
| January 2014 | Agreement on the Establishment of Joint Trade Committee and Preferential Trade Agreement. Tehran and Ankara signed a "preferential trade agreement" during Turkish PM Tayyip Erdoğan's trip to Iran aimed at paving the ground to boost trade to $30billion by 2015. Turkey is one of just twelve nations with which Iran has signed preferential and free trade agreements. |
| June 2014 | Agreements on cooperation in the fields of tourism, customs, cultural heritage, higher education and mailing services signed during the visit of Iranian President Hassan Rouhani's visit to Turkey. |

Source: Nader Habibi, "Growing Economic Relations Despite Western Sanctions," *Middle East Brief*, Crown Centre for Middle East Studies (Brandeis University), No. 62, May 2012, p. 4, http://www.brandeis.edu/crown/publications/meb/MEB62.pdf; Gareth H. Jenkins, "Occasional Allies, Enduring Rivals: Turkey's Relations with Iran," *Silk Road Paper*, Central Asia-Caucasus Institute Silk Road Studies Program, May 2012, pp. 51-53; Mustafa Aydin and Damla Aras, "Political Conditionality of Economic Relations between Paternalist States: Turkey's Interaction with Iran, Iraq and Syria," *Arab Studies Quarterly*, vol. 27, nos. 1&2 (Winter/spring 2005), p. 32;various news websites.

### *Bilateral Trade*

Rising trade volumes between the two countries reflect the immense potential for further development and diversification. Bilateral trade has grown rapidly in the ten-year period from $2.4 billion in 2002 to $22 billion in 2012 with an increase in the percentage share of Iran in the total volume of Turkish trade from 1.7 per cent to 5.6 percent. This makes the Islamic Republic, Turkey's sixth largest trading partner.[23] In 2007, trade reached $8 billion, 6.2 billion of which consisted of Turkey's energy imports from Iran.[24]While Iranian exports dropped precipitously to almost half in 2009 due to the global economic downturn, trade reached record levels in 2012, riding high on Turkey's export of gold and gold-plated silver to Iran in exchange for energy imports. Sanctions have decreased their total trade volume from $21.8 billion in 2012 to $14.5 billion in 2013 (See Table 2). [25]

Turkey has had a negative trade balance with Iran reflecting the high volume of energy import from the Islamic Republic. The trade deficit of goods with Turkey was $2 billion in 2012, a 432 percent decrease from $8.8 billion in 2011.[26] Iran and Turkey have signed a preferential trade agreement in January 2014 and hope to raise the value of their bilateral trade to $30 billion by 2015.[27]

**Table 2: Turkey–Iran Trade Relations, 2002–2013 (in million $)**

| | Turkey's Export to Iran/Iran's Import from Turkey | Turkey's Import from Iran/Iran's Export to Turkey | Total Trade | Balance of Trade (Turkey) |
|---|---|---|---|---|
| 2002 | 333.96 | 920.97 | 1,254.93 | -587.01 |
| 2003 | 533.79 | 1,860.68 | 2,394.47 | -1,326.89 |
| 2004 | 813.03 | 1,962.06 | 2,775.09 | -1,149.03 |
| 2005 | 912.94 | 3,469.71 | 4,382.65 | -2556.77 |
| 2006 | 1,066.90 | 5,626.61 | 6,693.51 | -4,559.71 |
| 2007 | 1,441.19 | 6,615.39 | 8056.58 | -5,174.20 |
| 2008 | 2,029.76 | 8,199.69 | 10,229.45 | -6,169.93 |
| 2009 | 2,024.55 | 3,405.99 | 5,430.54 | -1,381.44 |
| 2010 | 3,044.18 | 7,645.00 | 10,689.18 | -4,600.82 |
| 2011 | 3,589.63 | 12,461.53 | 16,051.16 | -8,871.90 |
| 2012 | 9,921.60 | 11,964.78 | 21,886.38 | -2,043.18 |
| 2013 | 4,192.51 | 10,383.22 | 14,575.73 | -6,190.71 |

Source: *Turkish Statistical Institute*

The trade between Turkey and Iran reflects a complementarity of interests. As an energy deficient country and hungry to fulfil its growing energy needs attendant with high growth, Turkey imports large amounts of oil and gas from Iran, which has these resources in abundance. On the other hand, Turkey supplies capital goods for Iran's weak industrial base to a great extent. Turkey's top five exports to Iran are iron and steel, textile yarn and fabrics, electrical equipment, automotive and spare parts. The top five imports are coal and raw petroleum materials, natural gas, plastics in primary forms, metals other than iron and organic chemicals. Iran ranked third among Turkey's export market in 2012; Iran was also Turkey's sixth largest supplier of imported goods in 2012.[28]

**Table 3: Position in Mutual Trade**

| **'Turkey' in Iran's List of Trading Partners** | |
|---|---|
| Export | 3rd |
| Import | 3rd |
| **'Iran' in Turkey's List of Trading Partners** | |
| Export | 3rd |
| Import | 6th |

Source: *Ministry of Economy, Republic of Turkey*

### *Natural Gas Imports*

The high volume of Turkish–Iranian trade driven by hydrocarbons underpins the economic ties between the two countries. Crude oil and natural gas account for 90 percent Iranian exports to Turkey.[29] Turkey's energy demand growth has been among the fastest in the world in 2010 and 2011; although slower economic growth in 2012 has brought down the natural gas consumption to some extent. Turkey can meet only 1.36 percent of annual consumption of natural gas from its domestic production, which has remained stagnant at 0.679 bcm[30] relying almost exclusively on imports (98.64 percent)[31] to meet domestic demand. The share of natural gas in Turkey's total primary energy supply increased at 32 percent in 2011 and it has overtaken oil to become the most important fuel in terms of volume consumed.[32]

Iran is the second largest supplier of natural gas to Turkey behind Russia. In 2012, out of the total consumption of 45.92 bcm of gas annually, Turkey imported about 18 percent or 8.2 bcm of natural gas from Iran (Table 4 & Figure 1).

**Table 4: Turkey's Natural Gas Import from Iran, 2005–2012**

| Year | Volume of Import from Iran (bcm) | Total Import Volume from Various Sources (bcm) | Percentage Share of Iran |
|---|---|---|---|
| 2005 | 4.248 | 26.571 | 15.98 |
| 2006 | 5.594 | 30.221 | 18.51 |
| 2007 | 6.054 | 35.842 | 16.89 |
| 2008 | 4.113 | 37.350 | 11.01 |
| 2009 | 5.252 | 35.856 | 14.64 |
| 2010 | 7.765 | 38.036 | 20.41 |
| 2011 | 8.190 | 43.874 | 18.66 |
| 2012 | 8.215 | 45.922 | 17.88 |

Source: *Doğal Gaz Piyasası Sektör Raporu 2013* (Natural Gas Market Sector Report), Natural Gas Market Department, Energy Market Regulatory Authority (EPDK), Republic of Turkey, p. 23.

**Figure 1: Turkey's Natural Gas Import by Source, 2012**

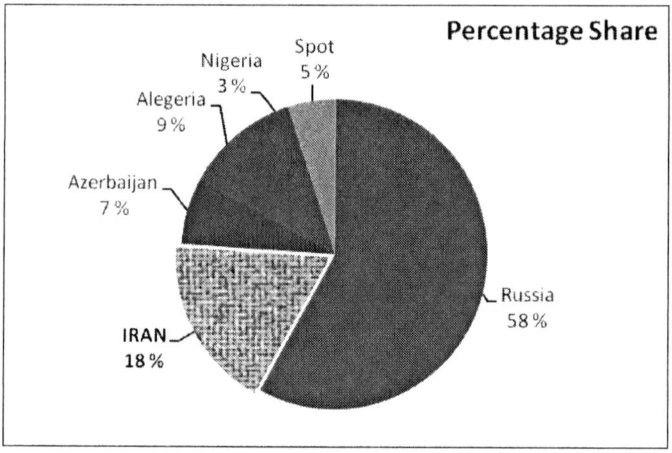


Source: *Doğal Gaz Piyasası Sektör Raporu 2013* (Natural Gas Market Sector Report), Natural Gas Market Department, Energy Market Regulatory Authority (EPDK), Republic of Turkey, p. 23.

Iran is contractually bound to export 10 bcm/year of natural gas to Turkey's state-owned Petroleum Pipeline Corporation (BOTAŞ) under a 25-year agreement signed in 1996 and activated in 2001.[33] Iran supplies Turkey with natural gas through the Tabriz–Ankara Pipeline, which connects Iranian natural gas reserves to Turkey's internal distribution network. However, Turkey's natural gas import from Iran is riddled with problems since the very beginning and was routinely marred by unexplained stoppages, mechanical failures and PKK attacks in the border region between Iran and Turkey and not in the least because of price issues.[34]

Since the beginning of Iranian natural gas exports to Turkey, there have been ongoing disputes between the two sides about either the volume or the price of the gas. In an apparent haste to push through a deal to enhance the credibility of his shaky government, Turkish Prime Minister Necmettin Erbakan agreed to pay a high price for gas and to a 'take or pay' provision which committed Turkey to paying for a minimum of 87 percent of the annual contracted volume regardless of how much it actually consumed. On June 24, 2002, Turkey halted importing natural gas from Iran on the ground that the quality of the gas was not up to standard and was not according to the contract conditions.[35] However, a more likely explanation appears to have been a low gas demand at that time and a desire to pressure Iran to renegotiate the price and the take-or-pay terms of the contract. In November that year, the Turkish government announced that it had negotiated a 9–12 percent price reduction with the rate reducing proportionately with the quantity of gas purchased. If Turkey purchases the entire annual contract quantity (ACQ), the reduction will be 12 percent. The take-or-pay level, which constitutes one of the most important contractual conditions, was lowered from 87 percent to 70 percent.[36]

Despite the 2002 agreement, gas delivery from Iran to Turkey has been plagued by disruption and the failure of Iran to supply the contractually obligated 10 bcm of gas a year. The pipeline was supposed to reach its full capacity of 10 bcm by 2007, but only 6.05 bcm was pumped through in that year, stopping supplies in January of that year—a month in which gas was urgently needed. Iran didn't supply enough gas to reach full capacity in the later years either, pumping 4.11 bcm in 2008, 5.25 bcm in 2009 and 7.76 bcm in 2010 reportedly owing to 'technical reasons,' which some Turkish officials believed had been diverted to meet Iranian domestic needs due to the blockage of Turkmen gas to Iran.[37] In addition, starting in 2006, the Tabriz–Ankara pipeline has been increasingly targeted by militant Kurds, leading to suspension of pumping for many days. These attacks have increased in frequency and damage. Flows were disrupted a number of times in 2012, with two such disruptions occurring during October alone.

Turkey has continued to push for further reduction in price since 2002. Of the natural gas that Turkey buys, Iran charges the most, and this is the main cause of strain between the two countries. Turkey currently buys a cubic metre of Azerbaijani gas for $330 and pays Russia $400 for the same amount. However, Iran sells its gas to Turkey for $505 for each cubic metre, which inflates Turkey's natural gas bill by an additional $800 million per year. The price of a cubic metre of natural gas is sold for $400 in international markets. The pricing issue coupled with the erratic flow of gas was cited as reasons why BOTAŞ applied to an international court of arbitration in 2012 over the gas price in a case that is still pending.[38] Turkey has plans to double the gas imports from Iran to meet growing domestic requirements, provided the price issue gets resolved.[39]

Despite the high price, Turkey's continued natural gas import from Iran is guided by certain economic imperatives. Energy consumption shows an upward trend in the country, largely due to gas-fired electricity generation, energy-intensive manufacturing as well as energy-intensive lifestyles in household, commercial buildings and transport. Energy consumption is growing faster than gross domestic product (GDP), leading to an increase in the total energy intensity; a general trend observed in other developing countries. The country's power generation sector consumes 48 percent of the total natural gas consumption (Figure 5). The electricity demand growth rate outstripped the GDP growth rate by 1.3 percent on an average between 2000 and 2011.[40] The high industrial consumption, 22 percent, is explained by high usage in cement manufacturing.[41] In the household sector and commercial establishment, natural gas is used mainly for heating, the demand for which shoots up in winters. A small amount of gas is used in energy transformation such as refining (Figure 2).

**Figure 2: Turkey's Natural Gas Consumption Profile, 2012**

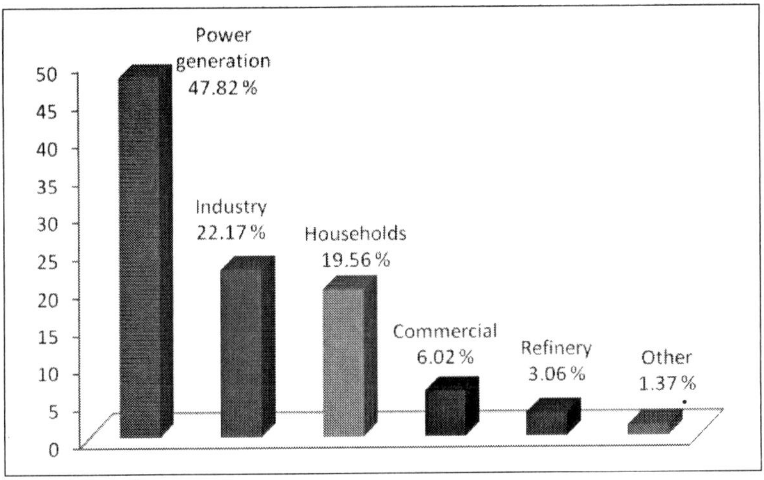


Source: *Doğal Gaz Piyasası Sektör Raporu 2013* (Natural Gas Market Sector Report), Natural Gas Market Department, Energy Market Regulatory Authority (EPDK), Republic of Turkey, p. 64.

In view of Turkey's growing demand for gas, Iran appears as the most attractive option owing to its geographical proximity, convenience of transportation via a pipeline, natural gas abundance and its need to sell gas for monetary gains in view of sanctions. Iran's vast reserves, the second largest in the world after Russia, make Iran a reliable supplier over a longer term. Because of the projected growth in the electricity demand, Turkey needs gas from Iran more than ever before. Driven by gas-fired electricity generation, according to BOTAŞ's forecasts in 2012, Turkey's gas demand will almost double from 45 bcm in 2012 to 81 bcm by 2030.[42] Although the government has taken a number of steps to increase energy efficiency in factories, Turkey would need to import gas in the medium-term to fulfil its requirements. Given that scenario, the demand for natural gas from Iran would increase proportionately. The Iranian natural gas also exhibits a high calorific value,[43] which also translates into value for money.

Turkey's natural gas trade with Iran is also a strategic necessity. Being an energy-dependent country, Turkey wants to diversify its sources to ensure security of supply. While Iran remains a strong source in view of its ample gas resources, concern over "its high price, quality [aspects], uncertain supplies, and the general frustration of doing business in Iran" has led Turkish energy planners "to focus their efforts on attaining more Azeri gas in the short term and Iraqi as well as Turkmen gas over the longer term."[44] It is no accident that Turkey's natural gas import has diversified over the years with increase in imports from other sources, including those from Iran (Table 5).

**Table 5: Turkey's Natural Gas Imports from Various Sources, 2005–2012 (bcm)**

| Years | Russia | Iran | Azerbaijan | Algeria | Nigeria | Spot | Total |
|---|---|---|---|---|---|---|---|
| 2005 | 17.524 | 4.248 | 0 | 3.786 | 1.013 | 0 | 26.571 |
| 2006 | 19.316 | 5.594 | 0 | 4.132 | 1.100 | 79 | 30.221 |
| 2007 | 22.762 | 6.054 | 1.258 | 4.205 | 1.396 | 167 | 35.842 |
| 2008 | 23.159 | 4.113 | 4.580 | 4.148 | 1.017 | 333 | 37.350 |
| 2009 | 19.473 | 5.252 | 4.960 | 4.487 | 903 | 781 | 35.856 |
| 2010 | 17.576 | 7.765 | 4.521 | 3.906 | 1.189 | 3.079 | 38.036 |
| 2011 | 25.406 | 8.190 | 3.806 | 4.156 | 1.248 | 1.069 | 43.874 |
| 2012 | 26.491 | 8.215 | 3.354 | 4.076 | 1.322 | 2.464 | 45.922 |

Source: *Doğal Gaz Piyasası Sektör Raporu 2013* (Natural Gas Market Sector Report), Natural Gas Market Department, Energy Market Regulatory Authority (EPDK), Republic of Turkey, p. 23.

There are other constraints relating to the Turkish–Iranian gas outlook, which could undermine future energy relations. For instance, Turkey aspires to become a transit corridor for pipelines carrying Iranian and Central Asian gas to Europe. Iran has indicated a preference for other routes—the so-called Islamic pipeline going through Iraq, Syria and the Mediterranean—and opposes the Trans–Caspian pipeline to transfer Central Asian gas to Europe via Turkey.[45] More specifically, while Turkish energy officials maintain, "Turkmen gas transit through Turkey is an unchanging condition for Iranian gas transport to Europe via Turkey," Iran, which is a importer of natural gas through pipeline from Turkmenistan that often frees its own gas for exports at higher price to Turkey, is opposed to the idea to "avoid possible future competition with Turkmenistan for European markets."[46]

### *Crude Oil*

In 2013, Turkey's total liquid fuel consumption averaged 714,000 barrels per day.[47]Only 11 percent of the crude oil consumption was met from domestic production in 2012; almost all the rest was imported from Iran, Russia, Saudi Arabia, Iraq, Libya and Kazakhstan, through pipelines and by tanker ships.[48] Since 2010, Iran has become Turkey's single largest source of oil, providing a majority 51 percent of the total import. In 2012, Iran retained its position as the single largest supplier of Turkey's crude at 39 percent. Russia, once the largest source country of Turkey's crude oil, has fallen behind the West Asian suppliers in terms of volume and is now the fourth-largest supplier of crude oil to Turkey. Even as suppliers have diversified, import from Iran has remained the highest for three consecutive years (Table 6). According to the IEA, Turkey's crude oil imports are expected to double over the next decade.[49] Despite strong relations between Turkey and Iran, oil trade between the two countries is fraught with certain risks effecting security of supply. One such security risk is the volatile environment around the Strait of Hormuz and possible disruption of oil trade. Another risk is the EU and US sanctions on Iran's energy trade that hampers stable supply.

**Table 6: Turkey's Crude Oil Imports, 2010–2012 by countries (1,000 tonnes)**

| Country | Amounts | | | Share (%) | | |
|---|---|---|---|---|---|---|
| | **2010** | **2011** | **2012** | **2010** | **2011** | **2012** |
| Iran | 7.261 | 9.287 | 7.561 | 43 | 51 | 39 |
| Russia | 3.320 | 2.131 | 2.113 | 20 | 12 | 11 |
| Iraq | 2.001 | 3.071 | 3.739 | 12 | 17 | 19 |
| Saudi Arabia | 1.953 | 1.967 | 2.823 | 12 | 11 | 15 |
| Kazakhstan | 1.786 | 1.186 | 1.414 | 11 | 7 | 7 |
| Libya | - | - | 1.019 | - | - | 5 |
| Nigeria | - | - | 397 | - | - | 2 |
| Syria | 406 | 255 | - | 2 | 1 | - |
| Italy | 110 | 116 | 258 | <1 | <1 | 1 |
| Azerbaijan | - | 81 | 161 | - | <1 | <1 |
| Total | **16.837** | **18.092** | **19.485** | **100** | **100** | **100** |

Source: *Petrol Sector Report 2013*, Petroleum Market Department, Energy Market Regulatory Authority (EPDK), Republic of Turkey, p. 32.

### *Turkish Investments in Iran*

Turkey prides itself on positive relations with virtually all of its neighbours, in accordance with 'zero problems with the neighbours' policy. Iran seeks outlets to avoid isolation and has assiduously courted trade ties with its neighbours, chiefly, Turkey. According to some sources, there are 200 small Turkish companies that have invested in Iran.[50] A majority of these are relatively small and mainly confined to white goods, household textiles, packaging, furniture and automotive supply industry. Many of the smaller investments are reportedly offices to support sales and marketing activities rather than manufacturing or provision of services. Nonetheless, in recent years Turkish firms have won large contracts in Iran's construction sector. One of the largest such projects, is that of the Özal Investment Group, which is managed by Zeynep Özal, the daughter of former Turkish president Turgut Özal. The $400 million project is a thirty-two storey commercial-retail complex in Tehran.[51] No official figure is available, although in early 2010 the annual value of projects undertaken by Turkish contractors was estimated to be around $1billion.[52]

Till 2014, the only sizeable Turkish investment in Iran was by Gübretaş, Turkey's second largest producer of chemical fertilisers. A consortium led by Gübretaş purchased 96 percent shares of Iran's state-owned Razi Petrochemical Company—one of the largest producers of fertilisers and feedstock in the region—for $656 million in February 2008.[53]The Turkish company was the sole bidder for the plant that was sold as part of Iran's privatisation programme. Located in the Masher free-trade zone in southwest Iran, the Razi plant remains Turkey's largest foreign investment by a Turkish company in any country. It has an annual production of about 3.5 million tonnes of fertiliser,[54] of which a substantial portion is exported to North Africa, China and India.[55] While Turkish firms have learnt the value of quality and price in order to stay afloat in the European market, in Iran they have a 'competitive edge' due to Iran's 'relatively autarkic and isolated' economic system. Turkish firms held 44 projects in Iran with a total value of $4.6 billion until the end of May 2013.[56]

### *Iranian Investment in Turkey*

Iran's investment interest in Turkey has been rising with the AKP's business-oriented foreign policy, especially since 2010, as Iranian companies started facing enquiries in European countries for their possible involvement in Iran's nuclear programme. Subsequently, with the sanctions, companies from Iran were subject to a more restrictive business environment in Dubai, the traditional Iranian investment destination in West Asia. The AKP's opposition to third-party EU and US sanctions (in addition to United Nations Security Council's sanctions) and Ankara's efforts to negotiate a resolution of the Iranian nuclear crisis—as well as the Turkish government's repeated assertions that Tehran was not building nuclear weapons—convinced Iranian businesses to move over to Turkey, where they believed they could function more freely and could still reintegrate into the global economy. From 1954 onwards until 2003, the number of Iranian-owned companies in Turkey was 416. It shot up to 716 firms in 2009. Within three years, from 2010–12, the number of Iranian businesses has increased by 40 percent to 1789 (Table 7).

**Table 7: Number of Iranian-Owned Businesses in Turkey, Year-Wise**

| Year | Number of Iranian-owned Companies established |
|---|---|
| 1954-2003 | 416 |
| 2004 | 113 |
| 2005 | 109 |
| 2006 | 98 |
| 2007 | 95 |
| 2008 | 131 |
| 2009 | 170 |
| 2010 | 418 |
| 2011 | 590 |
| 2012 | 781 |
| Total | **2921** |

Source: TurkStat; "Iranian Investment in Turkey on Rise: Cooperation Body, *Hurriyet Daily News*, June 9, 2014,http://www.hurriyetdailynews.com/iranian-investment-in-turkey-on-rise-cooperation-body.aspx?pageID=238&nID=67601&NewsCatID=345.

Despite the rise in numbers, virtually all the Iranian-owned companies remain very small. Around half of them are engaged in wholesale or retail trade, with the remainder in services or small-scale manufacturing. Jenkins notes that in 2010, foreign direct investment (FDI) from Iran totalled $42 million, compared with $4.72 billion from EU countries, which accounted for 75.1 percent of Turkey's total FDI of $6.29 billion for the year. Of the 590 Iranian-owned companies existent in 2011, 181 (30.7 percent) had capital of less than $50,000 and another 343 (58.1 percent) capital of $50,000–$200,000. Only 19 (3.2 percent) had capital of over $500,000.[57] Till 2012, Iranian direct investments in Turkey exceeded $110 million and FDI of Iran in Turkey (stock) was $101 million in the same year. [58] Earlier in 2013, Iran reportedly placed $7–8 billion in cash in a Dubai-based fund earmarked for investment and the acquisition of companies in Turkey.[59]

The only large-scale Iranian investment in Turkey in 2013 was Bank Mellat. With branches in Istanbul, Ankara and Izmir, Bank Mellat had total assets of $2.11 billion, ranking it 21st of the 44 banks active in Turkey. Traditionally, Bank Mellat has concentrated on providing trade financing and services, such as letters of credit and letters of guarantee, particularly for bilateral trade between Iran and Turkey and for joint efforts on Iranian and Turkish projects.[60] Initially it benefitted from rising US pressure on the activities of Iranian financial institutions, by securing businesses that Turkish banks were afraid to handle. However, the bank itself came under scanner when the UN Security Council passed Resolution 1929 on May 9, 2010, which named Bank Mellat's Malaysian subsidiary (First East Export Bank) of facilitating transactions for Iranian nuclear, missile and defence industries.[61] Due to international sanctions imposed on the bank, the size of its assets declined by eightfold in a year; the bank's report on its 2012 finances has revealed this and it continues to suffer a serious meltdown in its Turkish assets.[62]

Though the AKP government refused to suspend the bank's operating licence as demanded by the US, Turkish financial sector has reportedly severed all links with the bank to avoid ouster from American market under US sanctions.[63] In what has been a reprieve, Bank Mellat will be removed from the sanctions list of the United Kingdom after its

Supreme Court in June 2013 found no evidence that the Iranian Bank had helped to fund Iran's nuclear programme. The bank had appealed against measures imposed by the UK Treasury in 2009, forbidding any company operating in Britain from dealing with it. The Treasury acted to weaken Iran's nuclear and ballistic missile programmes by excluding Bank Mellat from the financial sector. The US, however, still retains sanctions against Bank Mellat.[64]

Iranian firms operating from Turkey reap more than one benefit: they are able to trade with European markets, which is often impossible when operating from inside Iran because of the sanctions. While most of these supply needed commercial goods to the isolated Iranian market, there are concerns that many of these companies may be fronts used by the Iranian government to circumvent Western sanctions. This may also constitute a smuggling route for machinery and other low-end commerce that Iran cannot import or engage in due to sanctions.

### *Tourism*

Turkey's large trade deficit with Iran is partially offset by a growing number of Iranian tourists in the country every year, boosted by reciprocal free travel regime without visa. During 2010–11, approximately 2 million Iranians visited Turkey but that number dropped sharply to around 1 million in 2012, reflecting an economy shaky enough due to international embargoes.[65] Iranians constitute the fourth-largest group of foreign tourists in Turkey thanks to visa-free travel, with nearly 2 million visitors in 2010 and 2011. This fell off significantly in the first five months of 2012 in the face of growing bilateral political differences over Syria and Iraq and sharply reduced Iranian purchasing power.[66] No concrete data is available on the number of Turkish tourists visiting Iran, although in early 2012 Turkish tourism agencies estimated that it was less than 20,000 per year.[67] One reason is Iran's strict dress code that turns out to be a deterrent for many female visitors not accustomed to a strict Islamic dress code.[68]

## Constraints

Despite the growth in trade relations, Turkey's businesses routinely face difficulties in Iran stemming from the country's erratic rules and cumbersome legal system. They also express great frustration in navigating the complex, opaque, and corrupt business environment in Iran. Turkish exports to Iran face high custom duties, especially on consumer goods, in addition to stiff taxes levied on foreign-owned trucks entering the country and calculated on the minimum amount of fuel the truck is likely to use, making transportation prohibitively expensive.[69] The cumulative effect of these factors meant that price of Turkish goods rose when they reached the Iranian market making them less competitive. Turkey's overland trade with the Central Asian Republics (CARs) has also suffered in the face of the high cost of transporting goods across Iran to Central Asia. In addition, Turkish firms usually find it difficult to secure financing services for trade with Iran (except for Bank Mellat) due to threat of Western sanctions. Banks in Turkey are reluctant to provide guarantees against export to Iran and the Iranian financial sector is underdeveloped, leaving them with few viable options.[70] Iran's economy has also become more dependent on Turkish trade with sanctions isolating it from the international banking system.

Iran has also failed to honour several investment deals from the Turkish side. For instance, the Turkish–Austrian consortium (TAV) was chosen to build and operate a new terminal in 2003 at Imam Khomeini International Airport in Tehran. However, the Revolutionary Guard seized the terminal just hours after it opened in May 2004, alleging that Turkish firms were too close to Israel and a Turkish consortium operating the terminal would pose a threat to national security. However, many think the real reason was that a company close to the Guards had lost its bid for the tender. In another similar case, in February 2004, Turkcell, Turkey's largest mobile phone operator, signed a three-billion dollar contract with Iran to extend its network into the country, after winning the tender to take a 51 percent share in a newly-created mobile telephone licensee called Irancell. The deal was then changed in the following February by the Iranian Parliament (*Majlis*), whereby the share of Turcell was reduced to 49 percent, because of the Turkish telephone operator's alleged "Zionist links." Turkcell refused to accept the reduced share or spend the $370 million licensing fee for the network. In October 2005, a 49 percent share in Irancell was sold to MTN of South Africa, leaving Turkcell with significant losses. It was later revealed that the Conservative members of the Majlis vetoed the deal to weaken Reformist President Mohammad Khatami's government.[71] Some voices in Iran are also not keen on expanding commercial ties with Turkey, as they believe the strong market for their country's goods and energy is in Asia.

In contrast, Iranian companies in Turkey face fewer hurdles to free business, as the environment is relatively more stable and businesses enjoy more rights. All in all, Iran has gained much more than Turkey in this partnership in terms of actual material and larger strategic advantages. Difficulties in securing a hassle-free trade with Iran and large trade deficits have been persistent pathologies of Turkey's trade ties with the Islamic Republic.

## Impact of Sanctions

Since 2007, Turkey has become a conduit for importing machinery and products that Iran cannot import through normal channels because of the numerous sanctions imposed on the latter for its nuclear programme. While Iran has access to markets in China, Russia, Turkmenistan and Iraq, access to Turkish market has played a crucial role in counteracting the impact of sanctions. "Iran views Turkey as a valuable partner for neutralizing the international economic sanctions and reducing her international isolation; and by deepening its economic interdependence with Turkey, Iran is also trying to discourage Turkey from supporting the sanctions itself," writes Nader Habibi. He adds, "The impact of sanctions on Iranian economy would be far more severe than otherwise."[72] The high volume of hydrocarbon export deepens Turkey's dependence on Iran, as Tehran reaps the benefit of a favourable balance of trade scenario. In other areas of trade as well, Iran has been a greater beneficiary. In general, growing economic ties with Turkey has given Iran numerous advantages; not the least, allowing it to circumvent a host of painful sanctions.

Like other trading partners of Iran, Ankara has been under intense pressure from Washington to cut down on economic ties with Tehran. Turkish private sector banks started avoiding transactions involving Iran in mid-2010 with Security Council resolution 1929 and with the imposition of additional sanctions by the EU and US. By 2011, only state-owned Halkbank still offered financial services for trade with Iran. It even handled payment for European banks, which were disinclined towards any financial dealings with Iran for fear of overstepping EU sanctions. Similarly, when the Reserve Bank of India scrapped the Asian Clearing Union (ACU) payment mechanism following tougher US sanctions on Iran's financial sector under the United States' CISADA in December 2010, Indian refiners started directing oil payments through Halkbank.[73] However, by December 2011, it appeared that Ankara was less willing to antagonise US not in the least as a consequence of creeping tensions with Iran over Syria and Iraq. That resulted in Halkbank's refusal to entertain new financial transactions involving Iran.[74]

Huge energy dependence on Iran warrants that Turkey maintains and even deepens economic relations with Iran. Sanctions imposed by the US under National Defence Authorization Act (NDAA) 2012 caused great concerns in Turkey as it had a bearing on Turkey's energy import from Iran. In the backdrop of the controversy over Iranian nuclear programme, section 1245 of the NDAA imposed unilateral sanctions against the Bank Markazi, the Central Bank of Iran. As the Act required the US President to deny foreign banks or financial institutions that did business with Iran's Central Bank access to US financial markets, it had immediate impact on how Turkey processed the Iranian oil and gas bills. These new measures were aimed at reducing foreign demand for Iranian oil by punishing dealings with Bank Markazi, the clearinghouse for crude oil and gas transactions, in the hope of starving the Islamic Republic of crucial state revenue and forcing it to give up its nuclear programme.

Sanctions on transactions unrelated to petroleum took effect 60 days after the bill was signed into law, while sanctions on transactions related to petroleum were effective from a minimum of 180 days after the bill's signing in January 2012.[75] But, recognising the need to avoid upending global financial health, the sanctions allowed the US administration to make exemptions to countries that 'significantly' reduced their volume of purchases of crude oil from Iran, determined on a case-to-case basis.

By the end of 2012, Turkey's import of Iranian oil declined by 12 percent. Turkey received a waiver from the United States for the fourth time in November 2013 for reducing purchase of Iranian oil.[76]

The US sanctions legislation also hit hard Turkey's ability to pay for its Iranian natural gas imports. However, a sanction loophole allowed Turkey and Iran to carry on energy trade through an informal 'gold-for-energy' strategy, proving a major respite to the Iranian economy. Because US sanctions prevented Turkey from paying in dollars or euros, Turkey through the state-owned Halkbank, started paying for Iranian natural gas in Turkish Liras, which was of limited value for Iran in the international market due to its inconvertibility, but was used to buy gold in Turkey. This gold was then transferred or sold in Dubai, where it was recorded as Turkish gold sold to the UAE, and then shipped to Iran. It was then re-exported to Iran or sold for foreign currency or used for import purchases in that country.[77] According to Turkish Statistics Institute data, in February 2013 Turkey exported almost $120 million in gold to Iran and in March Turkish gold exports to Iran soared to almost $381 million.[78] Imports of bullion from Turkey jumped to 126 tonnes in 2012 from one tonne in 2011, according to data from the International Trade Centre[79] thus becoming the 'gas for gold' scandal.

Iran seems to have used this method to repatriate hard currency till the introduction of NDAA 2013 (in operation since July 2013) that included sanctions prohibiting the transfer or sale of gold or other precious metals to Iran, representing an escalation of US efforts to stop this oblique method of payment for Iranian energy exports. However, the November 2013 interim agreement signed in Geneva between Iran and the Western powers provides for modest sanctions relief in exchange for Iran agreeing to freeze several components of its nuclear programme including relaxation on oil sales and removal of certain sanctions on gold and precious metals. Iran is still likely to be barred from accepting precious metals as payment for oil and gas or any other sanctioned transaction. Ankara has also stated its intention to increase oil imports from Iran by 30 percent. This means that Turkey could continue to pay for its discounted Iranian oil in Turkish Lira, which must remain in Turkish bank accounts and be spent on Turkish products.[80]

Sanctions run counter to Ankara's strategy of using deepening commercial ties to foster cooperative relations with Tehran and efforts to broker a resolution of the Iranian nuclear crisis. Turkey is keen to advance bilateral trade and economic cooperation with Iran in the wake of the Geneva deal. In an effort to keep the pressure on Iran, the United States, adamantly held the view that substantial sanctions on Iran should remain until a final agreement is reached, and warned Iran's trading partners not to relax the implementation of sanctions. A day before Erdoğan's much-publicised visit to Iran on January 28, 2014, the US Undersecretary for Terrorism and Financial Intelligence, David Cohen reminded Ankara that Tehran was still under sanctions and that "businesses interested in engaging in Iran really should hold off. The day may come when Iran is open for business, but the day is not today."

## Conclusion

Despite the external challenges posed by US policy, Turkey and Iran are likely to continue their economic cooperation. It is not an easy proposition for Turkey to reduce its dependence on import of hydrocarbons from Iran. Even if Ankara were to source its crude oil from alternative suppliers in the region, finding alternative sources for natural gas would be certainly more difficult. That alone will maintain Iran's importance in Turkey's strategic calculations. Turkish–Iranian ties could, however, face considerable challenges from the failure to address continuing irritants, such as fuel taxes, non-tariff barriers, lack of clarity on trade regulations in Iran and delayed or non-implementation of bilateral agreements. Those could divert Turkish businessmen from Iran to search for a more conducive and predictable economic climate. It must also be borne in mind that there are few instances of enduring economic cooperation between the two states amidst a lot of intentions. While economic dependency of Iran and Turkey has increased in recent years with the active encouragement of the governments of the two countries, regional developments have fuelled tensions and conflict of interests. The two economic partners are on the opposite sides in the context of the civil war in Syria. They have also emerged as competitors for investment and trade in Iraq and disagree on ways to deal with the autonomous Iraqi Kurdistan. Nonetheless, both countries have handled these issues cautiously lest they should impinge on trade and economic ties that are equally crucial and complementary.

## Notes

1. Peter Harling & Hugh Pope, "Turkey and the Arab Uprisings: From 'Zero Problems' to Losing Count", *ekathimerini.com*, November 25, 2011http://www.ekathimerini.com/4dcgi/_w_articles_wsite3_1_25/11/2011_416462.
2. H. Akin Ünver, "How Turkey's Islamists Fell out of Love With Iran", *Middle East Policy Council*, Vol. XIX, No. 4 (Winter 2012), http://www.mepc.org/journal/middle-east-policy-archives/how-turkeys-islamists-fell-out-love-iran?print.
3. According to Yeşilbursa, "the Regional Co-operation for Development (RCD) was set up by the regional members of the Central Treaty Organization (CENTO), Iran, Turkey and Pakistan, in July 1964 to strengthen their socio-economic development. However, a number of financial, political and administrative difficulties made progress under RCD slow. Despite assurances to the contrary, the probable impetus behind the formation of RCD was the unease with the politico-military aspects of CENTO. However, RCD's political significance grew steadily, and that of CENTO declined correspondingly. Nevertheless, recognizing that RCD could not provide an effective military substitute, Iran and Turkey still attached value to CENTO. After twelve unsatisfactory years, the three regional Heads of State held a summit in Izmir on 22 April 1976, making amendments to the 1964 declaration. The Treaty of Izmir, Turkey, was signed in 1977 as the legal framework for RCD. Yet, RCD was unsuccessful. In January 1985, Turkey, Iran and Pakistan established a new organisation called the Economic Co-operation Organization (ECO)." Behçet Kemal Yeşilbursa, "The Formation of RCD: Regional Cooperation for Development", *Middle Eastern Studies*, Vol. 45, Issue 4 (2009), pp. 637–660; Tareq Y. Ismael and Mustafa Aydın (ed), *Turkey's Foreign Policy in the 21st Century: A Changing Role in World Politics* (Surrey, UK: Ashgate, 2003), p.182; Nurul Islam, "Regional Co-Operation For Development: Pakistan, Iran and Turkey", *Journal of Common Market Studies*, Vol. 5, Issue 3 (March 1967), pp. 283–301.
4. Shireen Hunter, *Iran's Foreign Policy in the Post-Soviet Era: Resisting the New International Order* (Santa Barbara, California: Praeger, 2010), p. 158.
5. See Ziya Öniş, "Turgut Özal and His Economic Legacy: Turkish Neo-Liberalism in Critical Perspective", *Middle Eastern Studies*, Vol. 40, Issue 4, (2004), pp. 113-134.
6. Cengiz Dinc and Mustafa Yetim, "Transformation of Turkish Foreign Policy toward the Middle East: From Non-Involvement to a Leading Role", *Alternatives: Turkish Journal of International Relations*, Vol. 11, No. 1 (Spring 2012), p. 71; See "Turgut Özal Period in Turkish Foreign Policy: Özalism", *USAK Yearbook of International Politics and Law*, Vol. 2 (2009), pp. 153-205.
7. Shireen Hunter, *Iran's Foreign Policy in the Post-Soviet Era*, p. 158.
8. Robert D. Kaplan and Reva Bhalla, "Turkey's Geographical Ambition", *Stratfor (Geopolitical Weekly)*, August 12, 2014, http://www.stratfor.com/weekly/turkeys-geographical-ambition-0#axzz3A6w9wskH.
9. Itmar Rabinovich and Haim Shaked, *Middle East Contemporary Survey, 1984–*

*1985*, Vol. 1 (Tel Aviv: Dayan Centre for Middle Eastern and African Studies, 1987), (Distributed by Westview Press), p. 454.

10. Cengiz Çandar, "Turgut Özal's Foreign and Security Policy Revisited," *Hurriyet Daily News*, April 25, 2000, http://www.hurriyetdailynews.com/default.aspx?pageid=438&n=turgut-ozals-foreign-and-security-policy-revisited-2000-04-25.
11. Nader Habibi, "Growing Economic Relations Despite Western Sanctions," *Middle East Brief*, Crown Centre for Middle East Studies (Brandeis University), No. 62, May 2012, p. 2; http://www.brandeis.edu/crown/publications/meb/MEB62.pdf.
12. Ramazan Gözen. "Turgut Özal and Turkish Foreign Policy: Style and Vision", *Dış Politika/Foreign Policy* (Ankara), Vol. 20, Nos. 3-4 (1996), pp. 69-101.
13. Moshe Gammer (ed), *Caspian Region: A Re-Emerging Region*, Vol. 1 (London: Routledge, 2004), p. 110.
14. Fevzi Bilgin, *Resolving Turkey's Kurdish Issue* (Rethink Institute: Washington DC, 2012), p. 3; Nader Entessar, *Kurdish Politics in the Middle East* (Plymouth, UK: Lexington Books, 1020), p. 128; Marc Champion, "PKK Revokes Cease-Fire in Turkey", *Wall Street Journal*, February 28, 2011, http://online.wsj.com/news/articles/SB10001424052748704615504576172122380315948.
15. Aliza Marcus, *Blood and Belief: The PKK and the Kurdish Fight for Independence* (New York: New York University Press, 2007), p. 121.
16. Mustafa Kibaroğlu, Ayüegül Kibaroğlu, *Global Security Watch—Turkey: A Reference Handbook* (Westport, CT: Greenwood Publishing, 2009), pp. 153-54; David L. Phillips, *From Bullets to Ballots: Violent Muslim Movements in Transition* (New Jersey: Transaction Publishers, 2009), p. 129.
17. Habibi, May 2012, p. 2.
18. Ömer Taşpinar, "Turkey's Strategic Vision and Syria", *The Washington Quarterly*, Vol. 35, No.3, p. 128.
19. Lyubov Grigorova Mincheva, Ted Robert Gurr, *Crime-Terror Alliances and the State: Ethnonationalist and Islamist Challenges to Regional Security* (Abingdon, Oxon, Routledge, 2013), p. 59; Stephen Larrabee, Alireza Nader, *Turkish–Iranian Relations in a Changing Middle East* (Santa Monica, CA: Rand, 2013), p. 11.
20. OECD Outlook 2010 and the Turkish Statistical Institute; "GDP Growth (percentage)," The World Bank, http://data.worldbank.org/indicator/NY.GDP.MKTP.KD.ZG.
21. Christopher Hobbs, Matthew Moran, *Exploring Regional Responses to a Nuclear Iran: Nuclear Dominoes?* (New York: Palgrave Macmillan, 2014), p. 70.
22. Suleyman Elik, *Iran–Turkey Relations, 1979–2011: Conceptualising the Dynamics of Politics, Religion and Security in the Middle-Power States* (Abingdon, Oxon: Routledge, 2012), p. 175.
23. Turkish Statistical Institute (TurkStat), www.turkstat.gov.tr.
24. *Iran Ülke Bülteni* [Iran Country Bulletin], Foreign Economic Relations Board (DEIK), March 2008.
25. TurkStat.
26. Ministry of Economy, Republic of Turkey, http://www.economy.gov.tr/index.cfm?sayfa=countriesandregions&country=IR&region=4.
27. "Iran, Turkey Call for Closer Bilateral Relations", *Press TV*, May 16, 2014, http://www.presstv.com/detail/2014/05/16/362859/iran-turkey-urge-broader-relations/; "Iran, Turkey Trade Should Reach $30 Billion: Minister", *Hurriyet Daily News*,

July 29, 2013, http://www.hurriyetdailynews.com/iran-turkey-trade-should-reach-30-billion-minister.aspx?pageID=238&nID=51657&NewsCatID=344.

28. Ministry of Economy, Republic of Turkey, http://www.economy.gov.tr/index.cfm?sayfa=countriesandregions&country=IR&region=4.
29. Ministry of Foreign Affairs, Republic of Turkey, http://www.mfa.gov.tr/turkey_s-commercial-and-economic-relations-with-iran.en.mfa.
30. "Turkey", *US Energy Information Administration* (EIA), April 17, 2014, http://www.eia.gov/countries/cab.cfm?fips=tu.
31. *DogalgazPiyasasiSektorRaporu2013* (Natural Gas Market Sector Report), Natural Gas Market Department, Energy Market Regulatory Authority (EPDK), p. 30.
32. "Turkey: Oil and Gas Security, Emergency Response of IEA Countries", *International Energy Agency*, 2013, p.3.
33. "Natural Gas Exports from Iran: A Report Required by Section 505 (a) of the Iran Threat Reduction and Syria Human Rights Act of 2012," *EIA*, U.S. Department of Energy (Washington, D.C.), October 2012, http://www.eia.gov/analysis/requests/ngexports_iran/pdf/full.pdf, p. 5.
34. Anthony H. Cordesman, Bryan Gold, Robert Shelala and Michael Gibbs, "U.S. and Iranian Strategic Competition Turkey and the South Caucasus", *Centre for Strategic and International Studies,* June 6, 2013, https://csis.org/files/publication/130612_turk_casp_chap9.pdf, p. 17.
35. See, "Iran Resumes Gas Exports To Turkey With 9% Price Discount", *Middle East Economic Survey*, Vol. 45, Issue 46, November 18, 2002, http://archives.mees.com/issues/509/articles/21369;"Turkey Halts Iran Gas Imports, But Tehran Denies Quality", *Middle East Economic Survey*, Vol. 45, Issue: 37, September 16, 2002, http://archives.mees.com/issues/500/articles/21006.
36. Elin Kinnander, "The Turkish–Iranian Gas Relationship: Politically Successful, Commercially Problematic", *Oxford Institute for Energy Studies*, January 2010, http://www.oxfordenergy.org/wpcms/wp-content/uploads/2010/11/NG38-TheTurkishIranianGasRelationship-ElinKinnander-2010.pdf, p. 9.
37. Ibid, p. 10; *DogalgazPiyasasiSektorRaporu2013* (Natural Gas Market Sector Report), Natural Gas Market Department, Energy Market Regulatory Authority (EPDK), p. 23; Fahri Türk, "Natural Gas as a Foreign Policy Weapon: The Turkish–Iranian Gas Crisis of January 2007", *Konrad Adenauer Stiftung*, http://www.kas.de/wf/doc/kas_13056-544-2-30.pdf?080316141644.
38. "Azeri and Iranian Gas Supply Failure Fuels Shortage Concerns", *Today's Zaman*, February 07, 2012, http://www.todayszaman.com/news-270766-azeri-and-iranian-gas-supply-failure-fuels-shortage-concerns.html.
39. "Turkey May Double Iran Gas Purchase if Price Issue Solved: Energy Minister", *Hurriyet Daily News*, January 30, 2014, http://www.hurriyetdailynews.com/turkey-may-double-iran-gas-if-price-issue-solved-energy-minister.aspx?pageID=238&nID=61798&NewsCatID=348.
40. *Turkish Energy Market: An Investor's Guide 2012*, Energy Market Regulatory Authority (EPDK), Republic of Turkey, p. 21.
41. The ratio of energy costs reach up to 60 percent and even 70 percent in the sector's aggregate bills. See Serhan Ünal and Eyüp Ersoy, "Political Economy of Turkish–Iranian Relations: Three Asymmetries", *Ortadoğu Etütleri*, Vol. 5, No. 2 (March 2014), p. 153.
42. Gulmira Rzayeva, "Natural Gas in the Turkish Domestic Energy Market: Policies

and Challenges", *The Oxford Institute for Energy Studies*, February 2014, http://www.oxfordenergy.org/wpcms/wp-content/uploads/2014/02/NG-82.pdf, p. 1.

43. "Key World Energy Statistics 2012", *International Energy Agency, 2013*, p. 60.
44. Stephen J. Flanagan, "The Turkey-Russia-Iran Nexus: Eurasian Power Dynamics", *The Washington Quarterly*, Vol. 36, No.1 (Winter 2013), pp. 170-71.
45. Stephen J. Falangan et al., "The Turkey, Russia, Iran Nexus: Driving Forces and Strategies", *Project Report* (Abbreviated Edition) of the Centre for Strategic and International Studies (CSIS), March 2013, http://csis.org/files/publication/130318_Flanagan_TurkeyRussiaIran_web.pdf; Bijan Khajehpour, "The Role Of Economic & Energy Relations With Turkey And Russia In Iran's National Strategy", International Workshop on "The Turkey, Russia, Iran Nexus: Economic and Energy Dimensions" hosted by The Economic Policy Research Foundation of Turkey, Ankara, March 29, 2012, CSIS, http://csis.org/files/attachments/120529_Khajephour_Russia_Turkey_in_Iran_National_Strategy.pdf
46. Pinar Dost-Niyego and Orhan Taner, "Turkish–Iranian Rapprochement and the Future of European and Asian Energy", *Issue Brief of the DinuPatriciu Eurasia Center, Atlantic Council*, April 2014, http://www.atlanticcouncil.org/publications/issue-briefs/turkish-iranian-rapprochement-and-the-future-of-european-and-asian-energy.
47. *BP Statistical Review of World Energy*, June 2014, p. 9.
48. There is no oil pipeline between Iran and Turkey.
49. "Turkey", *EIA*, April 17, 2014.
50. Cordesman et al., June 6, 2013, p. 31.
51. "Dokhtar-e raisjomhourAsbaghTurkyedar Iran Foroushgah do tabaghehmisazad, (in Farsi)", *Asr Iran,* June 21, 2011, www.asriran.com.
52. Jenkins, "Occasional Allies, Enduring Rivals: Turkey's Relations with Iran", p. 61.
53. "Investor's Presentation", January 2014, http://www.gubretas.com.tr/FILES/Gubretas_InvestorPresentation_January2014.pdf.
54. Taylan Bilgic, "Iran Sanctions Reprieve Lifts Turkey's Gubretas: Istanbul Mover", January 21, 2014, *Bloomberg News*, http://www.bloomberg.com/news/2014-01-21/iran-sanctions-reprieve-lifts-turkey-s-gubretas-istanbul-mover.html.
55. Abdullah Bozkurt, "Turkey's Gübretaş eyes Global Expansion in Fertilizer Industry", *Today's Zaman*, November 4, 2008, http://www.todayszaman.com/news-157739-turkeys-gubretas-eyes-global-expansion-in-fertilizer-industry.html; https://npk101.wordpress.com/2012/02/28/201202-turkey-gubretas-is-seeking-to-ensure-its-phosphate-supply/.
56. Ministry of Economy, Republic of Turkey, http://www.economy.gov.tr/index.cfm?sayfa=countriesandregions&country=IR&region=4.
57. Jenkins, May 2012, p. 65; "FDI in Turkey", *Iran–Turkey Trade*, http://www.iranturkeytrade.com/index.php/en/turkey-guide/turkey-business-guide/fdi-in-turkey.html.
58. Ministry of Economy, Republic of Turkey, http://www.economy.gov.tr/index.cfm?sayfa=countriesandregions&country=IR&region=4; Ministry of Foreign Affairs, Republic of Turkey, http://www.mfa.gov.tr/turkey_s-commercial-and-economic-relations-with-iran.en.mfa.
59. Jamie Dettmer, "Turkey And Iran Accused Of Oil-For-Cash Sanctions Scheme", December 28, 2013, http://www.thedailybeast.com/articles/2013/12/28/turkey-and-iran-accused-of-oil-for-cash-sanctions-scheme.html.

60. Bank Mellat, https://www.mellatbank.com/en/banking_services.php; Jenkins, pp. 66-66.
61. "Security Council Imposes Additional Sanctions on Iran", June 9, 2010, Security Council SC/9948, http://www.un.org/News/Press/docs/2010/sc9948.doc.htm.
62. "Iranian Bank in Turkey Hit by US Sanctions", *Today's Zaman*, April 21, 2013, http://www.todayszaman.com/news-313321-iranian-bank-in-turkey-hit-by-us-sanctions.html
63. "Iran's Bank Mellat: All Turkey's Banks have Cut Link with Us", *Haaretz*, May 18, 2011, http://www.haaretz.com/news/world/iran-s-bank-mellat-all-turkey-banks-have-cut-links-with-us-1.362577.
64. "Iran's Bank Mellat Wins Ruling over Treasury", *The Telegraph*, February 24, 2010, http://www.telegraph.co.uk/finance/newsbysector/banksandfinance/7307874/Irans-Bank-Mellat-wins-ruling-over-Treasury.html; Tom Arnold, "UK Rules in Favour of Iran's Bank Mellat over Sanctions", June 20, 2010, http://www.thenational.ae/business/industry-insights/economics/uk-rules-in-favour-of-irans-bank-mellat-over-sanctions.
65. "Iran Nuclear Deal: Welcome Expectation for the Turkish Tourism Industry", December 14, 2013, *eturbonews.com*, http://www.eturbonews.com/40738/iran-nuclear-deal-welcome-expectation-turkish-tourism-industry.
66. "Number of Tourists from Iran Visiting Turkey Drop by 41 Percent", *Today's Zaman*, July 10, 2012,http://www.todayszaman.com/news-286112-number-of-tourists-from-iran--visiting-turkey-drop-by-41-percent.html.
67. Jenkins, May 2012, p. 59.
68. Lisa Daftari, "Iran Makes Pitch for Tourists as Americans Languish in its Prisons", *Fox News*, January 23, 2014, http://www.foxnews.com/world/2014/01/23/iran-makes-pitch-for-tourists-as-americans-languish-in-its-prisons/.
69 "Turkish–Iranian Business Council Convenes in Tehran", *Journal of Turkish Weekly*, March 12, 2008.
70. Falangan et al., March 2013, p. 9; Jenkins, May 2012, p. 58.
71. For the two botched projects see, Daphne McCurdy, "Turkish–Iranian Relations: When Opposites Attract", *Turkish Policy Quarterly*, Vol. 7, No. 2 (2008), p. 92; "Turkey–Iran Mobile Deal 'at Risk'", *BBC News*, 15 February 2005, http://news.bbc.co.uk/2/hi/business/4264483.stm; "Men of Principle", *The Economist* 19 July 2007, http://www.economist.com/node/9466902; Jenkins, May 2012, p. 62; "Irancell: Talks between MTN and Turkcell Collapse", *TeleGeography*, March 13, 2012, http://www.telegeography.com/products/commsupdate/articles/2012/03/13/irancell-talks-between-mtn-and-turkcell-collapse/.
72. Nader Habibi, May 2012, p. 5-6.
73. Jonathon Burch and Ebru Tuncay, "Halkbank to Handle Iran Payments So Long as Legal", *Reuters*, www.reuters.com, January 26, 2012.
74. Nidhi Verma, "BPCL Unable to Pay for Iran Oil via Turkey", *Live Mint*, December 15, 2011, http://www.livemint.com/Politics/BFDgr7I3DoEumarOiNbp9I/BPCL-unable-to-pay-for-Iran-oil-via-Turkey.html.
75. See Anthony H. Cordesman, Bryan Gold, Chloe Coughlin-Schulte, "Iran: Sanctions, Energy, Arms Control, and Regime Change", *A Report of the CSIS Burke Chair in Strategy*, Centre for Strategic and International Studies, January 2014, p. xii.
76. Timothy Gardner, "U.S. Extends Iran Oil Sanctions Waivers to China, India, South Korea", *Reuters*, November 29, 2013, http://www.reuters.com/article/2013/11/29/

us-usa-iran-waivers-idUSBRE9AS0QM20131129; "US Renews Iran Sanctions Waivers for Turkey, China, Others", *Today's Zaman*, June 6, 2013, http://www.todayszaman.com/news-317517-us-renews-iran-sanctions-waivers-for-turkey-china-others.html.

77. For 'gold-for-energy' see Nader Habibi, "In the Shadow of Sanctions", in Parvin Alizadeh, Hassan Hakimian (ed), *Iran and the Global Economy: Petro Populism, Islam and Economic Sanctions* (London: Routledge, 2013), p. 185; see also Nader Habibi, "The Iranian Connection in Turkey's Corruption Scandal", Iran Matters, Belfer Center (Harvard University), January 6, 2014, http://iranmatters.belfercenter.org/blog/iranian-connection-turkey's-corruption-scandal
78. John Daly, "Iran Gets Creative Over Energy Payments from Turkey and Pakistan", OilPrice.com, July 22, 2013.http://oilprice.com/Geopolitics/International/Iran-Gets-Creative-Over-Energy-Payments-from-Turkey-and-Pakistan.html.
79. Nicholas Larkin and Indira A.R. Lakshmanan, "Iran Gold Sanctions Easing Seen Having Little Price Impact", *Bloomberg*, November 25, 2013,http://www.bloomberg.com/news/2013-11-24/iran-gold-sanctions-easing-seen-having-little-impact-on-prices.html.
80. Jonathan Schanzer, "Turkey Cashes in on the Iran Talks", *Reuters*, December 12, 2013, http://blogs.reuters.com/great-debate/2013/12/12/turkey-cashes-in-on-the-iran-talks/.

# 6
# The Arab Spring and the Turkish Model

*Anita Sengupta*

In the aftermath of the events in Egypt and other Middle Eastern countries in February–March 2011, expectations were once again raised that Turkey would serve as a moderate model that would be emulated by these states.[1] There was speculation that the 'Turkish Model' was being studied by those seeking reform and a change of regime in Egypt. Projection of the Model as 'moderate' and 'useful' was made from divergent viewpoints and by actors with a very varied understanding of the Model. As a useful alternative strategy that is being put forward by the West as a counterbalance in the face of initiatives that could prove to be detrimental to their interests in the region, the Model was projected as an alternative in the face of the spectre of the success of the Muslim Brotherhood in Egypt. Representatives of the Muslim Brotherhood, on the other hand, stated that the 'moderation' of the Turkish AKP represented a model for the Egyptian Islamic Movement.[2] What the Turkish Model exactly constitutes, has however, been an important arena of political contestation in Egypt since then and competing interpretations of the model have been put forward. Various wielders of power in Egypt have selectively used Turkey's experience with democratic institutions to justify and advance a variety of initiatives. The earliest mention of the Turkish Model in the post-Hosni Mubarak public debates occurred in the summer of 2011 when military leaders made references to Turkey's 1982 constitution which allowed the military a great deal of influence and immunity. The appeal of the Turkish experience to the Muslim Brotherhood was rather different. As opposed to the constitution-centric vision that the military espoused, the Brotherhood was more focused on the ruling AKP and the party's perceived success in the realm of economic management and to some extent, foreign policy.[3]

This vision of an alternative also came from within Turkey. Namik Tan, the Turkish Ambassador in Washington, noted that Turkey was unique in the Muslim world to have a parliamentary system and a functioning free market adding that the country might be an 'inspiration' for the Middle Eastern countries.[4] Tan went on to note that Turkey always had had close relations with its immediate region. Turkey became hugely popular during the Tahrir demonstrations in Egypt. This has been supported by the fact that the Turkish Prime Minister Recep Tayyip Erdogan and President Abdullah Gul had publicly urged the Egyptian President Hosni Mubarak to resign. In fact Erdogan's call on Mubarak to resign was broadcast live throughout the Arab world and his speech at the Tahrir Square strengthened his image as a leader in the 'Arab street'. Also Turkey's attack on Israel over the last two years has made Erdogan the most popular leader on the 'Arab streets' and there is a renewed Turkish interest in its Middle Eastern neighbourhood. Interestingly enough, the only Turkish experience that seemed to be worthy of emulation, at this stage, was that of the ruling AKP ignoring the original Turkish Model based on secular modernity and the role it played in the post-colonial Middle Eastern history.

Turkey's position, of course, has not been without criticism. It has been noted that Turkey's main aim has been to improve relations with countries in the Middle East in the course of a policy of 'zero-problems' with neighbouring countries through improving dialogue, commercial ties and acting as a mediator. As a result Turkey's foreign policy has prioritised rapprochement in its neighbourhood and support for human rights and 'democracy' has not been unconditional.[5] For instance, it is being argued that the Turkish Prime Minister's celebration of democracy in Egypt lacks credibility, since the Turkish leadership had displayed no concern for democratic reform when mass protests were suppressed in Iran after the elections in 2009. The concern seems to be in cases where the Islamists are in opposition; contrary to expectations of a 'democratic' pulse as the principle motivating factor.

Similarly, Turkey has abstained from publicly condemning Colonel Qaddafi's position and has been opposed to the imposition of sanctions and military measures.[6] Turkish diplomacy towards the Libyan crisis ended with the evacuation of a majority of its citizens from Libya and extending help to the US and other countries in the evacuation operations. Turkey's position in Libya is rooted in its significant investments in the country and the fact that a large number of Turkish citizens are working and doing business in Libya.[7] The expanding domestic economic interests and regional dynamism represented by business constituencies that support the ruling AKP has seen the emergence of new Anatolian businesses competing against the traditional metropolitan businesses in western Turkey. These have acted as strong advocates for further Turkish expansion into the Middle East rather than the European markets. And, it has been noted, Turkey was mindful of these interests and investments when Ankara's stand towards Libya was formulated.[8]

This anomaly was also evident in Turkey's relations with Sudan. The government of Omar al-Bashir has been indicted of atrocities against the people. With its economy in dire straits the regime in Khartoum has been faced with demonstrations. However, Turkey is eager to expand business cooperation with Africa. Also, the African Union voted overwhelmingly for Turkey to win a seat on the UN Security Council. President Gul in turn promised that Turkey would be the 'voice of Africa at the Security Council'. Turkey has supported postponement of charges against al-Bashir and while being outspoken in his criticism of Israel's recent war in Gaza, Erdogan has said little about the violence committed in Darfur. When the popular protests in Tunisia and Egypt spread to Sudan resulting in crackdown on protesters and the media, there was no reaction from Ankara asking the Sudanese government to respect the will of the people. However, sanctions were imposed against Syria for its anti-opposition crackdowns including freezing of state assets, suspension of ties with Syria's central bank and ban on all military sales. The Turkish Prime Minister noted that these sanctions were carefully implemented so as not to harm the Syrian people.[9]

However, it can be argued that irrespective of the country's record of support for democracy abroad, Turkey constitutes a model due to its own democratic record and level of economic success in recent years. The representation of Turkey as a model of democracy within Islam is not new.[10] The Bush administration presented Turkey as a model within the framework of the Greater Middle East initiative. This image is supported by the AKP which portrays itself as a 'conservative democratic' party which is politically and economically liberal while being sensitive to certain societal values and traditions. There has been a tendency to read the current experiment in Turkey as the successful political integration of an Islamic movement within democracy. This has however raised questions about whether the AKP's denial of its Islamic connection is simply a compromise between the state and the AKP, or whether it indicates the ability of the Turkish system to transform political Islam.[11] The political opposition within Turkey, nevertheless, disputes this image and there is a debate on the 'moderation' of the AKP regime particularly with the arrest and implication of a large number of individuals in what is termed as the 'Ergenekon' affair.[12] Following five years of legal proceedings the court delivered life sentences to seventeen formerly prominent figures of the military establishment along with politicians, academics and journalists raising concerns about the freedom of speech and media and the independence of the judiciary.[13] Similarly in the aftermath of the Gezi Park events there were reports of adverse action against a number of journalists who had reported on the events in the media.[14] This has brought into question Turkey's commitment to 'democratic ideals'; a commitment that is being increasingly stressed upon by the European Union. Both the British Prime Minister David Cameron and the EU Foreign Policy Chief Catherine Ashton expressed concern about the events in Gezi Park and Taksim Park. There has also been for some time frustration about the government's stand on issues ranging from property development and media rights to the role of religion and access to alcohol, all of which are viewed as attempts to impose conservative values on a secular society.

A number of writings in the immediate post-Gezi Park period stressed that what the protesters wanted was a guarantee that the Turkish government would respect the difference among its citizens and there would be no AKP-inspired behavioural norms on Turkish citizens.[15]

The events followed by the refusal of the Prime Minister to accept the legitimacy of the grievances strengthened these concerns. In fact, even prior to the events surrounding Gezi Park, the death of thirty four civilians on December 28, 2011 due to bombardment on a Kurdish village by the Turkish Air Force had been considered to be excessive. Similarly, the Prime Minister's policy of active involvement in the Syrian civil war has been blamed as the cause of the explosion of two car bombs in the town of Reyhanli adjacent to the Syrian border resulting in the death and injury of civilians on May 11, 2013. It is still too early to predict what kind of alternatives will emerge or what impact the events will have on the forthcoming local and general elections, the presidential elections, the new constitution process, the proposed presidential system, the Kurdish initiative, domestic calculations and the balance of political parties and the economy in Turkey. However, what is generally defined as the 'Turkish Model' is once again at crossroads, at a juncture from where various alternative futures are possible. Its identification as 'secular, democratic and liberal' is at the heart of debates as there is a search for social, economic and political options in Turkey.[16]

Despite such contradictions, however, an interesting analogy was made based on the fact that just as Kemal Ataturk had once been the inspiration for mid-twentieth century Middle Eastern modernisers like the Egyptian President Gamal Nasser and Anwar Sadat or Tunisia's first President Habib Bourgiba, the current Turkish Prime Minister, who has claimed success as a moderniser with significant economic progress during his tenure and the success of the policies of the AKP, is a suitable example for emulation. Pro-government commentators in the Turkish media argued that what is happening in North Africa, which is popular uprisings against authoritarian 'secularist' states, is another version of what has recently happened in Turkey, where a popular Islamic force represented by the AKP defeated an 'authoritarian' state structure. This in its turn has given rise to the apprehension that rather than acting as a 'moderating' agent, events in the Middle East may actually radicalise Islam within Turkey. What is undoubted is the fact that a remake of the Middle East is inevitable. What remains debated is whether in this emerging Middle East Turkey would project itself in a leadership role.

Since 2011, the Turkish foreign policy doctrine has been challenged by political changes and growing instability in the Middle East. One of the flagship initiatives of the current government, the zero problem approach to its neighbours, no longer corresponds to the situation on the ground. And Turkey has been forced to take sides. In his victory speech in June 2011, Erdogan promised to adapt Turkey's foreign policy to a changing regional environment and announced Turkey's support for democratic forces across the Middle East and North Africa. Similarly Davutoglu argued that the political transitions in the Arab countries were natural and inevitable and that the best course of action is to develop a sound understanding of the causes of this transformation and develop suitable strategies to cope with the changes.[17] This is not the first time that Turkey has had to reinvent its foreign policy as a result of changes originating beyond its borders. In the early 1990s following the disintegration of the of the Soviet Union, relations with Turkey's neighbours (the Balkans, the Caucasus, Central Asia, Middle East and the Black Sea) gained in importance and Turkey added to its traditional foreign policy soft power instruments such as trade and cultural co-operation. Turkey also made its Western and European aspirations compatible with increasingly diversified foreign policy priorities. It is perhaps disproportionate and premature to draw a parallel between the Arab Spring and the disintegration of the Soviet Union. However, seen from Ankara, the fall of regimes in its southern vicinity, the rise of Islamist parties, the growing regional competition for leadership in the Middle East and the spectre of sectarian conflicts spreading near Turkey's borders raise many concerns. Moreover, the coincidence of these regional turbulences and transformations on a global scale in Europe and mounting opposition to its domestic policies magnify the challenges to Turkey's foreign policy.

On the one hand, these factors are accelerating Turkey's evolution from a status quo power to a more assertive and interventionist actor. On the other, they are also paving the way for a more pragmatic foreign policy. Turkish diplomats when asked about the validity of the principles that guided Turkey's foreign policy until 2011, argue that the values, the vision and the doctrine of Turkish foreign policy was uncontested but they have acknowledged that actions on the ground have to take note of profound changes in the regional context. In the aftermath of the Arab Spring, writings on Turkey's ability to emerge as a role model for the Middle East began with the argument that Turkey's importance was in terms of a 'demonstrative effect' where the example of earlier transitions would provide models for subsequent efforts.[18] In this sense it was assumed that the 'Turkish Model' would apply to the Arab world not so much because of what Turkey does but because of what it is. In the light of the crackdown on protestors in the Gezi Park and Taksim Square this analogy now seems to be problematic. The second point is the cultural affinity between Turkey and the countries in the region. This argument is based on the fact that in essence the countries of the Middle East and North Africa would find Turkey's own experience more meaningful and see it as more relevant than similar experiences of non-Muslim nations. The domestic transformation of Turkey over the last decade enhances the effectiveness of cultural affinity. As political parties, with political Islamist traditions, were declared winners of parliamentary elections in Tunisia, Egypt and Morocco, discussions on the model were revitalised. However, as Tarik Oguzlu notes, the countries in the region differ from each other in terms of their internal dynamics as well as the particular role conceptualisation that they assign to themselves.[19] Similarly, H Akin Unver argues that the new Arab regimes do not enjoy the AKP's advantage of functioning as a democratically legitimate government within fully sovereign states. These movements have in fact gone 'back to the future' and operate in a situation of uncertainty.[20] Despite this there was a perception that the Turkish Model is useful both from a domestic as well a foreign policy perspective. This has been supported by statements from Turkish leaders like Erdogan who during a visit to Egypt pointed out that secularism and plural democracy could be compatible.

Turkish foreign policy under the AKP has come to articulate a vision for improving relations with all neighbours, particularly by privileging the former Ottoman space in the Middle East where agreements are being negotiated for a free trade zone and an eventual Middle Eastern Union. The growing economic and political engagement of Turkey with the Middle East has already led to significant realignment in the region. In order to come to an understanding of this it would be necessary to take note not just of Turkey's current strategy towards its neighbourhood but also Turkey's position within the broader global arena and particularly in the EU accession process. At the present moment Turkey's relations with the EU has reached an all time low. Issues of human rights, democracy and Islam continue to mire the accession process in controversy. Incidentally, it is 'success' in these fields that is being projected by the US in its current designation of Turkey as a 'model' in the Middle East. In fact, even majoritarian interpretations of 'democracy' have been questioned in the course of the protests in Turkey as well as the military coup in Egypt that ousted the Egyptian President Mohammed Morsi. After a three-year hiatus the possibility of a new round of accession negotiations have reemerged after Germany withdrew opposition prompted by Ankara's crackdown on street protests. The European Commission also praised recent judicial reforms and the government's September 30, 2013 democratisation package. However, it also noted that the majority of the criticism directed towards Turkey was in the fields of human rights and freedom of expression.[21]

The viability of the 'model' has thus re-emerged in transition debates. This viability needs to be examined at two levels: at the level of domestic compulsions faced by Turkey and at the international level where the model is being projected as an alternative by the US. A very large part of the domestic debate is around issues involving 'negation' of a heterogeneous past and attempts at homogenisation of Turkish society and the subsequent aspiration of some of its citizens to a distinctive religious or ethnic identity. This debate includes within itself the Kurdish policy of the state and the attitude of the state towards other minorities, the question of the headscarf (the recent lifting of the ban on headscarves in state institutions being significant in this context), attitudes towards Islamic institutions and organisations, the position of women, the question of human rights etc. At the international level the debate is centred round the acceptability of Turkey as an international player and here the issues include the projection of Turkey as the link between the 'East' and the 'West' in a post-Cold War scenario, the long-denied EU membership, Turkey's position within the global economy, the question of Armenia and Cyprus, transformation of Turkish policy towards its neighbourhood, and a change in Turkish stance towards its old allies, the US and Israel.[22]

There is however, no real consensus on what the model actually means.[23] Perception about the model varies from inside and outside as do its connotations. Andrew Mango notes "...the Republic of Turkey is a model of a secular, democratic, Muslim country aiming to achieve Western standards in partnership with the West by applying liberal free market policies".[24] Some definitions are based on Turkey's confinement of Islam to the private domain while others focus on a constitutional system that guarantees Turkey's secular character and an acknowledgement of the role of armed forces as guardians and protectors of the constitution.[25] Among diverse understandings of the model, American policy makers emphasised Turkey's secular and multi-party electoral system alongwith its market economy. From the American perspective the Turkish military is the balancer against radical groups both from the Marxist and radical Islamic ideologies.

While perceptions and connotations have differed there is a broad consensus on the fact that the Turkish Model is essentially based on its secular character. It has been argued that Turkish secularism was not about the separation of state and religion but about the submission of religion to the reason of the state, promotion of an acceptable 'state Islam' and the judgement of non-conforming Islams as potential threats to the 'secular' regime.[26] Hence, secularism in Turkey involved not only the disestablishment of Islam, but also its different establishment in accordance with the new basis of legitimacy of separation of religion and state. The AKP's interpretation of this has been identified as 'new Islamism'. For the AKP, Islamisation is not to be achieved through the state. The state is important only for opening new spaces for individuals and society as a whole by assuring basic rights and liberties. 'New Islamism' aims to engage in politics on the basis of social legitimacy and socio-economic compromise. Change is achieved by liberating societal dynamics and allowing them to be reflected in politics. With respect to world politics, 'new Islamism' reflects a reevaluation that sees civilisational dialogue between the Islamic and the Western worlds as essential. Globalisation has become a constant point of reference for the AKP leadership and the European Union is seen as its embodiment. Domestically, 'new Islamism' has developed a culture of compromise. As a result the leadership has refrained from political polarisation and has distanced itself from insisting on solving issues that that could generate strong polarisation. As such the AKP represents a compromise between democracy and Islamic identity and the management of tensions by peaceful means. A new term 'conservative democracy' is being used to define the 'new Islamism' of the AKP.[27]

In addition, it is important to note that from the 1980s the Turkish economy became integrated with the world economy and registered satisfactory growth. Since 2002 the economy started to display sustained growth and inflation was brought down to single digits. The government has pursued important structural reforms like liberalising electricity, sugar and tobacco prices, reducing agricultural subsidies, reforming the banking system and strengthening independent regulatory structures. Structural reforms boosted market confidence and strengthened the government's hand in managing the financial position. In 2010, Turkey posted a GDP growth rate of 8.9 percent. In 2011, the growth is estimated to be 5.5 percent. In comparison the EU faces a projected growth of 1.8 percent in 2011.[28] However, despite steady growth over the past six years and the projection of Turkey as one of the fastest recovering economies, there are also reports that there is a rapid expansion in the current account deficit, foreigners are cutting Turkish debt and currency exposure, fiscal policy needs to be tightened and youth unemployment is high for a country where the average age is twenty eight. There are also fears of the return of a persistent imbalance in the Turkish economy.[29]

In any case it is now being argued that the Turkish model has become dysfunctional for Turkey's long-standing aim to join the EU as a full member.[30] Accession negotiations were restarted by the AKP Prime Minister Erdogan in 2005 prompting the argument that staunch proponents of the Turkish model (the Kemalist elite, the centre-left and centre-right political parties and the military establishment) have become a major source of resistance to Turkey's integration with Europe. The only exception has been some sections of the business elite, which broke ranks with the political elite in the mid-1990s. In contrast the model's critics are now ardent supporters of the EU accession process. Yet, an air of crisis seems to be hanging over the accession process where ambitious plans for political deepening have run into trouble while monetary cooperation has not opened to the political union.[31] The debate on the possibilities of Turkey's membership in the EU is centered around two groups of issues; the EU requirement for modernising economic, political and legal systems and adjusting them to EU membership and a second group of factors that are subjective in nature—the civilisational, cultural, historical and geographical specifics and the complexity of the EU's domestic situation. It is argued that while Turkey is moving towards compliance with regard to many of the first group of requirements, the situation will be more complicated with regard to the second group.[32]

A significant part of the changes within Turkey has been reflected in the process of constitutional amendment which was prioritised by the AKP in its second term in power. Although the AKP asked a panel of legal experts to draft a constitution, its inability to garner broader support for constitutional reform and resistance from the opposition put the issue on a back burner. Instead, it opted for limited revisions mainly intended for removing restrictions being encountered by female students wearing the headscarf. This initiative led to a closure case against the AKP and allegations that it had become the focal point of anti-secular activities.[33] In March 2011 the government announced that instead of rewriting the constitution it would opt for a smaller package of amendments that would redefine the powers and composition of state agencies. The AKP's problems in the so-called 'Kurdish opening' also forced it to re-conceptualise the issue of giving greater rights to Turkish citizens of different backgrounds and present it as a broad-based 'democratic opening'.

It is in this context that the June 12, 2011 Parliamentary elections assume importance. In the course of the campaign, both the AKP as well as the main opposition party the CHP committed themselves to introducing a democratic 'civilian constitution' after the elections. Although on the surface there exist a broad consensus on the need to draft a new constitution, contradictory opinions dominate on the issues of contention that have plagued Turkish politics over the years—the

Kurdish issue, the question of the place of religion in society and the role of the military. The AKP launched its election campaign with the slogan, "Vote for AK Party. Write your own Constitution" a clear reference to the AKP agenda for a new constitution to replace the one that came into force in 1982 during a period of military rule and which has been widely criticised for limiting individual rights. The new constitution is expected to strengthen democracy and pluralism. Among the changes that would be sought for would be a directly elected President of seven years, restriction of the political role of the military and a change in the headscarf policy; all issues that have led to debates between the government and the opposition. The EU has also repeatedly called on the AKP to reform the Turkish legal system, including restructuring the Supreme Board of Prosecutors and Judges (HSYK).[34]

The AKP required 367 out of a total of 550 seats to approve a new constitution on its own. The 49.9 percent vote that it received gave it 326 seats, requiring it to seek agreement from other parties.[35] Mr. Erdogan admitted that the election results indicated that the new constitution should be created through agreement and negotiation and that the AKP would be respectful towards the rights of all sections of the state.[36] As the cross-party parliamentary commission began the task of drafting a new constitution, the CHP demanded an overhaul of the amendments made in 2010 which it said had increased the control of the government over the judiciary. The BDP on the other hand insisted that no constitutional provision should be considered to be untouchable.[37]

While domestic issues would require negotiation, Mr. Erdogan left no doubt that the election outcome has strengthened Turkey's role in the region. In his victory speech at the AKP headquarters in Ankara he said

> Believe me, tonight Sarajevo has won as much as Istanbul has ...Beirut has won just as much as Izmir has, the West Bank and Gaza have won just as much as Diyarbakir has. Tonight the Middle East, the Balkans and the Caucasus have won just as much as Turkey has.[38]

A major challenge faced by Turkey has been in the arena of foreign policy where 'appropriate' policies have been sought in Turkey's historically troubled relations with its neighbours like Greece and Armenia. Turkey's improvement of its relations with these two states has been a major pre-requisite for the advancement of the pre-accession processes. As a member of the EU, Greece has identified the solution of disputes in the Aegean as an issue linked to Turkey's prospective membership. Similarly the establishment of EU neighbourhood policy necessitates the establishment of relations with Armenia. The EU does not characterise the current relations between Armenia and Turkey as 'good neighbourly'. The European Parliament also aims for Turkey's recognition of the Armenian genocide. On the other hand, key domestic elements of concern remain—the issues like gender role within the state exemplified by the debate around the headscarf and the rights of minorities alongwith related questions of democracy and human rights. This debate goes beyond the necessity of conforming to the political criteria of Copenhagen to the challenge of identity-related arguments. Identity-related arguments are best exemplified through what is referred to as the 'Kurdish question' in Turkey. The question of the Kurds in Turkey has both domestic and international dimensions and over the years it has exemplified both the identification of the state as less than 'democratic' and the efforts by the state to move beyond this identification. It also portrays the complexities within Turkish society and brings to the forefront debates around the nature of the Turkish model and the rhetoric that has been built around it. As a consequence it also throws light on whether the model would remain a 'myth' or transcend into reality.

The projection of the Turkish model as an alternative in the Middle East in recent times has emphasised the rhetoric surrounding the myth of the model and has once again raised questions about whether the Turkish model as an alternative makes sense both from a historical as well as a contemporary perspective. As new political landscapes emerge in the Middle East, debates on the Turkish model also assume various forms ranging from those that point to its fragility to others which focus on its advantages. It is fair to argue that the 'new' Turkish model epitomised by the AKP rather than the traditional classical Turkish model based on state modernisation led by secular elites has caught the imagination of large segments of the Arab society. The AKP experience represented a more flexible and nuanced understanding of secularism and allowed more space for religion in public space and everyday life. The AKP was also seen as more 'globalist' since it was willing to develop strategies to capitalise on the benefits of global integration. But it is also true that the "Turkish model" is something that cannot be readily replicated. The AKP Model can be replicated only by countries that have already switched to a functioning and legitimate democratic system; its success being paradoxically rooted in a strong independent and secular-democratic system and its simultaneous critique of and outgrowth from it. The new Arab leaders do not enjoy the advantage of functioning as a legitimate government within independent sovereign state systems. This has prompted the argument that in such circumstances they should begin with looking into the Kemalist model rather than the one developed by the AKP.[39]

## Notes

1. See for instance, Mathew Brunwasser, "Turkey as a Model Democracy for Middle East", *The World*, Global Perspectives for an American Audience, February 21, 2011, http://www.theworld.org/2011/02/turkey-as-model-democracy-for -middle-east/. Here he cites Hugh Pope, Turkey/Cyprus director at the International Crisis Group as pointing to the projection of Turkey as a model. See also Karem Oktem, "Turkey Remains an "Angry Nation" but could still Serve as a Democratic Inspiration", *The Turkey Analyst*, vol. 4, no. 5, 7, March 2011.
2. See Halil M. Karaveli and Svante Cornell, "Turkey and the Middle Eastern Revolts: Democracy or Islamism?" *Turkey Analyst*, vol. 4 no. 3, 7, February 2011 where they cite Tariq Ramadan (the grandson of Hasan al-Banna, the founder of the Muslim Brotherhood).
3. Hesham Sallam, "Obsessed with Turkish Models in Egypt", *Jadaliyya*, June 30, 2013.
4. Comment made by Namik Tan at a panel discussion at the John Hopkins School of Advanced International Studies, cited from 'US Ambassador: Turkey May Be an Inspiration for Middle Eastern Countries', *Trend,* 08.03.2011, http://en.trend.az/regions/met/turkey/1841736.html.
5. See for instance Paula Sandrin, "Unrest in the Middle East, the Turkish Response and the Turkish Model", *Political Reflection Quarterly*, vol. 2, no. 1, March-April-May 2011. Also see Halil M. Karaveli and Svante E. Cornell, "Turkey and the Middle Eastern Revolts: Democracy or Islamism?", *Turkey Analyst,* vol. 4, no. 3, 7, February 2011.
6. More recently however, there are reports that Turkey has established contacts with the Libyan opposition. The main concern is that Libya should not become a second Iraq.

7. For details see Joshua Walker, "Turkey's Regional Leadership in the Middle East: Principle or Realpolitik?" *Turkey Analyst*, vol. 4, no. 6, 21 March 2011.
8. Walker "Turkey's Regional Leadership in the Middle East: Principle or Realpolitik?".
9. "Turkey Declares its Sanctions on Syria", *Hurriyet Daily News*, 1 December 2011.
10. In fact, even prior to the Arab Spring Turkey's position as an initiator of reforms was debated in writings like Aysegul Sever, "Turkey's Constraining Position on Western Reform Initiatives in the Middle East", *Mediterranean Quarterly*, vol. 18, no. 4, Fall 2007. See also Abdullah Gul, "Turkey's Role in a Changing Middle East Environment", *Mediterranean Quarterly*, vol. 15, no. 1, Winter 2004.
11. See for instance, M. Hakan Yavuz, "The Role of the New Bourgeoisie in the Transformation of the Turkish Islamic Movement", in *The Emergence of a New Turkey, Democracy and the AKP Party*, Salt Lake City: The University of Utah Press, 2006.
12. The Ergenekon affair involves investigations against a group of people who were accused of alleged involvement in a plot to overthrow the AKP government and includes hundreds of senior military officials, journalists and academics.
13. Guney Yildiz, "Ergenekon: The Court Case that Changed Turkey", *BBC News Europe*, 5 August 2013.
14. Andrew Rosenthal, "Punishing Journalists, Subverting Press Freedom", *The New York Times*, The Opinion Pages, July 24, 2013.
15. Bayram Balci, "Protests a Needed Tonic for Turkey's Democracy", *World Politics Review*, June 28, 2013.
16. There have been commentators who have also argued that the new situation is a new stage of the model where the weakness of the political opposition has been compensated by public mobilisation in Turkey. What is optimistic is the ability of the civil society to challenge the government without organised political parties. See Bayram Balci, "Protests in Turkey: the end of the Turkish Model?", *Foreign Policy Journal*, June 29, 2013.
17. Cited from Eduard Soler i Lecha, "The Conceptual Architecture of Turkish Foreign Policy: An Update in the Light of Regional Turbulence", *Documentos CIDOB*, 18 June 2012.
18. Sinan Ulgen, "From Inspiration to Aspiration: Turkey in the New Middle East", *News Analysis*, Carnegie Europe, 7 December 2011.
19. Tarik Oguzlu, "Is the 'Turkey as a Model' Idea Turning into Reality from Perception?", *ORSAM Foreign Policy Analysis*, 5 December 2011.
20. H Akin Unver, "The Forgotten Secular Turkish Model", *Middle East Quarterly*, vol. 20, no. 1, Winter 2013.
21. Justyna Pawlak, "EU Revives Membership Talks with Turkey after Three Year Hiatus", *Reuters*, Brussels, October 22, 2013.
22. Turkey's position in the EU makes up a significant volume of the debates on the future of Turkey. See for instance, Bruce Kunilholm, "Turkey and the World in Twenty Five Years: Thinking About the Future", *The South Atlantic Quarterly* , vol. 102, no. 2/3 Spring/Summer 2003.
23. See F. Murat Ozkaleli and Umut Konuloglu Ozkaleli, "The Myth and the Reality about Turkish Model-Democratization in the Muslim World", Paper presented at the annual meeting of the American Political Science Association, Philadelphia, PA, August 27, 2003, http://www.allacademic.com/meta/p62697
24. Andrew Mango cited from Ozkaleli and Ozkaleli, "The Myth and the Reality about

Turkish Model-Democratization in the Muslim World".

25. For details of the arguments see Ozkaleli and Ozkaleli, "The Myth and the Reality about Turkish Model-Democratization in the Muslim World".
26. Menderes Cinar and Burhanettin Duran, "The Specific Evolution of Contemporary Political Islam in Turkey and its 'Difference'", in Umit Cizre (ed) *Secular and Islamic Politics In Turkey: The Making of the Justice and Development Party*, Abingdon, Oxon: Routledge, 2008.
27. The AKP developed its normative framework through its official publication, *Conservative Democracy*. The book defines the AKP's conservatism as an ideology that stresses common sense, prudence, and gradual change. It rejects rationalist utopias, Jacobinism and social engineering. At a conference organised to elaborate on the Party's conservative and democratic stand, Erdogan emphasised that the AKP's understanding of conservatism did not mean the conservation of established institutions and relations but implied the protection of important values and principles while pursuing progress. The attempt was to synthesise local and universal values, tradition and modernity and morality and religion. For details see Ahmet Kuru, "From Islamism to Conservative Democracy: The Justice and Development Party in Turkey", Paper presented at the annual meeting of the American Political Science Association, Marriot, Loews, Philadelphia and the Pennsylvania Convention Centre, Philadelphia, PA, August 31, 2006, http://www.allacademic.com/meta/p151181_index.html

    'Conservative democracy' has defined the expression of the AKP's will to internalise international norms. Having accepted human rights, democracy and the rule of law as universal values the AKP embraced dominant Western values while remaining committed to conservative Islamic roots. During its term in government the AKP has introduced significant political and economic reforms to consolidate Turkish democracy on the Copenhagen Criteria. Despite difficulties in the process of integration, the AKP has taken steps to ensure the implementation of reforms in line with European standards. In a number of instances these reforms address issues related to the core elements of Turkey's political structures and dynamics. These include reducing the influence of the military in politics, eradicating the death penalty, abolishing the State Security Courts, strengthening gender equality, broadening the freedom of the press, aligning the judiciary with European standards and establishing the supremacy of international agreements in the area of fundamental freedoms over internal legislation.
28. Justin Vela, "Turkey: How Long before the Boom turns to Bust?", *Eurasianet,* June 28, 2011.
29. Delphine Strauss, "Turkey's Economy: Warning Signs?" September 2, 2010, blogs.ft.com/beyond-brics/2010/09/02. See also Ibon Villelabeitia, "Scenarios—Why is Turkey June 12 Vote Important?", *Reuters*, June 6, 2011.
30. See Mehmet Ugur and Nergis Canefe, "Turkey and the European Integration, Conclusions", in Mehmet Ugur and Nergis Canefe (eds) *Turkey and the European Integration, Accession Prospects and Issues*, London and New York: Routledge, 2004. Since the signing of the Association (Ankara) Agreement of 1964, Turkey's relations with the European Union, then referred to as the European Economic Community, has passed through various phases. In 1987 Turkey applied for membership which was rejected in December 1989 citing a number of shortcomings. It was obvious that Turkey, due to its size and structure could not

be easily assimilated within the EU. Turkey is less developed and more populous than most of the other member states which would mean that its membership would accord to it a greater number of seats than most of the other members. The debate on Turkish membership is also closely related with the question of determining the limits of the European Union and its extension, not just in geographic terms but also in terms of cultural affinity. It is not surprising therefore that Turkey took over twelve years from its March 1987 accession application to the achievement of formal candidate status at Helsinki in December 1999. A further six years elapsed before the official opening of entry negotiations in October 2005. On the other hand, it has been argued that the intensity of the debate within Turkey demonstrates that the question of membership extends beyond that of entry to a multilateral forum and is in actuality a debate on the question of Turkey's identity.

31. Susannah Verney, "The Dynamics of EU Accession: Turkish Travails in Comparative Perspective", in Susannah Verney and Kostas Ifantis (eds) *Turkey's Road to European Union Membership, National Identity and Political Change,* London and New York: Routledge, 2009.
32. Pavel Varbanets, "A Turkic Alliance: Possible Alternative to Turkey's Unrealized EU Membership?", *Central Asia and the Caucasus,* no. 1 (55), 2009.
33. Saban Kardas, "Constitutional Amendments Further Polarize Turkish Politics", *Eurasia Daily Monitor*, vol. 7, Issue 87, May 5, 2010.
34. For details of the proposed changes see Gareth H. Jenkins, "Turkey's Constitutional Amendments: One Step Forward, Two Steps Back?", *Turkey Analyst*, vol. 3 no. 6, 29 March 2010.
35. The AKP required 367 seats to pass the constitutional amendment on its own. With more than 330 seats it would be possible for the AKP to make the changes with a public referendum. With less than 330 seats it is now bound to seek consensus among other parties in the Parliament.
36. The CHP has won 26 percent of the vote and the MHP 13 percent. This becomes all the more significant given the strong showing by the Kurdish independent candidates. Thirty five have won seats and this will give them a voice in the Parliament and also put pressure on Erdogan to address their grievances. Without a 'supermajority,' a referendum on a new constitution with a Presidential system is likely to trigger debate. The CHP also admits that there is need to modernise the constitution but it is deeply suspicious of Erdogan and the AKP. Kurdish nationalists want a redefinition of the citizenship clauses which could provoke a backlash from the nationalists. And any attempt to amend the first four clauses of the constitution, which describes Turkey as a secular state, would galvanise secularists, who in 2008 had organised mass protests against the AKP's attempt to lift a ban on headscarf in universities.
37. "Turkish Charter Panel Convenes as Cracks Emerge", *Hurriyet Daily News,* Tuesday October 18, 2011.
38. Thomas Seibert, "Election Victory for Erdogan Boosts Turkey's Standing in the Region", *The National,* June 14, 2011.
39. Akin Unver, "The Forgotten Secular Turkish Model".

# 7
# Israel and Turkey: Revisiting the Alliance?

*Priya Singh*

---

## Introduction

Relations between Israel and Turkey were formalised in March 1949. Military, strategic, and diplomatic cooperation between Turkey and Israel were accorded precedence by both countries as they had shared apprehensions about the regional insecurities in the Middle East.[1] According to a *New York Times* report in 1999, the strategic partnership between the two countries had the potential to alter Middle East politics.[2] Trade and tourism were flourishing, the Israel Air Force (IAF) practiced manoeuvres in Turkish airspace and Israeli technicians were modernising Turkish combat jets. There were also plans for high-tech cooperation and water sharing. However, relations between Israel and Turkey assumed a different trajectory during the term of Recep Tayyip Erdoğan as Turkish Prime Minister. Though Erdoğan had paid an official visit to Israel in 2005 and at the outset appeared to endorse a *status quo* attitude, his strong anti-Israeli rhetoric is regarded to have signified an intended shift of Turkish interests in the Middle East and a change from secular Israeli-oriented to Islamist pro-Arab stance of the Turkish Republic. Most conspicuously, the relations deteriorated after the *Gaza War* of 2008–2009 and the *Gaza flotilla* raid of 2010. In March 2013, Israel apologised for the raid, initiating the path for stabilised relations.[3] However, despite US mediation, no substantial progress had been achieved in reconciliation through 2013.[4] With the scandal over alleged Turkish involvement in the revelation of Israeli special agents in Iran in October 2013, the relations between Israel and Turkey touched a new low. Turkey recognised the State of Israel in 1949. Turkey's first diplomatic mission in Israel was a "Legation" and was officially inaugurated on January 7, 1950 and the first Turkish Chief of Mission, Seyfullah Esin presented his credentials to Chaim Weisman, President of Israel.[5] However, the Turkish Legation was downgraded to the level of "Charge d'Affaires" after the Suez Canal Crisis on November 26, 1956. In 1958, Israeli Prime Minister David Ben-Gurion and Turkish Prime Minister Adnan Menderes met secretly to discuss a "peripheral pact," which included public relations campaigns, exchange of intelligence information and military support. In 1967, Turkey joined the Arab condemnation of Israel after the Six-Day War and called for Israel's withdrawal from the occupied territories but abstained from voting in favour of a clause referring to Israel as an "aggressor state." At a meeting of the Organization of the Islamic Conference (OIC) in Rabat, Morocco, Turkey opposed a resolution calling for severing diplomatic relations with Israel. As a result of the positive developments in bilateral ties, the Turkish mission in Tel-Aviv was upgraded back to the level of "Legation" in July 1963 and further upgraded to the level of "Embassy" as of January 1980.[6] On Israel's annexation of East Jerusalem and enunciation of Jerusalem as its eternal capital, the representation was relegated to the level of "Second Secretary" on November 30, 1980.[7]

The essay attempts to highlight the relationship between Turkey and Israel, which has been largely governed by the concept of uncertainty/ inconclusiveness for decades. While the 1990s witnessed a growing understanding in their bilateral relations in tandem/or along with Israeli–Palestinian peace talks, the subsequent decade saw strains emerge in the relationship that reached an all–time low beginning with the *Israeli blockade of and incursion into Gaza* in 2008–09 and then the *Mavi Marmara incident* in 2010.[8] In other words, until recently, the "special relationship" between Israel and Turkey seemed resilient. Reinforced by shared perceptions of the threats and opportunities in their regional environment and concretised by an extensive network of joint initiatives in trade, intelligence and defence, the Turkish–Israeli alliance blossomed in the 1990s. Any differences that arose between these two regional giants paled in comparison to the predominant empathy and mutuality of interests that existed between them. At least that is the impression one got at the time. Underneath the apparent façade of goodwill between the two countries lay a growing gap in values and political cultures that set the stage for a deterioration of relations as two major crises transpired. The first of these was Israel's offensive against the Gaza Strip in the winter of 2008–09, followed a year and a half later by Israel's attack on the *Mavi Marmara*, a Turkish-flagged ship attempting to deliver humanitarian aid to the still-besieged Gazans. The divergence in values between the two countries began to take shape at the turn of the twenty-first century, and accelerated after Recep Tayyip Erdoğan became PM in 2003. At one point, Israel and Turkey were extraordinarily akin in their political makeup, policies toward minority groups and foreign policy predilections. Both countries fancied themselves as lone democracies in a region besieged with authoritarian regimes. Turkey and Israel also shared a comparable assessment of their regional environment. From the vantage point of Turkish officials, Syria's clandestine sponsorship of the Kurdish insurgency in south eastern Turkey fit into the same category as Syria's support for the war waged by Hizbullah against Israel in southern Lebanon. Thus, Israel and Turkey were natural allies in the struggle to keep in check Syria's policy of advancing its interests in the region through the manipulation of violent non-state substitutes. However, fundamental changes gathered momentum during Erdoğan's tenure in office that reoriented Turkey's political values and regional outlook and, by extension, its relationship with Israel. The most significant change by far was that Turkey became markedly more democratic than it was a decade ago in a wide range of areas, including enforcement of the rule of law, protection of civil rights and liberties, and the assertion of civilian control over the military. Particularly impressive were the significant concessions the Turkish government made toward Kurdish cultural rights; the most important one being the granting of a license in January 2009 for a 24-hour Kurdish language television channel.

On the other hand, Israel tightened its grip on the Palestinians over time. Meanwhile, expansion of Israeli settlements in the West Bank and East Jerusalem and expropriation of huge tracts of Palestinian-owned land continued rapidly, quashing the territorial basis of a two-state solution, while Gaza had to contend with a siege that restricted its access to a wide range of commercial goods. Apart from a brief respite in the early days of the Oslo Accords (roughly 1993–1995), as well as recent measures to ease some restrictions on freedom of movement, Israel has not engaged in a credible attempt to accommodate Palestinian aspirations that matched Turkey's overtures to the Kurds during the early phase of Erdoğan's tenure. Erdoğan's robust endorsement of the Palestinian Authority's bid to gain admission to the UN as a full member state and his championing of the Palestinian cause in general, as well as Turkey's demand that Israel meet a certain minimal moral threshold in its treatment of Palestinians as a condition for friendship placed at risk billions of dollars' worth of military contracts and other cooperative ventures without any compensating benefits, save for the intrinsic value of being on the "right side of history." As Richard Falk commented, "[T]his [Turkish] stand on behalf of the victimized population of Gaza represents a rare display of placing values above interests. The people of Gaza are weak, abused, and vulnerable. In contrast, Israel is a military powerhouse, prospering, a valuable trading partner for Turkey."[9] Turkey's democratic deepening versus Israel's democratic deficit was evident in the divergent styles of diplomacy each state employed to cope with the tensions that arose between them both before and after the flotilla attack.

After almost four years of diplomatic stalemate, Israel apologised to Turkey for the killing by the Israeli Defence Forces (IDF) of eight Turkish nationals and one Turkish American during the *Gaza Flotilla* raid in May 2010. The apology was brokered by US Secretary of State John Kerry in the run up to President Barack Obama's visit to Israel, leaving the US President to bask in the diplomatic limelight at a time when the prospects for reviving a genuine Middle East peace process appeared to be dim. In Israel the agreement was presented as a major foreign policy success for the newly established Netanyahu government, though there were criticisms from the likes of Avigdor Lieberman, who dubbed it as a serious mistake. In Turkey too, Prime Minister Erdoğan celebrated the agreement as a clear cut diplomatic victory, since Israel caved in to the Turkish demand for an apology and promised financial compensation for the families of the victims. Beyond an apology and compensation, the third Turkish demand for normalising relations with Israel—the lifting of the Gaza blockade has not been met. Therefore the Gaza blockade and more broadly the Israeli–Palestinian conflict, thus continues to be the continuing determinant of the Turkish–Israeli relationship, which has intermittently gone through ebbs and flows/ ups and downs reflecting the wider trends in the Middle East conflict. However, a return to the heydays of the 1990s when Turkish–Israeli partnership flourished against the backdrop of the Oslo peace process appears doubtful/is debatable though not impossible.

## *The 1990s*

As George Gruen argues, Turkey's relations with Israel have been governed by the concept of "ambivalence" for decades.[10] Although Turkey recognised Israel in 1949, relations were governed by Turkey's quest to balance its relations with both Israel and the Arab world. Turkey downgraded its diplomatic post to Israel in 1956 to that of chargé d'affaires after the Suez Crisis, and further downgraded diplomatic relations after the 1980 Jerusalem Act.[11] According to some experts, the re-upgrading of diplomatic representation to the ambassadorial level on December 19, 1991 came as a surprise to the Israeli side.[12] This upgrade came six weeks after the peace talks based on UN Resolutions 242 and 338 began at the Madrid Conference. The link between Turkey's closer relations with Israel and the peace process should be underlined here, since it is discernible as a factor in subsequent relations as well.[13] Some analysts described the developing relationship between Turkey and Israel at the beginning of the 1990s as "the newest and at the same time the most controversial aspect of Turkish foreign policy in the post-Cold War Middle East."[14] The main motive behind this move related to Turkey's efforts was to balance threats from its southern neighbours. The fact that Syria had signed a military training agreement with Greece in 1995 in a way justified the alliance. Both Turkey and Syria had wanted to surround the other at the time through strategic alliances and Turkey, by allying herself with Israel, achieved military supremacy over its rivals in the region. During the 1990s Turkey had faced increasing challenges not only from its southern neighbours but also from the West, which had become increasingly critical of Turkey's human rights record, especially regarding the Kurdish issue. Turkey was finding it hard to obtain Western technology and military equipment during the 1990s, including from the U.S. In the opinion of some analysts, the alliance with Israel[15] was a pragmatic approach by which the military-bureaucratic elite could counter the challenges posed by Turkey's European allies.[16] Their common stance against terrorism, common interests in Central Asia, and economic concerns were also important to this alliance but were of secondary importance. The idea among Turkish policy-makers was that Israel's privileged relationship with, and the "powerful Jewish lobby" in, the United States could be important at a time when Turkey was trying to secure a place for itself in the changing world order.[17]

At the domestic level, the 1990s witnessed the expansion of the role of the military in Turkish politics, which evolved out of the challenge posed by the Kurdistan Workers' Party (PKK) issue. This was also true of its role in foreign policy-making, especially with respect to Turkey's relations with the Middle East. Thus, the securitisation of Turkish foreign policy increased the military's power within the country. This argument is important when considering that the driving force behind the Turkish–Israeli alliance was the military. The same logic would be used to argue against relations in recent years. A series of high-level visits between the two countries was made from 1992 onwards, which resulted in a series of comprehensive agreements in 1996 in the military, economic, and technical fields. In February 1996, a military training agreement was signed "to facilitate cooperation between the two countries in military education through a series of measures including joint air force training, naval visits, military personnel exchange and joint training in military academies."[18] During President Demirel's visit to Israel in March 1996, agreements on free trade, promotion of bilateral investments, and prevention of double taxation were signed. Cooperation in areas such as investment, construction, manufacturing, environment, water and land conservation, technical cooperation and joint enterprises began to expand as a result of agreements. These agreements became significant in the diversification of relations and in creating constituencies that went beyond the state level in relations between the two countries. Even though the agreements between Turkey and Israel were never officially declared to be a formal alliance, and although it was emphasised that they were not intended against a third party, this led to an uproar in the Arab world.[19] Lebanon's *al-Safir* wrote that the alliance was directed against all Arabs, and that it exclusively served Israeli interests at the expense of Arab and Muslim interests. In other words, the alliance was portrayed as an attempt to oppress Arabs, with Turkey once again acting on behalf of Western interests in the region.[20]

Agreements between Turkey and Israel reached their peak during a period in which Necmettin Erbakan of the Welfare Party had been Prime Minister of Turkey, ruling the country in a coalition government with the True Path Party of Tansu Çiller. Keeping in mind the Islamist rhetoric of the party and its leader, this was quite unexpected. Necmettin Erbakan was known to have made statements such as all the "viruses" of Turkish economy and society—those of rent and dependence on the international market—could be traced to the ills of the "Jewish-led world economy." The on-going domestic economic system privileged only a handful of the population—the happy minority—who owed their situation in society to the "Jewish order" that also informed the Turkish socio-economic structure. When the Welfare Party came to power, Erbakan claimed while running for office, they would eliminate all traces of this "Jewish-based system" and reorient Turkey from the Jewish-led West (including the European Union[EU]) towards the Muslim world. Given that they came to power on the promise of revoking all agreements signed with Israel, the undertones behind the Turkish Israeli relationship under Erbakan's premiership tell a lot about the forces that drive such alliances. These relations actually became an issue through which the political body and the military attempted to assert authority over each other. The securitisation of foreign policy issues and especially the perception of threat from the Middle East increased the role of the military in Turkish politics during the 1990s. This was also a time when societal polarisation between secularists and Islamists reached their peak. Turkish–Israeli relations therefore became an issue the military-bureaucratic elite wanted to enhance as a demonstration of their anti-Islamist orientation, while Islamists wanted to limit it based on ideological reasons. The power of the military at the time, however, as well as the increasing opposition from the population at large to Erbakan's radical rhetoric, led to the formation of a coalition government. This in turn compelled him to sign these agreements with Israel, despite some initial resistance. In spite of this resistance from the Welfare Party, Chief of General Staff Hüseyin Karadayı visited Israel in February 1997, and the visits of Israeli Foreign Minister Davis Levy and Defense Minister Yitzhak Mordechai to Ankara during the same period "proved that Turkish–Israeli relations were expanding despite the WP's opposition." In fact joint naval exercises with Israel (dubbed Reliant Mermaid) were also held in January 1997 despite this resistance.[21]

### *The 2000s*

From late 1990s onwards, Turkish foreign policy has witnessed a series of changes that have continued in the 2000s. Regional and international developments during this period have had a deep impact on the country's foreign policy and affected Turkish–Israeli relations. Turkish–Israeli relations have been influenced by changes in Turkish foreign policy-making and orientation after 1998, and continued during the 2000s. Turkey's relations towards its southern neighbours in general began to turn from conflict to a cautious rapprochement during this period. Turkey was also granted the status of candidate by the EU during this period, which led it to embark on an ambitious reform programme at home. This process, coupled with the de-securitisation of foreign policy, put Turkey's foreign policy on a new path that emphasised cooperation and the adoption of a more EU-style foreign policy orientation and instruments.[22] Hard security issues seemed to be downplayed during this period, and the role of the military in foreign policy-making decreased, while soft power began to be emphasised. As Kirişçi argues, this became a period during which Turkey came to realise the need to address security issues "not solely with traditional mechanisms but also economic cooperation and regional interdependence."[23] Jung contends that with the end of the military threat from the PKK, and with domestic policies focused on the EU reform process, Turkey would be able to play a new role in Middle Eastern politics as a "benign regional power," with its military-driven foreign policy replaced by a network of multi- and bilateral ties in political, economic, and cultural fields.[24] This region-based foreign policy—adopted under the coalition government and Minister of Foreign Affairs İsmail Cem, which emphasised Turkey's more independent role in its region, and which called for close relations with all neighbouring regions, had an important role in this context. The Middle East had an important place in this policy, and relations with the Arab countries and Iran took a new turn during this period, sowing the seeds of cooperation for the following years. In thinking about the impact that such cooperation with the Arab countries and Iran would have on relations with Israel, it was emphasised that closer relations with Muslim countries did not have to be at the expense of relations with Israel. As Cem articulated, "We cannot give up one of our friends in favour of another."[25] Cooperation in political, economic, and military issues continued unabated, but these began to find a lower profile in the press beginning at the end of the 1990s. This period could be considered one of normalisation for Turkey's relations with the Middle East in general, both with the Muslim countries and with Israel. Thus, the transition from an intense "strategic alliance" to a "common balanced relationship" with Israel began during this period.[26]

The coming to power of 'The Justice and Development Party' (*Adalet ve Kalkinma Partisi*) AKP in the November 2002 elections had been significant in bringing a new perspective to Turkish foreign policy, building on changes that were already taking shape under the previous coalition government. Having its roots in the Islamic-oriented Welfare Party of Erbakan, the AKP's ascendance to power in a single party government was positively received in the Muslim world in general. Although relations with Israel continued and even flourished during Erbakan's coalition government in 1996–97, the future of the "alliance" under the AKP, which was seen by many as the continuation of the Welfare Party, was questioned by many circles in both Turkey and Israel during this period.[27] Some writers in Turkey even saw Turkish–Israeli relations and its future as a test case for the AKP's Western orientation, the sincerity of its respect for the secular Republic and their claims of ideological change from political Islam to conservative democracy.[28]

Prime Minister Erdoğan visited Israel in 2005 offering to serve as a Middle East peace mediator and looking to build up trade and military ties. Erdoğan brought a large group of businessmen on his two-day trip, which included talks with Prime Minister Ariel Sharon and President Moshe Katsav. Erdoğan also laid a wreath at the Holocaust memorial, Yad Vashem.[29] Erdoğan reaffirmed that his Justice and Development Party regarded anti-Semitism as "a crime against humanity." He added that Iran's nuclear ambitions were a threat not just to Israel but to "the entire world."[30] A joint Israeli-Palestinian industrial park was being developed under Turkey's patronage. Israeli President Shimon Peres and Palestinian Authority President Mahmoud Abbas addressed the Grand National Assembly of Turkey a day apart. Peres described Turkey as an "important player in the Middle East in relation to the United States, Syria and the Palestinians, as well as us." [31] According to a report in the *Jerusalem Post*, a spokeswoman for the Syrian Foreign Ministry said that Turkey was serving as a "channel of communication" between Syria and Israel.[32] On a three-day visit to Ankara in November 2007, Israeli President Shimon Peres met with Turkish President Abdullah Gül, and addressed the Grand National Assembly of Turkey. Gül promised to help free three abducted Israeli soldiers: Gilad Shalit, Ehud Goldwasser and Eldad Regev.[33]

The Turkish government's condemnation of the 2008–2009 Israel–Gaza conflict strained relations between the two countries. In December 1987, Turkey had already declared support for the Palestinians' right to self-determination. In 2004, Turkey had denounced the Israeli assassination of Sheikh Ahmed Yassin. It described the Israeli policy in the Gaza Strip as "state-sponsored terrorism."[34] There were demonstrations across Turkey against Israeli actions in Gaza.[35] On March 5, 2009, the Israeli daily newspaper *Haaretz* reported that "secret reconciliation talks at the highest level" had been held to get the Israeli–Turkish relations back on track.[36] This report was cited in the Turkish press.[37] On October 11, 2009, a military aerial exercise was to consist of Turkey, Israel, the United States and Italy. However, Turkey barred Israel from the Anatolian Eagle military exercise. In October 2009, following Turkey's prohibition of Israel's participation in the Anatolian Eagle military exercise, Israeli Prime Minister Benjamin Netanyahu objected to Turkey as a mediator, stating "Turkey can't be [an] honest broker," between Syria and Israel.[38] Erdoğan harshly criticised Israel's conduct in Gaza at the World Economic Forum conference in Davos, Switzerland in early 2009.[39] In October 2009, *Ayrılık*, a prime-time serial on Turkish state television channel TRT 1 featured fictionalised scenes of Israeli soldiers shooting Palestinian children and mistreating elderly Arabs.[40] Israeli Foreign Minister Avigdor Lieberman criticised the programme and rebuked the Turkish Ambassador in front of assembled media. Lieberman subsequently apologised after Turkey threatened to withdraw its ambassador. After Hamas leader Khaled Mashal paid an official visit to Turkey, relations began to cool off. In January 2010, Israel protested when an episode ("Ambush") of the Turkish soap opera *Valley of the Wolves* depicted Israeli intelligence spying inside Turkey and kidnapping Turkish babies.[41] The series depicted a fictional Mossad attack on the Turkish embassy in Tel-Aviv in which the ambassador and his family are taken hostage. On January 11, 2010, Israeli Deputy Foreign Minister Danny Ayalon met with Turkish ambassador Ahmet Oğuz Çelikkol, who was seated on a stool that was lower than Ayalon's. Ayalon allegedly turned to his aide and quipped, "The main thing is that you see that he is seated low and that we are high ... that there is one flag on the table (the Israeli flag) and that we are not smiling."[42] Moshe Ya'alon, Israel's Minister of Strategic Affairs accused Turkey of cooperating with Hamas and Iran. According to the Shin Bet, Hamas established a command post in Turkey and has used it to recruit operatives and oversee operations in the Middle East. [43]

### *The Mavi Marmara Episode and the Aftermath*[44]

On May 31, 2010, nine activists (eight Turkish citizens and one Turkish-American with dual citizenship) were killed and many more wounded by Israeli troops and seven Israeli soldiers were injured on the *Mavi Marmara*, part of the "Gaza Freedom Flotilla,"[45] a convoy of six ships carrying 663 people from 37 nations, including pro-Palestinian activists.[46] Following the raid, which took place in the Mediterranean Sea in international waters,[47] tension between the two countries mounted. One of the ships taking part was flying a Turkish flag. Erdoğan described the raid as "state terrorism." Turkey recalled its ambassador from Israel, and summoned the Israeli ambassador to demand an explanation. The Turkish Foreign Ministry stated that the incident could lead to irreparable consequences in bilateral relations. On September 2, 2011, Turkey downgraded diplomatic ties with Israel and suspended military cooperation after the UN released its report of the *Mavi Marmara* raid.[48] A statement from the Israeli Prime Minister's office said, "Israel hopes to find a way to overcome the dispute and will continue to work towards this goal." Turkey demanded an Israeli apology and compensation over the May 31, 2010 incident aboard the *Mavi Marmara*. The Israeli government refused to offer one.[49] In September 2011, Turkey expelled Israel's ambassador after a UN report found that the blockade of Gaza was legal according to international law although excessive force was used during the time of embarking.[50] Israeli officials stated that they hoped to restore ties but reiterated that they would not apologise.[51] Meanwhile Hamas commended Turkey's decision.[52] Kemal Kiliçdaroğlu, Turkey's opposition leader, condemned the downgrading of relations with Israel, stating "No good can come of it and there is no need for us to risk our interest with petty action."[53] Faruk Logoglu, a deputy chairman of the opposition Republican People's Party, criticised Erdoğan stating that "The probability that (Turkey's ruling) party has carried Turkey to the brink of a hot conflict is saddening and unacceptable." Alon Liel, a former Israeli ambassador to Turkey, stated that it was unlikely that Turkish forces would penetrate Israeli waters, but speculated that Turkey might disrupt future Israeli gas exports to Cyprus and warned of a new Turkish–Egyptian alliance that could isolate Israel in the Mediterranean.[54] Israeli Defense Minister Ehud Barak predicted that the rift would pass in time.[55] At the U.N. General Assembly in September 2011, U.S. President Barack Obama in fact urged Erdoğan to resolve the crisis with Israel.[56] The Turkish Foreign Ministry urged the international community and the United Nations particularly to take the required initiatives to stop Israel's military operation in Gaza in late 2012, which it described as another example of Israel's hostile policies and its foreign minister Ahmet Davutoğlu saw in this attack another example of Israel's "crimes of humanity."[57] Erdoğan described

Israel as a "terrorist state" that "massacres innocent children."[58] During his speech in Vienna on March 1, 2013 at a United Nations event, he went on to describe Zionism as "a crime against humanity" saying, "It is necessary that we must consider—just like Zionism, or anti-Semitism, or fascism—Islamophobia."[59] In response, both Benjamin Netanyahu and Shimon Peres condemned the remarks and argued that Erdoğan's statements were based on ignorance and they would ignite the flames of hatred.[60] On March 20, 2013, Erdoğan began an official visit to Denmark with an effort to clarify his remarks that he had made on February 27 at a UN conference in Vienna referring to Zionism as a crime against humanity. "Let no one misunderstand what I said. Everyone knows that my criticism [of Israel] focuses on some critical issues. It's directed especially toward Israeli policies on Gaza," as such his comments were not anti-Semitic but rather a criticism of Israel's policies.[61]

As a consequence of US pressure on both sides, efforts at reconciliation took off in early 2013. On March 22, 2013, during a phone call with Erdoğan, Israel's Prime Minister Benjamin Netanyahu apologised for the *Gaza Flotilla* incident. An official statement by the Israeli government said that Netanyahu expressed regret over deterioration in bilateral relations and described the incident as unintentional, regretful and—according to an investigation—involving "operational errors." Erdoğan later issued a statement, where he accepted the apology on behalf of the Turkish people. Israel also vowed to compensate the victims' families. An Israeli statement first said that the countries had agreed to restore normal diplomatic relations, including the return of ambassadors and cancellation of Turkish legal proceedings *in absentia* against Israeli troops involved in the raid, but this statement was later omitted. U.S. President Barack Obama, whose visit to Israel coincided with the development and who was credited with brokering the reconciliation, said that the U.S. "attached great importance to the restoration of positive relations between [Israel and Turkey] in order to advance regional peace and security."[62] In August 2013, the *Hürriyet* reported that Erdoğan had stated to a meeting of the AKP's provincial chairs that Israel was responsible for the recent military coup in Egypt which overthrew Mohammad Morsi. Erdoğan reportedly stated "Who is behind this?

Israel. We have evidence"—specifically, Erdoğan cited a video posted online of Tzipi Livni speaking with French intellectual Bernard-Henri Levy. Erdoğan claimed that Levy had stated that "Muslim Brotherhood will not be in power even if they win the elections, because democracy is not the Ballot box." However, according to the *Hürriyet*, what Levy actually stated was that "the Muslim Brotherhood arrives in Egypt; I will not say democracy wants it, so let democracy progress. Democracy is not only elections, it is also values...I will urge the prevention of [the Muslim Brotherhood] coming to power, but by all sorts of means."[63] The Israeli Foreign Ministry spokesman later stated that Erdoğan's accusation was "a statement well worth not commenting on."[64]

### *Inferences*

There are explanations at every level to what factors have drawn Turkey and Israel apart and led to deterioration in relations during the 2000s. At the domestic level, the changing Turkish foreign policy from late 1990s appeared to require less Israeli cooperation. The consolidation of relations with the Arab countries, especially after the AKP came to power, may have contributed to this development. At the regional level, the Palestinian issue and the Iraq War seem to reveal the diverging interests of Israel and Turkey, while at the same time drawing Turkey closer to the Arab countries. If not for these two issues, the decline in relations would not have been so visible.[65] The international context as well, coupled with the strain on relations with the U.S., gave Turkey more room to manoeuvre regionally, as well as with regard to its relations with Israel. It is imperative to note that all these factors have contributed to the crises from the late 1990s onwards until 2009, on a cycle of crisis-cooperation-crisis. However, since 2009, with a stronger AKP in power as well, relations acquired a harsher tone and crisis became a more enduring feature. The *Mavi Marmara* incident has been especially significant in highlighting the importance of the Palestinian issue. Somewhere between Operation Cast Lead and the *Mavi Marmara* incident, two lines of argument have developed in Turkey, which have strengthened over time. One of these questions the future of Israel. For example, in a conference held in Istanbul before the Arab Spring, it had been openly argued by one of the speakers that Israel will not be able to survive in its region and that its borders will need to be reconsidered. Accordingly, the strength of the AKP and Erdoğan in the Middle East may result in a borderless region, considering the potential success of economic integration projects at the time, and Israel, by remaining out of this game, will not be able to survive such developments. The Kurdish issue and the deaths of Turkish citizens resulting from the *Mavi Marmara* incident seem to have reinforced these ideas. Another, more neutral, line of argument emphasises the personalities of the leaders on both sides and ideas and images the two leaderships have about each other, which result in the emergence of a fourth level, a personal level, contributing to the deterioration in relations. The Turkish as well as the Israeli leadership have seldom harboured genuine empathy for the other.[66]

On the one hand, the AKP government has strengthened its rule in power, the peace process is on hold, and no real progress has been achieved on that front; at the moment there does not seem to be any motivation in either Turkey or in Israel to normalize the relationship. However, on the other hand, the Arab Spring is again changing the dynamics of the region. As argued above, one of the reasons that led to a decline in Turkey–Israel relations was the changing relations of Turkey with the Arab countries in the beginning of the 2000s, especially with Syria and Iran and the decrease of Turkey's threat perception from and increasing shared interests with these countries. Ironically, a decade later and mainly as a result of the uprisings in Syria, Turkey is finding itself increasingly distanced from Syria and Iran and beginning to share common perceptions with Israel, although at different levels of priority. Yet, the relationship is far from a sheer balance of power calculation at this moment in time. The relationship with Israel is too impaired to lead to cooperation in regional politics. Even if the two countries could attempt to develop their relations and some progress could be achieved diplomatically, the fate of relations will continue to be subject to developments in the peace process and in the Palestinian issue, and thus seem as though they will remain equally fragile for the foreseeable future.

At the time of writing this paper, Israel and Turkey are reportedly on the brink of restoring full diplomatic relations.[67] In the midst of a chaotic election year in which Erdoğan faces domestic political criticism over his increasingly authoritarian and Islamist policies, as well as the presence of growing regional threats like Syria and Iran for both Israel and Turkey, the question that arises is what would normalisation offer to the former allies? In the words of Michael Koplow, "The domestic situation in Turkey is extremely tense and polarized....Turkey is quickly hardening into duelling camps of people who believe every allegation that is made against the government and people who believe that none of the allegations have a shred of truth to them."[68] Since taking office more than a decade ago, Erdoğan's biggest claim to success has been the stability he has brought after decades of military coup d'états. Under his leadership, the economy has dramatically improved and the country's international profile has grown. Nonetheless that success has dwindled over the past year, with a growing number of Turks becoming disillusioned with Erdoğan's increasing authoritarian policies, including attacks on the media, judicial system and military as well as political corruption in his AK party and a stalling economy. This came to a head last summer when protests termed as "Gezi Park Protests" erupted in Istanbul and quickly spread to other major Turkish cities. The opposition in Turkey—led by the Republican People's Party, or CHP, a centre-left socialist party created by Mustafa Kemal Ataturk, the founder of modern Turkey—gained momentum ahead of the March 30 municipal elections. Leading up to the elections, Erdoğan faced increased criticism over the government's decision to block Twitter and YouTube. "The government has been waging a battle with its former ally, the Gülen movement (a more moderate Islamist movement led by exiled Turkish scholar Fethullah Gülen), and has [also] been dealing with leaks, allegations of large-scale corruption, protests in Istanbul, Ankara, and other cities," Koplow contended. Yet Erdoğan and his AK party won the local elections. As of early March 31, AKP led with nearly 47 percent of the nationwide municipal vote, well surpassing the 39 percent it had garnered in the last local elections in 2009. Analysts speculate that the results will encourage Erdoğan to either mend party rules to seek a fourth term as prime minister or to run for president later this year. "This nation has given a message to Turkey and to the world," Erdoğan said, according to Turkey's *Daily Hurriyet* newspaper.[69]

Amid the domestic upheaval, Israel and Turkey are reportedly nearing a deal on restoring ties. According to Turkish Deputy Prime Minister Bulent Arinc, a deal under which Israel would pay compensation to the families of the Turks killed abroad the *Mavi Marmara* could be signed as early as April, the *Daily Hurriyet* reported. "The gap between the expectations of the two sides is closing," Turkish Foreign Minister Davutoglu told *AFP* "Progress has been made to a great extent, but the two sides need to meet again for a final agreement."[70] A flotilla compensation deal would lead to a restoration of full diplomatic ties between Israel and Turkey, including the reopening of embassies. There have even been reports that Erdoğan would visit Israel and the Palestinian territories. While reports of the deal have appeared in Turkish media and have cited Turkish leaders, the Israeli government has denied that a deal is imminent. Koplow considers the impetus for reconciliation on the Turkish side has come from two sources—pressure from the U.S., and a string of foreign policy failures over the past year, asserting to the effect that "The Turkish government believes that making up with Israel will alleviate some of the recent tension with the U.S., and President Obama reportedly emphasized his expectation that Erdoğan make tangible moves toward patching things up." The U.S. has been highly involved in resurrecting the relationship of its two key Middle East allies. In March 2013, during his publicised trip to Israel, President Barack Obama persuaded Israeli Prime Minister Benjamin Netanyahu to call Erdoğan and apologise for the deaths of the Turkish citizens aboard the *Mavi Marmara.* After the call, Erdoğan's office issued a statement saying that Turkey valued its "friendship" with Israel. Yet since then, negotiations on restoring ties have been sluggish, despite several rounds of talks over compensation. Some in Israel are sceptical of Erdoğan's true intentions in the negotiations. "I'm not certain that Erdoğan is committed to a deal, as long as he demands the removal of the blockade on Gaza, there is no deal as far as Israel is concerned," according to Efraim Inbar. While it remains uncertain if Erdoğan is truly motivated to restore ties with Israel, on a geopolitical level, a Turkish–Israeli alliance would enable both countries to confront a myriad of regional threats. "An Israeli–Turkish alliance makes sense in a lot of ways. Both countries have need of countering and containing Iranian regional influence, both countries border an increasingly unstable Syria and both countries can benefit from Israel's natural gas finds as Turkey is a large energy importer while Israel is now poised to be an exporter," Koplow contends. He further opines, "Turkish domestic politics reward Israel-bashing, and Turkey's open support for Hamas and the Muslim Brotherhood, do not endear it to Israelis. Israel is extremely unpopular with Turkish voters, and so no party in government is going to go out of its way to cultivate strong ties with Israel." Like most Muslim leaders, Erdoğan has taken up the Palestinian cause to bolster his political standing. According to Inbar, "there definitely is a widespread sympathy for the Palestinians among the Turks, this puts Israel at a disadvantage." At the same time, despite the secular opposition's recent gains ahead of municipal elections, there still isn't a viable alternative to Erdoğan that Israel could establish warmer relations with. As Koplow puts it, "Erdoğan's future looks weaker than it once did, but there is no plausible opponent who can replace him in the foreseeable future. Turkey's opposition parties are largely feckless and do not compete on a national scale with the AKP." While it is unlikely that Turkish–Israeli ties will return to their pre-Erdoğan days, it is felt that an arrangement similar to what Israel and Egypt share—here the countries don't have a particularly warm relationship, but cooperate on economic and security matters—could be an option. As such, despite potential political drawbacks of restoring relations for Erdoğan who will probably continue to promote the Palestinian cause and criticise Israel, Inbar still believes it is in Israel's long-term interest to work with Turkey when he makes the statement that "Turkey is an important regional actor, it is a country with a large Muslim identity, and we would like to have relations with these types of countries, because we would like to dilute the religious dimensions to the Arab-Israeli conflict," and adds that "The ball is not in Jerusalem's court, it is in Ankara's."[71]

From an understanding and analysis of the vacillation in the Israel-Turkey relations over the last two decades or so, it can be inferred that one of the reasons for the endurance of the Turkish–Israeli relations despite far-reaching changes in Turkey's foreign policy in the decade of the 2000s is that the two states have no serious problems at the bilateral level. They have never engaged in a war with each other, nor do they pose a strategic menace to one another. On the contrary, the general positive historical bonds between the two nations have contributed to this longevity. [72]

## Notes

1. Akram T. Hawas, "The New Alliance: Turkey and Israel: Is it a Course towards New Division of the Middle East?", The Fourth Nordic Conference on Middle Eastern Studies: The Middle East in Globalizing World, Oslo, August 13-16, 1998: http://org.uib.no/smi/pao/hawas.html
2. Stephen Kinzer, "Quake Relief Shows Israel Feels Deeply For Turkey", August 28, 1999: http://www.nytimes.com/1999/08/28/world/quake-relief-shows-israel-feels-deeply-for-turkey.html
3. Sara Sidner. Ivan Watson and Joe Sterling, CNN, "Israel to Turkey: We Apologize for Deadly Raid on Gaza-Bound Flotilla", March 24, 2013: http://edition.cnn.com/2013/03/22/world/meast/israel-turkey-apology
4. Joel Greenberg and Scott Wilson, "Obama Ends Israel Visit by Brokering End to Dispute with Turkey", March 22, 2013: http://www.washingtonpost.com/world/middle_east/obama-ends-israel-visit-by-honoring-historic-figures/2013/03/22/7a489fc4-92e9-11e2-ba5b-550c7abf6384_story.html
5. Washington Institute, *Timeline of Turkish-Israeli Relations*: http://www.washingtoninstitute.org/documents/44edf1a5d337f.pdf
6. Washington Institute, *Timeline of Turkish-Israeli Relations*: http://www.washingtoninstitute.org/documents/44edf1a5d337f.pdf
7. *Relations between Turkey and Israel*: http://www.mfa.gov.tr/relations-between-turkey-and-israel%20.en.mfa
8. See Carol Migdalovitz, "Israel's Blockade of Gaza, the *Mavi Marmara* Incident, and Its Aftermath", Congressional Research Service (CRS), June 23, 2010; http://www.crs.gov
9. Cited from Matthew Weiss, "Talking Turkey: The Underlying Causes of the Israeli-Turkey Rift", Middle East Institute, Singapore, Policy Papers Series; www.mei.nus.edu.sg
10. George Emanuel Gruen, *Turkey, Israel and the Palestine Question, 1948-1960, A Study in the Diplomacy of Ambivalence* (PhD Dissertation, New York: Columbia University, 1970).
11. Efraim Inbar, *The Israeli-Turkish Entente* (London, King's College, Mediterranean Programme,2001), p.16.
12. Süha Bölükbaşı, "Behind the Turkish-Israeli Alliance—A Turkish View", *Journal of Palestine Studies*, vol.29, no.1, 1999, p.30.
13. Meliha Altunışık, "The Turkish-Israeli Rapprochement in the Post-Cold War Era", Middle Eastern Studies, vol.36, no.2, 2000, p.172.

14. Different terms have been used by different analysts to describe the growing ties between Turkey and Israel. For Bölükbaşı, it was "alliance," for Bengio, "alignment," for Altunışık, "rapprochement," for Inbar "entente" for Robin, "axis" etc.
15. Dietrich Jung and Wolfango Piccoli, "The Turkish Israeli Alignment: Paranoia or Pragmatism?" *Security Dialogue, vol.* 31, no. 1, 2000, pp. 91-104.
16. See Ofra Bengio, *Turkish-Israeli Relationship: Changing Ties of Middle Eastern Outsiders* (Gordonsville, VA, Palgrave Macmillan 2004).
17. *Hurriyet*, February 12, 1996: www.hurriyetdailynews.com
18. Sabri Sayari, "Turkey and the Middle East in the 1980s", *Journal of Palestine Studies*, vol. 26, no. 3, 1997, p.49.
19. Jung and Picolli, "The Turkish Israeli Alignment: Paranoia or Pragmatism?" p. 10.
20. Gencer Özcan, "The Military and the Making of Foreign Policy in Turkey", in *Turkey in World Politics: An Emerging Multiregional Power* ed. Barry Rubin and Kemal Kirişçi (London: Lynne Reiner Publishers, 2001), p. 23.
21. Kemal Kirişçi, "The Future of Turkish Foreign Policy towards the Middle East", in *Turkey in World Politics: An Emerging Multiregional Power* ed. Barry Rubin and Kemal Kirişçi (London: Lynne Reiner Publishers, 2001), pp. 93-94.
22. Talip Küçükcan and Müjge Küçükkeleş, "European Views of Turkish Foreign Policy", *Insight Turkey*, vol. 15, no. 1, 2013, pp. 127-144.
23. Kirişçi, " The Future of Turkish Foreign Policy towards the Middle East."
24. Jung and Picolli, "The Turkish Israeli Alignment: Paranoia or Pragmatism."
25. Özlem Tür, "Turkey and Israel in the 2000s–From Cooperation to Conflict", *Israel Studies*, vol. 17, no.3, 2012, p. 51.
26. Ibid.
27. *Milliyet*, September 21, 2003.
28. *Milliyet*, August 9, 2001.
29. Greg Myre, "Turkish Leader Visits Israel, Offers to Help with Peace Process", Greg Myre, New York Times *New York Times*, May 2, 2005.
30. "Turkey and the Middle East, Erdogan's Travels, The Turkish Prime Minister's Visit to Israel was Aimed Partly at America", *The Economist*, May 5, 2005.
31. Yaakov Katz, "Israel May Sell Arrow and Ofek to Turkey", *The Jerusalem Post*, November 2, 2007.
32. "Damascus Confirms Channel with Israel", *The Jerusalem Post*, March 30, 2008.
33. Yaakov Katz "Peres, Gul at Odds over Iran Nuke Threat", *The Jerusalem Post*, November 13, 2007.
34. "Stormy Debate in Davos over Gaza, Turkish PM Walks Out after Verbally Clashing with Israeli President over Gaza War", *Al Jazeera*, January 29, 2009.
35. "Hundreds of Thousands Protest in Turkey against Israeli Offensive,"*Hurriyet*, January 4, 2009; http://arama.hurriyet.com.tr/arsivnews.aspx?id=10695842
36. "Livni, Turkish FM Hold Secret Reconciliation Talks", *Haaretz*, March 5, 2009.
37. "Turkey, Israel in Secret Talks for Swift End to Diplomatic Crisis", *Hurriyet*, March 2009.
38. "Netanyahu: Turkey Can't be 'Honest Broker' in Syria Talks," *Haaretz*, October 18, 2009.
39. "Stormy Debate in Davos over Gaza, Turkish PM Walks Out after Verbally Clashing with Israeli President over Gaza War", *Al Jazeera*, January 29, 2009.
40. "Turkish TV Show has IDF Soldiers 'Killing' Palestinian Kids", *Ynetnews,* June 5, 2010.

41. "Israel-Turkey Tensions High over TV Series", *CNN*, January 12, 2010; http://edition.cnn.com/2010/WORLD/meast/01/12/turkey.israel/index.html
42. "Ayalon to 'Behave Diplomatically' in Future", *Ynetnews*, January 13, 2010; http://www.ynetnews.com/articles/0,7340,L-3833669,00.html
43. Yaakov Katz, "Shin Bet: Hamas Operating in Turkey, China", *The Jerusalem Post*, August 9, 2011; http://www.jpost.com/Middle-East/Shin-Bet-Hamas-operating-in-Turkey-China
44. For details on the Gaza Blockade and the *Mavi Marmara* incident, see Carol Migdalovitz, "Israel's Blockade of Gaza, the *Mavi Marmara* Incident, and Its Aftermath", Congressional Research Service (CRS), June 23, 2010; http://www.crs.gov
45. Black, Ian and Haroon Siddique, "Q&A: The Gaza Freedom Flotilla", *The Guardian*, May 31, 2010; http://www.theguardian.com/world/2010/may/31/q-a-gaza-freedom-flotilla
46. Tia Goldengerb, "Pro-Palestinian Aid Flotilla Sets Sail for Gaza", May 30, 2010; http://www.utsandiego.com/news/2010/may/30/pro-palestinian-aid-flotilla-sets-sail-for-gaza/
47. Noah Kosharek, Liel Kyzer, Barak Ravid, "Israel Transfers Hundreds of Gaza Flotilla Activists to Airport for Deportation", *Haaretz*, June 1, 2010; http://www.haaretz.com/news/diplomacy-defense/israel-transfers-hundreds-of-gaza-flotilla-activists-to-airport-for-deportation-1.293634
48. "Turkey Condemns Israel over Deadly Attack on Gaza Aid Flotilla", London: *The Telegraph*, May 31, 2010; http://www.telegraph.co.uk/news/worldnews/middleeast/palestinianauthority/7789077/Turkey-condemns-Israel-over-deadly-attack-on-Gaza-aid-flotilla.html
49. "Turkey Downgrades Ties with Israel", *Al Jazeera*, September 02, 2011; http://www.aljazeera.com/news/middleeast/2011/09/2011927226423902.html
50. Sebnem Arsu and Alan Cowell, "Turkey Expels Israeli Envoy in Dispute over Raid", *The New York Times*, September 2, 2011; http://www.nytimes.com/2011/09/03/world/middleeast/03turkey.html?_r=1&ref=middleeast
51. Maayan Lubell, "Israel Hopes to Mend Ties with Turkey: Govt Official", *Thomson Reuters Foundation*, September 2 2011; http://www.trust.org/item/?map=israel-hopes-to-mend-ties-with-turkey-govt-official
52. "Hamas Welcomes Turkey Move to Expel Israeli Envoy", *The Egyptian Gazette*, September 2 2011; www.egyptiangazette.net
53. Aviel Magnezi, "Erdogan Painted Himself into a Corner", *Ynet news.com*, April 9, 2011; http://www.ynetnews.com/articles/0,7340,L-4117626,00.html
54. Selcan Hacaoglu and Aron Heller, "Turkey: Israel Possibly Target of More Sanctions", *Huffington Post*, September 6, 2011; http://www.huffingtonpost.com/2011/09/06/turkey-israel-sanctions_n_950017.html
55. "Barak on Turkey: This Wave will Pass", *Ynetnews*, September 8, 2011; http://www.ynetnews.com/articles/0,7340,L-4119539,00.html & Herb Keinon, "Erdogan Threatens to Send Gunboats with next Flotilla," *The Jerusalem Post*, August 9, 2011 http://www.jpost.com/Diplomacy-and-Politics/Erdogan-threatens-to-send-gunboats-with-next-flotilla
56. Benhorin, Yitzhak, "Obama Urges Erdogan to Resolve Crisis with Israel", *Ynetnews*, September 21, 2011; http://www.ynetnews.com/articles/0,7340,L-4125187,00.html

57. "Turkish FM Defines Israeli Attack on Gaza as A Crime of Humanity", *The Journal of Turkish Weekly*, November 16, 2012; http://www.turkishweekly.net/news/144847/turkish-fm-defines-israeli-attack-on-gaza-as-a-crime-of-humanity.html
58. Emre Peker, "Turkey Labels Israel a Terrorist State", *The Wall Street Journal*, November 19, 2012; http://online.wsj.com/news/articles/SB10001424127887323353204578128880612421650?mg=reno64-wsj&url=http%3A%2F%2Fonline.wsj.com%2Farticle%2FSB100014
59. Nathaniel Botwinick, "Turkish PM Erdogan: Zionism Is 'a Crime Against Humanity' Like 'Anti-Semitism or Fascism'", *National Review Online*, February 28, 2013; http://www.nationalreview.com/corner/341877/turkish-pm-erdogan-zionism-crime-against-humanity-anti-semitism-or-fascism-nathaniel-b; Joe Sterling and Jill Dougherty, "Kerry Calls Turkish Prime Minister's Remark about Zionism 'Objectionable'", March 1, 2013, *CNN*; http://edition.cnn.com/2013/03/01/world/meast/turkey-israel/index.html?iref=allsearch
60. "Israel: Turk's Remarks Criticised", *The New York Times*, February 28, 2013; http://www.nytimes.com/2013/03/01/world/middleeast/israel-turks-remarks-criticized.html?_r=1&
61. Gavriel Fiske, "Turkish PM Says Zionism Comments Misinterpreted", *The Times of Israel*, March 20, 2013; http://www.timesofisrael.com/turkish-pm-says-zionism-comments-misinterpreted/
62. Joel Greenberg and Scott Wilson, "Obama Ends Israel Visit by Brokering End to Dispute with Turkey", *The Washington Post*, March 22, 2013; http://www.washingtonpost.com/world/middle_east/obama-ends-israel-visit-by-honoring-historic-figures/2013/03/22/7a489fc4-92e9-11e2-ba5b-550c7abf6384_story.html
63. "Israel Behind Coup to Oust Morsi, Turkish PM Erdoğan Says", *Hurriyet*, August 21, 2013; http://www.hurriyetdailynews.com/turkey-has-evidence-that-israel-was-behind-egypt-coup-erdogan.aspx?pageID=517&nID=52876&NewsCatID=338
64. Gavriel Fiske and Stuart Winer, "US, Egypt Pan Turkish PM for Saying Israel Ousted Morsi", *Times of Israel*, August 20, 2013; http://www.timesofisrael.com/us-pans-turkish-pm-for-saying-israel-ousted-morsi/
65. Ofra Bengio, "Altercating Interests and Orientations between Israel and Turkey: A View from Israel", *Insight Turkey*, vol. 11, no.2, 2009, pp. 43-55.
66. "Will Regional and Domestic Challenges Force Renewed Israel-Turkey Normalization?", April 3, 2014; http://www.algemeiner.com.
67. "Israel and Turkey: Old Friends Can't be Foes", February 22, 2014; http://english.alarabiya.net/en/views/news/world/2014/02/22/Israel-And-Turkey-Old-Friends-Can-t-Be-Foes.html
68. "Will Regional and Domestic Challenges Force Renewed Israel-Turkey Normalization?"
69. "Ibid.
70. "Turkey-Israel Relations 'Close' to Normalization: FM Davutoğlu"; www.hurriyetdailynews.com
71. "Will Regional and Domestic Challenges Force Renewed Israel-Turkey Normalization?"
72. Bengio, "Altercating Interests and Orientations between Israel and Turkey."

# 8
# Turkey's Middle Eastern Policy: A European Attitude

*Davood Kiani*

## Introduction

During the recent decade, Turkey has tried to introduce itself not only as a Middle Eastern actor but also as an active member of the Islamic world and a European and development-oriented Muslim country through taking initiative in regional and international relations. Turkey has found a significant role and status in the Middle East and plays an important role in regional equations. In addition to active participation in solving regional crises, it has not forgotten its cultural role and has tried to portray itself as a modernist and Islamic country on the international scene. However, Turkey is not going to jeopardise its national interests to obtain that status. The actions made by Turkey during recent years indicate that it intends to realise its goal which is presenting a new face of itself as a bridge between the Islamic world and the West by adopting a realistic approach and pursuing moderate stances.[1] It seems that Turkey has managed to achieve this goal to a great extent.

An important point is that Turkey is trying to become a major regional actor instead of having a neutral role in the Middle Eastern affairs. Since the beginning of the third millennium, Ankara has showed that it is dissatisfied with its weak role and status in the Middle East and has tried to play new regional roles by making efforts including playing a mediatory role between Palestine and Israel, paying attention to the Conference of Arab League, participation in the UN peacekeeping force in Lebanon,[2] collaborating with NATO forces in Afghanistan, founding

D-8 group, playing a role in Iran's nuclear programme and establishing balanced relations with Syria, Iran and Iraq. Besides, Turkish leaders have tried to play a more effective role in solving Balkan crises and disputes in the Caucasus and Central Asia.

On the other hand, Turkey continues its efforts to join the EU. Since the establishment of the Republic of Turkey, the top priority of its foreign policy has been forging close relations with the West and especially with Europe. Although, Turkey's relations with the U.S. and Europe have experienced so many ups and downs, in a general perspective, Turkey has never put aside the West from its top priorities in its foreign policy agenda and this has remained intact up to now.[3]

This article tries, in addition to examining the reasons for changes in Turkish foreign policy towards the Middle East and the Islamic world after coming to power of the Justice and Development party, analyse the attitude of Westerners, especially Europeans towards this development. However, Turkey as the heir of the Ottoman Empire can play both a facilitating and a constraining role in implementing the EU policies towards the Middle East. It is worth noting that before the collapse of the Ottoman Empire in 1923, it dominated the Arab world and North Africa for four centuries.

This article is organised in three sections. In the first section, Turkish foreign policy, especially after the coming to power of the Justice and Development Party, is studied. In the second section, Turkey's status in the EU security policy and strategy is examined and in the final section, the EU attitude towards Turkey's regional policies in the region is explored.

## Foundations of Turkish Foreign Policy

Essentially, the foreign policy of governments reflects the definition made by the ruling elite of themselves and their government. Despite changes and revisions made in the Turkish foreign policy based on changing regional and international circumstances, it can be said that Turkish foreign policy orientations are much influenced by principles involved in the foundation of the modern Turkey that could be called Kemalism.[4] Kemalism is based on six principles stipulated in the Constitution of 1937:

(i) Nationalism; (ii) Secularism; (iii) Republicanism; (iv) Populism; (v) Statism; and (vi) Reformism.[5]

The aforementioned principles, in many cases, have had direct impact on Turkish foreign policy. Turkish leaders inspired by these principles constructed a society characterised by two factors: the first of them made Turkey distant from regional countries and their problems and the second led Turkish foreign policy towards the West;[6] therefore, until the 1960s that Turkey had not faced regional problems in its foreign policy, regional issues were of second hand importance.

In the light of the abovementioned principles, Turkey has defined the following policies as its strategies of foreign policy:

- Exploiting Western economic and industrial power;
- Making efforts to be identified as a European nation and to be accepted in the Western civilisation;
- Not intervening in the Middle Eastern countries;
- Avoiding intervention in disputes between regional countries;
- Expanding bilateral relations with all regional countries;
- Expanding economic and trade relations with regional countries.

Given the philosophy of the founders of the Republic of Turkey, the Look to the West policy as the first principle of Kemalism, had influenced Turkish foreign policy stances towards the Middle East, so that after the Second World War, the Middle Eastern region had been of second hand importance for Turkish foreign policy.[7] Nationalist Turks believe that Turkey has become a European country since the conclusion of the Carlowitz Treaty in 1699 and the Paris Peace Treaty of 1856 has reemphasised this.

Based on the heritage of Kemalism, for a long time, religion had been considered a sign of traditional regimes and governments and at the same time laicism had become a boundary between intellectualism and dogmatism, progress and conservatism, and finally modernity and tradition. Laicism considered religion as something outside of the realm of society and as a personal affair. Kemalism built the laic republic of Turkey by equating Islam with economic, political, cultural and social backwardness and religion was subjected to the secular government of Turkey.[8]

Radical changes in the scene of international politics and their impact on Turkey, on the one hand, and the relative political maturity of parties and groups in this country, on the other hand, entered Turkey into a new stage of radical changes. Economic and political policies of Turgut Özal during the 1980s interpreted in political circles as Turkey's *Glasnost* and *Perestroika* and the consequences of the end of the Cold War have strongly influenced Turkish foreign and domestic policies.[9] The implementation of these policies along with the weakening of the durable and historical tradition of statism in Turkey paved the way for the growth of a civil society and a relatively powerful private sector during the 1990s and the beginning years of the 21st century.[10] This led to the extensive entrance of Islamists into the political scene. However, this trend was gradual and finally was accepted by the secular elite and the military as a fact.

## Coming to Power of the Justice and Development Party and the Construction of a New Identity for Turkey

Cultural and political identity with the society, capitalism, and Turkey's enthusiasm to join the EU are among the determining factors for the coming to power of the Justice and Development Party in 2002.[11] Recep Tayyip Erdoğan, leader of Justice and Development Party, was clever enough to realise that reforms prescribed by the EU, called Copenhagen criteria, were leading to the consolidation of democracy as well as the weakening of the military and secular parties. For this reason, the most important goal of Justice and Development party was giving priority to civil society over garrison state. Erdoğan has an extraordinary skill for establishing contact with ordinary people and at the same time, has necessary prowess for pursuing and implementing his policies and promises. From Justice and Development party leaders' point of view, the EU is somewhere in which military institution is subject to civil institution and in case of Turkey's joining the EU, it would be possible to protect Turkey, like the new Europe, forever from a military coup.[12]

For this reason, Justice and Development party has placed membership in the EU on its foreign policy agenda (Hale, 2006: 160)[13] and thereby attracted the support of the majority of the middle class, businessmen, and many liberal intellectuals. Egemen Bağis, Turkish minister for EU Affairs and chief negotiator of Turkey in accession talks with the European Union said: "We are located in the extreme western point of the east and in the extreme eastern point of the west. We are the representative of international values. 25 million European Muslims and 5 million Turkish Diasporas in Europe are closely monitoring the process of Turkey's membership in the EU..."[14] From a certain angle, the emergence and victory of Justice and Development party is considered a destructuring action, but the emphasis made by the party on democracy, free market economy, and Western legal and value system is in fact respecting the democratic rule in the political scene of Turkey.

After coming to power, Justice and Development party declared that Turkey is in a unique situation for serving as a bridge and making conciliation between Islam, democracy and secularism. Turkey protested against the idea of the "clash of civilizations" and at the same time, Washington wanted to introduce Turkey as a role model for the Islamic world.[15]

Since 2002 that the Justice and Development party has come to power, Turkish foreign policy has been theorised by Ahmet Davutoğlu, the Turkish foreign minister.[16] Davutoğlu who studied international relations and taught for many years in universities in Turkey and Malaysia and also is recently being considered as the potential successor of Erdoğan, reflected his views in a book titled *Strategic Depth*. He argues that Turkish foreign policy does not enjoy equilibrium and much emphasis on relation with Western Europe and the U.S. while neglecting relation with other countries, especially, in the Middle East is a mistake. He believes that the republic of Turkey has neglected relation with the countries situated in North Africa and in the Middle East and today Turkey needs to play greater roles. The leaders of Justice and Development Party want to reach an equilibrium point against their dependencies on the West and do not intend to shift their policy of alliance with the West. The Justice and Development Party in its proceeding on this new path, is trying, in domestic issues, to return to its original and historical bases and to obtain national consensus along these lines. This would be the reminiscent of a Turkey which is the heir of a multi-national Empire dominating the Middle East, North Africa, Balkans, and some parts of Central Europe. This emphasis on the Ottoman heritage is not a part of the Islamisation of Turkey and its foreign policy; rather it is an action for adjusting Kemalism with Turkey's geopolitical realities.[17]

In Davutoğlu's belief, Turkey like Russia, Egypt and Iran is a multi-faced country with multiple identities and should formulate its foreign policy accordingly. Turkey is neighbouring the Middle East, the Caucasus, Europe and Balkans, but it is not considered a part of them. However, it should have constructive interaction with all of them. Orienting towards one side creates disequilibrium in the Turkish foreign policy. He argues that Turkey enjoys strategic depth because of its particular geographical and historical situation. For this reason, Turkey is among the small countries that could be called central powers. He believes that Turkey should not limit itself to playing a regional role in Balkans or the Middle East, because it is a central and not a regional power—therefore, it should have a leadership role in several regions, something that gives strategic importance in the international system.[18]

The components of the doctrine of strategic depth developed by Davutoğlu are as follows: (i) Turkey should play an active role commensurate with its glorious history and geographical depth; (ii) to better performing this role, Turkey should invest in its soft power, because it has historical and cultural ties with all of the abovementioned regions; (iii) internal political institutions of Turkey could serve as a role model for regional countries; (iv) Turkey's economy is a powerful arm for supporting these relations; (v) Turkey should play an important role in the management of international and regional crises; (vi) Turkey can remove the need for foreign intervention by economic, political and security cooperation with regional countries; and (vii) instead of insisting on joining the EU and paying heavy costs for this, Turkey should focus on regional countries, especially those ones that in the past had been under the rule of the Ottoman Empire.[19]

Analysts evaluate the new Turkish foreign policy as Ankara's new role in the international equations; a role similar to that of the Ottoman Empire during the last five centuries. Therefore, Turkey's new foreign policy was defined as neo-Ottomanism with the following characteristics:

- Operationalising the politics and adopting the policy of "zero problems with neighbours": Along these lines, Turkey tries to solve its politico-cultural differences with its neighbours and some ethnic groups in the region including Kurds and also with Armenia. Turks invoke a Turkish proverb suggesting that "a good neighbour is closer than a brother"; therefore, Turks want to end the decades of distrust with their neighbours.[20]
- Relative satisfaction with this policy in the east and west: neo-Ottomanism is no longer the Turkish Empire in Balkans and the Middle East, rather it is combined with a moderate secularism in domestic affairs and an active diplomacy in foreign affairs. According to this approach, Turkey's behaviour is formed by the power of political, economic, diplomatic and cultural norms as well as its influence in the territories that had belonged previously to the Ottoman Empire.
- Flexibility for adjustment: Neo-Ottomanism regards Turkey as a regional superpower. This strategic vision reflects the historical experiences of Eastern Roman and Ottoman Empires. Turkey tries to set aside dogmatism in the realm of international politics and to find a place for itself in the international equations by adopting flexibility.
- Accepting the importance of the Islamic world: Kemalism claims that Turkey is more characterised by its Western identity rather than Eastern identity and places Turkey's Western identity in opposition to its Islamic identity and legacy.[21] Flexibility and pragmatism are missing in Kemalist policies regarding the East, while neo-Ottomanism accepts it as a geopolitical fact.
- Developing coordinated relations with the world powers: Turkey has established balanced relations with the five permanent members of the Security Council. Davutoğlu said in the Conference of foreign diplomats residing in Turkey that Turkey should become one of the ten most developed countries in the world by 2023 at the 100th anniversary of the establishment of the republic of Turkey and to realise this goal, it seeks to forge balanced relations with its neighbours and world powers. He believes that foreign policy is dynamic, while Turkish foreign policy orientation was static lacking

> an historical–geopolitical identity. He believes that because of the lack of a sound understanding of Turkey's facts regarding identity, this country got into trouble with its neighbours. This strategy did not achieve anything for Turkey, except that all of Turkey's energy was spent on managing problems with its neighbours.[22]

In Erdoğan's belief, Turkey is the only country in the Middle East which could interact with a set of heterogeneous countries and regions such as Iran, Israel, the U.S., Arab nations, and Europe; an advantage considered as Turkey's soft power that only few countries are enjoying. Turks believe that to compensate their historical humility by Europeans, they should be forcing Europeans to supplicate them, because Turkey is situated in a critical region being important in terms of energy and political considerations and it is Europe that needs Turkey. Turks believe that Turkey has soft power for managing problems in the Islamic world and the West should admit it because Turkey is among the top 50 most-populated countries in the world with a Muslim majority and is the only country that is a member of NATO and in the process of joining the EU. According to this attitude, before the official declaration of the victory of the ruling Justice and Development Party in the elections in June 2011, Erdoğan beside his wife, Amina, appeared in the balcony of the central office of his party in the downtown of Ankara and addressed a huge crowd of his cheering supporters. He said that it was a victory "for Bosnia as much as Istanbul, Beirut as much as Izmir, Damascus as much as Ankara, Ramallah, Nablus, Jenin, Western Bank, Quds, Gaza as much as Diyarbakir. It was a victory for the Middle East, the Caucasus, Balkans and Europe."[23]

The geographical map Erdoğan drew in his speech contains territories that had formed in the past the Ottoman Empire. The Erdoğan government well knows that for realising its goals, it should attract the positive view of the public opinion in the Arab world and one of the tactics in this regard is supporting the rights of Palestinians. Today, while Arab public opinion witnesses the inertia and fragility of their conservative and unelected government, it is the modern and at the same time, Islamist government of Turkey that is on the forward front of confronting Israel and apparently pays the costs of its action.

Therefore, despite the fact that Arabs historically have not had a positive mentality towards Ottoman Turks and their long domination over Arab territories, they see that Ankara with its power can stand up against the expansionist policies of the Tel Aviv rulers and defend the rights of Arabs and Palestinians.[24]

The difference between the status and approach of Turkey and those of its rival countries is that Turkey's power and its options for solving that Middle East crisis have a pragmatist nature, while the approach taken by some other Islamic countries are much more idealistic. Having adopted a realist approach instead of a sentimental and ideological approach, the Turks tend to attract the support of the international community and the world public opinion and other governments by advancing constructive solutions while relying upon their power. This distinctive feature has made Ankara's statesmen hopeful for obtaining the leadership of the Islamic world, a position achieved by its historical and geographical similarities with the West making this country the best option and channel for establishing communication between the West and Islam. The leaders of the Justice and Development Party, were formerly Turks who had had a strategy but not an ideology. Now, Turkey is seeking to inject ideological content into its national strategy and foreign policy.

## Interactions between Europe and the Middle East

The EU policy towards the Middle East is essentially influenced by the three factors of geographical closeness, energy security, and historical memory. For this reason, the EU considers other existing issues in the Middle Eastern region such as terrorism, arms race, Palestinian–Israeli peace process in the framework of abovementioned factors which influence each other. In addition to factors such as geographical closeness and energy security, historical memory of Europeans, especially European countries such as Britain, France, Italy and Germany shows that each of them has been interested in or has had influence on, according to different issues, one or more Middle Eastern countries. Due to the unpleasant historical record of some of these countries that had resulted from their past actions, their leaders have tried to pursue an independent policy towards the Middle East to clean this negative image. Obviously, because of the lack of active participation of Europe along with the strategic failure of the U.S. (because of the influence of the Israeli and Jewish lobby in the process of policy-making in its foreign affairs resulting in the lack of innovation in approaches taken by Washington) they incurred heavy security and political costs at the regional and international levels.

The three abovementioned factors have led the EU to make the providing of stability in the Middle East as its main strategy for the region. Stability in the Middle East not only increases the level of security in Europe and prevents many cases of illegal immigrations to this continent but also ensures energy transfer to European markets and the development of economic relations with regional countries.

Along these lines and to prevent the paying of more political and security costs in the Middle East, the EU and European powers have pursued and implemented the following security strategies:

- Advocating democracy and its promotion;
- Making efforts to create an international order based on multilateralism;
- Confronting traditional and modern threats.

On the other hand, Brussels pursues its "stabilization" strategy in the Middle East in the framework of different and at the same time, overlapping levels of partnership. Therefore, it can be said that the EU Middle Eastern policy for realising the abovementioned strategies focuses on these areas:

- European–Mediterranean partnership
- Europe–Persian Gulf partnership
- Participation in Palestinian–Israeli peace process.

World developments during the past two decades, especially those related to the Arab Spring, have provided new opportunities for major regional and extra-regional powers to play an active role. In the process, a new room for manoeuvre has been opened for European powers. Following September 11, 2001, the EU has tried to pay more attention to the Middle Eastern issues; the relevant four cases will be discussed here.

### *Terrorism*

In a list presented by Javier Solana, the then EU's high representative for Common Foreign and Security Policy, terrorism is defined as a strategic threat for the EU. From Solana's point of view, Europe is not only a target for terrorist operations but also it is a place for the growth and formation of terrorist groups. September 11 attacks brought about a paradigmatic change in the international politics and also changed the perception of the global phenomenon of terrorism and how to confront it. Along these lines, given the terrorist attacks on Madrid and London after the September 11 events, European countries felt more than ever the necessity of countering this threat.

### *Weapons of Mass Destruction*

The danger of the proliferation of the weapons of mass destruction is one of the other security concerns of the EU indicated in its new security document. According to this document, the proliferation of the weapons of mass destruction is among the greatest security threats against the EU. Generally, this document mentions three dangers related to the proliferation of these weapons at the global level and especially, in regions such as the Middle East:

The first danger is the proliferation of biological, chemical and radiological agents in regions such as the Middle East. This threat results to some extent from the previous use of these agents in the region by the Iraqi government during its eight-year war with Iran in Halabja. The horrific memory of this event led European countries to emphasise the necessity of controlling and eradicating these agents in other parts of the world.

The second danger is the proliferation of nuclear weapons. This technology has developed especially increasingly after the collapse of the Soviet Union. The obtaining of nuclear weapons by countries such as North Korea, India and Pakistan has heightened the danger of the occurrence of arms race among regional countries. On the other hand, all the efforts made for creating a Middle East free of nuclear weapons have failed. The existence of Israel in this region and its equipment with nuclear weapons has added to security concerns.

The third danger is the probability of terrorist groups' access to these weapons. According to this document, terrorist groups' access to the weapons of mass destruction could pose threats unknown until now for the EU. The extra-territorial nature of these threats makes countering them too difficult, if not impossible.[25]

### *Ethnic Disputes*

With the disintegration and division of Yugoslavia, the EU contemplated the danger of regional disputes within its borders. Failure in confronting this phenomenon by European countries increased the EU concerns over the occurrence of similar events. The existence of different and sometimes divergent stances (like differences between Britain and France, on the one hand and Germany on the other hand over how to deal with events in Yugoslavia) intensified these concerns. According to the new security document, regional disputes could destroy the life of people, social and economic infrastructures and threaten the freedom of societies and human rights including the rights of minorities. These disputes could bring about extremism, terrorism and failed states. The instances of these disputes could be seen in the Middle East comparable to what is happening in Iraq and Afghanistan or what has occurred as a result of Arab revolutions in Egypt and Syria. According to analysts, one of the reasons for the reluctance of the West to intervene militarily in Syria against Bashar al-Assad is their concern about the coming to power of extremists and Salafists under the guise of opposition forces.

### *Energy Security*

Increase in the EU demand for energy, on the one hand, and the domination of Russia over the EU markets on the other hand, have led European countries to devise a new strategy to diversify their energy sources. The concerns of the EU about providing energy security dates back to the Arab oil embargo in the early 1970s. This embargo made clear three issues for the EU. First, it reminded EU countries that there is a pressing need for them to cooperate and coordinate their efforts in policy-making in the field of energy security. Secondly, an institutionalised mechanism for increasing cooperation to face these kinds of events in the future is necessary. Thirdly, a consensus should be built that European countries should adopt a clear strategy preventing them from becoming the victim of energy policies in the future. In 1991, the EU declared its Energy Charter Treaty aimed at increasing cooperation in the field of energy and diversifying the sources of energy supply to the EU. This declaration was a prelude to the European Energy Charter Treaty in 1994 which was implemented in 1998 and provided a framework for international cooperation in the field of energy security. So far, 15 European countries have signed this treaty. It was an effort to provide grounds for increasing the level of investments in energy sector, to establish an energy free market, to freely transfer energy via pipelines, and to create a mechanism for the settlement of disputes. Diversifying energy sources and also using alternative energies have been among the solutions presented by the EU to deal with the energy issue. However, the heavy cost of using alternative energies has forced the EU to consider seriously using oil and gas production centres, especially those located in the Persian Gulf.

## Turkey and Security Issues in Europe

Turkey has introduced itself as a security actor in Europe since the 1950s by joining the North Atlantic Treaty Organization (NATO). Also, Turkish leaders are always trying to show their capabilities in security issues to the EU.[26] However, at the time of the ratification of the new EU political and security document in 2003, Turkey's membership of the EU was not mentioned. Turkish officials worried that this new document substitutes NATO's security policies, because in that case, it would be likely that Turkey will be left aside by the European security system and the EU on the whole. From the analysts' point of view, the reconstruction of European security after the Cold War has not been in the favour of Turkey. With the reduction of the level of military threats, Turkey could no longer present itself as an important member of the European system.[27]

After initial efforts to Europeanise the security of the EU and with the revival of the Western European Union (WEU) in 1992, Turkey could obtain a place for itself in the EU security system. This initial optimism for Europeanising security ended with the efforts made by Britain and France for operationalising ESDP in 1998 in the framework of the Saint-Malo

Summit. With the ratification of this programme, WEU lost its existential philosophy and Turkey's hope for playing a role in the EU was dashed.[28] Therefore, Turkey's participation in the EU security system was limited to the cases in which the EU needed Turkey's collaboration. However, Turkey could use its veto power in NATO for putting European countries under pressure. Given the fact that NATO is the main institution providing security for the EU which is lacking an efficient military force, Turkey could pursue its policies through NATO. Turkey's efforts for re-entering European security system led to the holding of a conference with the participation of both sides in 2001 in Ankara and also the ratification of the Nice Implementation Document (NID). Based on the Ankara agreement, Turkey could automatically participate in Berlin Plus operations.[29] Also, according to the Nice Implementation Document, the EU operations outside its borders are dependent on negotiation and agreement with the country in which the operation is to be carried out. At the same time, to alleviate Turkey's concerns, the EU declared that participation in Berlin Plus operations is only possible for those European countries that are members of NATO or have joined the programme of Partnership for Peace. Therefore, Cyprus was left aside by the scope of these operations. Generally, by the concluded agreements, Turkey relinquished its veto power in NATO and EU could begin its operations in the framework of Berlin Plus in 2003. Despite the fact that Turkey and the EU have reached some agreements, they still have some differences on certain subjects, including differences on the manner in which Cyprus can participate in the EU military and security operations and on the issue of which items should be included in the operations of Berlin Plus. Although due to these differences, Turkey did not participate in some of the EU operations in Georgia and Iraq; however, in Turkey's view, the EU security policies have had direct impact on Turkey's security, because seven operations out of the twelve operations carried out under ESDP and also nine other supplementary operations have taken place in the borders of this country.[30] Being aware of the necessity of cooperation on security issues, Turkey and the EU could pass and implement bilateral agreements. Changes in the security situation in the international system after 2001 have been one of the main factors of expanding cooperation between the two sides:

First, Turkey as one of the greatest energy importers is considered an important market for oil and gas exporting countries. On the other hand, Turkey's geographical situation has made it a transit route for transferring energy from regions such as the Middle East, Central Asia and the Caucasus, and also the Mediterranean and Black Sea.

Increase in the EU's demand for energy led the EU to have a special look at Turkey. According to the estimates made by the International Energy Agency (IEA), the EU's demand for oil and gas has increased annually by 2.9% from 2000 to 2010 and it will amount to 1.6% from 2010 to 2030.

Given the EU's pressing need for energy, this factor has become one of EU's security concerns. Turkey's location in the route of energy transfer gives a special status to this country. About 70% of the world oil and gas sources are produced and transferred in the northern, southern and eastern parts of Turkey. Being aware of this situation, Turkish leaders are trying to construct and use pipelines for transferring energy to EU countries. Among them the following pipelines could be mentioned:

- Baku-Tbilisi-Ceyhan pipeline transferring Azerbaijan's oil to Turkey via Georgia's soil. This pipeline transfers one million barrels oil per day.
- Baku-Tbilisi-Erzurum pipeline transferring the gas of Shah Deniz field in Azerbaijan to Turkey via Georgia. This pipeline was operationalised in 2006 and its capacity of gas transfer amounted to 26 million cubic meters in 2012.
- Blue Stream pipeline transferring the gas of Russia to Turkey via Moldavia, Ukraine and Romania.
- Pipeline between Turkey, Greece and Italy transferring the gas of the Caspian Sea and the Middle East to Europe in the framework of the programme of transferring oil and gas to Europe.

Among other instances, we can mention the Iraq pipeline systems transferring the oil of Kirkuk to Turkey and also the gas pipeline between Iran and Turkey. This contract was signed in 1996 between the two countries transferring gas from Tabriz to Turkey. One of the other energy pipelines that are too important for the EU is the Nabuco line.

This contract was signed in 2009 based on the Ankara agreement and by which the natural gas of Azerbaijan, Turkmenistan and other Caspian Sea basin countries including Iran is transferred to Turkey. The capacity of this gas pipeline is 310 billion cubic meters.[31]

Turkey has introduced itself as an important country in ensuring the energy security for the EU by successfully implementing these projects. Its status is especially strengthened when Russia and European countries enter into conflict with each other over energy exports. For example, differences between Russia and Ukraine in 2009 led to the gas export stoppage from Russia to Europe. Also, European countries urged substituting other energy producing countries for their oil and gas imports in their green energy document due to their vulnerability against Russia's domination over the EU energy market and Russia's political exploitation of its situation. In this document, regions such as the Caspian Sea basin and the Middle Eastern countries have been mentioned. The entrance of these regions into the European energy market provides opportunity for Turkey to play an important role as a transit route for exporting energy to Europe.

Second, with the emergence of terrorism as a security threat in the 21st century, Turkey seized the opportunity to introduce itself as a main actor in struggling against terrorism. Struggling against terrorism is among the common interests between Europe and Turkey. On the other hand, in struggling against terrorism, paying attention to both military and civil capabilities seems necessary. On the one hand, Turkey has acquired both of these capabilities relying upon its experience in struggling against the PKK terrorist group. During recent years, Turkey has found new methods for struggling against terrorist groups through countering PKK. On the other hand, Turkey, on some occasions, has trained the military for struggling against this phenomenon. Finally, Turkey is the only Muslim secular country with a liberal economy in the Middle East. In fact, since the establishment of the Republic of Turkey in 1923, this country has not challenged the European style of life and its modernist values.

The next issue regarding terrorism is related to the efforts made by the European countries and also the reconstruction of their relations with the Islamic countries, especially those situated in the Middle Eastern region.

European countries and the U.S. after coming to power of Obama have placed this policy among their priorities. Turkey as an Islamic country enjoying deep religious, cultural and historical ties with other Islamic countries, on the one hand, and as a country with cultural affinities with the West, on the other hand, has tried to serve as a bridge between the West and Islam.[32] Therefore, Turkey as the country with membership in institutions such as G 20, NATO and Islamic Cooperation Organization can facilitate relations between the West and the Islamic world.

Generally, it seems that Turkey enjoys enough civil capabilities to pursue the EU policies in struggling against terrorism. Turkey could be considered an appropriate country to cooperate in confronting this security phenomenon. Its military strengths and also its historical and cultural ties have provided grounds for struggling against terrorism as well as reducing pessimism between the West and the Islamic world. Turkey could play an important role in neutralising Islamophobia in Europe.

## Turkey, Middle East and the European Union

There is a theoretical complexity in analysing the nature of the European Union foreign policy. Some scholars call the EU as a civilian power, others regard it like a normative or trade power. I am not sure which kind of concept provides a comprehensive understanding of European Union. But I am confident that when the EU comes to the Middle East, it becomes apparent as a geopolitical power because interest and security are top priorities of this Union in the region.

Before explaining the European approach towards Turkey's Middle Eastern foreign policy it is necessary to attract attention to my two pre-assumptions regarding European policy in the Middle East.

- Europe tacitly tries to make the ethnic, identity and religious cleavages in the region alive.
- Among the three possible models of interactions between the three great powers of the region (Iran, Saudi Arabia and Turkey) which include hegemonic model, integration or cooperation model and balance of power model, the EU has long chosen the last one in order not to see establishment of a regional bloc against its interest and security.

Europe has a number of security, economic and identity concerns in the Middle East. These concerns include: security of Israel, security of energy and security of its social identity because of its geographical closeness to the region. Due to these three security concerns, European strategic choice in the Middle East is based on the stabilisation strategy. That is why the Union supports stability in the region more than change.

In this context, Turkey is the key player in meeting European concerns. This country was one of the counties which had recognised Israel in 1949 and the two countries changed diplomats in 1952. The main reason of this was Turkey's wish to reinforce its position in the Western alliance. Despite some tensions between Turkey led by AKP and Israel in the recent decade, Ankara is still committed to fully supporting the peace process treaties.

The shift in Turkish foreign policy regarding regional issues could be seen in Turkey's proactive behaviour towards the Middle East, especially during the recent years. Although, Turkey has deep religious, cultural and historical ties with the Middle Eastern countries, since long time ago and especially during the domination of the Kemalist discourse over its foreign policy, it somehow neglected the Middle East in its foreign policy. This pessimism towards the Middle East resulted to some extent from the prevalent attitude among Turkish leaders that Arab countries were responsible in the collapse of the Ottoman Empire following the First World War.[33]

The coming to power of Justice and Development Party brought about a change in Turkey's attitude towards the Middle East. Emphasising Turkey's cultural and historical affinities with regional countries, new Turkish leaders expressed their will to increasingly play a role in regional affairs. They have tried to establish strategic relations with Middle Eastern countries by leaving aside their previous pessimism towards the region. Making efforts to forge closer relations with Syria (of course before the recent developments in Syria which led Turkey to change radically its policies towards Bashar al-Assad government) can be analysed in this new context. The two countries concluded an agreement to cancel the visa regime. Also, they agreed to establish the Strategic Cooperation Council. Turkey's efforts for closer relations with

Iraq, especially in confronting terrorist actions made by the PKK group have intensified during the recent years. The two countries have signed 48 separate agreements on different issues so far.[34] Also, Turkey has tried to reduce its tensions with the Kurdistan territory, a region that is important to Turkey in terms of security.

One of the other dimensions of Turkey's regional policy in the Middle East are its efforts for mediation in regional disputes. Turkey has played an active role in negotiations for the settlement of the Palestinian issue.[35] Turkey has been the host of five rounds of negotiation between Syria and Israel. It has sent 1000 soldiers to participate in the United Nations Interim Force in Lebanon (UNIFIL). Also, it facilitated negotiations between Mahmoud Abbas and Palestinian officials.

The shift in Turkish foreign policy orientations has made the EU faced with the difficult task of interpreting these developments. Since the beginning of Turkey's accession talks with the EU in 2005, the Middle East has become a test for the degree of accommodating Turkish foreign policy with the values and Middle Eastern policy of European countries. As said before, the emergence of new security issues in the post-Cold War era such as terrorism, ethnic and regional disputes, weapons of mass destruction and energy security have made Europe dependent on the Middle East's security. This has been reflected in the revision of the EU security strategy and the ratification of Brussels 2003 security document on the one hand, and the EU has placed cooperation with other countries in its foreign policy agenda to confront the abovementioned threats on the other. In the process, Turkey has acquired a special status in the EU security strategy in terms of military and civil capabilities. It has a high potential for contributing to the EU security policies due to its force size and military equipment as well as civil characteristics such as geographical situation. Being aware of these characteristics, Turkish leaders have always showed their willingness to provide the EU with its capabilities. Turkey's geographical closeness along with its religious, historical and cultural affinities with the Middle East have provided this possibility for Ankara to play an active role in the new security issues in the EU. Security issues mentioned by the EU according to its new security document are all related somehow with Turkey's situation. Therefore,

Turkey can be an important actor for the EU. Recent developments in the Middle East showed that Turkey in addition to military strengths has extensive potentials in terms of civil capabilities. These characteristics make Turkey an important country for the long term strategy of the EU.

Generally, Turkey's mediation despite its failure between Iran and the West to solve Iran's nuclear dossier, participation in the Middle East peace negotiations, making contact with Hamas movement to encourage it to negotiate with Israel or supporting democratic movements in the Arab world, especially the events in Syria which made Ankara opposed to the Bashar al-Assad government, are instances commensurate with the EU's Middle Eastern policy based on stabilisation to preserve its security and economic interests.

However, the strengths of Turkey's Middle Eastern diplomacy for the EU, are considered its weaknesses. Turkey's action in preserving its political relations with Iran and the continuation of its economic relations with it, despite extensive financial sanctions against Tehran are among the cases that the EU is not happy with it, especially in the condition that Turkey has lowered the level of its economic relations with Iran. Welcoming heightened tensions with Israel aiming at attracting the Arab world public opinion is one of the other of Turkey's Middle Eastern policies denounced by European officials to such an extent that this policy has become one of the other negative factors for Turkey's membership in the EU. Interestingly, since the beginning of Turkey's accession talks with the EU (2005), Turkey has tried to use the Middle East as an advantage for consolidating its diplomatic relations with the EU. Turkish officials first tried to advance Turkey's influence in the Middle East to instigate the EU to accept Turkey's accession. For this reason, the Turks underestimated the EU's foreign policy towards the Middle East. Conversely, some European countries regard Turkey's eastern policy, especially towards the Middle East, as business-like. These countries, especially France express the view that Turkey is too closed to the Middle East to become an EU member. From this point of view, Turkey's accession to the EU means Europe's neighbourhood with Iran, Iraq and Syria that is a neighbourhood with the regions that the EU has tense relations with. Although, given the general approach of the EU to Turkey which is based on opposing its membership, it seems that the neighbourhood of Europe with the abovementioned countries is a pretext rather than an argument. Of course, the stances of European countries regarding Turkey's membership in the EU are not consistent. While France is strongly opposed to Turkey's membership, Britain agrees to it and Germany's stance is close to that of France.

With the beginning of accession talks, Turkey adopted a different policy from that of its European partners towards the Middle East. In fact, Turks tried to adopt a balanced foreign policy towards the countries situated in this region. On the other hand, Turkey has occasionally tried to pursue a close rivalry with the EU in the Middle East.

In general, it can be said that there is a kind of competition and cooperation model between Turkey and the EU in the Middle East. While Turkey is an appropriate option for implementing the EU security strategy and also the general policy of stabilisation that EU is pursuing in the Middle East, European countries are worried about the proactive behaviour of Turkey towards the Middle East during the recent decade that does not aim at their envisaged stability rather it seeks to revive Turkey's historical influence that the Ottoman Empire enjoyed in the past.

## Notes

1. Mohsen Moradian, *Turkey's Strategic Estimates* (Tehran: Abrar Moaser International Research Cultural Institute Publication, 2006), p. 579.
2. Volker Perthes, "Turkey's Role in the Middle East: An Outsider's Perspective", *Insight Turkey*, 12, no. 4 (2010), p.4.
3. Ehsan Aalaei, "The U.S. Status in Turkish Foreign Policy in the Post World War Era", 2010, p.2 http://www.irtt.ir/articles/international_policy/post_429.php
4. Tahaii, Seyed Javad, "Kemalism: The Elements of Crisis in Turkish Foreign Policy Attitude". *Rahbord Quarterly*, no. 21 (2001), p.204.
5. International and Political Studies Institute, *Turkey Green Book* (Tehran: Ministry of Foreign Affairs Publication, 2007), p.210.
6. Erik Cornell, *Turkey in the 21 Century* (London: Routledge, 2001), p.34.
7. Graham E. Fuller, *The Center of Universe: Geopolitics of Iran*. Translated by Abbas Mokhber (Tehran: Markaz Publication, 2000), pp.115-116.
8. Omer Taspinar, "Turkey's Middle East Policies: Between Neo-Ottomanism and Kemalism". Carnegie Paper, September 2008.
9. Moradian, *Turkey's Strategic Estimates*, p.526.
10. Aalaei, "The U.S. Status in Turkish Foreign Policy in the Post World War Era", pp. 1-2.
11. Farhad Attaei, "A New Attitude in Turkey's Regional Policy" *Middle East Studies Quarterly*, no. 19 (Fall 1999), p.107.

12. Rahman Ghahramanpoor, "A Series of Analyses on Political Developments in Turkey", 2010, http://fa.merc.ir/archive/article/tabid/62/articleType/CategoryView/categoryid/11/Default.aspx
13. William Hale, *Christian Democracy and the AKP: Parallels and Contrasts* (London: Routledge, 2006), p.160.
14. Seyed Assadollah Athari, "The Goals of Justice and Development Party in Accessing to EU", 2010, http://fa.merc.ir/archive/article/tabid/62/articleType/ArticleView/articleid/123/------2--.aspx
15. Moradian, *Turkey's Strategic Estimates*, p.590.
16. Perthes, "Turkey's Role in the Middle East: An Outsider's Perspective", p.2.
17. Gharamanpoor, "A Series of Analyses on Political Developments in Turkey".
18. Saeed Shokoohi, "A Study of the Components of Davutoğlu 's Strategic Depth Doctrine", 2011, p.1-10, http://strategicreview.org/1390/02/25
19. Ibid., p.4.
20. Gharamanpoor, "A Series of Analyses on Political Developments in Turkey".
21. Soner Cagaptay, "Is Turkey Separating from the West". Translated by Mohammad Mazhari, 2010, www.bashgah.net
22. Keyhan Barzegar, "Iran-Turkey Relations: Their Impact on Israel's Political-Security Strategies". *Strategic Studies of the Islamic World Quarterly*, 11, no. 44 (2010).
23. Mehrdad Farahmand, "Erdogan and His Ambition for Reviving the Ottoman Empire", 2011, http://www.bbc.co.uk/persian/world/2011/06/110614_132_mf_turkey.shtml
24. Maziar Aghazadeh, "Recep Teyyep, the Conqueror or Sultan Mohammad Erdogan", 2010, http://www.asriran.com/fa/news/119423
25. Kristi Raik, "Between Activeness and Influence: The Contribution of New Member States to EU Policies towards Eastern Neighbors". Policy Study Commissioned by the Open Estonia Foundation, September 2006.
26. Pinar Bilgin, "A Return to Civilizational Geopolitics in the Mediterranean? Changing Geopolitical Images of European Union and Turkey in the Post Cold War Era". *Geopolitics*, 9, no.2 (2004), p.347.
27. Bac, Meltem, Muftuler, "Turkey's Role in EU Security and Foreign Policies". *Security Dialogue*, 31, no. 4 (2000), pp.489-502.
28. Mahmut, Bali Aykan, "Turkey and European Security and Policies Identity/Policy (ESDI/P): A Turkish View". *Journal of Contemporary European Studies*, 13, no. 3 (2002), p.335.
29. Ibid, p.346.
30. Ihsan Kizitlan, "Improving the NATO-EU Partnership: A Turkish Perspective". *Turkish Policy Quarterly*, 7, no. 3 (2008): 33-46.
31. Bulent Aras, "The Nabucco Natural Gas Pipeline from Opera to Reality". Foundation for Political, Economic and Social Research (SETA), *Policy Brief*, no. 3 (2009), p.21.
32. Taspinar, "Turkey's Middle East Policies: Between Neo-Ottomanism and Kemalism", p.3.
33. Ibid., p.13.
34. Tarik Oguzlu, "Soft Power in Turkish Foreign Policy", *Australian Journal of International Affairs*, 61, no. 4 (2007), p.32.
35. Ibid., pp.23-31.

**Bibliography**

Aalaei, Ehsan. "The U.S. Status in Turkish Foreign Policy in the Post World War Era", 2010 http://www.irtt.ir/articles/international_policy/post_429.php

Aghazadeh, Maziar. "Recep Teyyep, the Conqueror or Sultan Mohammad Erdogan", 2010, http://www.asriran.com/fa/news/119423

Aras, Bulent. "The Nabucco Natural Gas Pipeline from Opera to Reality". Foundation for Political, Economic and Social Research (SETA), *Policy Brief*, no. 3 (2009)

Athari, Seyed Assadollah. "The Goals of Justice and Development Party in Accessing to EU", 2010, http://fa.merc.ir/archive/article/tabid/62/articleType/ArticleView/articleid/123/------2--.aspx

Attaei, Farhad. "A New Attitude in Turkey's Regional Policy" *Middle East Studies Quarterly,* no. 19 (Fall 1999).

Aykan, Mahmut Bali. "Turkey and European Security and Policies Identity/Policy (ESDI/P): A Turkish View". *Journal of Contemporary European Studies*, 13, no. 3 (2002).

Barzegar, Keyhan. "Iran-Turkey Relations: Their Impact on Israel's Political-Security Strategies". *Strategic Studies of the Islamic World Quarterly*, 11, no. 44 (2010).

Bilgin, Pinar. "A Return to Civilizational Geopolitics in the Mediterranean? Changing Geopolitical Images of European Union and Turkey in the Post Cold War Era". *Geopolitics*, 9, no.2 (2004).

Catapagay, Suter. "Is Turkey Separating from the West". Translated by Mohammad Mazhari, 2010, www.bashgah.net

Cornell, Erik. *Turkey in the 21 Century*. London: Routledge, 2001.

Farahmand, Mehrdad. "Erdogan and His Ambition for Reviving the Ottoman Empire", 2011, http://www.bbc.co.uk/persian/world/2011/06/110614_132_mf_turkey.shtml

Fuller, Graham. E. *The Center of Universe: Geopolitics of Iran.* Translated by Abbas Mokhber. Tehran: Markaz Publication, 2000.

Ghahramanpoor, Rahman. *International Security: Opportunities, Threats, and Challenges Facing the Islamic Republic of Iran.* Tehran: Abrar Moaser International Research Cultural Institute Publication, 2004.

Ghahramanpoor, Rahman. "A Series of Analyses on Political Developments in Turkey", 2010 http://fa.merc.ir/archive/article/tabid/62/articleType/CategoryView/categoryid/11/Default.aspx

Hale, William. *Christian Democracy and the AKP: Parallels and Contrasts*. London: Routledge, 2006.

International and Political Studies Institute, *Turkey Green Book*. Tehran: Ministry of Foreign Affairs Publication, 2007.

Kizitlan, Ihsan. "Improving the NATO-EU Partnership: A Turkish Perspective". *Turkish Policy Quarterly*, 7, no. 3 (2008).

Moradian, Mohsen. *Turkey's Strategic Estimates*. Tehran: Abrar Moaser International Research Cultural Institute Publication, 2006.

Muftuler, Bac, Meltem. "Turkey's Role in EU Security and Foreign Policies". *Security Dialogue*, 31, no. 4 (2000).

Oguzlu, Tarik. "Soft Power in Turkish Foreign Policy", *Australian Journal of International Affairs*, 61, no. 4 (2007).

Perthes, Volker. "Turkey's Role in the Middle East: An Outsider's Perspective". *Insight Turkey*, 12, no. 4 (2010).

Raik, Kristi. "Between Activeness and Influence: The Contribution of New Member States to EU Policies towards Eastern Neighbors". Policy Study Commissioned by the Open Estonia Foundation, September 2006.

Shokoohi, Saeed. "A Study of the Components of Davutoğlu's Strategic Depth Doctrine", 2011, http://strategicreview.org/1390/02/25

Tahaii, Seyed Javad. "Kemalism: The Elements of Crisis in Turkish Foreign Policy Attitude". *Rahbord Quarterly*, no. 21 (2001).

Taspinar, Omer. "Turkey's Middle East Policies: Between Neo-Ottomanism and Kemalism". Carnegie Paper, September 2008.

# 9
# A New World Order and its Impact on Turkey–EU Relations*

*Emirhan Göral*

## Introduction

The fall of the Berlin Wall in 1989 was not simply a unification process of a divided nation, but rather a sign of global change in the international political system. The dissolution of the Soviet Union followed that path by the end of 1991, and it was a clear evidence of the end of the bipolar structure. The winner of the Cold War was the United States as the only existing superpower. Following the next two decades, no clear rivalry for the global power competition has taken place and the US has enjoyed a peculiar unipolar moment throughout the history of international relations.

However, the system of international politics necessitates a balancing among its most powerful actors. After two decades of US dominance in global politics, other major actors have begun to criticise the ongoing unipolar structure. The main reason for this challenge to the unipolar world may be explained by a very basic realist assumption. Accumulation of power in one party usually triggers a counter balancing effort among other major international actors. American unilateralism and use of military power without consulting international organisations have literally made other major powers anxious about the intentions of the US. In more concrete terms, other major powers—including the Cold-War US allies—have made some declarations about their interests in the end of the existing unipolar system.

Among the academic circles, on the other hand, there have been discussions about the non-existence of balancing behaviour by other powerful actors. Other major powers have not gone too far beyond the level of showing their discontent with the existing system. Yet, in this hazy atmosphere of the international system, some major European countries, especially France and Germany, have performed different foreign policy choices when compared to the previous decades. Particularly the defenders of the realist-based approaches have suggested various explanations about the anomaly of the current structure of the system.

The unipolar moment has begun to erode by the developments that have taken place in the post-2001 world. The tragic September 11 events resulted in an unprecedented US policy championed by neo-conservatives. The operation in Afghanistan was followed by the invasion of Iraq in 2003. The unilateral policies introduced by the Bush Doctrine[1] of the United States have found a deep response among major international actors including the former Cold War allies of the US. The divided response of the European Union (EU) members against the Iraqi War was a clear example of soft balancing against the superpower, which threw the feeler for understanding how much free space was available for unilateral action.

Europeans somehow imposed soft balancing against the US as well as the then-ongoing criticisms of China and Russia. The potential of other major powers against the United States cannot be ignored. For instance, revenues from energy trade have helped Russia to improve its international reputation as a former superpower. With a miraculous economic development level, China has begun to emerge as a potential superpower, which may overtly express its discontent with the unipolarity and US political decisions at global level. In other words, Russia and China as well as some of the leading EU member states have begun to criticise the US very harshly in the international arena, which has caused the current unipolar moment to be questioned seriously.

In the hazy structure of international politics, it is very difficult for states to define a prompt foreign policy. Without having sufficient national capacity[2] it is very difficult for an international actor to define a specific role in current international politics. Considering this difficulty, almost every major power (at global or regional level) tries to calculate foreign policy options and find a viable external policy that may serve the national interests at a substantially greater degree among the alternatives. Every actor has different options, which may result in different consequences depending on the structure of international system.

The foreign policy choices of actors in this period may make a country prosperous and politically stable in a peaceful environment or may put in a difficult position of enmity particularly within its neighbourhood. Being aware of the difficulties carried by the changing nature of the international system, Turkey tries to follow a more active foreign policy in order to create a zone of stability in its neighbourhood. When compared to the Cold War years, Turkey directly interferes with regional affairs and develops special relations with most of the countries in the Middle East and North Africa (MENA region), Central Asia, the Caucasus, and the Balkans. Turkey's strenuous efforts to provide stability particularly in its close proximity has resulted from a combination of several primary factors, which include: (i) current structure of the international political system; (ii) economic development that Turkey has experienced for the last two decades; and (iii) personal influence of Ahmet Davutoğlu, Turkish PM's foreign policy advisor (2003–09) and Foreign Minister (2009–14).

From this point of view, the primary purpose of Turkey's active foreign policy has similarities with the EU's neighbourhood policy, because both policies pursue security and stability in the bordering countries and regions. Therefore, EU–Turkey relations are directly affected from and shaped by the change in international structure. This chapter tries to analyse the probable consequences of structural changes in the international system on EU–Turkey relations. In the following parts of this study an analytical view of the current international order will initially be evaluated in order to shed light on the behaviours of international actors. The policies of the EU and its major powers will be examined briefly. Finally, Turkey's foreign policy choices will provide an insight for deriving a conclusion on the impact of international political system on the Turkey–EU relations.

## Defining the New Structure of the International Political System

The current international political system is a tumultuous order in that there is no dominant power with the ability to control all other international actors. Different from a state structure, where a politically powerful government can define constitutional rules and put sufficient pressure on domestic actors to obey the laws, the current international system does not allow a clearly defined global constitution. Therefore, the current international system is somehow anarchic in nature. This anarchic nature requires each and every actor to guarantee its survival by following a specific foreign policy in line with its own capabilities.[3] In other words, great powers in the system normally follow more independent policies, while middle-range powers and smaller countries prefer to be more congruent with the foreign policies of their allies.

Throughout the 19th century, this global order resulted in a balance of power among several great powers. This power contest brought two great catastrophic consequences during the first half of the 20th century. After the end of World War II, the world turned into a new structure. The war-prone multipolar structure turned into a bipolar world which is divided by clear-cut lines between Western countries under US leadership and Eastern countries under Soviet influence. The lack of nuclear capability made the non-aligned countries less powerful when compared to the two superpowers.

The end of the Cold War paved the way to an unprecedented structure in the anarchic international system. This unipolar world was a very new phenomenon and was intrinsically expected to end in a short time due to the potential threat derived from the overwhelming power of the sole superpower.[4] However, the structural change has not been realised for more than two decades for several reasons. Firstly, the presence of US military forces in different parts of Europe provides stability by balancing the regional powers. The same reasoning was quite relevant for the Far East. Secondly, the United States has been extremely powerful when compared to others but this does not trigger others' incentives for balancing because the US power is not threatening. Finally, even if it would be threatening, the aggregate power capabilities of other major powers have not been sufficient to balance the US power. Whatever the genuine reason for the lack of balancing is, the prevailing unipolar world is going to change sooner or later due to structural pressures.

Mearsheimer argues that the US grand strategy during the 1990s and 2000s has aggravated the anti-American sentiments among other major powers instead of providing the persistence of US global dominance.[5] Naturally, the United States is expected to follow a foreign policy that helps to protect its interests in an anarchic world. In that sense, three particular regions are vitally important for the United States: Europe, Northeast Asia and the Persian Gulf. Europe and Northeast Asia are important because the powerful states in these regions may well turn into threatening rivals for the United States. Persian Gulf, on the other hand, is crucial for the rich energy resources.[6] The American activities in these regions could be respected at a certain level unless US policies are perceived as a threat by the other powerful actors. In the following decade after the end of the Cold War, other major powers had not engaged in any overt balancing behaviour. However, by the end of 2003, the US policies—particularly in the Middle East—accelerated the demand for a shift in the global structure in favour of a multipolar world. Consequently, the rising powers have obviously started to question the gaps in the current structure and voiced their grievances about the unipolarity. In this new situation, "how and when this change will take place" largely depends on foreign policy choices of other major powers.[7]

## European Union and the New World

As mentioned earlier, the end of unipolarity may result in two probable new structures of international political system. The first alternative for unipolarity is a bipolar world, in which a second major power rises to the status of a superpower. In such a polarity, China would be the most probable candidate for the status of an alternative superpower to the United States. China's incredible economic growth in the last two decades made the country the most probable superpower if the world turns into bipolarity.[8] In this case, other powers are expected to take part according to their perceived power structure. In a bipolar world between the United States and China, major European actors' preferences would mostly be shaped by several factors including threat perception, societal affinity and existing alliance partnership structure.

First of all, both the United Kingdom and other major continental powers in Europe would take the geographical threats into account when they calculate primary security concerns. European security is much more sensitive against the power of US when compared to threats coming from China. In other words, the Chinese potential to threaten European security is not as impressive as the United States. Although US and Europe have a clear and long standing security cooperation, any severe disagreement would cause serious security problems for Europe particularly after the disappearance of the Soviet threat. This security gap for Europe is still relevant. Therefore, Europe may be inclined to take part with the US in post-unipolarity if the world is divided into two spheres of influence between China and the US. Secondly, internal politics would be a factor for European powers to align with the United States in a bipolar world. The relations between the United States and most of the European countries have been based on centuries-old friendship. Both American and European societies are much more sympathetic to each other than they are to China. As a consequence of these social linkages, domestic pressures on European governments may enforce them to prefer the United States. Finally, there is an existing alliance system between the Europeans and the Americans. NATO has proved its validity on many different occasions and has provided comfort to Europeans in terms of security. The cost of changing such a deep-security partnership would be high enough to convince European leaders to stay within the NATO alliance. All these three factors may help to confirm that Europeans would get in an alliance partnership with the United States in a possible rivalry between China and the US. In addition to this, despite there being no clear European interests in the Asia-Pacific, the EU and the US are not on diverging policies on strategic issues with respect to this region.[9]

However, the second alternative, multipolarity, for the current order is more probable since the other powers are also capable enough to take part as major actors of a multipolar world. Among them Russia, Germany, France, Japan and the United Kingdom can be mentioned as well as some other regional powers like Brazil, India, Mexico, South Korea or Turkey.[10] The reactions of some major European Union members against the US invasion of Iraq proved a clear shift from European consent to unipolarity.[11] Some of the bigger NATO members reacted severely against US policies and their attitude could help prevent the US intervention in Iraq. All those diplomatic and institutional difficulties that were implemented mainly by a group of countries led by France and Germany in the EU as well as Turkey in NATO have been regarded as a new type of balancing against the United States. Among some pundits, this new balancing is called soft balancing and has been discussed in detail.[12] When the previous Russian and Chinese grievances about the US dominance are taken together with the newly emerged European responses, one may argue that the unipolar structure is experiencing hard times with the pressure of multiple actors in a new structure.

Considering the current capabilities of major actors, a shift to multipolarity may seriously be expected. In a multipolar world, the preferences of European powers will be quite significant for global balances since the European countries—as a Union—constitute the largest economic entity on the global scale as well as one of the most influential political actors. In other words, any foreign policy choice that European countries prefer may matter much more than many other actors in defining the new global order. In contrast, however, the unity among the EU members is in serious question as it was clearly depicted during the 2003 Iraqi War.[13] Furthermore, there are discussions on the inability of the EU to act as a great power because of the existing member state policies.[14] Therefore, foreign policy strategies of the EU for a multipolar world are difficult to estimate under the current circumstances and this will consequently affect Turkey's policy choices since the EU is an indispensable factor in Turkish foreign policy.

## Turkey and the Difficult Path in the New Era

Along with the current developments in world politics, Turkey has become an important international actor, which may have considerable weight in power configurations of the future multipolar world. There are several factors that make Turkey an important regional actor. First of all, the recent economic development level of the country as well as its human capital has turned Turkey into a reliable partner in its region. Secondly, the strategic location of Turkey is another crucial asset for the country that any potential major power of a multipolar would like to ally with. Last but not the least, Turkey has cultural, ethnic and/or religious ties with different groups living in its close neighbourhoods. Put it differently, Turkey may have influence over the Balkans, the Caucasus and Central Asia, the Black Sea, and the Middle East and North Africa. Without any doubt, this leverage, which has been acquired from the past, increases Turkey's significance as an ally for potential great powers of the post-unipolar world.

In the hazy atmosphere of international politics, Turkey is normally engaged in increasing its own capabilities in order to survive in an anarchic world. Turkey, in this regard, not only improves in term of economic development, but also develops national military systems and builds up military equipments[15]. This is one of the indications that show how Turkey is being prepared for a multipolar world in terms of internal balancing.

On the other hand, Turkey does not have sufficient resources to become a full-fledged great power. The reasons for Turkey's insufficiency to become a great power in a multipolar world are various: First of all, Turkey does not have a nuclear capacity which may be evaluated as condition for being a great power. Germany, for example, does not have any nuclear weapon, but has the technological capacity to produce immediately. Turkey, on the other hand, searches for foreign support even for building a nuclear power plant. Therefore, Turkey lacks technological innovations in terms of nuclear capacity. Secondly, Turkey does not have sufficient energy resources. One may say that most of the other major powers do not have their own energy resources. Although some major powers do not have energy resources, they have developed alternatives including enhanced nuclear capabilities, using renewable energy resources as well as engaging special relations with energy-producing countries. Turkey, however, could achieve very little developments so far in terms of relief from its energy deficiency. Last but not the least, Turkey has certain problems with regard to internal politics. Although the Justice and Development Party (JDP) has enjoyed sufficient political support and does not need a coalition partner in government, the public unrests that started in June 2013 as well as the complicated Kurdish question inhibit Turkey's political stability, which in turn make it very difficult to be a great power without domestic political stability.

Considering Turkey's current position, one may argue that Turkey does not have sufficient capabilities to balance other major powers in a multipolar world. A country with insufficient balancing capabilities would naturally search for external balancing activities, which are primarily based on forming alliances with other countries with equivalent power. In this regard, Turkey has engaged a policy of cooperation and normalisation with its neighbouring countries. The zero-problem policy of Turkey's Foreign Minister Davutoğlu might well serve to this policy. This policy is based on Davutoğlu's vision[16] on Turkey's activism in its environment, which had been previously dominated by the Ottoman Empire. The ability to implement such a comprehensive foreign policy, on the other hand, is not a very easy task. For instance, the zero-problem policy has proved insufficient as far as Armenia and Syria are considered due to various reasons that Turkey cannot fix by its own efforts.

## Shaping Turkey–EU Relations in a Multipolar World

The accession process of Turkey to the EU has been a question of more than 50 years. The initial application of 1959 could not be finalised because of certain impediments derived both from Turkey's insufficiency to fulfil certain criteria and from anxieties among various EU (European Economic Community or EEC as it was known earlier) members. However, the reshaping of international politics may give rise to new developments in the Turkey–EU relations. Analysing through the lenses of polarity, two probable conclusions can be drawn for Turkey's membership. The first alternative in a brand new world is a bipolar order with two superpowers, which are the United States and China. In this case, EU may have three probable alternative foreign policy choices: First alternative is to go on with the current alliance structure based on Atlantic ties. Second alternative is to put an end to its close relations with the United States and prefer to develop special relations with China. The third alternative foreign policy, on the other hand, may be to stay indifferent with the new polarity by following a neutrality policy. As mentioned earlier, the first option is the most likely alternative among others for Europe.

Turkey has also similar alternatives in a bipolar world. However, Turkey's alternatives may be more susceptible to other actors' choices when compared to the EU. Turkey may either be associated with one of the poles, or prefer to be neutral. In that sense, Europe's neutrality would promote Turkey to be neutral. Considering the close ties with the Western world based on more than 60 years, Turkey's current NATO alignment may be more meaningful for security concerns unless the EU prefers non-alignment or China. An alignment with the similar camp, may make the probability for Turkey's EU membership considerably very high. Moreover, Russia's security cooperation with China may increase Turkey's chance for EU membership. On the other hand, if Turkey prefers to engage in a new alliance with China and others, or prefers neutrality, it would mean a total collapse for Turkey's EU membership candidacy.

However, as mentioned earlier, the structure of international politics may shift into multipolarity as well. In a multipolar global order, the US, China, Russia and some other major powers may attain great power status. The EU, as a collective body of states acting together, may behave as a unique international actor and become one of the major powers in multipolarity.[17] If EU can achieve unity in foreign policy, it will probably be one of the most influential actors in international politics. In that case, Turkey may have different alternatives ranging from alliance membership with one of the poles to independent actorness based on neutrality. Because of its geostrategic location, Turkey may need to engage in an alliance with a major international actor. While bandwagoning maybe an alternative for Turkey, selecting one of those great powers as a close partner and disregarding relations with others entails certain risks, such as entrapment or abandonment.[18]

Turkey's EU accession process may at a great extent be affected by Turkey's foreign policy behaviour. If Turkey prefers bandwagoning with the Union, the membership process may certainly gain impetus and Turkey may become a member in a very short time. On the other hand,

Turkey's alliance with another great power in a future multipolarity may totally collapse Turkey's EU bid or suspend the relations until the alliance structure changes. Finally, although very difficult to maintain in a multipolarity—Turkey's independent status may cause the continuation of the accession process without any particular change in its current nature as if it is nothing more than an economic cooperation at the level of a customs union.

## Conclusion

Since the beginning of the Turkey–EU relations, there have been various factors affecting Turkey's accession to the European Union. The underdeveloped Turkish economy when compared to the EEC as well as the potential of a huge wave of immigration from Turkey to Europe were the main concerns of the member states in previous decades of Turkey's accession process. However, the recent economic development of Turkey has made it clear that there are additional considerations impeding Turkey's membership. Cultural and religious differences as well as Turkey's potential power in EU's decision making are some of the factors currently shaping Turkey–EU relations. As the European Commission clearly states almost in every progress report, Turkey's failure to fulfil political aspects of the Copenhagen Criteria and gaps in implementing *acquis communautaire* are among other obstacles in Turkey's relations with the EU. However, there is a very critical factor that has the capacity to change Turkey–EU relations abruptly. The structure of international relations may enforce both Turkey and the European countries either to develop a close alliance or to become rivals depending on other actors' decisions.

A probable change in unipolarity will naturally require the defining of new foreign policy strategies both for Turkey and the EU. As long as those strategies come into line with each other properly, Turkey's accession process to the EU may be positively affected from structural changes. Otherwise, the accession process may be suspended or may totally collapse due to the alliance formation in a new world. In short, this chapter argues that defining or assuming of foreign policy options for the EU and Turkey in a future international political structure is not possible at the moment. However, the chapter suggests that the association process will be extensively shaped by the shift from a unipolar world to a brand-new world order.

## Notes

* This study is a part of project (SOS-D-101013-0408) supported by the Marmara University, Scientific Research Commission.

1. Bush Doctrine is the concept that defines the unilateral policies of the US President George W. Bush. Those policies include withdrawing from ABM treaty, rejecting the Kyoto Protocol as well as the policy of preventive war. For an early critic of Bush Doctrine, see Jervis, Robert (2003). "Understanding the Bush Doctrine", *Political Science Quarterly,* 118 (3), pp. 365-388.
2. This capacity mostly includes own natural resources, military power, economic capabilities based on trade surplus and political stability at the domestic level.
3. Perpetual anarchic structure of the system was primarily mentioned by the founder of neo-realism. See: Waltz, Kenneth N. (1979). *Theory of International Politics*, Massachusetts: Addison-Wesley Publishing, pp. 102-129.
4. John J. Mearsheimer (1990). "Back to the Future: Instability in Europe after the Cold War", *International Security*, 15 (1), pp.5-56 ; Christopher Layne (1993). "The Unipolar Illusion: Why New Great Powers Rise", *International Security*, 17 (4), pp. 5-51; Kenneth N. Waltz (1993). "The Emerging Structure of International Politics", *International Security*, 18 (2), pp.44-79.
5. John J. Mearsheimer (2011). "Imperial by Design", *The National Interest,* No.111, pp. 16-34.
6. Mearsheimer, 1990: 12-13.
7. Schweller and Pu contend that the timing and method of structural change will depend on three main policy preferences of major powers. Major actors may prefer to be supporters, spoilers or shirkers. Schweller, Randall L. and Pu, Xiaoyu (2011). "After Unipolarity: China's Vision of International Order in an Era of US Decline", *International Security,* 36(1), pp. 41-72.
8. Christopher Layne (2008). "China's Challenge to US Hegemony", *Current History,* 107 (705), pp.13-18.
9. Terry Narramore (2008). "China and Europe: Engagement, Multipolarity and Strategy", *The Pacific Review,* 21(1), pp.87-108.
10. Randall Schweller (2011). "Emerging Powers in an Age of Disorder", *Global Governance,* 17, p.295.
11. For a detailed analysis of European reactions on a unilateral Iraqi operation, see: Brooks and Wohlforth (2005). "Hard Times for Soft Balancing", *International Security,* 30 (1), pp. 93-103.
12. For a comprehensive analysis of soft balancing, see Robert A. Pape (2005). "Soft Balancing against the United States", *International Security,* 30(1), pp. 7-45; T.V. Paul (2005). "Soft Balancing in the Age of U.S. Primacy", *International Security,* 30(1), pp. 46-71.
13. Stanley Hoffmann, (2003). "US-European Relations: Past and Future", *International Affairs,* 79 (5), pp. 1034-35.

14. Toje, Asle (2011). "The European Union as a Small Power", *Journal of Common Market Studies,* 49 (1), pp. 43-60.
15. Turkey's defence industry was extremely dependent on external producers during the Cold War years. In the 1990s, Turkey has developed special relations particularly with Israel in improving its defence capabilities. Recently, Turkey is in an effort to develop several national military systems including a new national military vessel project known as Milgem (Enginsoy, 2011a); domestic missile systems (Enginsoy, 2011b); and defence information systems (Baysal, 2013).
16. For a more comprehensive evaluation of Davutoğlu's foreign policy approach, see Ahmet Davutoğlu (2010). *Stratejik Derinlik: Türkiye'nin Uluslararası Konumu (41. Baskı),* İstanbul: Küre Yayınları.
17. There are discussions about EU's ability to act as a unique body at the international level. EU's decision making process at foreign policy level requires a complex intergovernmental process that hampers EU from implementing prompt decisions in cases of urgent international action. Zielonka analyzes EU's external policy with respect to those of the United States, China and Russia to understand the main differences. Zielonka, Jan (2011). "The EU as an International Actor: Unique or Ordinary?", *European Foreign Affairs Review,* 16 (3), pp. 281-301.
18. For a detailed analysis see: Serhat Güvenç and Özel, Soli (2012). "NATO and Turkey in the Post-Cold War World: between Abandonment and Entrapment", *Southern European and Black Sea Studies,* 12 (4), pp. 533-553.

**Bibliography**

Baysal, Ercan (2013). "TÜBITAK Develops Information Systems for Use in Defense", *Today's Zaman, 4 March 2013.* Retrieved from: http://www.todayszaman.com/news-308721-tubitak-develops-information-system-for-use-in-defense.html

Brooks and Wohlforth (2005). "Hard Times for Soft Balancing", *International Security,* 30 (1), pp. 72-108.

Davutoğlu, Ahmet (2010). *Stratejik Derinlik: Türkiye'nin Uluslararası Konumu (41. Baskı),* İstanbul: Küre Yayınları.

Enginsoy, Ümit (2011a). "Turkey to Unveil its Own Made Warships", *Hurriyet Daily News, 25 September 2011.* Retrieved from: http://www.hurriyetdailynews.com/default.aspx?pageid=438&n=turkey-to-unveil-its-own-made-warships-2011-09-25.

Enginsoy, Ümit (2011b). "Turkey Develops Domestic Missile, Rocket", *Hurriyet Daily News, 19 June 2011.* Retrieved from: http://www.hurriyetdailynews.com/default.aspx?pageid=438&n=turkey-develops-domestic-missile-rocket-2011-06-19.

Güvenç, Serhat and Özel, Soli (2012). "NATO and Turkey in the Post-Cold War World: between Abandonment and Entrapment", *Southern European and Black Sea Studies,* 12 (4), pp. 533-553.

Hoffmann, Stanley (2003). "US-European Relations: Past and Future", *International Affairs,* 79 (5), pp. 1029-1036.

Jervis, Robert (2003). "Understanding the Bush Doctrine", *Political Science Quarterly,* 118 (3), pp. 365-388.

Layne, Christopher (1993). "The Unipolar Illusion: Why New Great Powers Rise", *International Security,* 17 (4), pp. 5-51.

Layne, Christopher (2008). "China's Challenge to US Hegemony", *Current History,* 107 (705), pp.13-18.

Mearsheimer, John J. (1990). "Back to the Future: Instability in Europe after the Cold War", International Security, 15 (1), pp.5-56.

Mearsheimer, John J. (2011). "Imperial by Design", *The National Interest,* No.111, pp. 16-34.

Narramore, Terry (2008). "China and Europe: Engagement, Multipolarity and Strategy", *The Pacific Review,* 21(1), pp.87-108.

Paul, T.V. (2005). "Soft Balancing in the Age of U.S. Primacy", *International Security,* 30(1), pp. 46-71.

Pape, Robert A. (2005). "Soft Balancing against the United States", *International Security,* 30(1), pp. 7-45.

Schweller, Randall (2011). "Emerging Powers in an Age of Disorder", *Global Governance,* 17, pp. 285-297.

Schweller, Randall L. and Pu, Xiaoyu (2011). "After Unipolarity: China's Vision of International Order in an Era of US Decline", *International Security,* 36(1), pp. 41-72.

Toje, Asle (2011). "The European Union as a Small Power", *Journal of Common Market Studies,* 49 (1), pp. 43-60.

Waltz, Kenneth N. (1993). "The Emerging Structure of International Politics", *International Security*, 18 (2), pp.44-79.

Waltz, Kenneth N. (1979). *Theory of International Politics*, Massachusetts: Addison-Wesley Publishing.

Zielonka, Jan (2011). "The EU as an International Actor: Unique or Ordinary?", *European Foreign Affairs Review,* 16 (3), pp. 281-301.

# 10
# Turkey's Dream of the European Union Membership and the Protracted Hurdles to it

*Indrani Talukdar*

Considering the latest democratisation package unveiled by Turkey on September 2013 as a "positive" sign,[1] the EU governments agreed to restart entry talk after a three-year pause. The decision was taken after the European Union's progress report[2] on Turkey was published on October 16, 2013.

Talks between Turkey and the European Union on November 5, 2013 over accession were not successful as expected. The reason behind it was the protracted issue of the Cyprus conflict and the violation against human rights which took place in the form of violent suppression of mass demonstrations in Turkey in May and June 2013. According to the EU *acquis communautaire*, the EU's rules and regulations, Turkey has made it only 1/35th of the way through the checklist of legislative and policy moves required for membership.[3] The slow progress made by Turkey and the continuous refusal to accept it as a member by the EU, leading to stalemate, creates doubts about the genuineness from both the sides.

The decades-old history of engagement between Turkey and the European Union has covered a multitude of issues, highlighting its association with Europe as the epitome of the country's integration in the league of Western civilisation. Membership in NATO and its application to the EU have been the moves to achieve it. But the road to Europe has been complex and unpredictable; something that often resembles a roller-coaster ride.[4]

Turkey and the EU have not achieved the optimal level of cooperation which they are capable of. Turkey dreamt of associating itself with Europe from the period of the Ottoman Empire's rule; however, with different objectives related to its national interests including its identity, with the main aim of protecting Turkey's survival as a state.

The affiliation process with Europe has undergone a transition of phases which can be divided into three: the Ottoman Empire, Kemal Attaturk and post-Attaturk. Likewise, Europe constructed its association with Turkey from the Empire's time with the objective of achieving its national interests and security in the region. It manoeuvred its way through associations and agreements with Turkey and at the same time kept a distance from the country. Europe has engaged with Turkey through the 'carrot and stick' policy. It has been unable to completely either assimilate Turkey or disassociate with it. This dilemma in Europe of not letting go of Turkey is because of the latter's geostrategic position which lies between the West and East.

## Genesis of the Relationship between Turkey and Europe: During the Ottoman Empire

The genesis of the relationship in a constructive manner between Turkey and Europe was at the onset of the 16th century. The Ottoman Empire was the epicentre of trade and commerce and the seat of Islamic leadership and Europe, on the other hand, was evolving as a great house of power through its discoveries and inventions of science and technology. It was also the seat of Catholic Christianity. The evolution in both the worlds (the Ottoman and Europe) led to exploration and extension of their relationship.

The Ottomans felt the first European penetration during the period of capitulations, based on economic privileges. Although the association between the Empire and Europe was limited to economy, however over a period of time, it started encompassing other facets of political, defence and social sections in Turkey. The Western ideas of liberalism and modernisation based on European Enlightenment and French Revolution had started filtering into the Turkish society. These led to reforms under *Tanzimat*; however it was not that successful as the Ottoman Empire had still not embraced the European ideas completely. Europe took advantage of the Empire's initiation in its Westernisation process as it helped the West in securing its position in this part of the region through the latter's alliances and agreements.

The bonhomie between the Empire and Europe was reciprocated when Turkey was implicitly accepted as a European power in 1856 when it was included in the *Concert of Europe* due to its alignment with France and Britain during the Crimean War. For the first time, Europeans formally recognised the Turks as a part of the European society of states, although this change was totally restricted to state-to-state relations and had nothing to do with cultural issues. This arrangement of bilateral relations minus cultural aspect suited the monarch. The cultural aspect of the Westernisation project in Turkey was carried out by Europe-educated intellectuals.[5]

The Ottoman Empire was clear in its objective of strengthening its relationship with Europe, with its focus to abreast itself in terms of Westernisation and modernization without altering the Empire's Islamic identity. With the dissemination of liberal ideas from the West along with its expansionist/imperialist policies, the Empire was facing crisis within the country in the form of disintegration in nationalism and weak militarisation. This had led to the unsustainable administration of the Empire, ultimately leading to its collapse. There was chaos within Turkey as there was a struggle simmering within the Empire to preserve its Islamic identity, nationalism and modernisation. Amidst this dichotomy of preserving the Empire's Islamic identity and opening itself to ideas of Westernisation, Turkey attached itself to Europe. This attachment to the West led to the introduction of a new geographical identity for Turkey: a Eurasian identity.

## Turkey and Europe during and after Attaturk's Time: the 'Look West' Policy

From the ashes of the Ottoman Empire, the phoenix of the Turkish Republic under General Mustafa Kemal Ataturk arose. From 1923 onwards, the Turkish Republic took on the task of converting Turkey into a modern Westernised nation.[6] The tussle between its Islamic identity and the desired identity of being a European country began. The founders of the Republic initiated radical social and cultural changes, which is often referred to as 'Cultural Revolution'. The long term goal of this was to catch up with the West. 'Westernisation' to the republican leaders of Turkey, meant establishment of a strong, unified national state enjoying full political and economic independence where secularism, nationalism and positivism provided the driving force instead of religion.[7] Therein, underlies the profound European influence on the construction of Turkey's national identity and polity which influenced the formulation of its 'Look West' foreign policy. The initiation of this 'Look West' policy could be felt from the Ottoman Empire's period—however with different connotations. During Attaturk's time this policy was to change Turkey's identity from an Islamic country to a Western country; however in the Ottomans' time, the policy was to be at par with Europe without reorienting its Islamic identity.

Turkey embarked upon the securing of membership in Western and European organisations. In 1948, Turkey was admitted to the Organisation for Economic Cooperation and Development (OECD), followed by the Council of Europe in 1949 and the NATO in 1952. The Western project, for the Turkish elites, meant as being a part of the integration process in Europe with the aim of eventual membership of the European club.[8] Around 1958, the European Economic Community (EEC) was created and by 1959, the EEC began negotiations with Turkey on an Association Agreement. This Agreement became the first-ever contractual arrangement with a third country, signed in November 1963 in Ankara called the 'Ankara Agreement'. The preamble and article 28 of this agreement clearly mentioned the prospect of Turkey eventually becoming a member of the European Community.[9] This agreement was the cornerstone upon which Turkey–EU relations were built. The Association Agreement was supplemented by an Additional Protocol, which was signed in November 1970 and came into force in January 1973, establishing a timetable of technical measures to be taken for attaining the objective of the customs union which culminated in 1995. Despite considerable success in the relationship between Turkey and the EU, however, there are obstacles that have blocked Turkey's accession to the EU membership.

## Reasons for Non-Membership for Turkey

Turkey's non-acceptance in the EU and its having been kept in the 'waiting room'[10] status can be traced to the various reasons that the community has addressed. The EU is willing to offer Turkey a 'privileged partnership' position but not the full membership. It has cited political, economic and social issues, demographic and the Cyprus conflict as the main reasons behind the non-acceptance of Turkey in the EU. Apart from the general problems in Turkey, the Cyprus problem weighs more as it shows Turkey's attitude towards another country. From 1989, the EEC made it clear about the Cyprus issue being as one of the biggest obstacles in accepting Turkey as an EU member. Greece being an EU member and identifying Cyprus as its own extension politically, economically, culturally, socially and security-wise, has made the accession issue more complicated. Along with this issue, Turkey's non-European identity is also a challenge in the accession process. Although the EU is not overt about it but a Muslim country joining a European club is not too welcoming.

The relationship between Turkey and the EU has never been smooth from the beginning. Politically, the association between Turkey and the EEC from the 1960s till 1980s was not stable due to a variety of reasons but most importantly it were the military interventions in Turkish politics and its military interference in Cyprus during 1974. Around 1980s, the severe economic crisis and the coup d'état in Turkey led to the freezing of its relationship with the EEC. Relations between the two were gradually normalised after the restoration of a civilian government in 1983. However, the army's control over civilians, human rights violations and Greece's fearsome opposition to Turkey's membership delayed progress.

By the end of 1986, relations between Turkey and the EEC became normal that led to the application for full membership in 1987. Its application was not considered due to West Germany and Greece's objection, which influenced the EEC's decisions. The application of 1987 led to Turkey's third phase of European penetration post-Attaturk, which is of ambivalence.

## Greece and Cyprus becoming a Hurdle

The year 1989 proved to be critical for Turkey and the EU. The EC stated resolutely in 1989 that the evaluation of the political aspects of the application would be incomplete without taking into consideration the negative effects of the disagreements between Turkey and Greece, a member state, and the situation in Cyprus. Solving of the Cyprus conflict laid down the groundwork for assessing Turkey's genuineness of becoming an EU member. This stand of the EU gave Greece a leverage within the Union. In fact, the non-compromising position over the Cyprus conflict has signalled a non-European orientation of Turkey to the EU.

Turkey blames the influence of Greek pressure and had accused the EU of submission to Greek blackmail.[11] It severely criticised the European stand on Cyprus, repeating that it had not occupied Cyprus. In Turkey's eyes, the EU persisted in its erroneous assessment of the Cyprus question and thus had adopted a Cyprus policy based on the Greek view.[12] The rivalry with Greece has been a huge block for Turkey in attaining its EU membership. Turkey applied for an associate status on July 31, 1959 following Greece which had applied on July 15, 1959, Turkey's was rejected. But the EC promoted the Turkish application despite several EC members', notably France's, reservations on Turkey's European identity and "cultural" issues, due to the delicate situation share between the age-old rivals Greece and Turkey, both important NATO members.[13] In 1975 Greece applied for full membership and was accepted in 1981. Once it joined, Greece used the EU to advance its position in conflicts with Turkey over Cyprus and the air, sea and continental shelf borders in the Aegean Sea.[14] It blocked Turkish access to EU funds, development of the EU–Turkey Association and joint initiatives and vetoed Ankara's EU candidacy.[15]

Bilateral conflict with an EU member constitutes a natural barrier to full membership. Greece's early membership in the EU has acted as a constraint on the smooth development of Turkey–EU relations. In the Union, a small country like Greece[16] can also manage to make its voice heard concerning the issues of importance to its national interests. Wielding the veto stick in the Council of Ministers, Athens managed to influence the EU policy vis-à-vis Cyprus. The Greek pressure could be described as a negative influence as it led the EU, at times, to take certain unwanted decisions.[17] For example, the 1987 membership was rejected because of the Aegean Sea conflict between Turkey and Greece.

With Greece being an EU member and Cyprus applying for membership in 1990, it had led to more complications in the relationship between Turkey and the EU. For Turkey, Cyprus's accession meant that the Greeks would obtain a second veto against Turkey, in addition to their own. The state elite in Turkey had tended to interpret the EU's involvement in the dispute as a threat to the country's strategic interests in the Eastern Mediterranean. Since the time of Turkey's official application to the EC in 1987 and the Greek Cypriot application in 1990, Turkey's policy had been based on delinking the dynamics of its own relations with the EU from resolution of the dispute.[18] But the European Council after 1990s had explicitly linked the Cyprus problem to its relations with Turkey. However, to keep Turkey in the European sphere, in 1990 the European Commission adopted a set of proposals called "the Matutes Package" and in 1995 a Customs Union was reached between the two parties.

To further complicate things for Turkey, in 1993 the EU introduced membership requirements set by the Copenhagen European Council, which included stability of institutions guaranteeing democracy, the rule of law, human rights, respect for and protection of minorities. These criteria became an integral part of the Treaty of Europe through the adoption of the Amsterdam Treaty in May 1999. Democracy had thus become a non-negotiable condition for joining the EU.[19] In 1993, the EU accepted the Republic of Cyprus's candidacy, infuriating Turkey and Turkish Cypriots since the application was in effect on behalf of only the ethnic Greek part of the divided island.[20] However, Turkey kept its EU vocation alive by securing a Customs Union in 1995 to which Greece agreed but only after a date was set to begin membership talks for Cyprus.[21]

Nevertheless, the pressures from the EU (the stick) and potential membership of the EU (the carrot) had been influential in bringing about important changes in Turkey. The 1995 package of constitutional reform in Turkey adopted by the government in response to the European

Parliament's insistence on progress in democracy and human rights as preconditions for its admission to the Customs Union proves the country's commitment towards the EU. While entry into the Customs Union raised hope for Turkey's EU integration, the decision of non-inclusion of Turkey in the EU's enlargement process during the 1997 Luxembourg Summit by the European Council enraged the Turkish leaders.[22]

The root cause of this decision could be traced in the period 1995–1997. The relationship between Turkey and the EU had taken a turn for the worse. The period after 1995 coincided with unfortunate incidents such as the violent confrontation between the Turkish security forces and the Kurdistan Workers' Party (PKK) that led to harsh criticisms from the EU on failing to solve the Kurdish problem. The Turkish government, in turn, accused the EU of interfering in Turkish domestic affairs and of supporting the PKK's agenda to carve a separate Kurdish state from Turkey.[23] External factors such as the Aegean dispute, the crisis of the Rock of Kardak-Imia and the Cyprus issue between Greece and Turkey further complicated Turkey's relations with Europe.

### Double Standards on the EU's Part

Relations between Turkey and the EU reached their all-time low when in December 1997, the European Council decided not to include Turkey among the list of candidate countries for the next round of enlargement.[24] This was preceded in 1996 by a major crisis between Greece and Turkey when both countries came to the brink of a military confrontation over a tiny set of islands in the Aegean Sea.[25] These events had occurred in an environment characterised by the continuing armament of the Greek Cypriots by Greece as an effective deterrent against Turkey. Meanwhile, Greece took over the EU presidency in 1994 and made it clear in the Corfu Summit about the inclusion of Cyprus as an EU member. It marked the beginning of the 'give-and-take' historical compromise between Greece and the EU over Cyprus.

Meanwhile, the Customs Union Agreement was re-established in 1996 between the EU and Turkey, but the 1997 Luxembourg Council withdrew Turkey's eligibility for EU accession. During the 1997

Luxembourg summit, Greece was to assert its approval for the first-wave of candidates for the EU enlargement only if Cyprus was to be included and negotiations with it would begin. It could be seen that it was the Greek pressure on the EU that made the EU ignore the complicated situation of the Cyprus conflict and start with accession negotiations with Cyprus, hence degrading the EU's role as a catalyst in solving the protracted conflict between Turkey, Cyprus and the parties involved. The EU Commission announced in its 'Agenda 2000' report that the resolution of the Cyprus dispute should not be a precondition[26] (for Greek Cypriots) that would lead to the non-negotiation stand of the Greek Cyprus for a resolution with the Turkish Cypriots.[27] Also during that time, the situation between Turkey, Greece and Cyprus had turned volatile due to the S-300 missile crisis (early 1997–late 1998) and to make the situation complicated, the EU Commission with its *Agenda 2000* document gave a negative assessment of the political situation in Turkey. Turkey was excluded from the first wave of applicant countries for 'technical' reasons. It felt the decision was unjustified.

The uproar within Turkey was felt in Brussels and not wanting to lose a potential "gatekeeper"[28] in Turkey, the EU decided to draw up a strategy to prepare Turkey for accession. But the EU stopped the accession process by citing Turkey's non-conformity with the Copenhagen criteria both politically and economically. The EU gave clear signals to Turkey that to be a member it had to vigorously pursue its political and economic reforms, including alignment to human rights standards and practices of the EU; respect for and protection of minorities; the establishment of satisfactory and stable relations between Greece and Turkey; the settlement of disputes and support for negotiations under the aegis of the UN on a political settlement in Cyprus on the basis of the relevant UN Security Council decisions.[29] Turkey's entry was made conditional on certain values and principles.[30]

The conditions laid out by the EU were not well received by Turkey as it felt that they were unjustified. It was because Turkey felt angry and hurt as certain Central and Eastern European countries which were economically behind Turkey and were still nascent in democracy were given a membership status ahead of Turkey. For those countries, including Cyprus, there was a very clear prospect of membership, and even a timetable. While for Turkey there was none.[31] Relations were pacified during the Helsinki Summit in 1999, when the EU decided to give Turkey the candidate status for accession on the basis of the same criteria applied to the other candidates.[32] Behind this softening stand of the EU, there were many reasons.

One of the reasons was in the wake of the Kosovo War[33] where Europe needed Turkey as a NATO member. Another reason was related to the Cyprus issue where it had become clear that by excluding Turkey from the list of candidates, the EU was only hardening the Turkish position over the Cyprus issue. Therefore, the EU changed its policy towards Turkey by announcing Turkey's official candidature for membership at the European Council Helsinki summit. It was hoped that Turkey's accession process would contribute to the resolution of the Cyprus problem. The expectation was that Turkey, as one of the major actors in Cyprus, would modify its position to break the deadlock on the island. For Turkey, the Cyprus issue is a domestic political concern and it has tried to keep it separate from the EU accession process.[34] But the positive effect of the Helsinki decision accelerated the momentum of political and economic reforms in Turkey. Since then, Europeanisation became a strong instrument in shaping the country's domestic policies, accelerating the reforms and in transforming Turkey's approach towards foreign affairs issues.

Turkey opened itself to the EU *acquis* and the Europeanisation mechanisms and participated fully in the reform process. Membership in the Union was perceived as the ultimate requirement to fulfill the Kemalist imperative of identification with the Western modernity.[35] The year 1999 was important for Turkey. Apart from the Turkish membership application, the Kurdish violence came to an end after the capture of the PKK leader, Abdullah Ocalan in February 1999. In this capture, a major revelation was done by the Turkish government regarding Greece's involvement in protecting the rebel leader. It was an embarrassment for Greece but it remained defiant.[36] Apart from this, a general improvement in the political climate in Turkey occurred and the coalition government elected to power in April 1999 committed itself to reforms. This also coincided with a period when Greek–Turkish relations began to improve subsequent to the massive earthquakes that both countries suffered. The rapprochement between Turkey and Greece through the disaster diplomacy[37] brought a positive turn in the EU's attitude such as the 1999 Helsinki Summit decision. Greece lifted its veto to allow full Turkish candidature in 1999 and in turn, it won an important concession: that Cyprus could join the EU in return for a verbal promise that it would go along with the UN-led plans for a bi-communal solution to the island's division.[38]

The change in Greece's attitude towards Turkey was that both Greece and the EU understand the costs and benefits of Turkey's accession that relate to the realm of security. For countries like Greece and Cyprus, the understanding of national security was and is the primary reason behind the acceptance of Turkey's accession. Both the countries know that their national security hinges upon their relations with Turkey. But this acceptance has come with a price for Turkey, which the country is not comfortable with. Greece wants Turkey to fulfil the EU conditions regarding its neighbour such as solving the dispute regarding the Aegean Sea, Cyprus and the rights of the Orthodox community in Turkey, and also the rebalancing of Turkey's civil–military relations which would allow Greece to cut its defence budget. Turkey's accession is conceptualised through the lens of national security for Greece.[39]

## Benefits of the Helsinki Summit

The decision of 1999 set off a process of political reforms within Turkey. Initially, the reforms proceeded very slowly due to a weak coalition government. However, the elections in November 2002 brought in the government led by the Justice and Development Party (AKP) with a decisive majority in the Turkish Parliament[40] that saw expedited the reform process in Turkey. Prior to 1999, the European ambivalence toward Turkey's claims to full EU membership had created the appropriate climate for the rise of authoritarian brands of identity politics, namely, political Islam, as well as ethnic nationalism. Both had emerged as major threats to Turkish democracy in the 1990s; threats that had clearly facilitated the re-emergence of the military as a major factor in Turkish politics in the context of a fragmented party system and a weak Parliament.[41]

The new government formed by the AKP accelerated the reforms and adopted four major reform packages in a short span of time from January to June 2003 aiming at far-reaching changes in political system.[42] This government has been responsible for an important set of democratisation reforms, helping to move Turkey from a kind of representative, procedural democracy, which had been a reality for several decades, towards "substantive democracy", with significant improvements in the realm of civil and human rights such as freedom of expression, freedom of association, and civilian control of the military.[43] The democratisation process and the emergence of a sizeable pro-EU/pro-reform coalition in Turkey, within both the state and the society at large, had also precipitated a shift from a hard-line nationalistic stance. This change was clearly reflected in the approach towards the resolution of the Cyprus dispute. The AKP took a pro-active stance in it and strongly advocated the acceptance of Kofi Annan's Plan as the best option for resolving the Cyprus dispute.[44] However, the implementation of the reform packages was considered uneven by the EU. During 2004, Turkey took measures to ensure the proper implementation of the reforms. The process continued with an increasing pace so as not to leave any pretext for the EU to delay the start of accession negotiations. Although Turkey was far from meeting the criteria in rather sensitive areas such as legal procedures, property rights and internal management of non-Muslim religious communities, the status of the Alevis, and broadcasting in Kurdish, the EU's regular report in 2004 was quite favourable towards Turkey's performance in completing the requirements of the Accession Partnership.[45]

Despite taking important steps in domestic reforms, Turkey witnessed deterioration in the EU–Turkey relationship with objections rising from countries like Germany and France and the non-breakthrough in the Cyprus issue. In January 2004, Turkish Prime Minister Recep Tayyip Erdogan agreed with Kofi Annan, the then Secretary General, that if the two Cypriot leaders failed to reach any agreement then Turkey would allow Annan to "fill the gaps". The Turkish military also supported the Annan Plan of referendum. An important feature in the Cyprus case is that the AKP government[46] was the first government within Turkey that could break away from the hard-line stance over Cyprus. The EU granted Greek Cyprus membership which caused a furore within the Turkish circle which saw a hurried EU balancing the relationship with Turkey by its decision on December 2004 to open negotiations with the country on October 2005, though not immediately.

The EU leaders although agreed to open negotiations with Turkey in 2005 but five points in the agreement sparked severe reactions in Turkey: the issues of permanent derogations; the extension of the 1963 Ankara Agreement to the (Greek) Republic of Cyprus; the absorption capacity of the EU; a statement in the agreement that the negotiation process would be open-ended and the issue of the maintenance of good relations with Turkey's neighbours with particular focus on the Aegean issue. These points revealed that the method that the EU would apply to Turkey's integration would be different from the previous methods that the Union had applied for the former candidates and for Central and Eastern European Countries (CEECs).[47]

From the EU side, non-recognition and non-negotiation by the Greek Cypriots became critical in the Turkey accession process. The changing variables of the international arena after the Greek Cypriots were admitted to EU membership on May 1, 2004, created a new challenge for the AKP in terms of preserving its own domestic political power vis-à-vis the relationship with EU. The AKP government announced a Cyprus Action Plan on January 24, 2006, which aimed to end the isolation of Northern Cyprus in exchange for opening the ports and air space to Greek Cypriots and for resuming the settlement process under UN supervision. However, this Action Plan has not brought any concrete results for the resolution of the problem. The accession negotiations that started with the EU on October 3, 2005, had the settlement of the Cyprus issue as one of the conditions required to be met by Turkey for the success of negotiations.[48] The ambiguity of the EU has resulted in restlessness amongst the Turkish reformers. Turkish leaders including President Abdullah Gul and Foreign Minister Ahmet Davutoglu had spoken of the possibility of "alternatives" if the Cyprus problem was not solved by the end of 2009. Prime Minister Recep Erdogan had spelled out that Turkey wants a settlement to be agreed upon and if there was no solution due to a Greek Cypriot failure to compromise then Ankara said that it would push for something like recognition of a Turkish Cypriot state. Turkey has become demotivated because of EU's attitude. It has understood that no matter whatever it does, Turkey would not be accepted by Europe and that if it should help solve Cyprus, core EU states would find another issue to block the accession process.[49] This has led to the return of Turkey's harder attitude.

The accession talks that had formally started in late 2005 as per the decision of the December 2004 European Council meeting, did not radically improve Turkey's status within the EU. The reasons apart from the Cyprus issue were due to the European leaders' concerns about the potential costs of Turkey's membership for the EU (its size, demographic growth, level of economic development and its different culture and religion). Consequently, Turkey's eventual accession was tied to several non-Copenhagen criteria-related conditions including, inter alia, the EU's absorption capacity and affirmative votes of European nationals. Besides, the EU also made it clear that accession negotiations would involve an 'open-ended' process in which the outcome would not be predicted beforehand. The uncertainty surrounding Turkey's entry into the EU in spite of its impressive democratisation performance reduced incentives for the ruling AKP to push ahead with its reform agenda in the face of stiff resistance by the nationalist forces hell-bent on preserving the status quo. Once scepticism about the EU membership set in, public support for the painful domestic reforms showed signs of progressive decline.[50]

## Problems within Turkey due to the Non-Acceptance by the EU and the Beginning of a 'Look East' Policy

Emboldened by the receding 'EU-phoria', the state-centred, hard-line secularists raised the spectre of the AKP's secret Islamicising agenda and sought the closure of the party in March 2008 following its initiative to lift the headscarf ban on female university students. Uncomfortable with some key elements of the EU's conditionality (namely, recognition of Kurds as national minority with distinct cultural and linguist rights, deletion of the anti-terrorism law, restricted role of the NSC, democratic control of the armed forces and decentralisation of power), the Turkish military joined the civilian opponents in confronting the AKP.[51] In fact, during the Presidential election in April 2007, the military issued a dire warning to the government over the election of a president whose wife wears the headscarf. The e-memorandum was followed by stunning allegations of a plot involving *Ergenekon*—a sinister network of serving and retired military officers, intelligence operatives, journalists, businessmen and lawyers and judges—to plan wide-scale violence and provoke the military to step in. Amidst the political polarisation and an intense power struggle, the EU-driven reform process in Turkey had virtually stagnated since the end of 2005.[52] The Turkish referendum on the constitutional amendment package had ironically deepened social fragmentation, rendering it all the more difficult for the governing AKP to build a broad consensus on its democratisation project. The legal and political reforms that Turkey underwent between 2001 and 2005 had constituted a major leap-forward in achieving the status of liberal democracy. This transition, however, would have been impossible in the absence of a powerful and highly institutionalised EU anchor in the direction of full membership.[53]

But the year 2007 was a negative year for Turkey as there was unprecedented polarisation in Turkish politics. The conflict between the AKP and its secular opponents reached a crisis point over the election of a new President of Turkey. While this crisis was going on, the AKP deputies proposed a constitutional amendment package that involved changes in five articles and the addition of two provisional articles. The project was seen as the AKP's plan to get rid of the controls of military and judiciary, and turn the political system into a majority dictatorship, thus eventually paving the way for an Islamic regime. In Turkey the secularist considers the office of the Presidency as a symbol and the 'last citadel' of the secular republic, therefore election of any Islamist politician is vehemently opposed by the secularists. Ahead in 2007, when the candidature of Abdullah Gul as the President was contested, subsequently a crisis in the Parliament arose though ultimately Mr. Gul came out victorious.[54] Though there was fear looming within Turkey but the EU saw the electoral victory of 2007 as a positive signal. With this encouraging signal from the EU, Turkey also acknowledged its bit of work to streamline Turkey with the EU's standard.

In 2008 Mr Abdullah Gul, President of Turkey recognised that Turkey needed reform and requested support from the Turkish society[55] and a new National Programme for the Adoption of the EU *acquis* was signed, formally updating the road map for adopting the EU body of law for the first time since 2003. In 2009, Turkey showed its renewed will to revive its flagging convergence with the EU, when Prime Minister Erdogan upgraded the status of Turkey's main implementing institution for EU legislation, the EU General Secretariat, from the control of the Foreign Minister to the Prime Minister.[56] But the efforts went unrecognised as 18 chapters of the EU *acquis* out of the 35 chapters remained closed. The EU wants Turkey to open its ports and airports to ships and planes from the Greek side of Cyprus.

Both the sides had kept the negotiations open despite the obstacles which saw the launching of the 'positive agenda' between Turkey and the EU on May 2012. However, since July–December 2012, Turkey had frozen its relations with the EU because of the Greek Cyprus Presidency in the union. On February 2013, Turkey and the EU again started with their associations which led to the opening of another chapter but the violent suppression of mass demonstration against the Turkish government on May 2013 have again pushed the relationship to the backburner. The EU in October 2013 come out with its progress report which is a mix of praise and expectations from the community's side that led to the November 2013 talks regarding the negotiations. But the failure of the talks shows the protracted stalemate on the issue and also the disinterest on both the sides.

In fact, over time, with the failure on EU's part to tap into Turkey's potentialities because of the former's 'carrot and stick' policy, it can be seen how Turkey's current government is diverting Turkey from the EU towards the East, with its 'Look East' policy. With a new world order of mulitpolarity, where the prominence of the West is being diminished, there is growing disinterest in Turkey's part to be associated with this part of the world. Turkey under the AKP has been asserting its Islamic identity more than Atatturk's European identity. It wants to emerge as an individual Islamic regional power in West Asia, keeping a balance between West and East rather than be under the tutelage of the West. Hence, from Attaturk's 'Look West' policy, Turkey under the AKP is moving towards the 'Look East' foreign policy.

It might not be wrong to argue that Turkey is pursuing a covert policy of neo-Ottomanisation. During the period of Ottoman rule, the Empire was clear in its association with the West—economy and military alliances. It tried to stop the dilution of Turkey's Islamic identity. This was changed during Attaturk's time, who through his forceful imposition, deflected the country's course to an European identity. This policy was successful to a certain extent; however, a large section of Turkish society was left with dissent. During AKP's time, the government initially went along with the Europeanisation process as it helped in building its foundation to disseminate its ideology in the secular country. With the EU's ambivalent behaviour showcasing Turkey's incapability of being an EU member for various reasons including the identity issue and the membership of the Greek Cyprus in 2004, it has helped the AKP government to divert the Turkish people from the membership issue and keep Turkey's association with Europe in terms of economy. Also, there is a return of the hardline stand towards the Cyprus issue with complete support to TRNC by the AKP which was seen weak during the 2004 Annan Plan. Military wise also although Turkey is still a NATO member but the recent contract of September 2013 between Turkey and China to co-produce a long-range air and missile defence system (T-LORAMIDS) and integrate it into NATO's overall air defence architecture[57] is an indication of Turkey's covert diversion. In addition to these, Prime Minister Recep Erdogan's statement in January 2013 on considering an alternative in SCO (Shanghai Cooperation Organisation) because of the stalemate with the EU speaks in length about the fatigue and disinterest that Turkey is undergoing regarding the accession issue.

## Conclusion

The EU's change of position from 'yes' to 'yes-but', and from 'yes-but' to 'privileged membership' to the 'waiting room' option[58] has complicated the issue of the EU membership in Turkey, especially the section of people which identifies itself with Europe. However, for the AKP and its supporters, the EU accession process proved a boon for their religious freedom and identity. The latest 2013 reforms by the AKP government give out a mixed picture of deliverance and reluctance. On one hand, the government has lifted the ban on headscarves which will alter the Turkish society as most of the people identify themselves with their religion and on the other hand, the government has curbed the freedom of expression which was witnessed during the May–June 2013 Gezi Park suppression.

The AKP government's drive to move Turkey towards a conservative society and distancing itself from the EU membership highlights the government's objective of retaining the Islamic identity of the Ottoman rather than a secular one of Attaturk's. It understands the effect of becoming an EU member where the European ideas will seep into the Turkish society which the AKP especially Erdogan is against, such as freedom of alcoholism, abortion, condemnation of co-ed dormitories etc. The implication of AKP's latest steps in diverting Turkey from the West and attaching more to West Asia and Asia might help in strengthening its Islamic identity. But the government must be careful about various things that can be the future seeds of instability in this stable country such as it becoming the breeding ground for Islamist extremists, clashes between the majority and the minorities etc.

The EU on the other hand should be clear about its approach to Turkey's membership. The ambivalence exuded by the EU towards Turkey has not been in a positive context. One can understand that the non-acceptance of Turkey by the EU is a conscious decision to exclude a country of 76 million Muslim people which can alter Europe's identity but somewhere the community is betraying its EU motto 'United in Diversity' by vacillating in its commitment towards Turkey. The EU must understand that by including Turkey as a member it will help in building a 'global society of peace and creative coexistence'.[59] In the same manner, Turkey should keep its secularism intact and contribute towards this harmonious and creative coexistence with the European people. The coexistence will help in understanding the concept of *dependent origination* that would further help in creating sustainable development and peace all over the world.

## Notes

1. "Germany Gives Green Light to Open New Chapter in Turkey's EU Bid", *Hurriyet Daily News*, October 20, 2013. http://www.hurriyetdailynews.com/germany-gives-green-light-to-open-new-chapter--in-turkeys-eu-bid.aspx?PageID=238&NID=56541&NewsCatID=351
2. The progress report highlighted the protracted political and technical stalemate between both the parties.
3. James G. Neuger, "EU Resumes Turkey's Entry Talks, Presses Erdogan on Civil Rights", *Bloomberg Buisnessweek*, October 22, 2013. http://www.businessweek.com/news/2013-10-22/eu-resumes-turkey-s-entry-talks-presses-erdogan-on-civil-rights
4. Amikan Nachmani (2003), *Turkey: Facing a New Millennium-Coping with Intertwined Conflicts*, Manchester: Manchester University Press, p.55.
5. John Redmond (1993), *The Next Mediterranean Enlargement of the European Community: Turkey, Cyprus, and Malta?* Aldershot, Hants, England; Brookfield, Vt., USA: Dartmouth, 1993, p.21 and *International Crisis Group* (2008), "Turkey and Europe", p.1.
6. Ibid, p.21.
7. Korel Goymen (2007), "Interaction of Democracy and Islam in Turkey" in Zoya Hasan (ed) *Democracy in Muslim Societies: The Asian Experience*, London: Sage Publications, pp.221-222.
8. George Christou (2004), *The European Union and Enlargement: The Case of Cyprus,* New York: Palgrave Macmillan, p.126.
9. Article 28 states that 'as soon as the operation of the Agreement has advanced far enough to justify envisaging full acceptance by Turkey of the obligations arising out of the Treaty establishing the Community, the Contracting Parties shall examine the possibility of the accession of Turkey to the Community'. *Regular Report from the European Commission* (1998) "Turkey's Progress: Progress Towards Accession 1998", and Olli Rehn, Member of the European Commission, responsible for Enlargement (2006), "Turkey's Accession Process to the EU", *SPEECH/06/747*, Helsinki, 27 November.
10. Borut Grgic, "A New Strategic Outlook for Turkey", *ESI*, http://www.esiweb.org/pdf/esi_turkey_tpq_id_65.pdf, p.3.
11. Semin Suvarierol (2003), "The Cyprus Obstacle on Turkey's Road to Membership in the European Union" in Al Çarko Lu and Barry Rubin (ed.) *Turkey and the European Union: Domestic Politics, Economic Integration and International Dynamics*, London: Frank Cass and Company Limited, p.60.
12. Ibid, p.60.
13. Redmond, *The Next Mediterranean Enlargement,* p.25.
14. Greece's conflict with Turkey has been from ancient times. With time the standoff got aggravated when Greece fought its War of Independence in 1823 where it involved Cyprus for the first time. The 1921–22 war and the Cyprus invasion of 1974 along with the Aegean islet conflict of Imia/Kardak in 1996 shows the bitterness between both the NATO members. Greece aggravated the bitterness more by involving the international community. In 1954 Greece involved UN over the Cyprus issue which got ugly and till date is a conflict which remains unsolvable and with both Greece and Cyprus becoming members the conflict seems frozen. Greece

and Turkey also have similar histories of the political system where both were ruled by the military but Greece after the 1974 coup that led to the invasion of Cyprus changed its government to a democratic civilian government. Regarding Greece's accession to the EU, Greece was fortunate enough as during 1980s the EC started to expand its community where it embraced Greece, Spain and Portugal (For more details regarding the Greek-Turkish conflict one can refer to Amikam Nachmani (2001), "What Says the Neighbour to the West? On Turkish-Greek Relations", in Barry Rubin and Kemal Kirisci (eds) *Turkey in World Politics*, London: Lynne Rienner Publishers and for Turkey's involvement in Cyprus, the reason behind it one can consult Leontis Ierodiakonou (1971), *The Cyprus Question*, Stockholm: Almqvist & Wiksell and many other books dealing with the issue).

15. *International Crisis Group* (2008), "Turkey and Europe: The Decisive Year", Europe Report N°197 – 15 December, http://www.crisisgroup.org/~/media/Files/europe/197_turkey_and_europe___the_decisive_year_ahead.pdf, p.2.
16. This validates the eagerness of Cyprus (Greek side) for an early membership.
17. Suvarierol, "The Cyprus Obstacle", p.59.
18. Kivanc Ulusoy (2008), "Turkey and the EU: Democratization, Civil-Military relations, and the Cyprus Issue", *Insight Turkey*, Oct, 2008, p.9.
19. Aswini K. Mohapatra (2011), "Turkey's Transition to Liberal Democracy and the Issue of its EU Membership", *India Quarterly,* vol. 67, no. 2, p.151.
20. *International Crisis Group* (2008), "Turkey and Europe", p.2
21. Ibid, p.2.
22. Mohapatra, "Turkey's Transition to Liberal Democracy, p.157.
23. Kemal Kirisci (2004), "The December 2004 European Council Decision on Turkey: Is It an Historic Turning Point?"*MERIA*, vo.8, no.4, December, p.89.
24. In December 1997, the Luxembourg Summit had put Cyprus but not Turkey on the list for the next expansion round. Greece was not solely responsible, since a number of member states were disturbed by the Turkish hardliners' repeated threats of war against Greece, near civil war in the Kurdish south east and triple-digit inflation (also another *soft coup* had taken place in Turkey on 1997) (*International Crisis Group*, "Turkey and Europe", p.2).
25. Kirisci, "The December 2004", p.89.
26. "The Role of the EU in Turkish-Greek Relation", *Ankara Paper 10*, 2004, New York: Taylor & Francis Ltd, p.2.
27. Suvarierol, "The Cyprus Obstacle on Turkey's Road to Membership", p.60.
28. Turkey has zealously guarded one third of NATO's front line with the Warsaw Pact for 40 years. It has always tried to be in the forefront as a NATO member to protect Europe. However, lately there is a shift in Turkey's attitude regarding its commitment towards the NATO. Reasons are varied.
29. Christou, *The European Union,* pp.77-78.
30. Ibid, pp.77-78.
31. Turkish Prime Minister Mesut Yilmaz compared the German approach to European Union expansion with Adolf Hitler's "Lebensraum" drive for German settlement of Eastern Europe. Yilmaz accused the EU of discriminating against Ankara. He blamed the German government in particular for Turkey's omission. Julia Ferguson (1998), "Turkish PM says Germany seeks 'Lebensraum' via EU", 3 March, *Reuters.*
32. "Turkey and the EU: 2004 and Beyond", 3 and 4 October 2003, *LIEIS*, Luxembourg: Luxembourg Institute for European and International Studies, p.1.

33. Rana Deep Islam (2008), "The Accession of Turkey to the European Union: Security Implications for Transatlantic Relations", *DIAS Analyse* (Düsseldorfer Institut für Außen- und Sicherheitspolitik (DIAS) Nr.[29], Düsseldorf, Mai, p.10.
34. Suvarierol, "The Cyprus Obstacle on Turkey's Road to Membership", p.58.
35. Ioannis N. Grigoriadis (2006), "Turkey's Accession to the European Union: Debating the Most Difficult Enlargement Ever", *School of Advanced International Studies Review of International Affairs (SAIS)*, vol.26, no.1, Winter-Spring, p. 150.
36. Nachmani, "What Says the Neighbour", p.76.
37. For details regarding *disaster diplomacy* refer James Ker Lindsay (2000) "Greek-Turkish Rapprochement: The Impact of 'Disaster Diplomacy'", *Cambridge Review of International Affairs,* Autumn-Winter, vol xiv, no.1, pp.215-232.
38. *International Crisis Group*, "Turkey and Europe", p.2.
39. Nathalie Tocci (2007), "Conditionality, Impact and Prejudice in EU-Turkey Relations", *Quaderni IAI-TEPAV Report*, July Series 9, p.23.
40. Kirisci, 'The December 2004 European Council Decision on Turkey", p.90.
41. Ziya Onis (1999), "Turkey, Europe, and Paradoxes of Identity: Perspectives on the International Context of Democratization", *Mediterranean Quarterly*, vol.10, no.3, 1999, p.109.
42. Kivanc Ulusoy (2008), "Turkey and the EU: Democratization, Civil-Military Relations, and the Cyprus Issue", *Insight Turkey*, Oct, 2008, p.7.
43. Turkey was going through a difficult phase in its economy. Turkey needed the IMF funds to stabilise its own economy; therefore with the change in power under the AKP, lot of changes in both domestic and foreign policies were seen, including pro-active steps towards the Cyprus issue.
44. Ziya Onis and Suhnaz Yilmaz (2008), "Greek-Turkish Rapprochement: Rhetoric or Reality?" *Political Science Quarterly,* vol 123 No.1, pp.136-137. Meanwhile, in 2001 while the EU officials were encouraging the Turks and the Turkish Cypriots to work for a resolution, the EU on the other hand had taken the pressure off the Greek Cypriots by reiterating that the island would join the EU without the resolution of the dispute being a precondition. *Ankara Papers*, "The Role of the EU", p.5. The EU agreed upon inclusion of Cyprus in lieu of Greece's support for the enlargement process with the Central and Eastern European countries. Therefore, this ambiguity and partial behaviour of the EU had affected the relationship between it and Turkey. International Crisis Group, "Turkey and Europe", p. 1.
45. Ulusoy, "Turkey and the EU", p.7.
46. In 2010 the Turkish Prime Minister Recep Tayyip Erdogan sent a personal letter to Cyprus's Archbishop Chrysostomos, in a gesture indicating that he wants a quick solution to the Cyprus problem. Erdogan's letter to Archbishop Chrysostomos has been seen as a significant gesture, since the Archbishop is one of the most vocal critics of Turkey's policies on Cyprus, accusing Ankara of promoting a permanent partition of the island. "Turkish PM Sends Good-will Letter to Cyprus Archbishop", *Trend,* 9 March .2010, http://en.trend.az/regions/met/turkey/1650803.html.
47. Islam, "The Justice and Development Party", p.182.
48. Ayşe Aslihan Çelenk (2007), "The Restructuring of Turkey's Policy towards Cyprus: The Justice and Development Party's Struggle for Power", *Turkish Studies*, vol. 8, no. 3, p.359.
49. *International Crisis Group* (2009), "Cyprus: Reunification or Partition?" 30 September, pp.22-23, http://www.crisisgroup.org/~/media/Files/europe/201_

cyprus___reunification_or_partition.pdf.
50. Mohaptra, "Turkey's Transition to Liberal Democracy", p.158.
51. Ibid, p.159.
52. Ibid, p.159.
53. Ibid, p.159.
54. For details refer William Hale and Ergun Ozbudun (2010), *Islamism, Democracy and Liberalism in Turkey: The Case of the AKP,* New York: Routledge, pp.39-40 and also p.156. According to the opposition charges these changes were no more than "bubble wrap" used to conceal more invidious changes. It was because the core of the package was a major overhaul of the judiciary. This gave the President and the Parliament a greater say over the appointments of senior judges and prosecutors, and expanded the size of the constitutional court and that of the judicial body in charge of appointments. The opposition claims AKP would use the changes to pack the courts with Islamists, paving the way for religious rule. *The Economist* (2010),"Erdogan Pulls it Off", Sep 13th, 2010, http://www.economist.com/blogs/newsbook/2010/09/turkeys_constitutional_referendum.
55. Speech during the 24th meeting of the EU-Turkey Joint Consultative Committee (JCC) meeting, *The European Economic and Social Committee (EESC)* (2008), CES/08/35, Brussels, 15 April, http://www.eesc.europa.eu/activites/press/cp/index_en.asp, p. 1.
56. Ibid, p.1.
57. Burak Bekdil, "Chinese Air Defenses in Turkey a 'Virus' for NATO", *Hurriyet Daily*, October 15, 2013. http://www.hurriyetdailynews.com/chinese-air-defenses-in-turkey-a-virus-for-nato.aspx?pageID=238&nID=56239&NewsCatID=483
58. Grgic, "A New Strategic Outlook", p.3.
59. Daiskau Ikeda, "Compassion, Wisdom and Courage: Building a Global Society of Peace and Creative Coexistence", *Peace Proposal 2013*, http://www.sgi.org/assets/pdf/peaceproposal2013.pdf.

# 11
# The Gülen (Hizmet) Community in Slovakia and Bosnia: Transnational Movement as a Turkish Foreign Policy Actor

*Gabriel Pirický*

## Introduction

The transformation of Turkish political Islam during the past two decades had an immense impact on foreign relations of Turkey not in the least because of the expanding space for a more rationalist Islam after the triple victory of the Justice and Development Party (*Adalet ve Kalkınma Partisi, AKP*) in the general elections since 2002. On the one side, the AKP's attempts to introduce an Islam-based morality into Turkish politics was welcomed by various religious communities and *cemaats*; on the other side, diminished pressure from state authorities allows religiously oriented Turkish transnational movements to act more freely in their foreign activities.

The nature of socio-religious groups in Turkey changed significantly in the last decade and long established stereotypes are not reflecting the reality anymore. In fact, the sociopolitical atmosphere after the arrival of the AKP government to power bolstered more rationalist Muslim communities including the Hizmet Movement (formerly known as the Gülen movement) that use pragmatic and mostly non-confrontational methods on a large scale including in their activities abroad. The spiritual, economic and educational network around Fethullah Gülen is nowadays visible via educational programmes, publishing and business activities or media presentations throughout the world. A style of mobilisation based on personal networks loosely allied with domestic or foreign organisations has been termed "vernacular politics".

With the AKP's consolidation of power the Hizmet movement finally forged a closer alliance with Erdoğan's government becoming an important source of political and economic support both in Turkey and abroad. Therefore, it is completely natural to apprehend the movement as a foreign policy actor. Indeed, with loosening of boundaries between countries from Germany and the United States as far as Central Asia, pious Turks have entered into numerous transnational networks as important actors.

This contribution examines the above-mentioned processes and foreign activities in connection with the strategies of the Gülen-Hizmet movement in two ex-communist countries, Slovakia and Bosnia. Although, unlike in Bosnia, the Gülen movement is not a household name in Slovakia; it seems to be one of the most mature in terms of its methodology of interaction and of conflict resolution. Also, the two countries present in many respects a contrasting picture with, on the one side, vibrant domestic Muslim society recovering from a disastrous war in the Bosnian case, and on the other side, Slovakia that has only a tiny non-recognised Muslim minority living in a predominantly Catholic country. In examining these cases it becomes clear how important a role the Hizmet community plays in bridging Turkey with the outside world.

## Turkish Foreign Policy in the Age of 'Conservative Democracy'

Fethullah Gülen, a charismatic Islamic preacher, philosopher, mystic and writer, lives since more than a decade in Saylorsburg in the U.S. state of Pennsylvania, where he took refuge at the end of the 1990s when a judicial process against him began in his native Turkey, but stayed there even after his acquittal in 2006. In a survey organised by the *Foreign Policy* and *Prospect* magazines in 2008 Fethullah Gülen has come in first on a list of the top one hundred living public intellectuals. It is also highly symbolic for our discussion on Turkey's foreign policy that this leading figure ranked first in a magazine that has foreign policy as its main focus. At least since 2008 then, Fethullah Gülen may be considered as someone with an international prestige.

The Gülen community whose activities are centered mainly on education, media and business, can be described as one of the greatest and most distinctive in the entire Muslim world. The community has long ago expanded beyond the borders of Turkey and other Turkic countries, disseminating its message globally and gaining respect in various countries of Africa, North America and Europe. The movement gave birth to an alternative Turkish elite that is educated, enterprising, modern and yet anchored in moderate Sunni Islam. The Gülen movement succeeded in strengthening its economic and social base mainly thanks to the policies of the late Prime Minister and President Turgut Özal who was the father of Turkey's integration into the global economy after 1980. Its members are recruited from the conservative-oriented middle and upper class of Turkish society. In the field of business, media and secular education, they try to beat their competitors who are primarily from the ranks of the secular Turkish bourgeoisie, whereas the community's attempts to avoid direct political conflicts are largely successful. Moreover, the community is also active in non-profit organisations that focus on inter-religious dialogue and development aid. All in all, the movement is undoubtedly part of the process that Cihan Tuğal described as a "passive revolution" which aims at increasing the share of Muslim believers in the management of the institutions of the Republic of Turkey.[1]

Although the Gülen movement originally started its activities as a religious community it was rather quickly transformed into a socio-political movement as well. Notwithstanding that the movement always claims to be apolitical, similar statements do not fully grasp the actual situation on the ground. In fact, it gives preference to informal and network politics, though in recent years it became also more active in electoral politics.[2] It is undoubtedly true that Fethullah Gülen is not apolitical, but rather prefers approaches that could be described as "behind the scenes policy" (*politika üstü politika*). By publishing several daily newspapers and magazines as well as broadcasting TV programmes, the Gülen movement takes part in the public sphere and participates in political processes anyway. In previous decades, relations between the movement and the Turkish state varied between support by individual politicians including the centre-left PM Bülent Ecevit during 1980s, severe repression towards the end of the 1990s and increasing socio-political influence in the 2000s.

There has been much talk about the missionary activities of the movement. In this connection, it is perhaps reasonable to quote from David Tittensor:

> "the [Gülen] movement is a missionary organization—though not in the traditional sense...teachers are not the main agents of transmitting the message of Islam. Rather, this is undertaken by a select group of religiously inclined Muslim students that are identified and groomed in their formative years into *belletmenler* (study aids) that assist junior students in the dormitories and share houses, and act as proxies for the teachers, a process that allows the teachers to remain largely removed from the recruitment process, and maintain outwardly secular appearance of their institutions."[3]

It should be noted that there has been a gradual change in the name of the community which is now called by its members and sympathisers the Public Service Movement (*Hizmet Cemaati*). Those who are in the movement, label it with the word '*hizmet*', meaning Movement of voluntary service, where people come together not only on the basis of faith, but also in relation to more general human values, whether for education, health and charitable activities or commercial projects. The word *hizmet* has in recent years become so popular that even the ruling AKP party is often labelled as the 'Public Service Party' (*Hizmet Partisi*).

The Hizmet community has always been distinct from other Islamic communities in Turkey in its pro-state conformist attitude and its international aspirations. In fact, Gülen has been an effective international actor who placed his community in a different position in comparison with other Muslim communities in Turkey. The simple fact that the community with its nationalist version of Islam always fulfilled certain representative roles abroad made it undoubtedly an actor at the international level. Their efforts to reconnect Turkic people from Central

Asia or the Caucasus with their Turkic origins after almost a century of communist rule were implemented very much in harmony with the long-term foreign policy aims of the Republic of Turkey. In this context, representatives of the Gülen movement all over the world have always tried to develop good relations with Turkish diplomats.

In the meantime, political aspirations of the community reached the US establishment. Political Scientist Hakan Yavuz quoted one follower of Gülen as saying: "We have ties with almost all necessary networks in the United States. We have close ties with Hilary Clinton and some senators since the movement contributed to their election campaigns. We need to emulate the Jewish experience in America. Turkey is important but as long as the movement has close ties with the US establishment, Ankara will also listen to Hocaefendi".[4] The Gülen movement's institutions in the US such as Rumi Forum, Institute of Interfaith Dialogue or Atlas Foundation have been praised by influential politicians, for example ex-President Bill Clinton, Secretary of State Madeline Albright, James Baker or Hilary Clinton and many others. Furthermore, one of Gülen's financial advisers has been quoted as saying that if the movement transferred its power from abroad to Turkey it would become a political giant in Turkey.[5] The movement is even considered to be too pro-American (and even pro-Israeli) by some Turkish Islamist circles.

As early as in 1998 the Turkish daily *Yeni Yüzyıl* reported that "four thousand teachers work like diplomats in Gülen's schools abroad."[6] As Berna Turam mentioned in 2003, the community is proud to replace the state's functions at the international level, especially in Central Asia.[7] She reminded us that outside Turkey the schools opened by the community have "broader cultural and political agendas" and constitute "a major part of the pan-Turan ethnic politics that Gülen pursues in that region".[8] To open private schools in more than eighty countries (as of 2012) certainly requires experienced political lobbysts and the Gülen community has reached a stunning success in expanding its educational affiliates. Today, their 130 schools in the United States are outnumbered only by the Gülen-inspired schools in Turkey itself.[9]

According to Kösebalaban, Gülen's "vision of an ideal Turkish foreign policy differs from that held by other segments of the Islamic movement." In Gülen's vision Turkey is both Muslim and European and its foreign policy should acknowledge this fact. Although Turkey lacks common identification with the West, it desires to integrate with Western institutions.[10] Concerning Gülen's views he writes that "whereas the conventional map of the Islamic world takes the Middle East as its center, his cognitive map perceives Turkey to be at the center of a region comprised of the Balkans, Caucasus, and Central Asia".[11] Indeed, Gülen tries to fulfill his foreign policy vision mostly through the worldwide educational network. At the same time Kösebalaban argues that Gülen offers "an alternative vision of foreign policy" through the religious dialogue which he tries to construct with religious communities of different faiths. In 1998, Fethullah Gülen met with Pope John Paul II and several representatives of other religions in Turkey such as Patriarch Bartholomeos or the Chief Rabbi of Turkey David Aseo.

## Surpassing the Limits of Conventional Diplomacy: the Gülen–Erdoğan Axis

While in the past Gülen advocated for entente with Turkish Kemalists and the army—and against the Welfare Party (*Refah Partisi*) and its leader Necmettin Erbakan—after 2002 the movement converged with Prime Minister Recep Tayyip Erdoğan with whose political formation the AKP it formed a close alliance.[12] Both sides advocated for economic liberalism and religious and cultural conservatism as well as tried to establish themselves among the civilian and military bureaucracy. The Gülen community also became a network of power which secured lucrative positions in the administration and the business sector. The proliferation of opportunists who entered the ranks of the community for utilitarian reasons has augmented too. Both the movement and the current government have abandoned the inward-looking Kemalist concept of the Turkish foreign policy in favour of a more balanced policy of foreign engagement.

In the aftermath of 9/11 the Gülen movement received a lot of attention in the US and even more in countries where, as it was suggested, the community could be an example of moderate and modernist Islam. The rapid growth of conservative democracy linked with economic liberalism of the AKP was possible largely thanks to the existing vast network of Gülen followers organised as a web of associations. Some experts have identified the process promoted by the alliance of moderate Turkish Islamists (the AKP and the Gülen movement) as a religiously motivated project of Turkish imperialism.[13] According to Hendrick the AKP and the Gülen movement are two coalition forces that divide "the labor of the passive revolution between formal politics and market-based resource accumulation".[14] Hendrick also defines the "coalition's" foreign policy aims in terms of "aligning the AKP's policy of 'strategic depth' (i.e. its policy to broaden Turkey's bilateral relations with its regional neighbours, and with developing countries in Africa and Southeast Asia) with the Gülen movement's effort to deepen Turkey's cultural and economic relationships with developing countries the world over".[15] In a way, Gülen advocates similarly to what the Turkish foreign minister Ahmet Davutoğlu does for a balance between realism and idealism in foreign policy.

Formulated somehow differently Öktem states that:

> *"the AKP government opted for a new mode of engagement in the region, which significantly widened the scope of the country's regional influence. In cooperation with religious networks and charities from Turkey (especially the Gülen movement and Turkey-based foundations close to the government), foreign minister Abdullah Gül (now President) and his successor, Ahmet Davutoğlu, introduced a new policy perspective that surpassed the confines of conventional diplomacy and high politics, reaching out into the micro-level of community organisations and grassroots politics".*[16]

The Gülen Cemaati has supported Turkey's integration into the EU with "the belief that religious rights in Turkey would be better protected under the EU than they are currently under the Turkish constitution".[17] Ahmet Kuru suggested that more the movement started to benefit from globalisation, the more it became in favour of Turkey's membership in the EU.[18]

During the recent unrest in Turkey there has been much talk on the relationship between Islamic (conservative) and secular forces.

The fact that the Prime Minister's authoritarian style has been causing problems also with his potential voters and allies remained less noticed. Also, it is generally less-known outside Turkey that PM Erdoğan got into serious disputes with the Gülen community before the events in Istanbul's Taksim Square in June 2013 started. In this respect, in April 2013 the Gülen community issued a statement expressing deep concern over restrictions on the freedom of expression in Turkey. The fact that Fethullah Gülen openly spoke against the Prime Minister may have a deep impact in the near future on the course of events in the government and in Turkish society.

According to Yavuz, the current AKP government appreciates the support of the Hizmet community, but it is "very unhappy with the constant engagement of the movement in policy formulation".[19] Although generally in harmony with the Islamic facets of Erdoğan's foreign policy, it must be said, the movement has distanced itself from Erdoğan's government on certain foreign policy issues such as its very critical stance on Israeli policy or the waning enthusiasm for membership in the EU. Unlike PM Erdoğan, for example, Gülen has been critical of the Turkish flotilla that tried to help Palestinians in Gaza in 2010.[20] Consequently, Erdoğan despised this challenge to his authority although, at the same time, he was well aware that he needs the support of the community for electoral reasons. As it turns out, Bill Park says, "there has been, or is now, a long march through the institutions. Even in places like the foreign ministry, it seems that the followers of Gülen are starting to appear. What a lot of people tell me, in a way that I am starting to believe, is that they set up parallel structures within government institutions which might sometimes bypass the official structure of which they are part".[21]

Berna Turam underlines the importance of the "Turkish-ness" of the Gülen schools for the success of the community beyond the borders of the Republic of Turkey. She stresses that "the community expands its sphere of influence and power outside the national borders because of its national loyalties, not despite them".[22] In Central Asia, through activities of followers of Fethullah Gülen, transnationalism mixes with cultural pan-Turkism. Common roots (both existing and invented) or ancestors, blood brotherhood, similar customs, food or drink, all are used to refer to the shared Turkicness mixed with ethnic consciousness in Turkish Islam. In order not to fall into disgrace or not to risk conflict with the Turkish state, the Gülen network outside Turkey "has developed a more efficient and effective national identity... rather than an Islamic one," especially in the period before 2002.[23] This is also evidence that in its transnational activities Islamic networks are ready to suppress, at least partially, their vision of an Islamic mission. On the other side, borrowing Mücahit Bilici's argument, we notice that before 2002 the Islamic religion was acceptable and legitimate for the Turkish state only as far as it was part of the Turkish national identity, but it is not acceptable as religion pure and simple.[24] In Turkmenistan and Kyrgyzstan, two private institutions associated with people close to Fethullah Gülen, *Başkent* and *Sebat*, were active side by side with the official Turkish ministry of education (*Milli Eğitim Bakanlığı*). At "Turkish" schools in Kyrgyzstan or Turkmenistan it is a common thing to celebrate Turkish national holidays, including the date of Atatürk's passing.[25]

The Gülen movement, of course, is not the only Turkish actor outside Turkey. One of the most important actors is the state Sunni-Muslim "Church" organisation (*Diyanet*) that has long ago established its offices throughout the Balkan peninsula. Diyanet is probably, as Öktem says, "the world's largest and most centralised Muslim organization comparable in scope and capabilities only to the Vatican".[26] During the last ten years *Diyanet* has participated in construction projects throughout Central Asia and the Caucasus that resulted in the building-up of numerous mosques, as well as opening of several theological faculties and secondary schools, providing them with teaching personnel for Qur'anic courses and copies of Qur'ans in Arabic. A similar scenario has been welcomed by the West because the international community under its leadership considered the Turkish model of Islam acceptable and worth emulating in the ex-Soviet Turkic republics. The export of laicism (*laiklik ihracı*) belonged to the transnational activities of Turkish authorities as much as the delivery of imams for the places of worship in Germany.[27]

## The Gülen Movement and its Activities in Bosnia

Although the Bosnian Muslims are not ethnic Turks, for Turks they represent the last remnant of the once important Ottoman Muslim presence in the Balkans. It is sometimes said that up to four million Turkish citizens, who mostly came to Anatolia in the second half of the nineteenth and at the beginning of twentieth centuries, are of Bosnian origin.[28] In the Bosnian war between 1992–1995 Turkey strongly supported Bosnian Muslims on all important international platforms such as the NATO, the United Nations, the Organization of Islamic Conference and others. The common imaginary played an important role as the banners carried at a big protest meeting in Istanbul in February 1993 testified (the meeting was addressed by President Turgut Özal): 'Bosnia will not become a second Andalusia'.[29]

After the fall of communism in 1989 the first networks of Salafis and Jihadis spread in the Balkans, supported in the 1990s by donors from the Arabian peninsula. Then, Turkish networks replaced them. Unlike Wahhabis from the Gulf, Turks were considered by Western powers after 9/11 to represent a moderate state-controlled Islam. According to Solberg the Gülen movement is nowadays the most influential Turkish community in the Western Balkans with private education as its main field of activity.[30] Kösebalaban, for example, writes that Gülen perceives Turkey as the leader of the whole region with a specific Turkish interpretation of Islam, the pivotal state within the "Turkish sociocultural milieu".[31] The Gülen schools in the Balkans, as some say, resemble the American missionary schools which were active in the Ottoman Empire during the nineteenth century.[32] Yavuz mentions, however, that the community "so far did not make major inroads into non-Turkish Balkan Muslim communities".[33]

The Balkan region is in a sense vital for Turkey because it gives the rationale for the country to consider itself a European state, especially in terms of civilisation and identity. The Turkish involvement in the region in general and in Bosnia-Herzegovina in particular has been explained by foreign minister Davutoğlu mostly as a feeling of responsibility: "the territorial integrity of Bosnia-Herzegovina is as important for us as the territorial integrity of Turkey. The prosperity and security of Sarajevo is as important as the security and prosperity of Istanbul. This is not only the feeling of responsibility of our statesmen; this is the feeling and emotion of any individual Turk living in Turkey".[34] Another description attributed to the Turkish foreign policy in the Balkans has been connected with the term "new activism." To better explain this notion, Sabri Sayari clarifies the activist behaviour of Turkey within the region of the Middle East, Caucasus, and the Balkans by arguments emphasising the instability of the region as well as the influence of the diaspora minorities in Turkey.[35]

The Gülen community started its activities in Bosnia-Herzegovina in 1997. Because the Hizmet schools always follow the educational policy of the host country, they had to accommodate the Bosnian model that is multidimensional and in which religious classes are provided to Muslim, Catholic and Orthodox children separately. Only in Albania, secular education has been extended also to a religious one. This was due to the fact that the Gülen movement in 1995 took over the Albanian medreses jointly with *Komuniteti Musliman*, the Islamic community of Albania, when the Albanian Islamic Community was losing the financial support from the Gulf countries or was afraid of losing the medreses to the Wahhabis.

In Bosnia-Herzegovina, the Gülen schools function under the umbrella organisation called Bosna Sema Foundation. The schools, along with their dormitories, can be found in different cities throughout Bosnia—in the capital city Sarajevo, as well as in Zenica, Tuzla and Bihac. The education offered includes primary, secondary as well as university study programmes. The Bosna Sema owns three primary schools (in Sarajevo, Tuzla and Zenica), three high schools (Sarajevo College, the International School of Sarajevo and Una Sana College), and the Burch University in Sarajevo. In 2009–2010 the Burch University was attended approximately by 300 students. In 2011, according to the magazine *Student*, the university was attended already by 530 students, including 74 enrolled for doctoral or post-doctoral studies.[36]

In January 2011, *Today's Zaman* informed about the ranking of the Burch University which was chosen out of thirty universities as the best university in the country based on academic performance and educational criteria. The Bosna Sema, like any other among the Güleninspired educational facilities in foreign countries demonstrates its standards by organising Olympiads in mathematics, physics, biology, informatics or environmental projects. Otherwise, most of teachers at the Burch University come from Turkey, others are from Bosnia-Herzegovina, Uzbekistan, Malaysia, and Pakistan. Most of the sixteen professors come also from Turkey.

The university has been attended mostly by students from abroad, especially from Turkey. Female students would come to the Burch University because they can wear headscarves, whereas males have the possibility to keep Islamic-style beards. In Bosnia, no ban on wearing headscarves exists which makes the universities there even more attractive for young Turks. This freedom of outward religious expression together with the relatively short distance from Turkey and cultural similarities shared by the two countries are the main reasons why Sarajevo has a high standing among Turkish Muslim circles. Additionally, cheaper living standards in Bosnia and the possibility to avoid the highly demanding university entrance exam in Turkey is attracting students from Turkey as well.

However, education is not the only field in which the Gülen community has been involved in Bosnia. The construction company Prizma International as well as the tourist agency Fidan Tourism are both parts of the Gülen *cemaati* operating in the country. The Prizma International, for example, has participated in the construction of the Burch University and Fidan tours. As can be read on their official website, Prizma International was founded in 2004 as a small IT equipment business. Today, however, the company is engaged mainly in the field of construction although it also includes following activities: souvenir shop, school and office supplies, security systems, and a marketing studio. Moreover, the company reconstructed the Turkish Cultural Center named after *Yunus Emre* in Sarajevo and the Bosnian–Turkish business centre. Not surprisingly, Prizma International has been also reconstructing one of the biggest treasures of the Bosnian architectural heritage, the *tekke* in Blagaj; simultaneously rented by Fidan Tours, part of the Gülen community. The activities of the Gülen *cemaat*, including construction and tourism, can be considered as a step beyond the initial goal of promotion of the intercultural dialogue via education.

The community's national business association TUSKON (Confederation of Businessmen and Industrialists of Turkey) has also benefited from the Gülen movement's contacts with markets and both Turkish and local government officials. TUSKON's interest to be involved in the Balkan region was confirmed in September 2010 when it organised a conference in Bosnia which was attended by seventy businessmen and was led by the Turkish President Abdullah Gül under the heading "Turkey–Bosnia and Herzegovina Trade and Investment Forum." The very same month TUSKON also helped to organise a US Business Forum 2010 and the Balkan Leaders' Summit 2010 jointly with FEBA (Federation of Balkan American Associations) in New York. In July 2011, TUSKON and FEBA with joint efforts of Turkish, Balkan and US businessmen organised the Turkey-Balkans-America Trade and Investment Forum held in Istanbul. These meetings illustrate how the Gülen movement brings the attention of the Turkish businessmen to the region. It equally shows how Gülen's philosophy works in practice: the schools attract the businessmen, the businessmen invest.

The Turkish state also has its own rival educational activities in the country. The most important undertaking in this sense is the International University, founded by SEDEF (Sarajevo Education Development Foundation, established in 2004) and officially opened by the Turkish Prime Minister Erdoğan in April 2010. SEDEF, still another Turkish Islamic foundation consisting of Turkish businessmen and Bosnian intellectuals, has ties to *Deniz Feneri* (the Lighthouse), the biggest Islamic charity organisation in Turkey with further activities in the Balkans. In this way, various Turkish Muslim groups compete with each other outside the national territory as well.

One may argue that so far the Gülen movement in Bosnia-Herzegovina has been successful in promoting its own agenda as a foreign policy actor. The role of the Gülen community as the Turkish 'soft power' confirms that private actors are successfully challenging the state-centred perspective of Turkish foreign policy. The instruments of the Hizmet para-diplomacy are focused on education, business and media activities. With or without the consent of the AKP government it plays an important role in bridging Turkey and the movement with Western Balkans more generally and with Bosnia in particular.

## The engagement of the Gülen movement in Slovakia

Although the Ottoman Empire extended its frontiers well into central parts of the territory of the Kingdom of Hungary (of which Slovakia was a northern part) after the battle of Mohács in 1526, Islam hardly gained any ground there and very few towns, such as Esztergom and Visegrád on the Danube river, were inhabited exclusively by Turks.[37] Nevertheless, the southern borderland of what is today Slovakia had been an integral although often disputed part of the Ottoman empire during the 16th and 17th centuries. The city of Nové Zámky (Turkish *Uyvar*) to the east of Bratislava, Slovakia's capital, was the seat of the Ottoman province (*vilayet*) between 1663–1683. In fact, Uyvar was the most significant acquisition of the Ottomans in Slovakia.

Meanwhile, based on the findings of the Slovak Statistical Office, only 1212 people in Slovakia declared themselves Muslims in the 2001 census.[38] On the other side, Slovakia's Muslims estimate their numbers currently at some 5 thousand believers according to unofficial reports. In a conservative environment marked by Catholic tradition and post-communism, Muslims form an internally diverse and dynamic community of mostly temporary migrants. Muslims are concentrated in the capital Bratislava and several regional centres, as well as in Piešťany Spa. The number of Muslims in the neighbouring Czech Republic doubled in the past decade and similar trends are discernible in Slovakia too. Local Muslims are mostly well educated people and many of them are either students or enterpreneurs. Indigenous Muslims, however, are marginal in Slovakia. Generally, while Muslim immigrants are mostly male, among the Slovak converts women prevail over men in the ratio of six to four.[39] The majority of roughly 150 to 300 local Muslim converts are educated, young and women. With regard to their nationality, 'foreign' Muslims are mainly Arabs, Bosnians, Turks and Albanians, whereas Muslim converts are represented by Slovaks and Hungarians.

It cannot be overlooked that among the religious minorities in Slovakia, local Muslim communities especially receive wide media and political coverage. Noticeably, after 9/11 it is mainly the Muslims who are under scrutiny, not least because of their efforts to get permission to build a congregational mosque and to receive recognition from the Slovak state.[40] Since large segments of the Slovak society perceive Islam as a religion prone to violence and inequality, direct Muslim proselytism (*tebliğ*) is often understood in martial terms and encounters mostly negative reactions among the native population.

Although the Gülen movement is not a household name in the area, it seems to be one of the most mature in terms of its methodology of interaction. Hence, the concept of *temsil* or indirect mission as promoted by the Gülen community, based on moral conduct and good individual example including hard work, seems to be a much more convincing way of interaction and persuasion vis-à-vis the Slovak environment. The invocation of the Ottoman Empire's heritage nowadays helps the Gülen movement in the field of foreign policy and presents a possible rationale for their presence in Slovakia too.

In Slovakia, since 2011 the movement runs the Turkish–Slovak Alliance for Education and Development (TSAFED), a non-governmental and non-profit organisation with its seat in the capital Bratislava. It was established in order to develop mutually beneficial bilateral relations, especially in the field of education, research and business relations. Its educational branch, Bystra Education, has been established in 2005. It held, for example, a Turkish Day festival to promote Turkey and its culture via various activities: distributing Noah's pudding (*aşure*) on the streets, performing folk dance (e.g. *zeybek*) and whirling dervishes (*sema*), teaching people the traditional Islamic art of paper marbling (*ebru*) and calligraphy (*hat*). Again, they organise in Slovakia the European Olympiad in mathematics well-known as Pangea. In November 2008 the group co-organised the Slovak participation at the "Türkiye Mid-Eastern Europe Foreign Trade Bridge" in Istanbul that was organised by TUSKON.

On its internet pages TSAFED is trying to promote Slovakia under the heading 'Small country, big opportunities' as an ideal and safe investment destination for Turkish businessmen due to its economic and political stability as well as its membership in the Eurozone.[41] TSAFED's business partners, as can be read on its webpage, are the only companies which follow business ethics. Another aspect of TSAFED's activities in Slovakia is to establish a secondary school in Bratislava in the near future.

It is important to stress that Slovakia as a member of the European Union is being targeted by the community, I would argue, in connection with their mission to bring Turkey to the EU. Therefore, the movement cultivates its relations with the predominantly Christian countries of Central Europe—such as the Czech Republic, Hungary, Poland or Slovakia—in spite of the very small number of Muslims or Turks living there. It is perhaps best to see the community's activities here as the broadening of their diplomatic role in the EU countries that have joined the European Union only recently (in 2004).

**Final Remarks**

In the past, the Turkish military expressed its concerns over the international involvement of the movement fearing among others that Gülen will organise abroad a powerful lobby. In order to gain terrain in Turkey, however, the Gülen community had to appeal also to a global audience. Needless to say that they succeeded and the Gülen movement has an organisational network that now includes over 120 countries. The Hizmet schools worldwide are instruments of promoting Turko-Ottoman culture and Turkish language that are admired by Gülen himself. The Gülen schools are sometimes designated as 'ambassadors of peace.'

As this brief sketch shows, the followers of Gülen are very much motivated to burnish Turkey's image abroad and to put Turkey on the map of economically and culturally advanced countries. At the core, Gülen always tried to convince the Turkish public that he is working with and for the state. On the whole then, the use of nationalism and re-invocation of the Ottoman past by the community serve as foreign policy tools which should ensure positive relations with the Turkish state. Also, the convergence between activities and motivations of the Gülen movement and the AKP government goes far beyond anything that was imaginable before 2002. Nevetheless, the community represents a private and paralel diplomacy that is from time to time contesting the sovereignty of the state in the area of foreign policy.

What is still more important, is that the traditional inter-state model of foreign relations we have known from the past has become passé and what is unfolding here is a model based on a variety of actors. Turam argues that "the Gülen movement qualifies as an international bridge between the West and Islamic and Turkish ways of lives, especially by its emphasis on English instruction, universality of science, progress and secular education".[42] According to her, "it is important to note that the Gülen community initiates an international approach to education that involves educational policymaking in Turkey and in the host countries. In other words, the states recognise the Gülen community as an international actor and cooperate with it in formulating curricula. Because each curriculum reflects the educational policies of both Turkey and the host country, it should not contradict the national interest of any nation state".[43] For Gülen even non-religious education serves religious aims, the idea which appeals to many people outside Turkey, too.

In Bosnia and Herzegovina, unlike the Wahhabis and Salafis who focused on less educated segments of the population or Iranian networks that were interested mainly in coopting Bosnian intellectuals, the Gülen community is clearly middle and upper-class oriented. Turkey today is once again a Balkan power. The advantage of the Turkish networks vis-à-vis other international actors is twofold: a common historical legacy and similar Islamic practices (Sunni Hanafi) both in Turkey and Bosnia and Herzegovina.

Unlike Bosnia, Slovakia is neither a Muslim land nor a former part of the Ottoman Empire. But similar to the situation in Bosnia, the end of the communist regime enabled religious freedom and opened the door for various religious networks from abroad including the Gülen movement.

In 1992, Selim Deringil summarised that "the basic problematic of republican Turkish foreign policy has always been readjustment to secondary power status from an Imperial past".[44] With the economic power of the Turkish Republic rising, the AKP government tries to renew some of the pre-Republican grandeur of the Turkish foreign policy. It positions itself as a transnational Muslim power trying to revive a sort of Neo-Ottoman Commonwealth. The Gülen movement is without any doubts an important ally of the government in these endeavours and the major non-governmental Turkish foreign policy actor too. Be it as it may, the activities of the movement in both Bosnia and Slovakia seem to confirm this fact.

## Notes

1. See Cihan Tuğal, *Passive Revolution: Absorbing the Islamic Challenge to Capitalism*. Stanford, Stanford University Press, 2009.
2. M. Hakan Yavuz, *Toward an Islamic Enlightenment: the Gülen Movement*. Oxford, OUP, 2013, p. 200.
3. Unpublished lecture: David Tittensor: "Gülen's Schools and the Changing Nature of Islamic Mission: Exploring the Teacher-Student Dynamic", Middle East Studies Association, Denver 2012.
4. Yavuz, *Toward an Islamic Enlightenment: the Gülen Movement*, p.45.
5. Mucahit Bilici, "The Fethullah Gülen Movement and Its Politics of Representation in Turkey",*The Muslim World*, Vol. 96, No. 1 (2006), p. 7.
6. *Yeni Yüzyıl,* 26 January 1998.
7. Berna Turam, "National Loyalties and International Undertakings: The Case of the Gülen Community in Kazakhstan",Yavuz, M. H. – Esposito, J. L. (eds.): *Turkish Islam and the Secular State: The Gülen Movement*. New York, Syracuse University Press, 2003, p. 200.
8. In some countries very cautious diplomacy was needed from members of the movement to reach their goals. This was the case, for instance, in Turkmenistan during the rule of President Saparmurat Niyazov (*Türkmenbaşı*) with whom relations often switched from troubled to cordial. Turam, "National Loyalties and International Undertakings: The Case of the Gülen Community in Kazakhstan", p. 188.
9. Joshua Hendrick, *Gülen: The Ambiguous Politics of Market Islam in Turkey and the World*. New York–London, New York University Press, 2013, p. 7.
10. Hasan Kösebalaban, "The Making of Enemy and Friend: Fethullah Gülen's National-Security Identity", Yavuz, M. H. – Esposito, J. L. (eds.): *Turkish Islam and the Secular State: The Gülen Movement*. New York, Syracuse University Press, 2003, pp. 170–172.
11. Ibid., p. 173.
12. Yavuz, *Toward an Islamic Enlightenment: the Gülen Movement*, p. 228.
13. See Bayram Balci, *Missionaires de l'Islam en Asie centrale. Les écoles turques de Fethullah Gülen*. Paris, Maisonneuve&Larose, 2003.
14. Joshua Hendrick, "Globalization, Islamic activism, and Passive Revolution in Turkey: the Case of Fethullah Gülen", *Journal of Power* 2/3 (2009), p. 345.
15. Ibid. p. 351.
16. Kerem Öktem, "Global Diyanet and Multiple Networks: Turkey's New Presence in the Balkans", 4. Joshua Hendrick, "Globalization, Islamic Activism, *Journal of Muslims in Europe*, Vol. 1, No. 1 (2012), p. 31.

17. Burhanettin Duran, "JDP and Foreign Policy as an Agent of Transformation", Yavuz, M. H. (ed.): *The Emergence of a New Turkey: Democracy and the AK Party*. Salt Lake City, The University of Utah Press, 2006, p. 284.
18. Ahmet T. Kuru, "Changing Perspectives on Islamism and Secularism in Turkey: the Gülen Movement and the AK Party", *Muslim World in Transition: Contributions of the Gülen Movement* (International Conference Proceedings). Leeds Metropolitan University Press, 2007, p. 144.
19. Yavuz, *Toward an Islamic Enlightenment: the Gülen Movement*, p. 219.
20. In May 2010 the Israeli army attacked in international waters off the cost of the Gaza Strip the "Freedom Flotilla" including the Mavi Marmara Turkish ship that was carrying humanitarian help to Palestinians. Nine Turks were killed and the Turkish–Israeli relations deteriorated sharply. The world condemned the attack, yet Gülen criticised Muslim humanitarian organisations for not attempting to gain the legal consent of Israel.
21. Suzy Hansen, "The Global Imam", *New Republic* November 10, 2010 (available at http://www.newrepublic.com/article/world/magazine/79062/global-turkey-imam-fethullah-gulen).
22. Turam, "National Loyalties and International Undertakings: The Case of the Gülen Community in Kazakhstan", pp. 194–195.
23. Ibid. p. 193.
24. Bilici, "The Fethullah Gülen Movement and Its Politics of Representation in Turkey", p. 7.
25. Cennet Engin Demir, Ayse Balcı and Fusun Akkok, "The Role of Turkish Schools in the Educational System and Social Transformation of Central Asian Countries: the Case of Turkmenistan and Kyrgyzstan", *Central Asian Survey*, Vol.19, No.1 (2000), pp. 141–155.
26. Öktem, "Global Diyanet and Multiple Networks: Turkey's New Presence in the Balkans", p. 41.
27. Secularity (that is ideological secularism meaning to replace religion) not secularism is said to be the best term to describe Turkish *laiklik*. As an example of what secularity means it is instructive to quote from Turkish President Ahmet Necdet Sezer. In September 2004 during a symposium on religion organised by the state *Diyanet* he proclaimed to the astonishment of many participants that "secularism is a way of life, which should be adopted by an individual". A second example comes from the opening speech of President Sezer at the 21st World Congress of Philosophy in August 2003 in Istanbul, where he proclaimed that "philosophy must be modern and secular".
28. William Hale, *Turkish Foreign Policy 1774–2000*. London-Portland, Frank Cass, 2000, p. 261.
29. Ibid. pp. 260–261.
30. Anne Solberg, "The Gülen Schools: A Perfect Compromise or Compromising Perfectly?" 2nd Kotor Network Conference (2005), available on http://www.kotor-network.info/papers/2005/Gulen.Solberg.htm, accessed 11 August 2013.
31. Kösebalaban, "The Making of Enemy and Friend: Fethullah Gülen's National-Security Identity", p. 175.
32. Öktem, "Global Diyanet and Multiple Networks: Turkey's New Presence in the Balkans", p. 20.
33. Yavuz, *Toward an Islamic Enlightenment: the Gülen Movement*, p. 194.

34. Halit Eren (ed), *The Ottoman Legacy and the Balkan Muslim Communities Today. Conference Proceedings 16–18 October 2009*. Istanbul, Balkanlar Medeniyet Merkezi, 2011, p. 17.
35. Sabri Sayari, "The Turkish Foreign Policy in the Post-Cold War Era: The Challenges of Multi-Regionalism ", *Journal of International Affairs* Vol. 54, No.1 (2000), pp. 169–182.
36. N. Sarajlic, "Obrazovanje kao samostalan sektor djelatnosti." *Student* No. 86 (2011), p. 6.
37. See the headword "Madjar, Madjaristan" in EI$^2$ (1960-2003) *Encyclopaedia of Islam* (New Edition, Leiden, E.J.Brill), print edition V: 1010b.
38. Radovan Čikeš, "Registrácia cirkví a náboženských spoločností verzus náboženská sloboda", Moravčíková, M. and Lojda, M. (eds.) *Islam v Európe: náboženská sloboda a jej aspekty* , Bratislava, Ústav pre vzťahy štátu a cirkví–Centrum pre európsku politiku, Bratislava, 2005, p. 15.
39. Ivana Knapová, "Konverzia na islam na príklade slovenských žien." Unpublished M.A. dissertation. Trnava, Univerzita svätého Cyrila a Metoda, Slovakia, 2007, p. 42.
40. Slovakia is probably the only European country without a single mosque.
41. see www.tsafed.org
42. Turam, "National Loyalties and International Undertakings: The Case of the Gülen Community in Kazakhstan", p. 207.
43. Ibid. pp. 202–203.
44. Selim Deringil, "Introduction: Turkish Foreign Policy Since Atatürk." In: Dodd, C.H. (ed.): *Turkish Foreign Policy: New Prospects*. Huntingdon, The Eothen Press, 1992, p. 1.

**Bibliography**

Balcı, Bayram: *Missionaires de l'Islam en Asie centrale. Les écoles turques de Fethullah Gülen*. Paris, Maisonneuve&Larose, 2003.

Bilici, Mucahit: "The Fethullah Gülen Movement and Its Politics of Representation in Turkey", *The Muslim World*, Vol. 96, No. 1 (2006), 1–20.

Bougarel, Xavier: "Islam and Politics in the Post-Communist Balkans (1990–2000)", Keridis, D. and Perry, Ch. (eds): *New Approaches to Balkan Studies*, Dules, Brassey's, 2003, 345–360.

Bulaç, Ali: *Din-Kent ve Cemaat: Fethullah Gülen Örneği*. İstanbul, Ufuk Kitap, 2008.

Cenker, Michal: *Traditions Confronted: Muslim Migrants in Slovakia*. Saarbrücken, LAP LAMBERT Academic Publishing, 2010.

Clayer, Nathalie (2011), *Muslim Brotherhood Networks in South-Eastern Europe*, available on http://www.ieg-ego.eu/en/threads/european-networks/islamic-networks/nathalie-clayer-muslimbrotherhood-networks-in-south-eastern-europe/?searchterm=tariqa&set_language=en, accessed August 29, 2013.

Čikeš, Radovan: "Registrácia cirkví a náboženských spoločností verzus náboženská sloboda", Moravčíková, M. and Lojda, M. (eds): *Islam v Európe: náboženská sloboda a jej aspekty* , Bratislava, Ústav pre vzťahy štátu a cirkví–Centrum pre európsku politiku, Bratislava, 2005, 14–18.

Demir, Cennet Engin–Balci, Ayse–Akkok, Fusun: "The Role of Turkish Schools in the Educational System and Social Transformation of Central Asian Countries: the Case of Turkmenistan and Kyrgyzstan", *Central Asian Survey*, Vol.19, No.1 (2000), 141–155.

Deringil, Selim: "Introduction: Turkish Foreign Policy Since Atatürk", Dodd, C.H. (ed): *Turkish Foreign Policy: New Prospects*. Huntingdon, The Eothen Press, 1992, 1–8.

Duran, Burhanettin: "JDP and Foreign Policy as an Agent of Transformation ", Yavuz, M. H. (ed): *The Emergence of a New Turkey: Democracy and the AK Party*. Salt Lake City, The University of Utah Press, 2006, 281–305.

EI[2] (1960-2003) *Encyclopaedia of Islam*. New Edition, Leiden, E.J.Brill.

Eren, Halit (ed): *The Ottoman Legacy and the Balkan Muslim Communities Today. Conference Proceedings 16–18 October 2009*. Istanbul, Balkanlar Medeniyet Merkezi, 2011.

Hale, William: *Turkish Foreign Policy 1774–2000*. London-Portland, Frank Cass, 2000.

Hansen, Suzy: "The Global Imam", *New Republic* November 10, 2010 (available at http://www.newrepublic.com/article/world/magazine/79062/global-turkey-imam-fethullah-gulen).

Hendrick, Joshua: "Globalization, Islamic Activism, and Passive Revolution in Turkey: the Case of Fethullah Gülen", *Journal of Power* 2/3 (2009), s. 343–368.

Hendrick, Joshua: *Gülen: The Ambiguous Politics of Market Islam in Turkey and the World*. New York–London, New York University Press, 2013.

Karčić, Harun: "Islamic Revival in Post-Socialist Bosnia and Herzegovina: International Actors and Activities", *Journal of Muslim Minority Affairs*, Vol. 30, No. 4 (2010), 519–534.

Knapová, Ivana: "Konverzia na islam na príklade slovenských žien." Unpublished M.A. dissertation. Trnava, Univerzita svätého Cyrila a Metoda, Slovakia, 2007.

Kösebalaban, Hasan: "The Making of Enemy and Friend: Fethullah Gülen's National-Security Identity", Yavuz, M. H. – Esposito, J. L., (eds.): *Turkish Islam and the Secular State. The Gülen Movement*. New York, Syracuse University Press, 2003.

Kuru, Ahmet T.: "Changing Perspectives on Islamism and Secularism in Turkey: the Gülen Movement and the AK Party", *Muslim World in Transition: Contributions of the Gülen Movement* (International Conference Proceedings). Leeds Metropolitan University Press, 2007, 140–151.

Mendel, Miloš–Ostřanský, Bronislav–Rataj, Tomáš: *Islám v srdci Evropy*. Praha, Academia, 2007.

Öktem, Kerem: "Global Diyanet and Multiple Networks: Turkey's New Presence in the Balkans", *Journal of Muslims in Europe*, Vol. 1, No. 1 (2012), 27–58.

Pirický, Gabriel: *Islám v Turecku: Fethullah Gülen a Nurcuovia*. Trnava, UCM, 2004.

Pirický, G.: "Restrictive Legislation towards Minor Religions in Slovakia: the Case of the Muslim Community", *European Yearbook for Minority Issues 2007/8*, Leiden–Boston, Brill-Martinus Nijhoff Publishers 2010, s. 717–729.

Rüma, Inan: "Turkish Foreign Policy towards the Balkans: New Activism, Neo-Ottomanism or/so what?", *Turkish Policy Quarterly* Vol. 9, No. 4 (2010), 133–140.

Sarajlic, N: "Obrazovanje kao samostalan sektor djelatnosti." *Student* No. 86 (2011).

Sayari, Sabri: "The Turkish Foreign Policy in the Post-Cold War Era: The Challenges of Multi-Regionalism", *Journal of International Affairs* Vol. 54, No.1 (2000), 169–182.

Solberg, Anne: "The Gülen Schools: A Perfect Compromise or Compromising Perfectly?", 2nd Kotor Network Conference (2005), available on http://www.kotor-network.info/papers/2005/Gulen.Solberg.htm, accessed 11 August 2013.

Solberg, Anne R.: "The Role of Turkish Islamic Networks in Western Balkans", *Südosteuropa*, Vol. 55, No. 4 (2007), 429–462.

Tittensor, David: "Gülen's Schools and the Changing Nature of Islamic Mission:Exploring the Teacher-Student Dynamic", Unpublished lecture: Middle East Studies Association (46th Annual Meeting), Denver 2012.

Tuğal, Cihan: *Passive Revolution: Absorbing the Islamic Challenge to Capitalism.* Stanford, Stanford University Press, 2009.

Turam, Berna: "National Loyalties and International Undertakings: The Case of the Gülen Community in Kazakhstan", Yavuz, M. H. – Esposito, J. L. (eds): *Turkish Islam and the Secular State: The Gülen Movement.* New York, Syracuse University Press, 2003.

Yavuz, M. Hakan: *Secularism and Muslim Democracy in Turkey.* Cambridge, CUP, 2009.

Yavuz, M. Hakan: *Toward an Islamic Enlightenment: the Gülen Movement.* Oxford, OUP, 2013.

White, Jenny: *Islamist Mobilization in Turkey: A Study in Vernacular Politics.* Seattle, University of Washington Press, 2002.

White, Jenny: *Muslim Nationalism and the New Turks.* Princeton, PUP, 2013.

12

# Turkey's Cyprus Policy under the AKP

*Zeynep Didem Akınoğlu*

The long-running ethno-territorial conflict in the island-state of Cyprus is one of the world's intractable regional conflicts. Situated in the Eastern Mediterranean some 800 km to the east of Greece and about 70 km to the south of Turkey, and with an area of 9251 sq. km inhabited by over 1000, 000 people 77 percent of whom are of Greek extraction and 18 percent of Turkish origin, Cyprus remains divided since 1974.[1] It is the historic rivalry between Greece and Turkey, the two powerful regional actors, which has played the major part in the flare-up of an inter-ethnic conflict in this proverbial 'island of love.' Etiologically, therefore, roots of the Cyprus conflict may be traced to the rise of the two competing—Greek Cypriot and Turkish Cypriot—nationalism, but structurally it is linked to the hostile relational patterns between the two mainlands. In addition, the interposition of the UN peacekeeping forces in Cyprus since 1964 has shoved the conflict to a 'stable equilibrium from which it is difficult to budge the parties to the conflict.'[2] In other words, peacekeeping has hindered peacemaking by reinforcing the physical separation between the two communities and erecting the 'wall around them.'[3]

A series of developments in the recent years, notably the European Union's decision in December 1999 to accept Turkey's candidature for membership followed by the rise of the Justice and Development Party (AKP) to power and its de-securitised foreign policy pursuit have, however, stirred renewed optimism about the resolution of the Cyprus tangle. In this backdrop, this article will attempt to explain the factors accounting for the change in Turkey's Cyprus policy and assess its impact in terms of breaking the logjam in the process of a negotiated settlement of the conflict. It will be analytically useful to begin the discussion with a brief historical background of Cyprus, highlighting the island's geopolitical salience, the divisive role of the British colonialism and the two 'motherlands' in transforming apolitical religious division into mutual exclusive national identity and the structural flaws inherent in the post-independence political arrangement.

Historically, Cyprus changed hands several times due to its unique geographical location along the main routes between Europe and Asia and endowment of the copper deposits. In nine thousand years, every major and several minor empires in the eastern Mediterranean have conquered Cyprus.[4] Until the Roman Empire assumed the control of the island, Cyprus, for instance, had been under the influence of various nations. In 395 AD when the Roman Empire was split into two as the Western Roman Empire and the Eastern Roman Empire, Cyprus was declared as a province of the Eastern Roman Empire and remained under its influence until 1184, despite the interruptions. Under the rule of Roman Empire the people of Cyprus coming from different nations had been united in terms of language and religion and established the base of the Greek Cypriot community of contemporary Cyprus.[5] The first Islamic expedition to Cyprus had taken place in the tenure of Caliph Uthman by his Governer of Damascus Muawiyah. As a result of the second expedition in 654, Muslim population was accommodated on the island. During the Third Crusade, Richard I of England conquered the island. But, after a short period of time he sold the island to the Knights Templar then handed over the island to Guy de Lusignan in 1192. While Cyprus was under the Lusignan Rule between 1192 and 1498, the island came under Egyptian, Mamluk, Genoese and Venetian influence from time to time. In 1498 Venetians turned their de facto rule into de jure status and Cyprus officially came under the Venetian rule.[6]

In 1570 the Eastern Mediterranean, the Black Sea and the Red Sea were among the Ottoman lands, hence Turks were highly interested in the islands of the Mediterranean and they started to get the possession of the strategically important islands. From the perspective of the Ottomans especially after the capture of Rhodes in 1522, there were strong strategic and economic reasons to aim at the conquest of Cyprus.[7] Following the capture of the island, the Ottoman administrative system adapted and Anatolian people were settled on the island as a part of the *iskan* policy of the Ottoman Empire. During the Ottoman rule over the island which lasted for more than 300 years, the Turkish-Muslim and Hellenistic constituents of the island had grown separately and thereafter established a dual system distinct from each other.[8] The confrontation between the two constituents started only after the beginning of the activities for the Greek Revolt and efforts to achieve *Megali Idea* (Great Idea) in Cyprus following the independence of Greece from the Ottoman Empire. The effects of the Greek Revolt echoing in Cyprus were accompanied by the intensified campaign of Filiki Eteria which led to preparation for a revolt under the leadership of the church, but it was realised by the administration and prevented.[9]

The aftermath of the 1877–78 Russo-Turkish War was a turning point for Cyprus. This war created a shift in the European balance of power which had been established by the 1856 Paris Treaty in which the territorial integrity of the Ottoman Empire was secured by the European nations' guarantee. However, until the Russian troops had approached Istanbul, European powers did not act. The first European power to intervene was Britain as a consequence of her interests in Asia. Thus, Britain offered the Ottoman Empire to make an alliance treaty. According to the treaty which was signed in Istanbul on the June 4, 1878 "joint defence will be made against Russia, reforms will be made in those regions of Eastern Anatolia which are inhabited by Christians and Cyprus will temporarily be handed over to British rule".[10] Britain had taken over Cyprus' administration on July 15, 1878 and ruled the island as a protectorate until 1914, when Ottomans sided with Germany in the First World War. In 1914 "Britain annexed Cyprus and ruled it as a colony until 1960 when it became an independent republic."[11]

## Overview of Turkey's Cyprus Policy

### *From 1924 Lausanne Peace Treaty to the Foundation of the Republic of Cyprus*

In 1878, administration of Cyprus was handed over to Britain with the condition of continuity of sovereignty of the Ottoman Sultan over the island. In 1914, the Ottoman Empire joined Central Powers against the Allied Powers; then Britain announced the annexation of Cyprus. During the years of the First World War and the Turkish Independence War the island remained under British administration. Eventually, the Cyprus issue was included in Article 21 of the Lausanne Peace Treaty, which was signed on July 24, 1923, marking the end of the Turkish Independence War: "Turkey hereby recognises the annexation of Cyprus proclaimed by the British Government on the 5th November, 1915."[12]

The island under the British rule had witnessed acceleration of efforts of the Greek Cypriots in order to achieve *enosis* (union with Greece) beginning in 1931 and increasing especially after the Second World War. Though, Greek Cypriots' activities towards *enosis* led to tension at the Turkish Cyriot side, due to the context of the Cold War Turkey opted for maintenance of the status quo established by the Lausanne Treaty. Therefore, Republican People's Party (CHP) governments did not establish an active policy in the case of Cyprus, given that the Greek government had not taken the issue to the international area officially.

After 1950, the domestic change in Turkey and developments in Cyprus led Turkey to implement a Cyprus policy gradually. Following the elections held on May 14, 1950, the Democratic Party (DP) came to power. In the initial phase the DP government hesitated to come up with a new policy on Cyprus, hence it followed the same line as the previous government until 1954. On August 20, 1954 the Greek government requested the inclusion of right to self-determination in Cyprus in the agenda of the next session of the UN General Assembly. After rejection of the discussion of the issue in the UN General Assembly, the Greeks decided to go for an armed struggle and formed groups such as EOKA, OXEN, PEON.[13] At the same period of time that the issue was being taken to the UN thus becoming an international issue, EOKA started its operations and targeted Turkish Cypriots. After that "Turkey took her official position against Greek claims" then implemented the 'annexation thesis' which defended "Cyprus must be given back to Turkey since Britain had taken the island from Turkey."[14] When this strategy did not work, Turkey shifted to the *taksim* (partition) thesis. As from January

1965, Britian initiated the establishment of a liberal constitutional system within the context of self-government; accordingly Lord Radcliffe prepared a draft as the constitution of Cyprus. Since, Turkish Cypriots would be treated as a minority according to this proposal, Turkey rejected the Radcliffe constitution draft. Britain understood that consensus can not be reached by considering only one community's demands. In 1958 Britain suggested the MacMillan Plan which proposed bi-communual administration on the island.[15] The MacMillan plan was accepted by Turkey due to the fact that it did not leave space for *enosis* but it was rejected by the Greeks. All the diplomatic efforts resulted in a compromise between Britain, Greece and Turkey which "formalized the independence and territorial integrity of Cyprus by the Zurich-London agreements".[16]

In conclusion, in the period between 1950 and 1960 Greece and Greek Cypriots carried on their policy of *enosis* while Turkey adapted new policies according to the developments. Turkey firstly retained the policy of non-involvement in Cyprus affairs based on the argument that the island belongs to the British government and in case of a withdrawal, Britain would leave the island to Turkey. Firstly, when Britain gave signals of recognising Greek efforts, Turkey established the annexation thesis. Secondly, Turkey shifted to the *taksim* (partition) thesis which comprises the division of the island into two. Lastly, the confrontation of the theses of Turkish and Greek parties with the British imposition resulted in the Republic of Cyprus.

### *From 1960 to 1974 Turkish Intervention*

In the years following the foundation of the Republic of Cyprus differences occurred over the administrative issues of the island between the two communities which led to intercommunal clashes. Later on, amendments to the 1960 Cyprus Constitution, which would end the bi-communal feature of the republic, were proposed by the President Archbishop Makarios on November 30, 1964.[17] Meanwhile, the violence against Turkish Cypriots on the island had increased highly in 1963–64. When a solution within NATO was not accepted by President Makarios, Britain referred the issue to the UN Security Council on February 15,

1964. Eventually, "UN Security Council Resolution 186 was adopted on 4th of March 1964 which provided setting up of a UN Peacekeeping Force with the approval of the government of Cyprus and on 14th of March UN Peacekeeping Force in Cyprus (UNFICYP) arrived in Cyprus." The arrival of the UNFICYP did not stop the violence on the island.[18] Though, the Turkish Grand National Assembly authorised the government to use the Turkish Armed Forces if circumstances required it, Turkey did not go further than conducting reconnaissance missions over Cyprus. The years 1967–74 were a relatively calm period on the island; on the other hand, though, tension within the Greek community of the island was intiensified which led to the overthrow of Makarios by the supporters of EOKA member and *enosis* defender Nicos Sampson.[19]

In response to the coup d'etat Turkey intervened in Cyprus by depending on her status as a guarantor power according to the London-Zurich Treaties. Turkey's broader interest can be explained on the basis of the historical cause, the ethnic cause which was defined as security of the Turkish Cypriots and the strategic location of Cyprus in the Eastern Mediterranean. Turkey's military operation gradually resulted in the de facto division of the island.

### *1974–2002 Negotiations Period and European Union Involvement*

After 1974, although innumerable negotiations had taken place, the solution was not reached. The obstacle was both parties' approach to the negotiations as a zero-sum game. At the same time, Turkish Cypriots established an independent administration, the Turkish Federated State of Cyprus with Rauf Denktaş as President while Greek Cypriots' claims of Republic of Cyprus continued. Further, on November 15, 1993 when talks were suspended the Turkish Cypriots unilaterally proclaimed the Turkish Republic of Northern Cyprus (TRNC).[20] The reaction of the UN was the adoption of "Resolution 541 which declares TRNC as illegal and called on all countries not to recognise it."[21] In 1990s the efforts to bring a solution to the conflict including negotiations increased. Therefore, the parties reached a consensus on some issues alongwith confidence building measures.

Turkey's policy was not to make any linkage between the settlement of the Cyprus dispute and Turkey's EU membership. However, the 1999

Helsinki Summit of the EU stated the settlement of Cyprus issue to be a condition for the EU membership of Turkey; at the same time it was decided that the southern part of the island, the "Republic of Cyprus", could join the EU either unified or divided.[22] Following this decision, Turkey promoted a policy which "advocated legal partition of the island based upon the principle of two communities and two separate states."[23] At the last stage of the policy which sees the Cyprus problem as a national cause, Turkey stated that "Turkey and the TRNC would match any form of integration concluded between the Republic of Cyprus and the EU." Therefore, Turkey's reaction was to increase its integration with the TRNC to balance the EU's policies towards South Cyprus. This policy could not prevent South Cyprus from becoming a member of the EU, but in the long run these integration initiatives created tension in the Turkey–TRNC relations.

## Turkey's Cyprus Policy under the AKP

In the 2002 Parliamentary Elections AKP won the absolute majority and formed a single-party government that provided the potential to the new government to restructure the foreign policy of the country.[24] When the political situation which the AKP had inherited in the case of the EU accession is evaluated, it is seen that in the 1990s Turkey's determination for the membership had increased and the previous government had passed EU-driven reform packages which were supported by the public and institutions of the Turkish state.[25] Therefore, the domestic environment was suitable for continuing with a policy towards the EU accession of Turkey. On the other hand, initially there were doubts whether the AKP would follow the "country's traditional pro-Western policy"; in order to obliterate this scepticism, the leader of the party Tayyip Erdoğan, declared "his party's firm commitment to undertake all necessary steps to obtain a date for accession talks with the EU."[26] After declaration of their commitment to the EU accession, since the Cyprus question was a tough obstacle in Turkey's way to membership, the AKP decided to start from the most pressing issue.[27]

As mentioned before, the policy of Turkey was not to make any linkage between the settlement of the Cyprus dispute and Turkey's accession to the EU. However, decisions taken at the 1999 Helsinki Summit showed that settlement of the dispute began to be conditional for Turkey's membership. Once this linkage was established, Turkey's desire to be a part of the EU and Turkey's uncompromising attitude on the Cyprus issue became contradictory. Retrospectively, it can be argued that the shift in Turkey's Cyprus policy was essential to overcome the contradiction. Besides, the motives of the policy change were to illustrate that Turkey was not a party refraining from reaching a solution and in this way gaining the world's support; in order to achieve that the "UN was invited to take a more active role in the negotiations."[28]

The first initiative of the AKP was to propose the 'Belgian model' as a framework for solution which foresaw one state with two communities and the establishment of a state administration consisting of the two communities. This was the first clash between the state policy and AKP's upcoming new Cyprus policy of giving up the idea of confederation and accepting the federation formula.[29] After the proposal attracted widespread domestic criticism, the AKP stepped back and changed rhetoric, but continued with the efforts for a new Cyprus policy.

After the Greek Cypriot President Clerides and Turkish Cypriot President Denktaş met and agreed to begin direct talks, in November 2002 the UN General Secretary Kofi Annan submitted a settlement plan which widely known as 'Annan Plan' that was based on Swiss and Belgian government models and proposed the creation of a United Cyprus Republic covering the whole island except the British base areas in which Greek Cypriots and Turkish Cypriots joined together in one federal state.[30] But, neither the Turkish Cypriot side nor the Greek Cypriot side agreed to it. When Annan offered to submit a final revised plan, as the second significant effort to establish the new policy on the Cyprus issue, the AKP government decided to support the Annan Plan which was the last chance for the membership of the island to EU as a unified Cyprus.

The strategy of AKP between 2002 and April 24, 2004 (referenda of Annan Plan) can be defined "to prove the willingness of the Turkish party to pursue a solution through a positive attitude toward negotiations, to formulate a new stance based on the Annan Plan, to return to the negotiation table, and to end the status quo through a solution acceptable to both sides."[31] At the same time in December 2003 general elections were held in TRNC and the coalition forces which came together under the Republican Turkish Party (CTP) known as pro-solution and pro-EU party led by Mehmet Ali Talat came to power.[32] With this domestic political change in North Cyprus the political environment became more favourable to a fresh momentum for the resolution of the dispute. On the other hand the political developments on South Cyprus side were contrary. The 2003 general elections in South Cyprus brought Tassos Papadopoulos to power who was known for his hardliner position on the Cyprus issue. "The months leading to the referenda on the Annan Plan, Papadopoulos, with the help of many Greek Cypriot political and social elites created the conditions for a rejection of the UN resolution plan."[33] In referendums held in April 2004, sixty-four percent of Turkish Cypriots voted for the Annan Plan, whereas the overwhelming seventy-six percent of Greek Cypriots vetoed it[34] and South Cyprus under the label of the "Republic of Cyprus" entered EU. This outcome signified that Turkey and Turkish Cypriots were in favour of a solution even a compromise; this led to the sympathy of the international community, but in the process it did not turn into concrete gain. After the EU accession of South Cyprus, EU declared its determination to help Turkish Cypriots and address their long-standing international isolation, as a reward for their positive vote on the Annan plan[35] but as some scholars argued "the EU failed to reward the Cypriot Turks for the dramatic change in Turkey's policy and Turkish Cypriots' will for a solution".[36]

In order to show that Turkey was still committed to the settlement of the dispute, on January 24, 2006, Turkish Foreign Minister Abdullah Gul presented The Action Plan (known as the Gul Plan) to the Secretary-General in the form of a letter proposing the opening of Turkish ports, airports and airspace to Greek Cypriot ships and planes in exchange for "special arrangements for the practical inclusion of North Cyprus as an economic entity, into the European Union's customs union, unhindered direct trade between both sides of the island as well as with the outside world", opening of ports and airports of Northern Cyprus under the Turkish Cypriot management and inclusion of the Turkish Cypriots in international activities". It also called for talks among Turkey, Greece, and Turkish and Greek Cypriots.[37] On February 5, 2006 Papadopoulos repeated his three conditions for resuming the talks: no mediation, no timetables and referendum on a solution.[38] Following this statement, negotiations between Greek Cypriot leader Papadopoulos and Turkish Cypriot leader Talat resumed, but no result came out of it.

The discovery of gas and oil resources in the Eastern Mediterranean added a new aspect to the Cyprus dispute. In 2007, South Cyprus "signed an agreement with Lebanon to delimit an exclusive economic zone for oil and gas exploration in the Eastern Mediterranean". According to the Turkish and Turkish Cypriots' argument South Cyprus did not represent the whole island thus such agreements are not valid and those also ignored the rights of Turkish Cypriots.[39] As a counter it was declared that Turkey will start oil exploration in the Mediterranean through the Turkish Petroleum Corporation (TPAO). Moreover, the President of TRNC Derviş Eroğlu and Prime Minister of Turkey Tayyip Erdoğan signed a continental shelf delimitation agreement following which TRNC granted gas and oil exploration licences to the TPAO. Then, the TPAO started to collect seismic data in the TRNC's continental shelf region.[40] Lastly, the agreement between the TRNC Ministry of Economy and Energy and the TPAO on oil field services and production was signed which gave permission to the TPAO to conduct exploration, drill oil wells and run a drilling platform.[41]

Following the election of Christofias as the President of South Cyprus, the two leaders came together in March 2008 and "decided to start a process that would result in a comprehensive settlement. Negotiations started on September 3, 2008 with the common understanding that the final text would be put to public referendums." Negotiations have been conducted on four issues: territory, security, property and governance. Through this negotiation process many confidence building measures have been adopted. Besides, the leaders "reaffirmed their commitment to bi-zonal, bi-communal federation with political equality" in accordance with the relevant UN resolutions.[42]

Contemporarily, Turkey's Cyprus policy can be related to the two themes of Turkish foreign policy: de-securitisation of foreign policy and 'zero-problem with neighbours' policy. The widely accepted argument on the Turkish foreign policy is that after the end of the Cold War Turkey continued to securitise its foreign policy due to its issues with neighbouring states. Therefore, the process of de-securitisation of foreign policy started in the 2000s in response to the changing international and regional context. De-securitisation and 'zero-problem with neighbours' policy go hand in hand and support the "adoption of a win–win approach and an emphasis on dialogue and negotiation as means to solve disputes are now the characteristics of Turkey's external relations. Instead of seeing the regions around it as a source of risks, Turkey began to see them as areas where it could play a proactive role in the maintenance of peace and stability."[43] For the implementation of both policies to the Cyprus issue, Turkey continues the dialogue that started in 1999 with Greece to improve bilateral relations having faith that this will help all parties to move further in the settlement of the dispute in Cyprus. Moreover, Turkey sustains its support to negotiations under the auspices of the UN.

## Conclusion

As like any new policy, AKP's Cyprus policy has brought new prospects and also constraints to the long-standing dispute and to its two Cypriot and international parties. In the very beginning of its initiatives the AKP leadership itself expressed that Turkey's past policy choices had limited its options and gave arguments that shape the current policy to some extent; for instance, the foundation of TRNC, Turkey– TRNC integration process and the fact that Turkey gave consent to the membership of South Cyprus in 1995 and 1999.[44] After the AKP started to establish its policy, constraints appeared in the shape of criticisms and challenges. The main objections were from military circles and domestic constituents which consider Cyprus issue as a national cause. When the Annan Plan failed due to the veto of the Greek Cypriot side, the AKP gradually adopted a less-compromising attitude on issues such as opening of Turkish ports and airports for Greek Cypriot transport or Turkey's military presence on the island. This attitude was interpreted to mean that the AKP wants to sustain its domestic interests rather than the EU membership of Turkey.[45] In the case of the Turkish Cypriots, following the EU accession of South

Cyprus the pro-EU stance decreased. The EU proposed a trade agreement between Turkish Cypriots and EU member states in order to ease their international isolation which is pending because of the veto of South Cyprus.[46] The last phase of efforts for the solution for a unified Cyprus is the continuing negotiations between leaders of the Greek and Turkish Cypriot communities. However, a settlement has not been achieved and disagreements remain particularly regarding the "the status of Turkish armed forces on the island, the continuation of Turkey's guarantor status, the administrative structure of the new state, the internal boundaries of the constituent states, the property rights and the number of Greek Cypriots who would settle in the north of island following the settlement."[47] The main obstacle is the different perception of the Greek and Turkish sides. The Greek side wants to see improvement in the main issue areas and then go for a comprehensive settlement. On the contrary, the Turkish side perceives that Turkey and Turkish Cypriots have compromised enough in the course of time, but no result has come out of it. Therefore, the Turkish side wants to see settlement and then solve the rest of the problems.

## Notes

1. Europa Publications, *The Middle East and North Africa 2013,* London: Routledge, 2012, 59th edition, p. 262; *CIA, The World Factbook: Europe: Cyprus*, August 22, 2013, https://www.cia.gov/library/publications/the-world-factbook/geos/cy.html (accessed July 20, 2013).
2. F. O. Hampson , "Building A Stable Peace: Opportunities and Limits to Security Cooperation in Third World Regional Conflicts", *International Journal*, Vol. 45, no. 2, Sprong, 1990, p. 464.
3. V. D. Volkan, *Cyprus War and Adaptation: A Psychological History of Two Ethnic Groups in Conflict*, Charlottesville: University of Virginia, 1979, p. 145.
4. Glen Camp, "The Cyprus Problem: A Cold War Legacy", *Global Dialogue*, Vol. 3, 2001, p. 1.
5. Cyprus Turkish Cultural Association, *Kıbrıs'ın Tarihi Gelişimi ve Kuzey Kıbrıs Türk Cumhuriyeti,* (Ankara: Cyprus Turkish Cultural Association, 1984), pp. 2-6.
6. Ahmet C. Gazioglu, *Kıbrıs'ta Türkler: 1570–1878 (Turks in Cyprus: 1570–1878)* (İstanbul: Cyprus Research and Publication Centre, 2000), pp. 2-10.
7. Genelkurmay Askeri Tarih ve Stratejik Etüt Başkanlığı (ATASE), Kıbrıs'ın Fethi 1570–1571 (Ankara: Culture and Tourism Ministry Publications, 1986), pp. 12-13.
8. Sibel Akgün, "Kıbrıs: Doğu Akdeniz'de Egemenlik Mücadelesi," in *Dünya Çatışma Bölgeleri ve Konuları,* ed. Kemal Inat, Burhanettin Duran and Muhittin Ataman (Ankara: Nobel Publishing, 2010), pp. 728-750.

9. Sabahattin Ismail, *Kıbrıs Sorununun Kökleri* (Nicosia: Akdeniz News Agency, 2000), pp. 11-12.
10. Rıfat Uçarol, *1878 Cyprus Dispute & The Ottoman–British Agreement* (Nicosia: Rustem Bookshop, 2000), pp. 140-141.
11. John Reddaway, *Burdened with Cyprus* (Nicosia: Rustem Bookshop, 2001), p. 3.
12. Republic of Turkey, Ministry of Foreign Affairs, Lausanne Peace Treaty, http://www.mfa.gov.tr/lausanne-peace-treaty-part-i_-political-clauses.en.mfa (accessed June 20, 2013).
13. Esra Sarıkoyuncu Değerli, "Turkey's Cyprus Policy During Democratic Party Period (1950–1960)" *Journal of Gazi Academic View,* vol. vi, no.11, Winter 2012, pp. 85-101.
14. Mustafa Albayrak, "Türkiye'nin Kıbrıs Politikaları (1950–1960)" *Atatürk Araştırma Merkezi* Dergisi, vol. xvi, no. 46, March 2000, pp. 1-17.
15. Ibid. pp. 9-10.
16. James H. Meyer, "*Policy Watershed: Turkey's Cyprus Policy and the Intervention of 1974"*, WWS Case Study 3/00. http://www.wws.princeton.edu/~cases (accessed October 10, 2013).
17. Ahmet C. Gazioğlu, "Cyprus Was Ever Really United?", *Perceptions: Journal of International Affairs*, vol. vii, no.3 (June–August 2002) accessed http://sam.gov.tr/was-cyprus-ever-really-united/
18. Baskın Oran (ed), *Turkish Foreign Policy 1919–2006 Facts and Analyses with Documents* (Salt Lake City: University of Utah Press, 2010), pp. 436-437.
19. James H. Meyer, "*Policy Watershed: Turkey's Cyprus Policy and the Intervention of 1974"*, WWS Case Study 3/00. http://www.wws.princeton.edu/~cases (accessed August 19, 2013).
20. Nilgün Gülcan, "Chronology: Cyprus Issue", *The Journal of Turkish Weekly*, http://www.turkishweekly.net/article/55/chronology-cyprus-issue.html (accessed October 6, 2013).
21. Osman Ertuğ, "The United Nations' Approach to the Cyprus Issue and UNFICYP", *Perception: Journal of International Affairs* vol. vi, no. 3, September–November 2001.
22. Ayşe Aslıhan Çelenk, "The Restructuring of Turkey's Policy towards Cyprus: The Justice and Development Party's Struggle for Power", *Turkish Studies*, vol. 8, no. 3, September 2007, pp. 349-363.
23. Ibid. p. 351.
24. See, Ibid, pp. 349-363.
25. Müge Kınacıoğlu and Emel Oktay, "The Domestic Dynamics of Turkey's Cyprus Policy: Implications for Turkey's Accession to the European Union", *Turkish Studies*, vol. vii, no. 2, June 2006, pp. 261-273.
26. Ibid. p. 263.
27. Oran (ed), *Turkish Foreign Policy 1919–2006*, p. 927.
28. Çelenk, "The Restructuring of Turkey's Policy towards Cyprus," pp. 349-363.
29. Oran (ed), *Turkish Foreign Policy 1919–2006*, p. 927.
30. Carol Migdalovitz, "Cyprus: Status of U.N. Negotiations and Related Issues", CRS Report for Congress (Washington D.C. 2007).
31. Çelenk, "The Restructuring of Turkey's Policy towards Cyprus: The Justice and Development Party's Struggle for Power", *Turkish Studies,* vol. viii, no. 3, September 2007, pp. 349-363.

32. Kıvanç Ulusoy, "Europeanization and Political Change: The Case of Cyprus", *Turkish Studies*, vol. x, no. 3, September 2009, pp. 393-408.
33. George Kyris, "The European Union and the Cyprus Problem: a Story of Limited Impetus", *Eastern Journal of European Studies*, vol. iii, no. 1, June 2012, pp. 87-99.
34. Tarık Oğuzlu, "Turkey and the Cyprus Dispute: Pitfalls and Opportunities, *Ankara Bar Review*, vol. iii, no.1, January 2010, pp. 73-82.
35. Kyris, "The European Union and the Cyprus Problem: a Story of Limited Impetus", *Eastern Journal of European Studies*, vol. iii, no. 1, June 2012, pp. 87-99.
36. Morton Abramowitz and Henri J. Barkey, "Turkey's Transformers: The AKP Sees Big", *Foreign Affairs*, vol. lxxxviii, no. 6, November/December 2009, pp. 118-128.
37. Republic of Turkey Ministry of Foreign Affairs, "New Initiative by Turkey on Cyprus", (24 January 2006) http://www.mfa.gov.tr/new-initiative-by-turkey-on-cyprus.en.mfa
38. Carol Migdalovitz, "Cyprus: Status of U.N. Negotiations and Related Issues", CRS Report for Congress (Washington D.C. 2007).
39. Ibid. p. 14.
40. Zeynep Gürcanlı, "KKTC'de petrol arama çalışmaları başlıyor", *Hürriyet*, April 26, 2012. http://www.hurriyet.com.tr/ekonomi/20426323.asp
41. Anatolia News Agency, "Turkey, North Cyprus Sign New Energy Deal", *Hurriyet Daily News*, November 3, 2011. http://www.hurriyetdailynews.com/turkey-north-cyprus-sign-new-energy-deal.aspx
42. Oğuzlu, "Turkey and the Cyprus Dispute", pp. 73-82.
43. Republic of Turkey Ministry of Foreign Affairs, "Zero-Problem Policy with Neighbours", http://www.mfa.gov.tr/komsularla-sifir-sorun-politikamiz.tr.mfa
44. Çelenk, "The Restructuring of Turkey's Policy towards Cyprus", pp. 349-363.
45. Carol Migdalovitz, "AKP's Domestically Driven Foreign Policy", *Turkish Policy Quarterly*, vol. ix, no. 4, Winter 2010, pp. 37-45.
46. Kyris, "The European Union and the Cyprus Problem: a Story of Limited Impetus", *Eastern Journal of European Studies*, vol. iii, no. 1, June 2012, pp. 87-99.
47. Oğuzlu, "Turkey and the Cyprus Dispute", pp. 73-82.

# 13
# Uyghur Factor in Turkey's Relationship with China

*Mahesh Ranjan Debata*

## Introduction

Turkey's long nurtured dream to establish a pan-Turkic homeland stretching from the Balkans to the Great Wall of China to the east of Xinjiang Uyghur Autonomous Region has prompted the Turkish leadership to maintain a strong rapport with its Turkic cousins across the globe, including the Uyghurs of Xinjiang. Uyghurs, who share culture, history and folklore with the Turkish people, have been culturally, linguistically and historically part of a Turkish civilisation distinct from the Chinese civilisation.[1] Even during the rule of Eretna in 13th–14th centuries, Uyghur merchants were allowed to do business in Turkey.[2] In the contemporary times, Uyghurs preferred to live in Turkey in order to escape Chinese excesses, particularly since the communist takeover of China in 1949. During the Great Leap Forward and Cultural Revolution, many Uyghurs left Xinjiang for Turkey. Presently, over 50,000 Uyghurs are living in Turkey, out of which some 40,000 live in and around Istanbul only and rest live in Manisa, Kayseri, Anatolia and Izmir. Until the mid-1990s, Turkish leadership provided all possible help to the Uyghurs. However, Ankara changed its pro-Uyghur attitude and chose to make a favourable tilt towards Beijing through increasing trade contacts. The beginning was the establishment of diplomatic relations between Turkey and China in the year 1971 and the relationship blossomed throughout 1980s. Two reasons can be attributed to this development: a) China as one of the members of UN Security Council supported Turkey in all international issues related to it; and b) Ankara's wish to get market share from China.[3] Both now vow to enhance cooperation in important fields such as project contracting, finance, energy, railway and civil aviation. Besides, both the countries now have a common stand on separatism and terrorism, which was exhibited during the 2008 Beijing Olympic Games. Since 2003, Turkish security forces have been keeping vigil over the international terrorist infrastructure and their connections with Uyghurs. Against this background, this chapter highlights how the issue of Uyghurs has been an important factor in Sino-Turkish relations and also how it has affected both the countries. The chapter argues that the Turkish political leadership, which once patronised Uyghurs and made constant efforts to internationalise their cause, has changed its pro-Uyghur stance. The chapter further argues, since Turkey aims at becoming one of the world's 10 biggest economies by 2023, the Turkish leadership feels the need to strengthen relations with China, the no.2 economy in the world, and thus does want to sacrifice its greater interests for the sake of the Uyghurs.

## Uyghur Problem in Xinjiang

China's Xinjiang region, where over 10 million Turkic-origin Uyghurs live, has been experiencing separatism since 1949. Uyghurs demand a separate East Turkestan republic out of China.[4] While Uyghurs point at the Chinese policy towards Uyghurs as the root cause of all evils in Xinjiang, the Chinese accuse Uyghurs of not only harbouring three evil forces "separatism, religious extremism and terrorism", but also indulging in anti-national (anti-Chinese) activities. Since the Chinese government claims Xinjiang as its inalienable and inseparable part, it has a clear cut mandate in the region. This strategically important region has borders with eight countries, three being nuclear powers (Russia, India and Pakistan), three Central Asian countries (Kazakhstan, Tajikistan and Kyrgyzstan) with whom the Uyghurs share history and culture, Mongolia and the war-torn Afghanistan. Hence, the Chinese Central government feels Xinjiang as its jugular vein as far as the security and stability in its northwestern borderland is concerned. In addition, Xinjiang is dubbed as the gateway to the resource-rich Central Asia region through which China's energy needs can be satiated. In this context, Uyghur aspirations to get any favour from China—autonomy in the least, forget about a separate state of East Turkestan—gets a backseat. The top most agenda of the Chinese policy in Xinjiang is and has been to secure peace and stability in the region, even at the cost of Uyghurs. This seems to be the major cause of consternation among Uyghurs, who feel that the Central government's developmental effort in Xinjiang is only an eyewash and the hidden Chinese agenda is to control the region by hook or by crook. The bickering between the Uyghurs and the Chinese has pushed the region to a perpetual state of tension. And in the last 65 years since China's independence in 1949, the region has witnessed violent separatist and terrorist activities by Uyghur cadres followed by military crackdown by Chinese security forces, further leading to loss of lives and public property. The situation in Xinjiang has deteriorated in the last two decades since the end of the Cold War.

## Violent Separatism in Xinjiang since 1990s

Even though there were several violent attacks in Xinjiang from 1949 to 1990, the Baren incident on April 5, 1990 changed the format of separatist activities in Xinjiang, when Jeyidin Yusuf, a religious preacher, gave a clarion call to all Muslims of the region, especially Uyghurs, to launch jihad against Chinese infidels. The earlier ethnic tenor of the Uyghur movement in Xinjiang instantly got a religious overtone. Further, growth of religious extremism and terrorist activities in the post-Cold War world has adversely affected the situation in Xinjiang. One top Chinese official in Xinjiang, the Chief of the Public Security Department of Xinjiang, Zhang Xiuming, expressed serious concern over the situation in Xinjiang in the 1990s, which was being aggravated by four waves of terrorist activities: The first wave occurred from 1990 to 1995, when the terrorists considered themselves capable of grabbing power in Xinjiang by force, which featured a series of explosions and riots. The second wave in 1996 and 1997 was characterised by chain assassinations. The third wave was from the end of 1997 to 1999 featuring explosions and assassinations commanded by organisations outside China or foreign terrorists. The fourth wave started from the second half of 1999 onwards during which some transnational Islamic extremist organisations like Al

Qaeda, Taliban and Islamic Movement of Uzbekistan (IMU) were found for the first time developing their networks within China. Some East Turkistan terrorists were sent to China to set up armed forces and training bases and produce arms and ammunitions.[5] A document released by the Chinese Central government in 2002 went one step further. According to the document, "under the influence of extremism, separatism and international terrorism, part of the East Turkistan forces, inside and outside the Chinese territory, turned to splittist and sabotage activities with terrorist violence as the main means, even brazenly declaring that terrorist violence is the only way to achieve their aims".[6] The latest wave of violent activities, perhaps the most dangerous of all waves of terrorism, began with the Urumqi riots on July 5, 2009.

The situation in Xinjiang in the last six years has been very violent, the recent being an attack on a railway station in Urumqi on April 30, 2014 that killed three persons and injured over 70 people. On August 4, 2008, just four days before the Beijing Olympics 2008, a terror strike in the Kashgar city of Xinjiang left 16 policemen dead and 16 others injured. On July 5, 2009, an ethnic riot in Xinjiang's capital Urumqi resulted in the death of 197 people and left over 1,600 people injured. Later in August 2009, mysterious attacks with syringes were reported in Urumqi leading to injury to 531 people.[7] On June 24, 2010, Chinese security personnel had claimed to have unearthed a terrorist ring that had been behind a string of deadly attacks in the region, and arrested 10 people in this connection. On July 18, 2011, 20 protesters were killed in Khotan. Further, between July 31 to August 1, 2011, two attacks by alleged terrorists left 13 people dead in Kashgar, while security forces gunned down eight suspected Uyghur separatists. On February 28, 2012, rioters armed with knives killed 10 people in Yecheng town in Kashgar, while police shot two of the attackers dead. On June 29, 2012, six Uyghur men tried to hijack a plane that had taken off from Khotan but were thwarted by passengers and crew. Two of the men were killed in the struggle, and 24 crew members and passengers were injured. On April 23, 2013, gunfights broke out in the Bachu County leaving 15 police and community workers and six terrorists dead. On June 26, 2013, knife-wielding Uyghurs attacked police stations and other important Chinese installations in Lukqun township of Turpan killing 35 people.[8]

These violent activities not only tormented the restive northwestern region left and right, but also its reverberation was felt in the Chinese capital Beijing. On October 28, 2013, a Sports Utility Vehicle (SUV) knocked down pedestrians and burst into flames near Beijing's Tiananmen Square, killing two tourists and injuring over 40 people. This incident assumes importance because i) the incident occurred in one of the most heavily guarded areas of Beijing. Although there were major bomb blasts in Beijing in the 1990s that the Chinese government attributed to Muslim separatist groups, this was the first major suicide attack on Beijing in recent years; ii) the attack took place just weeks before the third plenum of Chinese Communist Party (CCP), which means the attackers had to contend with increased state security. If additional attacks were successfully carried out, they could prove extremely embarrassing for the CCP; and iii) Beijing apprehends an international connection to this attack, probably believing any Al-Qaeda group as its mastermind. This is being corroborated by one report by *Inspire Magazine*, an English-language publication by Al Qaeda's Yemen branch, which sought to inspire Muslims in English-speaking countries to carry out lone wolf or small cell attacks against the countries in which they live. The magazine contains stories glorifying jihad as well as ready-made instructions to carry out attacks. The second edition of the magazine encourages prospective terrorists to turn a pick-up truck into a human lawn mower by placing large steel blades on the vehicles for a large scale attack.[9]

## China's Response

China claims that its government has been doing the same, as any other country does to safeguard its unity and territorial integrity. In order to curb separatist and terrorist activities in Xinjiang, China has not only stuck to a sort of "carrot and stick policy"[10], but also implemented it astutely, sometimes ruthlessly. In addition, China has been able to mobilise the international community against violent separatist activities of the Uyghurs in Xinjiang. The international community treats separatism by Uyghurs as any other problem of separatism, and vehemently criticises the recent spate of violent attacks by Uyghurs in

Xinjiang, and even agrees to Chinese efforts to ward off separatism and terrorism. Some foreign powers, which had been sympathising with the Uyghurs and even supporting their movement, are now making a U-turn and focusing more on a warm relationship with China because of China's rise as a world power. Even a well-defined US policy supporting political rights, autonomy and cultural identity of Uyghurs has not been any help to them.[11] The linkage between the Uyghur separatists and some transnational terrorist organisations like the Al Qaeda has compelled all those who have been sympathising with the Uyghurs to rethink their stand on this sensitive issue. The world community denounces terrorism, not only in Xinjiang, but also in any part of the world, and also considers it as a common menace threatening peace, progress and prosperity of the society. The United States and other major powers have largely accepted China's contention that Uyghur separatists are part of a broader threat to stability posed by Islamic fundamentalists.[12] On the occasion of the 10th anniversary of the 9/11 attacks, China has called for a renewed and united international effort against terrorism seeking greater global support for its own battle against terror groups. China has also convinced its neighbours, the European Union and the Muslim world on the issue of Uyghurs. In addition, under the rubric of the Shanghai Cooperation Organization (SCO), China has legitimised its position on the Uyghurs due to which every SCO Summit since 2001 has been adopting a clause on three evils "separatism, extremism and terrorism."[13] Last but not the least, the international community understands the strength and stature of China[14] and hence does not want to meddle in its internal affairs. China, the second largest economy in the world, is a major investor with investments all across the globe. Turkey, one of the major support bases of Uyghurs and even where a substantial number of Uyghurs live at present, is now subscribing to the Chinese position on Uyghurs, which will be discussed here at length.

## Factoring Uyghurs in Turkey's Relations with China

Turkey, which has long served as a refuge for the Uyghur exiles from Xinjiang, is an important player so far as the issue of Uyghurs is concerned. As discussed earlier, Uyghurs are Turkic Muslims, who share their history and culture with the people of Turkey. So, it is natural for Turkey to express solidarity with the Uyghurs. It not only gave asylum to its Turkic speaking cousins from Xinjiang, but also patronised them and tried to highlight their cause at the international fora. One scholar describes Turkey's stand on Uyghurs as "a time-honoured commitment to Uyghur nationalism and its long term cultural and historical affiliation, ideological inspiration and material support for the realization of Eastern Turkestan vision."[15]

There is an American angle to how Turkey developed an interest in Uyghurs after the end of World War II. The beginning of Cold War witnessed the establishment of China as an independent country in 1949, which had an ideological affinity with the Soviet Union, as both followed the communist ideology. With Stalin in Soviet Union and Mao in China as two tallest leaders with one common ideology, the American leadership smelt danger. Many felt America would use the Uyghur card to check the rise of China, as the separatist overtone by Uyghurs was echoed at that point of time when Isa Yusuf Aleptkin and Muhammad Amin Bughra led a group of over 200 Uyghur families towards India in 1950. But America did not use the Uyghur card directly, but indirectly through Turkey, which later became a close US confidante and an important ally under the NATO alliance. Keeping in view the historical and cultural linkage between Turkey and Uyghurs, America insisted on Turkey to provide shelter to Uyghurs, who were refused asylum in India. Under this impression, Turkey became vocal against the Chinese excesses against its Turkic brethren. In an act of vengeance, Turkey not only accepted Uyghur exiles from Xinjiang through India, Pakistan, Afghanistan and even countries like Jordan, but also provided them place to stay, financial help and citizenship rights.[16] The sympathy towards Turkic cousins (Uyghurs), prompted Turkey to express solidarity with Uyghurs, which automatically became an anti-Chinese stand.

## Turkish Patronage to Uyghur Leadership

The Uyghur leader, the late Isa Yusuf Alptckin, who spearheaded the Uyghur movement for a separate East Turkestan Republic, sought refuge in Turkey just after China's independence in 1949. He struck an emotional chord with the Turkish people as well as the leadership. He was accorded state patronage to carry out pro-independence East Turkestan movement from the Turkish soil. Former Turkish President Turgut Ozal and Prime Minister Suleyman Demirel, who dreamt of a Turkic homeland stretching from the Balkans to the Great Wall of China to the east of Xinjiang, extended all kind of support for the independence of the ancient homeland of the Turkic people (East Turkestan). Under Ozal and Demirel's inspiration and patronage, Isa Yusuf Alptekin led the East Turkestan delegation at the World Turkic Congress, which was organised by the Turkish government from March 20–23, 1993 in Antalya, Turkey. The top Turkish leadership, including President Turgut Ozal, Prime Minister Suleyman Demirel and Vice Premier Erdal Inonu, not only graced the occasion, but also denounced Chinese atrocities against the Uyghurs in Xinjiang and called for liberation of Xinjiang from Chinese suzerainty.[17] Further in September and October 1995, the World Turkic Congress of Friendship, Brotherhood and Cooperation was held in the Turkish city of Izmir, and the Congress was opened by President Suleiman Demirel, who stressed the ties of "history, language and culture' that bind the Turkic peoples from China to the Balkans. A resolution was passed at the Congress to the effect that Eastern Turkistan would be represented at the World Turkic Congress.[18]

Isa Yusuf Alptekin's commitment to pan-Turkism earned him accolades on a personal basis and also compelled the Turkish authorities to encourage and advance the Uyghur cause. Isa was conferred with an Honorary Doctorate Degree from Seljuk University in 1994. Parks and streets were named after Isa. The Isa Yusuf Alptekin Park in the high profile Sultanahmet (Blue Mosque) section of Istanbul was one of such parks.[19] One such park named after Isa is also built in Ankara and another in Kayseri. Until the mid-1990s, Turkey's mainstream political parties sympathised with the Uyghurs, besides being personally committed to Isa Yusuf Alptekin, and hoped to restore Turkish influence in the region. During his visit to the Turkish capital Ankara in 1994, the Chairman of the Turkish Parliament and leaders of several political parties in Turkey—Chairmen of the *Motherland Party* and the *Welfare Party* and Bulent Ecevit, the Chairman of the *Democratic Social Party*—accorded him a ceremonial welcome. Even the Turkish National Television telecast live the funeral ceremony of Isa Yusuf Alptekin on December 17, 1995.[20] The present Turkish Prime Minister Recep Tayyip Erdogan was the Mayor of Istanbul at that point of time. However, After Isa Yusuf Alptekin's death, Turkey's pro-Uyghur stand and support for Uyghur activism underwent a paradigm shift.

Another Uyghur, who rose to prominence in Turkey, was General Mehmet Riza Bekin Pasha, an outspoken advocate of Uyghurs. After his studies at the Land Warfare School in Turkey in 1948, Riza joined the Turkish army. During the Korean War, Riza led the First Turkish Brigade Field Artillery Battalion as a ranking lieutenant. He served as assistant military attaché in Tehran, Iran, and in 1977 retired with the rank of brigadier-general. He was also the first Uyghur general in the Turkic world to serve under NATO. Active in Uyghur politics and education, he staged Uyghur-related human rights events in Turkey and founded the non-profit East Turkestan National Freedom Center, which supported Uyghur students in Turkey and around the world. Riza was elected President of the Istanbul-based Foundation for East Turkestan in 1986. From 1989–90, he served as a specialist for the Turkish Prime Minister in charge of a United Nations humanitarian aid programme to Afghanistan and Pakistan. He was an organiser of the first East Turkestan Congress, in Istanbul in 1992. Riza founded the East Turkestan Cultural Solidarity Association in 1994 and East Turkestan National Freedom Center in 1998.[21]

## Turkey's U-turn on the Uyghur Issue

When Turkey and China established diplomatic relations on August 5, 1971 after a hiatus of almost two decades, Uyghurs living in Turkey got the first low-intensity blow. Further, the whole 1980s witnessed a vibrant bilateral relationship between the two countries. The end of Cold War created a peculiar situation with USA as the sole superpower. At this juncture, a new development occurred when China began to rise as a global actor with a huge economy and military prowess. Like any other small but aspiring actor, Turkey realised and even believed China as a major force to reckon with, and thus Ankara chose to come closer to Beijing, giving less importance to the Uyghur issue. Two factors need to be underlined here. First, Turkey's trade relationship and economic partnership with China has ushered in a new era of Sino-Turkish relationship. Any country dreaming of being a developed economy in the present world, cannot ignore China, the world's second largest economy, which is aspiring to take over USA as the number one economy in the coming days. Turkey's aim to be among the top ten economies of the world by 2023 prompted it to establish a meaningful tie with the communist giant. Thus, it can be said that economic interests of a country are prior to any emotional interests and are above any ethnic, cultural and historical relationship. A common stand against separatism and terrorism is the other important factor. In China, there have been separatist and terrorist activities in Xinjiang and Tibet. Similarly, Turkey has a Kurdish problem. But the hidden factor behind Turkey's shifting stand on Uyghurs is perhaps China's veiled threat of providing support to Kurdish rebels.[22] Even the Uyghurs believe this as the major factor that compelled Turkish leadership to extend a hand of friendship to China, ignoring their Turkic brethren.

What added insult to the Uyghurs' injury was a bill passed by the Turkish Parliament in February 1998. According to this bill, the newly arrived Uyghurs from China would be granted permanent resident status instead of citizenship—the latter entailing full rights, duties and responsibilities. Further the bill said, Uyghurs could legally live and work in Turkey, but they could not join the armed forces and government organisations. Applied mainly to about 1,000 refugees, who had escaped Xinjiang, but had not yet been granted citizenship, the new regulation resulted in a considerable deterioration of Uyghurs' status, as they regarded permanent resident status as a certificate for second class citizens.[23]

The Turkish Prime Minister, Mesut Yilmaz sent a confidential circular order in 1998 to the Turkish government officials instructing them not to participate in any activities organised by the Turkey-based East Turkestan and Uyghur organisations. In that order, Yilmaz emphasised that the Uyghur community's activities might affect Turkish–Chinese relations.[24] In February 1999, Yilmaz while declaring Xinjiang as an integral part of China, stated that expatriate activities were stumbling blocks on the path of growing Sino-Turkish relations.[25] He even exerted pressure on an unidentified number of Uyghurs in Turkey in the early 2000s,[26] not to indulge in any anti-Chinese activities from Turkish soil. Ankara rejected Turkish visa to Rebiya Kadeer twice, who is the President of World Uyghur Congress and the tallest leader of Uyghur movement now. Both the countries have cooperated on counter-terrorism, especially during the time of the 2008 Beijing Olympic Games.[27] The Turkish government has taken a hard line against any separatist and terrorist activities aimed at establishing an independent East Turkestan. Since 2003, the Turkish security forces have been very vigilant about Al Qaeda activities and their possible connections with Uyghurs. Even one Turkish security official informed that "some of the recent immigrants, particularly Uyghurs and Chechens, who have spent some time in Afghanistan, then migrated to Turkey have had contacts with the Al Qaeda and links with local Al Qaeda cells in Turkey."[28] Further, with the help of Turkish authorities, Beijing has been engaged not only in collecting political and military intelligence in Turkey, but also in infiltrating Uyghur organisations through moles and sleepers.[29] Turkish approval of the recent Chinese accusation that some Uyghurs living in Turkey were indulged in fighting in Syria in August–September 2013 could be a perfect example of Turkey's changing stand on Uyghurs.

Turkey's commitment to a "One China" policy and strong emphasis on the territorial integrity and sovereignty of China has catapulted their relations to a new high and thus the Sino-Turkish strategic partnership 2010 has been ushered in. China has invited Turkish companies to conduct trade and investment in Xinjiang. The Xinjiang provincial government has allocated a large tract of land for a Turkish industrial zone in Xinjiang. And now Turkey has forged a military cooperation with China.[30] Further, China Southern Airlines has started direct flights between Urumqi and Istanbul in 2012. On the cultural front, both the countries have gone many steps ahead. China has established Confucius Institutes[31] in Turkey to popularise Chinese culture through the promotion of Chinese language, besides making an endeavour to minimise all sorts of Turkish patronage to Uyghurs. Xinjiang Art Theatre had sent a 40-member Song and Dance troupe to Turkey in 2012 as part of the Chinese Culture Year 2012 programme. An agreement was signed between Chinese Islam Association and Turkey's Religious Affairs Directorate in 2011, under which students from China will return to their native land after studying in Turkey.[32]

## Turkish Reaction to July 5, 2009 Incident

A new wave of violent ethnic clashes erupted between the Han Chinese and the Uyghurs in Urumqi on July 5, 2009 taking away around 197 innocent lives and injuring over 1,600 people. Turkey was the only country to openly criticise the military crackdown by the Chinese security forces against the Uyghurs in Xinjiang after the ethnic riots in Urumqi.[33] Turkish public, political leaders, business groups and mass media denounced Chinese action against Uyghurs. Turkish Prime Minister Recep Tayyip Erdogan rose to the occasion and vociferously criticised Chinese action against Uyghurs. While speaking at a press conference on the sidelines of the G-8 summit in 2009, Erdogan not only described Chinese action against the Uyghurs as "nearly genocide", but also threatened to raise the issue at the UN Security Council.[34] Since Turkey is a non-permanent member of the UN Security Council, the issue assumed significance. Even Prime Minister Erdogan asked Foreign Minister Ahmet Davutoglu to take stock of the situation and keep him informed. As a Special Envoy of Turkish Prime Minister Erdogan, Turkish State Minister Zafer Caglayan visited China on August 31, 2009, being the first Turkish Minister to visit China after riots in Urumqi in July 2009.[35] The Turkish Foreign Ministry even issued a statement emphasising Ankara's concerns over the Chinese actions in Xinjiang. Bulent Arinc, a co-founder of the AKP and deputy Prime Minister of Turkey, who was sympathetic towards Isa Yusuf Alptekin's campaign for the Uyghur cause, expressed solidarity with the Uyghurs. The Turkish Trade Minister, Nihat Ergun gave a clarion call to his fellow countrymen to boycott Chinese goods.[36]

Political leaders from various mainstream parties in Turkey castigated the Chinese action against Uyghurs. The *Nationalist Great Union Party* (BBP) leader, Yalcin Topcu urged the Turkish government to reconsider its relations with China and requested the Parliament to pass a resolution condemning the Chinese actions against Uyghurs. As many as 500 members of the nationalist *Alperen Ocaklari* group marched to the Chinese Consulate in Istanbul to lodge protest against Chinese action. The Turkish Education Personnel Union called upon the government to act and urged Prime Minister Erdogan to communicate their concerns to Chinese authorities. Devlet Bahceli, the leader of the *Nationalist Action Party* (MHP), criticised the Turkish government for not summoning the Chinese ambassador to the foreign ministry to protest against, what he described, "massacre against the Uyghurs."[37]

The Turkish media went one step ahead and did not hesitate to air its view condemning the Urumqi attacks. The *Hurriyet* alleged that the Chinese security agencies were responsible for the death of Uyghurs. The pro-government daily *Yeni Safak* accused the Han Chinese of burning Uyghur shops and dubbed the response by the international community against the Chinese government as inadequate.[38] One commentary in the *Bugun* with a caption "East Turkestan is bleeding", spelt out in strong words that "China should know when East Turkestan is hurt, Turkey is hurt". Further the *Sabah* opined that "Turkey cannot remain indifferent to the sufferings of its ancestral land". Reacting to tremendous Turkish response to July 5, 2009 that resulted in a sympathy wave for Uyghurs, Uyghur leader Rebiya Kadeer went to the extent of saying that "Turkey would not sell out the Uyghurs, who have Turkish blood in their veins."[39]

Even though the pro-government Independent Industrialists and Businessmen's Association (MUSIAD) in its statement called upon Turkish investors to refrain from doing business with China, the Turkish business community expresses eagerness to strengthen business relationship with China. The Vice Chairman of the Turkey–China Business Council, Yavuz Onay criticised the protests against China and accused the Uyghurs of being terrorists.[40] Even some reliable sources informed this author that Uyghur businessmen in Turkey, who have been gaining immensely from their business with China, did not support the Uyghur protests against the Chinese. Since China is an important export market for Turkish companies, it is believed that business with China can create hundreds of thousands of jobs all across Turkey. Turkish business groups identified textiles, leather goods, telecommunications, contracting services, agro-industries and spare parts production as suitable sectors for investment or joint ventures. Even the government seemed to be a little reluctant to snap trade ties with China as just a week before the July 5, 2009 Turkish President Abdullah Gul visited China during which eight Turkish companies signed contracts worth 3 billion US dollars with their Chinese counterparts. While delivering a speech at the Xinjiang University on June 28, 2009, Abdullah Gul reiterated that Xinjiang has been the linkage between the two countries.[41] This not only underlines the strengthening of mutual political trust between China and Turkey, but also injects pep into the economic partnership.

In the wake of the July 5, 2009 incident, both the countries were engaged in verbal duels due to which the relationship descended to a new low. However, the damage control exercises by the leaders of both the countries tried to bring down the mutual distrust. High profile leaders of both countries started dialogue to reorient the already bruised relationship. Chinese Foreign Minister Yang Jiechi broke the ice in January 2010 on the sidelines of the Afghanistan conference in Istanbul. Yang met Turkish Foreign Minister Davutoglu and discussed issues of mutual interest. In June 2010, Culture Ministers of both countries met during the Shanghai Expo 2010 Fair, where it was agreed that Turkey would host China Culture Year 2012 and China would host Turkey Culture Year 2013. Further, from August–September 2010, Erdogan's special emissary as well as the Turkish Trade Minister Zafer Caglayan went to Urumqi to attend the International Urumqi Trade Fair. Chinese Prime Minister Wen Jiabao visited Turkey in September 2010 during which the leadership of both countries agreed to cooperate in the energy sector, including nuclear energy. They expressed their aim to increase bilateral trade to 50 billion US dollars by 2015 and 100 billion US dollars by 2020. Turkish Foreign Minister Davutoglu paid a visit to China from October–November 2010, including a stopover at Urumqi and Kashgar. The year 2012 has been very eventful so far as the Sino-Turkish relationship is concerned. In February 2012, the then Chinese Vice President Xi Jinping undertook a visit to Turkey where big projects in strategic sectors like nuclear energy were signed. This was followed by a reciprocal visit by Erdogan to China, which started from Urumqi. Most importantly, Turkey was made a dialogue partner of the SCO in its Summit in June 2012.[42] This clearly indicates that the Sino-Turkish relationship is in an upswing mood, and perhaps the Uyghur issue gets a backseat in this process.

## Conclusion

Amidst 'sometimes strong' and 'sometimes strained' Sino-Turkish relationship, Uyghur pleas for greater recognition are likely to remain a major cause of concern. Uyghurs want Turkey to play an impregnable role for the Uyghur cause to establish a separate republic out of China and the Chinese government wants Turkey to refrain from giving even an iota of support to Uyghurs, and interestingly, Turkey is between a devil and the deep sea. The Uyghur endeavour to establish a separate nation out of the People's Republic of China has found few takers, even no takers at some point of time. The Turkish government seems determined not to let the Xinjiang issue spoil growing economic and political ties. Since, the Uyghur problem in Xinjiang is a political issue, and in the present-day world economic issues outflank political issues, Turkey does not want to sacrifice her economic interests with China for the sake of Uyghurs. A statement by the Turkish Foreign Ministry could be a pointer in this regard. On July 6, 2010, just a day after the first anniversary of the July 5, 2009 Urumqi riots, the Turkish Foreign Ministry stated that: "It is our expectation that the persons who are responsible for these incidents will be found as soon as possible and brought to justice. We believe that the necessary measures will be taken to prevent this kind of incident in the future in China, a country on the way to becoming more stable and prosperous. We extend our condolences to the people of the Xinjiang Uyghur Autonomous Region in particular and to the people of China in general, to the families of those who lost their lives and wish speedy recovery to those who were injured."[43]

## Notes

1. Eric Hyer, "China's Policy towards Uighur Nationalism", *Journal of Muslim Minority Affairs*, vol. 26, no.1, p. 80.

2. Eretna, a Uyghur Turk who created an independent principality in central Anatolia in 1339 AD after the collapse of the Ilkhanid Mongol Empire in 1335. For details, see John Freely, *The Companion Guide to Turkey*, Harper Collins, 1993, p.391; Bruce Alan Masters, Gábor Ágoston, *Encyclopedia of the Ottoman Empire*, Infobase, 2010, p.41.
3. Selcuk Colakoglu, "Turkey-China Relations; Rising Partnership", 2013, http://www.orsam.org.tr/en/enUploads/Article/Files/2013415_3selcukcolakoglu.pdf, p. 33
4. Uyghurs, in their quest for an independent republic, were able to establish the East Turkestan Republic in Xinjiang twice, first in 1933 and then in 1944.
5. Mahesh Ranjan Debata, *China's Minorities: Ethno-Religious Separatism in Xinjiang*, New Delhi: Pentagon, 2007, p. 165.
6. "'East Turkistan' Terrorist Forces Cannot Get Away With Impunity", Beijing: Information Office of the State Council, People's Republic of China, 21 January 2002 (Reproduced in *News from China*, 29 January-11 February 2002), p. 8.
7 "Victims of Syringe Attacks in Urumqi Rises to 531", 4 September 2009, online: http://english.cctv.com/20090904/110223.shtml (6 September 2009)
8. "11 More Terrorist Suspects Captured after Xinjiang Deadly Attack", www.xinhua.net, 29 April 2013.
9. Zachary Keck, "Al-Qaeda in Xinjiang Autonomous Region? Was the Attack on Monday in Tiananmen Square inspired by al-Qaeda?", *The Diplomat*, 30 October 2013.
10. The carrot side is all round prosperity of Xinjiang through social, economic, cultural and religious reform and the stick side is ruthless crackdown on the separatists, splittists and anti-Chinese elements. The measures taken by the Chinese authorities to checkmate the growth of separatist activities in Xinjiang include i) Economic development of Xinjiang, under the Great Western Development Programme, which is led by the Xinjiang Production and Construction Corps (XPCC) from the front; ii) Military strategy, with "Strike Hard, Maximum Pressure" campaign at the vanguard; iii) Diplomatic initiatives to stop some external forces who take active interest in the Xinjiang issue; and iv) Regional cooperation with some neighbours under the auspices of the Shanghai Cooperation Organisation (SCO). For details, see Note no. 4, pp. 187-209; Willy Lam, "Beijing's Carrot-and-Stick Strategy to deter Social Instability", *China Brief*, Vol. 9, Issue.3, 5 February 2009, p. 2.
11. Ellen Bork, "The Right Way to Help the Uyghurs", *Washington Post*, 10 July 2009, Online:http://www.washingtonpost.com/wp-dyn/content/article/2009/07/09/AR2009070902425.html. (11 July 2009).
12. Edward Wong, "Chinese Separatists Tied to Norway Bomb Plant", *New York Times*, 9 July 2010, p. 44.
13. For details, see Shanghai Cooperation Organization website http://www.sectsco.org
14 With a land mass spanning from Russia in the north to Vietnam and Thailand in the south, from India and Pakistan in the west to Korea and Japan in the east, China has the world's third biggest territory, with a total land area of 9.6 million sq. kms, next only to Russia and Canada. One out of five people in the world live in China (1.2 billion people). China is also the second largest economy in the world after the USA. Any country desiring to compete in the global market cannot ignore the gigantic and increasingly prosperous Chinese market. Besides, China is a big military power with the largest army in the world.

15. Yitzhak Shichor, "Ethno-Diplomacy: The Uyghur Hitch in Sino-Turkish Relations", *Policy Studies no. 53*, Washington DC: East West Centre, 2009, p. 24.
16. During this author's visit to Turkey in July 2011, one Uyghur living in Istanbul said that the Turkish government provided land to Uyghurs in Anatolia in 1950s. According to him, a substantial amount of Turkish currency (amount not specified) was also provided to Uyghurs.
17. "Alptekin at Turkic Conference", *Eastern Turkestan Information Bulletin*, Vol. 3, No. 2, April 1993.
18. "Turkey: Treatment of Uighurs (various spellings), particularly those who have been actively promoting the rights of Uighurs in China, and a group called 'Eastern Turkistan Foundation' in Istanbul", Research Directorate, Immigration and Refugee Board, Canada, 7 October 1999.
19. In August 1995, Chinese Ambassador to Ankara Wu Keming registered his protests before Recep Tayyip Erdogan (who was Mayor of Istanbul Metropolitan Municipality then) against the naming of this park in Isa's memory at the Sultan Ahmet area. For details, see Note no. 3, p. 35.
20. Debata, *China's Minorities: Ethno-Religious Separatism in Xinjiang*, p. 193
21. For more details, see http://www.rfa.org/english/news/uyghur/leader-02182010160741.html
22. Shichor, "Ethno-Diplomacy: The Uyghur Hitch in Sino-Turkish Relations", p. xi.
23. Ibid, p. 35.
24. Emrullah Uslu, "Are China's Uyghurs Operating an al-Qaeda Network in Turkey? Ankara and Beijing Discuss Cooperation against Terrorism", *Terrorism Monitor*, Vol. 7, Issue 30, p. 8, 1 October 2009.
25. Debata, *China's Minorities: Ethno-Religious Separatism in Xinjiang*, p. 193.
26. Lale Kemal, "Turkey should be Sensitive to the Plights of Uyghur Turks", *Today's Zaman*, 7 July 2009, Online: http://www.todayszaman.com/columnistDetail_getNewsById.action?newsId=180147 (15 July 2009).
27. Uslu, "Are China's Uyghurs Operating an al-Qaeda Network in Turkey? Ankara and Beijing Discuss Cooperation against Terrorism", p.9.
28. Ibid, p. 8.
29. Yitzhak Shichor, "Turkey Trot: Military Cooperation between Beijing and Ankara", *China Brief*, vol. 9, issue 8, 16 April 2009, p. 6.
30. Ibid.
31. METU Confucius Institute is the first of its kind in Turkey. It operates under the partnership of Middle East Technical University, Office of Chinese Language Council International (HANBAN), and Xiamen University, China, with the help of the Chinese embassy in Ankara. The METU Confucius Institute was inaugurated on November 28, 2008. China's growing global engagement requires promoting a deeper understanding of Chinese culture and contemporary China all over the world. As cultural and business ties between China and Turkey become more important, there is an increasing need to provide more opportunities to learn the Chinese language and introduce Chinese culture, history, economy, politics, and foreign policy to the academic community as well as the general public in Turkey. Both Turkey and China, having very distinguished cultural heritages, attach great importance to education. The institute offers general Chinese and business Chinese language courses to both METU students and the public. The business Chinese courses offered at the Institute promote a deeper understanding of China's business

climate, and help students overcome linguistic, geographical and cultural barriers, enabling them to achieve a higher communicative competence in business contexts. The Institute organises lectures, seminars, and workshops on Chinese culture and society. It also puts forth efforts to facilitate research on both Chinese culture and enhance the relationship between Turkey and China. METU's Technopark, the biggest and the most developed of its kind in Turkey, is a great asset in this endeavour. The major areas of activity of the Institute are given below:
The Institute offers an extensive programme of Chinese language training and teaching.
The Institute aims at promoting cultural exchange and friendly relations with China through enhancing the understanding of Chinese society and culture.
A primary concern of the METU faculty is directed towards the promotion of academic, scientific and technological links with China, with Chinese universities, academic institutions and research centres. The Center aims to strengthen and build new possibilities for exchange and collaboration in all fields; particularly in architecture and engineering, arts and social sciences, humanities and education.
The Institute aims to contribute to foster Turkish-Chinese economic relations. As with many other countries of the world, Turkey has been following China's fast track economic development closely and with appreciation.

32. "China Seeks further Engagement from Turkey in Xinjiang Region", 1 April 2012, http://www.todayszaman.com/news-276069-china-seeks-further-engagement-from-turkey-in-xinjiang-region.html
33. Even though the international community described the situation in Xinjiang as a matter of grave concern, it preferred to maintain silence on the entire episode.
34. Recep Tayyip Erdogan sympathised with Uyghurs, particularly Isa Yusuf Alptekin as discussed in this chapter in detail. But as the Chairman of Justice and Development Party (AKP) that came to power in 2003, Erdogan visited China where he advocated political and commercial cooperation between Turkey and China. He also gave statements against the separatist movement in Xinjiang. He also visited Urumqi in April 2012 as part of his Chinese sojourn.
35 Uslu, "Are China's Uyghurs Operating an al-Qaeda Network in Turkey? Ankara and Beijing Discuss Cooperation against Terrorism", pp. 6-7.
36. Emrullah Uslu, "Ankara's Reaction to Xinjiang Crisis Raises Bilateral Tension", *Eurasia Daily Monitor*, Vol. 6, Issue 135, 15 July 2009, pp. 1-2. Category: Eurasia Daily Monitor, Home Page, Turkey, China and the Asia-Pacific, Domestic/Social, Foreign Policy
37. Ibid.
38. Emrullah Uslu, "Ankara Anxiously Monitors the Xinjiang Crisis", *Eurasia Daily Monitor*, Vol. 6, Issue 130, 8 July 2009, pp. 1-2.
39. Matti Nojonen and Igor Torbakov, "China-Turkey and Xinjiang: A Frayed Relationship", http://www.opendemocracy.net/article/china-turkey-and-xinjiang-a-frayed-relationship (5 August 2009)
40. Teddy Ng, "Crackdown on Separatists, Xi says", *South China Morning Post*, 23 February 2012.
41. See Lale Kemal, "Turkey should be Sensitive to the Plights of Uyghur Turks".
42. See Colakoglu, "Turkey-China Relations; Rising Partnership".
43 Online: www.mfa.gov.tr, 6 July 2010.

# 14
# Geopolitics of Central Asia: The Changing Role of Turkey

*Mohammad Monir Alam*

The term 'geopolitics' is the key word in understanding the principal international power relations. In the intellectual discourse to understand fundamentals of Central Asian geopolitics it is all the more important. Interestingly, the ideas of classical geopolitics which were propounded by the Swedish political scientist Rudolf Kjellen, German geographers Friedrich Ratzel and Gen. Karl Haushofer who formed the 'Munich School' of political geography, were used by Adolf Hitler to justify German nationalism and the doctrine of Nordic superiority. But this led to the discrediting of all discourses of geopolitics of international significance. It was only with the beginning of the Cold War that the term 'geopolitics' began to be used in reference to theories and interpretations of international politics based on policies of great powers. Subsequently, the views of Alfred T. Mahan, a US naval officer, and British geographer Sir Halford Mackinder, on control of the sea as the key to world power and eventual emergence tempted by geography of a globally dominant empire located in the heartland of Eurasia occupied by Russia, were used to reinforce the Cold War. Mackinder in his later formulation expressed the view that the states of Western Europe and North America constitute a natural defence community which can balance the Eurasian heartland in population, resources and strategic potential.[1]

The 'Great Game' over Central Asia which Britain played against Russia was mainly explained in terms of the strategic significance of the region because of its geographical location as the gateway to the Indian sub-continent and the Persian Gulf. At present, the Central Asian–Caspian region with its large hydrocarbon reserves and natural gas resources has undoubtedly become a region of critical strategic importance and an object of international interests particularly between United States, Russia and China. According to Western experts' estimates the real hydrocarbon reserves in Central Asia are staggeringly large—perhaps equal to those of Saudi Arabia and Kuwait combined if both the onshore and offshore Caspian Sea resources are included.

In his work, *The Grand Chessboard: American Primacy and Its Geostrategic Imperatives,* President Jimmy Carter's National Security Advisor Zbigniew Brzezinski has tried to revive 'geopolitics' which was propounded by Mackinder and Mahan to prop up the North Atlantic alliance against the Socialist World during the Cold War era. In his book, Brzezinski promotes the idea that there is a 'zone of instability' that encompasses the Transcaucasus and Central Asia in which the intelligent chess player can manipulate the tribal, ethnic, or religious differences to his advantage.[2] A central theme of his book is to deny Russia any influence over developments in these newly independent Central Asian Republics. At the same time, Brzezinski has also advocated his theoretical support to the Anglo-American oligarchy's grab for the region's extensive oil, natural gas and mineral wealth.

Brzezinski has devoted a complete chapter to this end which he calls "The Eurasian Balkans". He writes:

> "In Europe, the word 'Balkans' conjures up images of ethnic conflicts and great power rivalries; Eurasia, too, has its 'Balkans'. They are located within that large geographic oblong that demarcates the central zone on instability... and that embraces portions of southeastern Europe, Central Asia and parts of South Asia, the Persian Gulf area, and the Middle East.... The Eurasian Balkans are of importance from the stand point of security and historical ambitions to at least three of their most immediate and more powerful neighbours, namely Russia, Pakistan and Iran with China also signalling an increasing political interest in the region. But the Eurasian Balkans is infinitely more important as a potential economic prize: an enormous concentration of natural gas and oil reserves is located in the region, in addition to important

> minerals including gold… A geostrategic issue of crucial importance is posed by China's emergence as a major power. Potentially, the most dangerous scenario would be a grand coalition of China, Russia, and perhaps Iran, an 'anti-hegemonic coalition' united not by ideology but by complementary grievances."[3]

After September 11, 2001, the US- led 'Operation Enduring Freedom' in Afghanistan has completely altered the traditional geopolitics of Central Asia. Taking advantage of the 'War on Global Terrorism' and military operations in Afghanistan, the United States has established several military bases in the Central Asian–Caucasus region which has added a new dimension in the regional geopolitics. The US military and security engagement with the Central Asian–Caucasus Republics has not only created a regional alignment after redrawing the geopolitical map of Central Asia, but has fundamentally altered the power balance. Moreover, it has also constrained the regional environment. The US's increased military involvement has also affected with profound impact the respective roles not only of Russia and China but also other regional powers—Turkey and Iran.

The present paper proposes to discuss geopolitics of Central Asia and the changing roles of Turkey towards the region primarily in the aftermath of the disintegration of the Soviet Union. This paper also focuses on the roles of Turkey in the changing geopolitical alignment in Central Asia in the wake of the US-led 'Operation Enduring Freedom' in Afghanistan and the 'Global War on Terror'.

## Turkey as a New Geopolitical Actor in Central Asia

The disintegration of the Soviet Union which led to the emergence of Central Asian Republics on the vast Eurasian landmass expanded the regional boundaries of West Asia. Both Iran and Turkey have been strongly affected by these radical transformations in their regional foreign policy environment. Leaders of both countries welcomed the disappearance of the military threat posed by the superpower and its Warsaw Pact allies. For more than forty years since the end of the Second World War, the perceived Soviet threat—a hostile superpower—was the principal guiding factor for both Iran and Turkey's regional foreign and national security policies.

Initially, the United States had not expressed its primary interests in the Central Asian region, but during the course of time, Washington sought to minimise regional instability by thwarting the influence of Iran—the so-called 'hostile regional power'. Later on, the US supported Turkey by trying to fortify their regional position. But Iran with its geographical proximity, its revolutionary doctrine and aspirations for regional hegemony and for the leadership of the world Islam, has similarly displayed a profound interest and made extensive efforts in Central Asia.

As already stated, after the demise of the Soviet Union it was perceived that Turkey might lose its strategic importance for the West in the post-Cold War era. During the Cold War, as a member of NATO, and neighbour of USSR, it had been granted political and military importance and economic rewards (economic and military aid). In many ways Turkey was treated by the NATO members as a more than equal partner than a Third World ally. But the fall of Soviet Union sharply reduced Turkey's importance to its Western allies. Its concern was also compounded by the strains with West European NATO allies over its desire to gain full membership in the European Community and the Western Union.[4] However, Turkish policy makers have maintained close political and military ties with the West as it is seen as essential for Turkey's national security, economic progress and democratic political development. But at the same time, Turkey's foreign policy has concentrated on finding new strategies to guard against its possible isolation from the emerging economic and political institution of Europe and to reassert its importance as a regional power.

The late Turkish President Turgut Ozal, the chief architect of Turkey's new foreign policy initiatives, advocated the finding of a new regional role for Turkey in the aftermath of the first Gulf War. Later on, his initiatives to establish the Black Sea Economic Cooperation Organisation intended to create a new regional politico-economic bloc was another example of Turkey's search for new strategies to reassert its regional importance.

The emergence of independent Central Asian Republics provided opportunities to Turkey not only to expand its influence, but also to establish political, economic and cultural relations. Turkey' involvement in the new geopolitical environment as a potential player in the region came mainly from the common ethno-linguistic relations between the Turks in Turkey and the nearly 50 million Turkic peoples who lived in Azerbaijan, Turkmenistan, Uzbekistan, Kazakhstan and Kyrgyzstan. Turkish leadership had a very optimistic view of economic and business opportunities in Central Asia and anticipated that Turkey's export-oriented economic growth strategy would benefit extensively from the growth of Turkey's regional ties and influence.[5] The establishment of official diplomatic ties between Turkey and the newly independent republics gave additional opportunities to the expansion of political and economic contacts.

Turkey's policy towards Central Asia is based on the following principles:

- Contributing to the consolidation of their state structuring,
- Supporting the political and economic reforms,
- Promoting their integration with the international community,
- Developing bilateral relations in all fields on the basis of equality, mutual interest and respect for sovereignty.

Leaders of Central Asian republics have sought Turkey's support in their efforts to become integrated into the international political and economic system, hoping that Ankara's close relations with Washington will help their entry into international political and financial organisations. Central Asian leaders were also impressed by Turkey's market-oriented economic policies and expected to receive technological help, managerial expertise and financial support from Turkey.[6]

The then Turkish Prime Minister, Suleyman Demirel, boasted in February 1992 of a "gigantic Turkish world" stretching from the Adriatic Sea to the Great Wall of China. Moreover, while touring Central Asia in May 1992, Demirel spoke out for forming a Commonwealth of independent Turkic states. But, even the first Turkic Summit held in Ankara in October 1992, which was attended by leaders of all Central

Asian Republics, provoked disappointment for Turkey. The Central Asian leaders had advocated for broader economic and political relations with other states, including Russia and Iran. Later on, immediately before the Fifth Turkic Summit in Astana in June 1998, Uzbek President Islam Karimov walked out by declaring that the summits should not consider political or security matters.[7]

However, Turkey's principal security concern has been that regional competitors, especially Russia and Iran can expand their own cultural and economic influence. In fact, the United States has continuously supported Turkey in becoming an important regional player possibly to serve as a role model for Central Asian Republics. The US strategy of promoting the 'Turkish Model' in comparison to the 'Iranian Model' was largely based on its fear that Islamic radicalism, supported by Iran, would make inroads into Central Asian region which might destabilise regional stability. In comparison with Iran, Turkey, with its pro-Western orientation in world politics, secular state institutions, democratic political process and market-based economic policies has more attraction for Central Asian Republics. At least in the initial stage, Turkey's foreign relations had acquired new political and economic dimensions. But for various reasons, Turkey's initial high expectations about the expansion of its influence in the Central Asian Republics have not been fully realised. As a member of NATO, Turkey could become an influential force in Central Asia, but has not been consistent in its strategic orientation. Currently, Turkish influence in the region has been significantly declined, but it must not be altogether discounted. Moreover, Turkey's self-image as "elder brother" for Central Asian republics has clashed with Uzbekistan's own aspirations to leadership. In fact, Islam Karimov has characterised the Uzbek view of Turkish pretensions: "Turkey wants us to become Turks. But we are Uzbeks, not Turks."[8]

Despite its social, economic, and strategic interests, Turkey's role in Central Asia has been very limited. This is due to the following reasons: (a) Geographical reasons (Turkey is far off from Central Asia), (b) Economic reasons (Turkey is not in a position to provide financial aid to the Central Asian Republics), (c) Geopolitical compulsions (Turkey can't afford confrontation with Russia, Russia is one of its main economic partners; over 90 percent of Turkey's trade with CIS states is with Russia and (d) The Central Asian apprehension of Turkish dominance in the region.

So far as defence relations between Turkey and Central Asian Republics are concerned, after the visit of General Dogan Giiresh, then Chief of the Turkish General Staff, in March 1993, to Kyrgyzstan and Turkmenistan, bilateral agreements on military training were concluded. Officers from the Central Asian Republics were enrolled in Turkish war academies. In a speech at the National Defense University in Washington, in February 1998, General Cevik Bir, the then Deputy Chief of the Turkish General Staff, noted that around 2300 cadets and officers from Central Asia and Azerbaijan had graduated from Turkey's war colleges, and another 1700 were continuing their training in Turkey.[9] Kazakhstan has also signed a military industrial cooperation agreement and a protocol on military training with Turkey. In fact, Turkey has been playing an important role in training Central Asian republics' new officer corps. At a meeting of the Military Committee of NATO in September 2000, H. Kivrikoglu (the Head of the General Staff of the Armed Forces of Turkey) proposed that Istanbul create a rapid-deployment force for the Balkans, Caucasus, and Central Asia. With a core of 1,500 officers, this formation should be able to expand to 50,000 or 60,000 military personnel in crisis situations. In the opinion of Kivrikoglu, Turkey is closer than the other NATO countries to the unstable crisis regions; situating staff headquarters here would have a restraining impact on the region.[10] Turkey is not extensively involved in arms production ventures with the Central Asian republics.

Turkey has played as an intermediary between NATO and Central Asian republics. In mid-1990s NATO officials delegated to Turkey the chief responsibility for promoting NATO's interests and concerns in Central Asia. At that time Turkey was the only NATO member which had military attaches stationed in the region. After Turkish lobbying, NATO opened a Partnership for Peace Programme (PfP), Commandership of Education Centre in Ankara in 1998, where participants from Central Asian republics attended courses.[11] In September 1997 the Centrasbat-97 military manoeuvres were held in Kazakhstan. In that series of exercises, soldiers from Kazakhstan, Kyrgyzstan, and Uzbekistan along with Turkish soldiers participated in a parachute drop exercise by US 82nd Airborne Division in Kazakhstan. The newly formed Central Asian peacekeeping battalion, composed of Kazakh, Kyrgyz and Uzbek units trained within the framework of the PfP, participated for the first time with US, Russian and Turkish troops in a peacekeeping and humanitarian aid exercise. The Centrasbat-98 exercise held in Kyrgyzstan and Uzbekistan also included units from Azerbaijan and Georgia along with Turkey. The Turkish military has also participated in NATO's other military exercises in order to strengthen strategic ties with the Central Asian republics. Gareth M. Winrow concluded:

> "The importance of Turkey's relations with Central Asia should not be exaggerated. Ties with the United States and the European Union are more crucial for Turkey. It is not a part of Central Asia. It is not able to play the role of a core state in the region. In spite of the rhetoric and Pan-Turkic groups in Turkey, a Turkic Commonwealth will not materialize. Central Asian leaders have preferred to diversify their contacts with the international community. Nevertheless, Turkey's involvement in Central Asia should not be downplayed. It is a major player in the pipeline politics game. Concerning energy security, though, it is only possible to speculate about the future. The pipeline politics game is a complex, dynamic and ongoing one. The future of Turkish–Uzbek relations remains uncertain. In military and defence matters, Turkey is an invaluable partner for many of the recently formed national armies in Central Asia and the Transcaucasus. Turkey, therefore, is likely to remain an important player in post-Soviet Central Asia and, in particular, in the Caspian region."[12]

## Turkey and the Geopolitics of Caspian Oil

Regarding Turkish policy towards the Caspian region and its hydrocarbon resources, different contradictory prepositions have been presented by Turkish, Western and Central Asian scholars. However, since energy security constitutes one of the extremely important components for sustained economic growth, Turkey has become a potential market for the oil and gas production of the Caspian region and Russia. Its energy demand has been increasing rapidly and will continue in the future as well. Turkey is estimated to import around 28 million tonnes of crude oil in the year 2001 and over 40 million tonnes by 2010. The increase in the demand for natural gas is even more striking. It is expected to rise from 10 billion cubic meters (bcm) in 2000 to over 30–40 bcm in 2010. At present, Turkey depends on imports for approximately 62.6 per cent of its energy consumption and for more than 95 per cent of the oil and gas it consumes.[13] Turkey is playing an increasingly important role in the transit of oil supplies from Russia, the Caspian region, and the Middle East to Europe, with the Turkish government deriving significant revenues from the transit fees. Significant volumes of Russian and Caspian oil move by tanker via the Turkish Straits to Western markets. Approximately 3.0 million bbl/d flowed through the Bosphorus and the Dardanelles in 2013 (approximately 2.5 million bbl/d of crude oil and 0.5 million bbl/d of petroleum products).[14] The major suppliers of crude oil for Turkey's domestic consumption are the Persian Gulf countries and Libya; the major supplier of natural gas is Russia. This trend has prompted Turkey to diversify its energy suppliers and to regard the Central Asian and Caucasus states as important energy partners.

But Turkey has encountered stiff competitions from the regional powers for transportation of the Caspian oil. In this context, Turkey has adopted an economic approach which is also dominated by environmental concerns and political considerations. However, apart from a number of existing pipelines to transport Caspian energy, Turkey has supported to build a pipeline from Azerbaijan through Georgia to Turkey's Mediterranean port of Ceyhan known as Baku-Tbilisi-Ceyhan (BTC) pipeline. Turkey is energetically promoting the BTC project, which will avoid all transport by sea through the Black Sea and the Turkish Straits. The United States is basically interested in isolating both Iran and Russia. The United States views the question of BTC oil pipeline routes as a crucial factor in the long-term geopolitical orientation of the region. Apart from the financial benefit and considerable share of the oil flowing through the BTC pipeline, Turkey does not want to antagonise Russia. Russia is Turkey's major economic partner and its most important energy supplier.

## Turkey's Politico-economic and Trade Policy

Turkey's current policy toward Central Asia is more realistic and has reachable goals. It aims to create an environment of cooperation. Initially, in the first 4 or 5 years following the fall of the Soviet Union, Turkish officials declared grand objectives for these countries that they were not able to meet: "romantic" declarations of intent based on a shared national and cultural heritage failed to materialise. From 1996 onwards, corrective measures were taken by the Turkish policy makers to shift to a more pragmatic foreign political stance in the region. In this new policy, the relationship between Turkey and the Central Asian Republics was defined first and foremost by shared economic interests. While Turkey's achievements are carried to the region by means of the state and civil society organisations it prioritises economic development and political stability in the Central Asian states. Flawed by many factors of instability such as growing nuclear activities, international terrorism, drug trafficking and illegal immigration as well as international competition for domination, Turkey's policy towards Central Asia seeks to contribute to peace and stability. The recently growing number of mutual visits between Turkey and Central Asian States reveals that the strong signs of Turkey's contributions to the region will continue which shapes its future policy as well.

Moreover, as a result of significant transformations over the last decade, Turkey has adopted a fiscal policy; a policy of Turkish activism on the foreign policy front. Its Foreign Minister Ahmet Davutoglu's strategic formulation of, 'zero problems policy with neighbours' brought dynamismtoTurkey'srelationswith most of its neighbouring and extended countries, including the Central Asian States. Throughout this period, economy and trade became the "practical hand" of Turkey's peaceful foreign policy.[15] As already mentioned, Turkey was among the first country to have recognised the independence of the Central Asian republics in 1991and the first to open embassies across the region. Building on cultural and linguistic similarities the Turkish government, private and civil societies have put an extensive effort in developing political, economic and social interaction between Central Asia and Turkey. Turkish-run universities and secondary schools, joint Turkic

TV channels, regular educational and cultural exchanges manifest an increased role of Turkey in the region.

The Turkish Cooperation and Development Agency since 1992 implemented numerous economic, social and cultural projects that aim to support nation-building processes in the region.[16] Turkey and Central Asian republics are members of Economic Cooperation Organisation (ECO) and Turkic Council. In fact, many Central Asians look at Turkey as an economic and democratic model of development. The recent surge of Turkish economy and its role in world affairs may have an even more influential role for the Central Asian people. Since 1991, Turkey has desired for a stable, independent and prosperous Central Asia as a policy priority in the region towards building free market economies and functioning democracies. The Foreign Minister said that Turkey and Central Asia have common historical, linguistic and cultural ties and Turkey has sought to increase engagement with this region on a broad range of issues. In this respect, the high level Strategic Cooperation Council (SCC) mechanisms have been established with Kazakhstan and Kyrgyzstan and the Cooperation Council with Tajikistan to provide a useful basis for further relations.[17] Turkey welcomes the peaceful and democratic change in Kyrgyzstan and supports the establishment of democratic rules and principles in the country. The strengthening of the political, social and economic climates in the Kyrgyz Republic is a key to regional peace and security. Kazakhstan also took an important step in the right direction in creating a multi-party system through nation-wide elections on January 15, 2012. Turkey encourages these efforts with a view that a democratic and stable Central Asia will better serve the interests of the whole Eurasian region. Turkey's economic relations with the Central Asian Republics have developed rapidly, and significant progress has been achieved in the fields of trade, transportation and communication.

In the sphere of economic cooperation, the Turkish International Cooperation Agency (TICA) has provided project assistance in various spheres of the economy. By 2001, the Turkish Exim Bank had granted credits to Central Asian Republics of around $ 800 million. According to official Turkish sources, by 2001 approximately 900 Turkish companies were active in the region. The private investments had reached the level of $ 3.5 billion, and the work of the construction companies valued $ 7–8 billion.[18] The loans given to the countries in the region through Exim Bank have reached the level of around 1 billion USD. Turkey has also provided around 1 billion USD in foreign aid to four Central Asian countries—namely, Kazakhstan, Kyrgyzstan, Uzbekistan and Turkmenistan over the last 20 years, which constitutes one fourth of its total foreign aid in the same period. The Turkish Cooperation and Development Agency (TIKA) was established in order to provide technical assistance to these countries.

Trade turnover between Turkey and Central Asian republics remained insubstantial. The figures for 1994 were less than $500 million, which was approximately only one quarter of the amount of the Turco-Russian trade in the same year.[19] In the initial years the imports and exports were very low. In 1990, before the disintegration of the Soviet Union the imports and export value was zero. In 1995, Turkey's imports and exports with all the Central Asian states were $273 million and $390 million respectively. In 2000, Turkey's total imports reached $549 million, $1,042 million in 2005, $3498 in 2008; but it declined in 2009 and reduced to $2228 million. In 2012 it reached $4806 million. For details, see Table 1.

**Table 1:- Turkey's Imports from Central Asia (in Million US$)**

| Country | 1990 | 1995 | 2000 | 2005 | 2008 | 2009 | 2011 | 2012 |
|---|---|---|---|---|---|---|---|---|
| Kazakhstan | 0 | 87 | 346 | 559 | 2332 | 1349 | 3020 | 3300 |
| Kyrgyzstan | 0 | 6 | 2 | 14 | 48 | 31 | 50 | 45 |
| Uzbekistan | 0 | 62 | 86 | 261 | 581 | 413 | 939 | 813 |
| Tajikistan | 0 | 6 | 17 | 47 | 148 | 107 | 324 | 345 |
| Turkmenistan | 0 | 112 | 98 | 161 | 389 | 328 | 392 | 303 |
| Total | 0 | 273 | 549 | 1042 | 3498 | 2228 | 4725 | 4806 |

Source: Turkish Statistical Institute, Istanbul

So far as Turkey's export is concerned, the total export to Central Asia in 2000 was $347 million, $929 million in 2005 and $2258 million in 2008. In 2008 it rose to $3480.8 million. Like imports export also declined in 2009 and it was $2124 million.[20] For details, see Table 2.

**Table 2:- Turkey's Export to Central Asia (in Million US$)**

| Country | 1990 | 1995 | 2000 | 2005 | 2008 | 2009 | 2011 | 2012 |
|---|---|---|---|---|---|---|---|---|
| Kazakhstan | 0 | 151 | 119 | 460 | 891 | 634 | 948 | 1060 |
| Kyrgyzstan | 0 | 38 | 21 | 90 | 191 | 140 | 180 | 257 |
| Uzbekistan | 0 | 139 | 83 | 151 | 337 | 279 | 354.5 | 449.8 |
| Tajikistan | 0 | 6 | 4 | 47 | 176 | 126 | 172 | 234 |
| Turkmenistan | 0 | 56 | 120 | 181 | 663 | 945 | 1490 | 1480 |
| Total | 0 | 390 | 347 | 929 | 2258 | 2124 | 3144.5 | 3480.8 |

Source: Turkish Statistical Institute, Istanbul

Turkey's volume of trade with the Central Asian republics was about $6.5 billion by the year 2010 and the total investments of Turkish companies in the region exceeded $4.7 billion. The total value of projects realised by Turkish contracting companies in the region has reached a level of around $50 billion. Nearly two thousand Turkish companies have been operating on the ground. The data reveals that, Turkey's imports and exports with three of the Central Asian States—Kazakhstan, Turkmenistan and Uzbekistan are in a commanding position but trade deficit is a regular feature with all the states. For details, see Table 3.

**Table 3:- Turkey's Ranking in Trade with Central Asian Republics (%) (As of December 31, 2012).**

| Country | Import | Ranking | Export | Ranking |
|---|---|---|---|---|
| Kazakhstan | 2.6% | 6 | 3.5% | 6 |
| Kyrgyzstan | 6.6% | 10 | 3.9% | 6 |
| Uzbekistan | 5.2% | 6 | 5.8% | 4 |
| Tajikistan | 5.4% | 4 | 9.8% | 2 |
| Turkmenistan | 8.0% | -- | 5.0% | -- |

Source: Turkish Statistical Institute, USAK-ISRO, Istanbul

Relations have also developed in the areas of culture and education. The International Organization of Turkic Culture (TURKSOY) was established in 1993 for the purpose of protecting the Turkic culture, art, language and historical heritage; introducing these values to the world and transferring them to the younger generations. Turkey has been carrying out a broad scholarship programme "Great Student Project" for students in the Central Asian countries. Many Turkish schools under the

Ministry of National Education or managed by private organisations exist in the Central Asian Republics. The Turkish–Kazakh International Hoca Ahmet Yesevi University operates in the city of Turkestan (Kazakhstan) and the Turkish–Kyrgyz Manas University is located in Bishkek (capital of Kyrgyzstan). Turkey pioneered the process of "The Summits of Turkic-Speaking Countries' Heads of States", held since 1992 in order to increase solidarity between the Turkic-Speaking Countries and to create new cooperation opportunities among them. This process has acquired an institutional structure through the Nakhichevan Treaty regarding the Establishment of the Cooperation Council of Turkic-Speaking States (Turkic Council) signed on 3rd October, 2009. The Secretariat of the Council was established in Istanbul and Ambassador (R) H.E. Mr. Halil Akıncı appointed as its first Secretary-General.

Turkey is now among the top six trading partners for all Central Asian economies, with enviable positions in key sectors such as food production and conditioning, construction, hotel management, financial services, oil and gas, as well as IT and telecommunication. Kazakhstan is the largest trading partner of Turkey from all the Commonwealth of Independent States (CIS). But, import and export figures are still below Turkey's full, optimal, economic potential, which constitutes both a challenge and an opportunity. Today's Turkey is aware of the importance of Central Asia while taking into account the existence of Russian, Iranian and Chinese interests in the region. In this perspective, Turkey should pursue and build on its pragmatic policy of the past few years by systematically privileging economic development, and thus avoid being distracted by purely political considerations. The rise in trade and investment flows with Central Asia and Turkey's belated willingness to revive the old "Silk Road" trade routes mean that Ankara has been making real progress in the mutually beneficial economic partnerships. Turkish firms have been established in the five republics of Central Asia. But this does not mean in any sense that Turkey is engaging with its "Eastern" Central Asian neighbours at the expense of the "rest". Quite the contrary: Turkey aims to position itself as a "central country" at the intersection of a geographically strategic region, a key Eurasian power within the European Union.[21] Hence, Ankara acknowledges that the same democratisation and Europeanisation processes that have helped Turkey to achieve its remarkable economic and political developments of the past 10 years have helped create the spillover commercial and diplomatic effects into its relations with its Central Asian neighbours. Finally, Turkey has brought economic and political stability to that crucial part of the world which constitutes a vital link between Western Europe and Asia. What Turkey expects from its European friends and allies is simply to be recognised as an equal, equally European, partner as it strives to further the security and welfare of the region.

## Conclusion

The emergence of Central Asia with its large hydrocarbon reserves and natural gas resources has undoubtedly become a region of critical strategic importance and an object of international activity particularly between United States, Russia and China. Simultaneously, it has also provided an exuberant opportunity to Turkey to re-link the two vital Islamic regions. In the wake of the disappearance of a hostile superpower and an anti-Muslim geopolitical environment, Turkish policy makers initially envisioned the establishment of a much needed strategic depth with enormous expectations for wider economic and cultural prospects. Apparently, even after more than two decades of independence, Ankara has failed to form a multi-lateral politico-economic and strategic arrangement based on ethno-religious and cultural solidarity with the Central Asian republics. Although, Turkey has tried to assume the role of a state-bridge as well as the representative of Western partners in the Central Asian region, it has failed to achieve its objectives because of certain internal and external constraints. From the beginning of its independence, Kazakhstan along with other republics was very critical about the pan-Turkic ideas of Turkey. Despite all efforts to develop cultural–political and economic relationships, Central Asian leaders have declined to accept Turkey as a 'big brother'.

However, taking advantage of the so-called 'Operation Enduring Freedom' in Afghanistan, the United States has established several military bases in the Central Asian–Caucasus region which has added a new dimension to the regional geopolitics. In this present strategic environment, both Turkish–Iranian geo-economic and strategic interests in Central Asia have been sharply affected. Although, Turkish–American strategic relations have strengthened since Turkey has become an important strategic partner of the US coalition forces in Afghanistan and West Asia. Turkish soldiers have also participated in the International Security Assistance Force (ISAF) in Afghanistan. Unfortunately, Ankara did not sustain its politico-economic interests in Central Asia. Moreover, after the US engagement and attack on Iraq and outbreak of the Arab spring movements Turkey has shifted its attention more to domestic concerns than to the Central Asian region. At the same time, Central Asian republics have also emerged as strategic partners of the United States.

But in the case of Iran, despite its hostility towards the Taliban regime, Iranian leaders have sharply condemned the US-led 'war on terrorism' in Afghanistan. Both conservative and reformists have expressed fears that US motives are not pious.[22] In the name of war on terrorism, US has established its military presence in Central Asia and the Persian Gulf, and is going to place its control upon the region's energy resources. In fact, the current geopolitical situation in the Central Asian region has provided favourable conditions to the United States to consolidate its position which has indirectly marginalised regional powers. But being the most important regional power and in its close geographical proximity, for future domestic energy security and to access new markets, Turkey has to reinvigorate its politico-economic and diplomatic thrust towards the Central Asian region.

## Notes

1. Devendra Kaushik, "The New Geopolitics of Central Asia: Russia, China and India", *Contemporary Central Asia*, Vol.III, No. 2, August 1999, (New Delhi), p. 13.
2. For details, see Zbigniew Brzezinski, *The Grand Chessboard: American Primacy and Its Geostrategic Imperatives,* (New York: Basic Books, 1997).
3. Muriel Mirak-Weissbach, "Zbigniew Brzezinski's Dangerous Chessboard", *EIR*, September 8, 2002, vol. 27, No. 35, p. 72.
4. For details, see Sabri Sayari, "Turkey: the Changing European Security Environment and the Gulf Crisis", *The Middle East Journal*, Vol. xvi, No. 1, Winter 1992, pp. 9-21.

5. See Sabri Sayari, "Turkey, the Caucasus and Central Asia" in Ali Banuazizi and Myron Weiner (ed), *The New Geopolitics of Central Asia and its Borderlands* (London: I.B. Tauris & Co Ltd. 1994), p.180.
6. For the detailed views expressed by President Islam Karimov and President Askar Akaev regarding the appeal of Turkish secularism, see Bress Brown, "Central Asia's Diplomatic Debut', *RFE/RL Research Report,* March 6, 1992. Also see, Sabri Sayari "Turkey, the Caucasus and Central Asia" p.179.
7. Roy Allison, "Central Asia: A Region in the Making", *Central Asia in a New Security Context*, (The Swedish Institute of International Affairs, Stockholm, 1999), pp.8-9.
8. Ibid.
9. "Turkey's Role in the New World Order: New Challenges", speech delivered by Gen. Cevik Bir at the Institute for National Strategic Studies, National Defense University, Washington, DC; Strategic Forum, No. 135, February 1998, cited by M. Laumulin, "Turkey and Central Asia", *Central Asian Affairs,* No. 3, posted on http://www.Kisi.kz/English/Geopolitics.
10. *http://www.Kisi.kz/English/Geopolitics.*
11. Gareth M. Winro, "Turkey and Central Asia" in R. Allison and L. Jonson (ed), *Central Asian Security: The New International Context* (London: RIIA/Brooking Institution Press, 2001), p.199.
12. Ibid, p. 230.
13. M. Laumulin, "Turkey and Central Asia", *Central Asian Affairs,* No. 3, *http://www.Kisi.kz/English/Geopolitics.*
14. Report of *US Energy Information Administration* available at http://www.eia.gov/countries/analysisbriefs/Turkey/turkey.pdf.
15. Salih Dogan and Mustafa Kutlay, "Turkey and Central Asia: Modern Economic Linkages Along the Silk Road", *Asie Centrale Et Caucase*, No, 38, 2011, p. 34.
16. Farrukh Suvankulov and Yunus Guc, "Who is Trading Well in Central Asia? A Gravity Analysis of Exports from the Regional Powers to the Region", *Eurasian Journal of Business and Economics*, Vol. 5, (9), 2012, p. 28.
17. Turkey Relations with Central Asia States, *Ministry of Foreign Affairs*, Republic of Turkey, available at http://www.mfa.gov.tr/turkey_s-relations-with-central-asian-republics.en.mfa
18. M. Laumulin, "Turkey and Central Asia", *Central Asian Affairs,* No. 3, posted on http://www.Kisi.kz/English/Geopolitics.
19. Gareth M. Winrow, "Turkey's Relations with Transcaucasus and the Central Asia Republics", *Journal of International Affairs*, Vol. 3, (4), 1996, p. 4.
20. Salih Dogan and Mustafa Kutlay, "Turkey and Central Asia: Modern Economic Linkages Along the Silk Road", *Asie Centrale Et Caucase*, No, 38, 2011, p. 35.
21. Ibid. p. 37.
22. *The Middle East Media Research Institute (MEMRI) Report*, (Berlin), November 12, 2001.

# 15
# Role of Turkey in Making Peace in Afghanistan

*Md. Rahat Hasan*

## Introduction

The stabilising or peacemaking efforts in Afghanistan took off against the backdrop of the American-led NATO intervention launched in the wake of the September 11, 2001 terrorist attacks. Since the initial military intervention in 2001, International Coalition forces led by USA have remained in Afghanistan conducting counterinsurgency operations and claiming to be involved in the reconstruction and peace-building process. The framework of post-conflict reconstruction programme of Afghanistan was established under the Bonn Agreement of December 2001 under the UN leadership. This document involved frameworks on political reform and security, which were planned to create conditions for the reconstruction process in Afghanistan.[1] Today, there is partnership between the Afghan government, United Nations Assistance Mission in Afghanistan (UNAMA) and NATO-International Security Assistance Force (ISAF) in providing reconstruction.[2] Apart from political transition, economic and infrastructure development are also widely considered by the international community as pivotal to Afghanistan's ability to shape its future. Donor aids constitute a large amount of Afghanistan's GDP. As a result of these efforts, Afghanistan, over the years, has been able to build democratic structures and progress has been made in key areas such as governance, security, economy, health, education, transport and agriculture.

In parallel to international efforts, Turkey is following an eclectic approach in Afghanistan in which it combines military approach with non-military contribution.[3] In recent years the Turkish foreign policy priority over Afghanistan is to improving regional cooperation in order to negotiate on how to work more efficiently for bringing peace, security and stability in Afghanistan; particularly offering a trilateral dialogue between Turkey, Afghanistan and Pakistan. Besides regional and trilateral meetings, there have been other diplomatic initiatives as well. The Istanbul Summit for Friendship and Cooperation in the Heart of Asia or "Istanbul for Afghanistan" Summit in January 2010 is an example of this. However, this regional diplomacy for regional cooperation to resolve the Afghanistan crisis was not without politics as India was not invited in the summit because of the apprehension of Pakistan. India's presence in Afghanistan remains a source of much misgiving within Pakistan. While Afghanistan looks towards India for greater cooperation, Pakistan appears determined not to allow such a scenario. Nevertheless, with a limited military presence, training, diplomatic initiatives and economic projects the role of Turkey in the post- conflict reconstruction of Afghanistan has been constructive. Accordingly, the paper first provides an overview of the international efforts for reconstruction in Afghanistan then highlights and examines Turkey's contributions within this larger context of international assistance.

## International Efforts in Making Peace in Afghanistan

After the overthrow of the Taliban regime, the United States and its allies realised that fighting terrorism required more than hunting down the al-Qaeda and Taliban. Thus, apart from a military solution, Afghanistan's reconstruction or state-building has been an essential part of NATO's strategy.

State building is a complex process, as it involves many strands of formal and informal institutions. Functionality and effectiveness of state institutions largely determine the governing capacity of the state. Four institutions of the state—Executive including public administration, Legislature, Judiciary and Security agencies are key institutions that define the modern states. Afghanistan, even as a non- modern, underdeveloped state, had all of them with variable capacities in each, but lost them in the wake of the civil war. Since the overthrow of the Taliban regime, the international coalition supporting Afghanistan's revival and restructuring has attempted to address state deficiency in these areas.

The reconstruction process in Afghanistan started after the Bonn Agreement in 2001 under the UN leadership. This document involved frameworks on political reform and security, which were planned to create conditions for the reconstruction process in Afghanistan. Under the Bonn Agreement, Hamid Karzai was appointed chair of a new transitional government in Afghanistan and reaffirmed as leader by an "emergency *Loya Jirga*" in June 2002. The new Constitution was approved in January 2004 by a "Constitutional *Loya Jirga*" (CLJ). The Constitutional *Loya Jirga* adopted the 162 articles of the Afghan Constitution. Under the Constitution a Presidential system with a bicameral Parliament was established. Presidential, Parliamentary and Provincial elections have been held twice so far and the last Presidential election was be held in May 2014. People behind the drafting of the Constitution provided institutional mechanism for the representation of women in the power structure. They have attempted to ensure this by providing for the equality of women under the Constitution and securing of 25 percents of seat of the *Wolesi Jirga* for women. For the *Meshrano Jirga*, President's appointees shall be 50 percent women. The Constitution also established a regular pattern of court systems, including High Court, Appeals Court and Supreme Court.[4]

Today, there is partnership between the Afghan government, United Nations Assistance Mission in Afghanistan (UNAMA) and NATO-International Security Assistance Force (ISAF) in providing reconstruction. UNAMA was established in March 2002 following the Bonn agreement. It is responsible for all the UN relief, recovery and reconstruction activities in Afghanistan. Its development programmes continue in coordination with the Afghan government's development strategy, focusing mainly on five sectors in Afghanistan: agriculture, energy, private sector development, capacity building and higher education and vocational training. In addition, while the political affairs division at UNAMA supports political outreach, conflict resolution, disarmament and regional cooperation, its human rights unit plays an important role in the promotion and protection of human rights in Afghanistan.[5]

Besides UNAMA, other UN bodies as well have an impact on Afghanistan's reconstruction, including the UN Development Program, the UN High Commission for Refugees and the UN Development Fund for Women. Likewise, non-governmental organisations, the World Bank and the Asian Development Bank have a significant place in the reconstruction efforts.[6]

Afghan-led governmental reform and institution-building programmes are under way, all with U.S. and other donor assistance, that include training additional civil servants, instituting merit-based performance criteria, hiring on qualifications rather than kinship and ethnicity and eliminating widespread governmental corruption. The key institution for regulating public institution and their administration is the Afghan Independent Administrative Reform and Civil Service Commission (IARCSC). Afghan ministries have been greatly increasing their staffs and technological capabilities (many ministry offices now have modern computers and communications, for example). Afghanistan Independent Human Rights Commission (AIHRC) acts as an oversight body over alleged human rights abuses. Since 2001, numerous television channels, newspapers, and other media firms were established (*Pajhok, Arina, Tolo News, Daily Afghanistan Outlook* etc.), giving Afghanistan some of the freest press.[7]

Apart from political transition, the International Security Assistance Force (ISAF) was created in accordance with the Bonn Conference. 46 countries including 28 NATO members sent their troops for the ISAF task in Afghanistan. The main objective of ISAF is assisting the government of Afghanistan in providing security and stability, in order to create the conditions for reconstruction and development. There are five main security tasks of ISAF: conducting security and stability operations; disarming illegally armed groups; facilitating bullets depository managements; providing post-operation assistance development and training the Afghanistan's National Security Forces (ANSF) so that they can effectively take over Afghanistan's security.[8] ANSF consist of three principle components: the Afghan National Army, the Afghan Air Force, and the Afghan National Police. The size of the Afghan army is roughly about 195,000 and they are trained by International Forces. The size of the Afghan Police is about 157,000. ANSF salaries are about $1.6 billion per year, paid by donor countries.[9] Presently, training of the Afghan army is carried by nine states: the US, Great Britain, France, Germany, Turkey, Romania, Mongolia, Canada and Estonia.[10]

In addition to ISAF, sixteen NATO countries lead 26 Provincial Reconstruction Teams (PRTs) operating across Afghanistan. Through its Provincial Reconstruction Teams (PRTs), ISAF tries to help the Afghan authorities to strengthen the institutions required to establish good governance and rule of law, and to promote human rights. PRT is a joint, integrated military–civilian organisation, staffed and supported by ISAF member countries, operating at the provincial level. The mission of the PRTs is to enhance security, extend the reach of the Afghan central government, and facilitate reconstruction. They are led by civilian agencies, supported by military Reconstruction projects, UNAMA and other provincial stakeholders.[11]

The framework for cooperation on reconstruction between the government of Afghanistan, the UN and the international community has been outlined and agreed to in a number of key documents and conferences including the Tokyo Conference of 2002 on reconstruction assistance to Afghanistan, the Berlin Conference of 2004 on Afghanistan, the London Conference of 2006, the Afghan Compact of 2006, the Paris Declaration of 2008, the Afghan Conference in London of 2010, Istanbul Process on Regional Security and Cooperation for a Secure and Stable Afghanistan in 2011 and recently the 2012 Tokyo Summit. The Istanbul Process was established to provide a platform to discuss regional issues, particularly encouraging security, political, and economic cooperation among Afghanistan and its neighbours. This region-led dialogue was launched in November 2011 to expand practical coordination between Afghanistan and its neighbours and regional partners in facing common threats, including counterterrorism, counternarcotics, poverty, and extremism. The United States and over 20 other nations and organisations serve as "supporting nations" to the process.[12] At the Tokyo Conference held in July 8, 2012, the United States and its partners pledged a total of US$16 billion in aid to Afghanistan up to 2015 for the socio-economic development of Afghanistan including:[13]

- The holding of credible, inclusive, and transparent elections in 2014 and 2015.
- Improved access to justice, and respect for human rights, particularly for women and children.
- Improved integrity of public financial management and the commercial banking sector.
- Improved revenue systems and budget execution.
- Efforts to re-build Afghanistan are showing some results. Ten million children have gone back to school. However, setbacks have occurred because of Taliban attacks on schools, causing some to close. The health care sector has made considerable gains in reducing infant mortality and giving about 65% of the population at least some access to health professionals. There has been substantial new construction, particularly in Kabul, including luxury hotels; Coca Cola bottling factory; apartment and office buildings; and marriage halls and other structures. Transportation system has also given priority in the Afghanistan Rebuilding process. Among major projects completed are the Ring Road, Qandahar to Tarin Kowt in Uruzgan province and road linking the Panjshir Valley to Kabul. A new bridge has opened over the Panj River, connecting Afghanistan and Tajikistan. Three railway projects are under way. One out of it, a 45 mile line from Mazar-i-Sharif to the border with Uzbekistan, was completed in March 2011. Other areas of development are agriculture, electricity and telecommunication.[14]

## Turkey's Efforts in Afghanistan Peace Making

Being a member country of NATO, Turkey remains in Afghanistan since the fall of the Taliban in 2001 and has been involved in the Afghanistan reconstruction process in parallel to international efforts. Turkey has been doing both military and non-military contributions to Afghanistan. Turkey's policy, although being a member of NATO, especially focuses on reconstruction and development activities, considering that a military solution alone could not resolve the problems in Afghanistan. While establishing peace and security, particularly in a country like Afghanistan is an important concern, other issues including reconstruction of economic and political institutions for ensuring social welfare, rebuilding of economy, increasing education level, raising the quality of life and improving the status of women are considered important as well.

The Turkish approach towards Afghanistan post-9/11 has been shaped by four main factors. The first one is Turkey's search for a new proactive foreign policy commonly referred to as the "New Foreign Approach". Turkey is searching for a greater role in regional and international affairs. Within this foreign policy approach, Turkish policy makers have used the concept of 'strategic depth' to conduct the Turkish foreign policy. 'Strategic depth', for them, is based on geographical and historical linkage.[15] Consequently, it is assumed that strategic depth places Turkey at the heart of many geopolitical areas of influence, enabling Turkey to play a more constructive role in multiple regions. The second main element of the new foreign policy approach is the search for 'zero-problem' with all neighbouring countries as well as development of political and economic relations.[16] Thus, while coordinating with the US and NATO in Afghanistan, Turkey also maintains cooperation with non-NATO countries such as Pakistan, hoping to strengthen regional cooperation for dealing with regional challenges.

The second factor is the "security interest". Turkey is highly concerned about challenges and risks in Afghanistan and Pakistan regarding terrorism and illegal drug trafficking, and is willing to cooperate in the fight against them. As long as Afghanistan is unstable, the whole region will be unstable, posing a security threat to Turkey. When Afghanistan becomes a secure and stable country, this will introduce wider stability in the region, bringing new economic benefits for the region in general and for Turkey in particular. Thus, Turkey has a shared interest with the international community in a stable Afghanistan with a regime that could promote economic development and social stability, thereby enhancing the security of the entire region.[17]

The third factor is the recent deepening of political and economic relations with Afghanistan. Turkey believes that if security in Afghanistan deteriorates, regional rivalries might intensify. Thus, Turkey has expanded its diplomatic energy in the recent years for reconstruction of politically and economically stabilised Afghanistan.[18]

Fourthly, Turkey has a strong historical and cultural relationship with Afghanistan. Though Turkey does not share a border with Afghanistan, over the years it has built close ties. In fact, Afghanistan established diplomatic relations with Turkey shortly after it gained independence in 1919 and was the second country to recognise the Republic of Turkey. The Afghan King Amanullah Khan headed the list of the foreign heads of state whom Ataturk received as guests in Ankara, which shows the political affinity between the two countries. King Amanuallah Khan introduced social, political and judicial reforms to modernise his country, while taking Turkey as a model. The two countries had signed numerous friendship and cooperation agreements since 1921. Furthermore, there is a positive attitude of the Afghan people towards Turkey, which is also related with friendly historical and cultural ties.[19] This has made it easier for Turkey to play an active role in Afghan reconstruction and in winning the hearts and minds of the Afghan people.[20]

**Noncombat Role and Civilian Provincial Reconstruction Teams**

Being concerned about bringing peace and stability to Afghanistan, Turkish military contributions to Afghanistan have been channelled through the ISAF. Turkey sent troops to Afghanistan on the condition that it would not deploy its troops for explicit counterinsurgency or counterterrorist operations.[21] It assumed the role of ISAF commander twice: first from June 2002–February 2003 (ISAF-II); and second from February 2005–August 2005 (ISAF-VII). During the first period Turkey, which initially had only 276 personnel, increased its troop number to 1300. During the ISAF-VII term, Turkey commanded 8,000 personnel from 30 countries, including 1,450 Turkish personnel.[22] During this period it also operated the Kabul International Airport. In addition, the Turkish Armed Forces took over the Kabul Regional Command (the Regional Command Capital) on November 1, 2009, and their mission has been extended by one-year periods since then. According to the website of the International Security Assistance Force, Turkey has 1,101 troops in Afghanistan as of June 2013, placing it 8th among the 50 ISAF nations.[23] Turkey is not planning to send more troops but it is willing to help the Afghans in the development of their security forces. Turkey is worried that too much emphasis on a more militaristic approach would complicate the situation in Afghanistan and this would in the end undermine the Afghanistan government. Moreover, according to the Turkish officials, in order to be successful in a strategy of Afghanistan, trust and support of the Afghans is required so that the Afghans would not perceive the security forces as occupiers. 'Afghanistan for Afghans' has been the motto of Turkey.

Perhaps more important than its military contributions are Turkey's social and cultural contributions. Turks run the Wardak and Jawzjan Provincial Reconstruction Teams (PRTs), the only PRTs run by civilian diplomats. They decided on this concept over a military-led PRT because they thought it would help them interact with local authorities and local people, enabling them to leverage their cultural ties and common values in fulfilling their mission.[24] This strategy has worked well. As Wardak Province Governor Halim Fedai says, "The Turkish programs are very sympathetic and acceptable to Afghans because they work within the Afghan culture and they are sensitive to Afghan values. We have a very good strong historical relationship with Turkey."[25]

The PRT in Wardak (a town 25 miles west of Kabul and one of the poorest provinces in Afghanistan) was established on November 12, 2006. This PRT cooperates with the Turkish International Cooperation and Development Agency (TIKA) (similar to the U.S. Agency for International Development) and has completed over 200 projects with its 130 employees.[26] Its stated goal is to focus on socio-cultural projects that can benefit the Afghan public in the fields of education, health and infrastructure with a view to enhance their quality of life. This has included restoring and building schools, hospitals and mosques, conducting health checks for people who live far away from city centres, training Afghan women to become midwives or nurses, building a sports complex at Kabul University, training Afghan police and military forces, training judges, prosecutors and mayors and building roads, bridges, and water wells. In addition to these activities, which are funded by the Turkish government, private Turkish entrepreneurs have invested over $2 billion in Afghanistan since 2002 in various projects. Following its success in Wardak Province, Turkey established the Jawzjan PRT in Shibirgan (the provincial center of Jawzjan) on July 21, 2010.[27]

## Capacity Development: Building Strong Indigenous Armed Forces

As an alternative to send more troops to Afghanistan, Turkey prefers to contribute by training the Afghan National Army (ANA) and Afghan National Police (ANP). Turkey is training the Afghan security forces in Turkey and sending them back while also training hundreds of the Afghan soldiers in Kabul. Turkish personnel in Afghanistan have trained over 12,500 Afghan personnel; another 3,300 have trained in Turkey. It is also leading a NATO training mission that plans to train 15,000 Afghan policemen over the course of a decade.[28] The ultimate goal is to build strong and indigenous armed forces such that the number of coalition combat forces in Afghanistan could be reduced. This is part of a broader effort to support plans to hand over security to Afghans by 2014 and reduce the role of coalition forces to logistics, intelligence, and medical and air transportation, instead of a combat role.

The Turkish police are also providing counternarcotics training to the Afghan police by hosting Afghan police at the Turkish Academy of International Narcotics and Fighting Organized Crime. This institution is under the Police Department's organised crime office.[29] Another field of capacity development is the specialised training for Afghan doctors in medical schools in Turkey. On December 10, 2011 the Health Departments of the two countries agreed to have Afghan doctors, nurses and midwives and other medical officials train in Turkish medical schools in programmes ranging from three months to one year.

## Diplomatic Initiatives: Afghanistan-Turkey-Pakistan

Under Turkey's new proactive foreign policy to increase regional cooperation through active diplomacy, trilateral meetings between Turkey, Afghanistan and Pakistan are continuing since 2007 to resolve the Afghanistan crisis. The purpose of this initiative is to improve relations between the two countries, whose ties are strained due to the Afghan belief that Pakistan supports the Taliban and that Pakistan's northwestern tribal regions are being used as a base for Taliban fighters seeking to overthrow the Afghan government. The first summit, which brought the leaders of Pakistan and Afghanistan together in Turkey, was held in 2007.

Since the start of this initiative, seven such summits have taken place (2007, 2008, 2009, twice in 2010, 2011, and 2012) at the presidential level. Each year the focus of the meetings has been different, but they generally involve dialogue on economic cooperation, cooperation in the fight against terrorism and cooperation in the intelligence, political and military fields, as well as security and training. These trilateral summits may not solve decades-long problems, but they serve to keep the lines of communication open. The leadership in Afghanistan and Pakistan welcomes these diplomatic initiatives by Turkey and views them as especially valuable due to Turkey's membership in NATO as well as its strong historical and cultural relationship with Afghanistan and Pakistan.[30]

Besides trilateral meetings, there have been other diplomatic initiatives as well. Turkey initiated the "Istanbul for Afghanistan" Summit (short for Istanbul Summit for Friendship and Cooperation in the Heart of Asia on January 26, 2010). This initiative brings together all the countries that border Afghanistan, with the goal of involving all those countries in finding sustainable solutions to Afghanistan's security and stability problems. The Presidents of Afghanistan, Pakistan, and Turkey, the first Vice President of Iran, the Special Representative of the President and the Minister of Foreign Affairs of China, and the Minister of Foreign Affairs of Tajikistan met in Istanbul upon the invitation of Turkey and signed the concluding Istanbul statement on Friendship and Cooperation. Representatives from the United States, the United Kingdom, Kyrgyzstan, Saudi Arabia, UAE, Russia, the Islamic Conference, France, Italy, Germany, Japan, the UN, EU and NATO attended as observers. Under this framework, these countries accept that they should take determined and coordinated action against challenges such as terrorism, extremism and illicit narcotic drugs. Both the Istanbul Regional Summit and the concluding statement were also important because they have underlined that regional cooperation starts from the region.[31]

However, this initiative for regional cooperation for resolving regional challenges was not without politics as India was not invited in the summit because of the apprehension of Pakistan. Despite its own economy facing a slow growth, India has invested heavily in

Afghanistan's reconstruction and development. India has contributed US$ 2 billion so far. India is the fifth largest donor to Afghanistan.[32] The funds have been spent on road construction and building projects approved by the Afghan government and local communities. India is also providing training assistance to Afghan administrators, teachers, medical staff and officer cadets but only within India. In October 2011, Indian Prime Minister Manmohan Singh and Afghan President Hamid Karzai signed a Strategic Partnership Agreement (SPA) which formalised cooperation on governance, economics, commerce, education, public administration and security enforcement.

Despite this largely development role in Afghanistan, India's presence in Afghanistan remains a source of much misgiving within Pakistan and especially for its military establishment. While Afghanistan looks towards India for greater cooperation, Pakistan appears determined not to allow such a scenario. It typically sees any Indian presence and influence in Afghanistan, even which is acquired through legitimate means, as being disadvantageous to its interest.

Aside from governmental initiatives, the Turkish private sector and business industry have also been cooperating with the Investment Support Agency of Afghanistan. The Turkish business community and chambers of commerce have agreed on "Cooperation on Energy and Mineral Resources" between the two countries, signed in February 2011. The memorandum of understanding calls for cooperation in energy and mineral resources; the first of its kind Afghanistan has signed with another country in the field of mining.

In a nutshell, although Turkey is reluctant to increase the number of troops, it plays an important role for the stability and reconstruction of Afghanistan with its assistance projects. The official and diplomatic level discourses demonstrate that Turkey feels responsible for improvement of conditions in Afghanistan considering that these efforts would provide long-term stability in the country.

## Conclusion

The progress Afghanistan has made since the Bonn Agreement (2001) offers ground for hope. Yet, an important dilemma that faces the international community in Afghanistan is how to better assist state-building while leaving more responsibility to the Afghans since the West has made up its mind to exit from Afghanistan by the end of 2014. After that date, NATO would continue to contribute to training and advising the Afghanistan National Army. This transfer of responsibility is taking place via the so-called "Transition" process.

Although, the Afghanistan National Security Forces have achieved some successes, the effectiveness, professionalism and state of readiness of this security forces is uneven. There is also a possibility of disintegrating of the ANSF along ethnic lines, in case the Taliban, a predominantly Pashtun-majority entity, successfully overruns Kabul after 2014. The way ANSF is targeting their Western trainers, a phenomenon commonly referred to as "Green on Blue Attack or insider attack", questions are also being raised about their motivation and interest to take on the Taliban in the post-withdrawal situation. Meanwhile, the Taliban and its *jihadi* allies, the *Haqqanis* and *Hezb-i-Islami*, remain well-established and strong and actively involved in a nationwide insurgency which includes hundreds of assassinations and suicide attacks. In recent days, both the Afghanistan and U.S have been in favour of negotiating a peace with Taliban that would give the Taliban some role in the future government. However, the reconciliation process with Taliban is yet to produce any result. There are other issues relating to inter-ethnic disharmony, pervasive culture of militancy, radicalisation, warlordism, rampant corruption, narcotic trafficking, growing public apathy—all of which are making matters worse.[33]

In absence of arrangements to supplement the capabilities of the Afghan security forces, common Afghan and security analysts pretend that the withdrawal of NATO forces will likely to create a security vacuum, particularly in the south-eastern provinces, and the Taliban are likely to fill it. Amid this post-2014 scenario, the role of Turkey has great importance.

Although Turkey is not about to increase its troop commitment further soon, its training of the Afghan military, along with its regional diplomatic initiatives aimed at reconciling Afghanistan and Pakistan as well as its economic reconstruction projects, are essential to promoting political stability and Afghanistan's post-conflict reconstruction. In addition, Turkey through its Provincial Reconstruction Teams (PRTs) in Wardak and Jowzjan Province train the Afghan Police, improve judicial administration, develop infrastructure, and support projects such as health and education which are aimed at raising the quality of life of the local population. Turkish civilian-run PRTs are very well received and readily accepted by Afghans because the teams working with indigenous forces are familiar with, among other things, local languages and cultures.[34]

Many European countries have already announced plans to end their missions; others are considering alternative strategies and policies that will stabilise Afghanistan after 2014. One of the options being discussed is transitioning the PRTs into purely civilian roles. The success of the civilian PRTs in Wardak and Jawzjan, initiated by Turkey, may offer a model for part of the contingent of U.S. troops that will stay in Afghanistan after 2014 as advisors and trainers.[35] However, this begs the question of whether civilian PRTs can sustain their efforts without the security umbrella that ISAF currently provides. The same issue also raises the question of how and whether Turkey can sustain a presence there, even in a noncombat role. This will, probably, depend on how much the U.S. eventually commits to Afghanistan beyond 2014.

In light of the above discussion one is led to the conclusion that Turkey's role in reconstruction of Afghanistan with both its hard and soft power assets and its eagerness to be a significant actor, can not be underestimated. The historical and cultural ties have made it easier for Turkey to establish credibility amongst the governments and the people of Afghanistan. Under Turkey's new proactive foreign policy to increase regional cooperation through active diplomacy, the Trilateral Summit process between Turkey-Afghanistan-Pakistan stands unique among other Afghan-related initiatives and this forum is making consistent contributions toward a peaceful Afghanistan. Besides regional and trilateral meetings, there have been other diplomatic initiatives as well like the Istanbul Summit for Friendship and Cooperation in the Heart of Asia or "Istanbul for Afghanistan" Summit in order to negotiate on how to work more efficiently for bringing peace, security and stability in Afghanistan. However, Turkey's need to be fair in its initiatives of regional cooperation for resolving Afghanistan crisis must include all countries of the region particularly India.

## Notes

1. Astri Suhrke, 2007: "Reconstruction as Modernisation: The Post-Conflict Project in Afghanistan", *Third World Quarterly*, vol. 28, no. 7, pp. 1298.
2. Nilufer Karacasulu, 2011: "Reconstruction of Afghanistan and the Role of Turkey", *USAK Yearbook of International Politics and Law*, vol. 4, p.190.
3. Ibid, p.177.
4. Helena Malikyar and Barnett R. Rubin, 2002: *"Center-Periphery Relations in the Afghan State: Current Practices, Future Prospect"*, Center on International Cooperation, December, p. 41.
5. Nilufer Karacasulu, 2011: "Reconstruction of Afghanistan and the Role of Turkey", *N. 2*, p. 191.
6. Ibid.
7. *US Department of Defence*, 2012: "Report on Progress towards Security and Stability in Afghanistan", pp. 72-73.
8. Nilufer Karacasulu, 2011: "Reconstruction of Afghanistan and the Role of Turkey", *N. 2*, p. 191.
9. Vishal Chandra, 2013: *India's Neighbourhood: The Armies of South Asia*, New Delhi, Institute For Defence Studies & Analyses, pp. 11-17.
10. Nilufer Karacasulu, 2011: "Reconstruction of Afghanistan and the Role of Turkey", *N. 2*, p. 190.
11. Kenneth Katzman, 2014: "Afghanistan: Post-Taliban Governance, Security, and U.S. Policy", *Congressional Research Service*, March 4, p. 36.
12. Nilufer Karacasulu, 2011: "Reconstruction of Afghanistan and the Role of Turkey", *N. 2*, pp. 191-192.
13. Kenneth Katzman, 2012: "Afghanistan: Politics, Elections, and Government Performance", *Congressional Research Service*, November 30, p. 36.
14. Kenneth Katzman, 2013: "Afghanistan: Post-Taliban Governance, Security, and U.S. Policy", *Congressional Research Service*, January 4, pp. 62-74.
15. Ahmet Davutoglu, 2008: "Turkey's New Foreign Policy Vision", *Insight Turkey*, vol. 10, no. 1, pp. 77-96.
16. Ibid. pp. 77-96.
17. Ihsan Bal, 2012: "Why is Turkey in Afghanistan?", *Journal of Turkish Weekly (JTW)*, May 2, Turkey.
18. Nilufer Karacasulu, 2011: "Reconstruction of Afghanistan and the Role of Turkey", *N. 2*, pp. 195-196.
19. Ihsan Bal, 2012: "Why is Turkey in Afghanistan?".
20. Aydemir Erman, 2010: "How Turkey's Soft Power can Aid NATO in Afghanistan", *New Perspectives Quarterly*, vol. 27, no. 2, p. 41.
21. Petros Vamvakas, 2009: "NATO and Turkey in Afghanistan and Central Asia: Possibilities and Blind Spots", *Turkish Studies*, vol. 10, no. 1, 2009, pp. 57-74.

22. Karen Kaya, 2013: "Turkey's Role in Afghanistan and Afghan Stabilization", *Military Review*, July-August, Defense Dept., Army, United States Army Command and General Staff College, p.24.
23. Ibid.
24. Richard Weitz, 2010: "Turkey's Efforts to Support Afghanistan Reconstruction", *Turkey Analyst*, vol. 3, no. 3, 15 February 2010; http://www.silkroadstudies.org/new/inside/turkey/2010/100215B.html
25. Karen Kaya, 2013: "Turkey's Role in Afghanistan and Afghan Stabilization", p. 24.
26. Ibid.
27. Ibid. pp. 24-25.
28. Ibid. p. 27.
29. Ibid.
30. Şaban Kardaş, 2013: "Turkey's Regional Approach in Afghanistan: A Civilian Power in Action", *Center for Strategic Research, Ankara*, April, no. 6, pp. 10-12.
31. Ibid. pp. 12-15.
32. Smruti S. Pattanaik, 2012: "India's Afghan Policy: Beyond Bilateralism", *Strategic Analysis*, vol. 36, no. 4, pp. 572-574.
33. Arvind Gupta, Ashok Behuria, Vishal Chandra and Smruti S. Pattanaik, 2012: "Post-2014 Afghanistan and India's Options", *Policy Brief*, Institute for Defence Studies and Analyses (IDSA), pp. 3-5.
34. Karen Kaya, 2013: "Turkey's Role in Afghanistan and Afghan Stabilization", p. 29.
35. Ibid.

# 16
# Turkey's Foreign Aid Programmes and its Foreign Policy Activism in Africa

*Ahmed Raza*

## Introduction

Although, as one part of the world is progressive, wealthier and shifting towards stabilised economy, a state of peace could not be attained in the whole world as a number of people have been still struggling with hunger, poverty and contagious diseases in another part of the world. International crime, wars and conflicts, trade in illegal drugs, and thousands of refugees from troubled zones have also contributed to the problems. In order to tackle these problems, which are being generally faced by the developing countries, global efforts have become the need of the times as it needs an appropriate infrastructure and sound economy. Therefore, the problems of nations are not only their own problems but the problems of the international community due to humanitarian feeling and everyone needs to discharge their own responsibilities. These global responsibilities led to the concept of foreign aid. Foreign aid is all aids given in kind and cash to support developing countries and find solutions to their developmental problems. In order to tackle these development problems globally, the United Nations developed its own institutions like the United Nations Development Programme (UNDP), International Trade Centre (ITC) etc. in the 1960s. However, these institutions have never been adequate to respond to the needs of the underdeveloped and developing nations. As a result of this, national development cooperation agencies were established to help alleviate the burden of the UN institutions. As well as the highly developed nations' agencies like the

United States Agency for International Development (USAID), Deutsche Gesellschaft fur Technische Zusammenarbeit (GTZ), Japan International Cooperation Agency (JICA), Canadian International Development Agency (CIDA), Department for International Development (DFID) etc., there emerged new donor countries to this equation in the recent decades as their economic situation began to allow them to help the outside world as well.[1] The emergence of new players in the donor community such as Turkey, India, South Korea, Mexico, Russia and China has also brought new impetus and opportunities to the global development community. But, in this context, Turkey represents a special case in the sense that on the one hand it is a recipient country, whereas on the other, it is also a donor country.

## Turkey's History as an ODA Recipient Country

The past six decades have witnessed Turkey's evolution from an aid recipient to an emerging donor country. Turkey has been an aid recipient country since the late 1940s. With the implementation of the Marshall Plan, Turkey was offered official development assistance (ODA). Turkey received $150 million of aid within the context of the Marshall Plan, which contributed a great deal to the economic development of Turkey in the 1950s. According to the figures provided by the US State Department, for the purpose of furthering Turkish economic development, the USA has also loaned and granted Turkey more than $12.5 billion in economic aid as of December 2005. In addition to the USA, Japan and Germany are the other two major donors for the betterment of Turkey's economic performance. Technical cooperation between Japan and Turkey started 45 years ago under the programme of 'Acceptance of Trainees'. Through JICA, Japan completed its 'development study' for Turkey in 1965, and its first project-type technical cooperation with Turkey was implemented between 1973 and 1979. Despite that interest, JICA's Turkey Office was only established in Ankara in June 1995. As of 2000, the total budget allocation for technical cooperation for Turkey amounted to roughly 31.46 billion Japanese yen (approximately $286 million). Germany started its technical cooperation with Turkey through its development cooperation agency, the Deutsche Gesellschaft fur Technische Zusammenarbeit, in

1970 within the framework of German–Turkish Technical Cooperation. On behalf of the German Federal Ministry for Economic Cooperation and Development (BMZ), GTZ provided assistance to a wide range of projects in different sectors of the Turkish economy during the 1970s and 1980s. As of 2003, Germany delivered 271 million worth of technical assistance to Turkey in the last 33 years.

### Emergence of Turkish Foreign Aid Programmes

Although Turkey still receives aid at a symbolic level, its stronger economic position and sense of responsibility for promoting international peace and prosperity have enabled Turkey to emerge as a new donor. It started its foreign aid activities programme on June 5, 1985 when it prepared a comprehensive aid package worth $10 million to the Sahel countries under the coordination of the Under-secretariat of State Planning Organization of Turkey (SPO). Since then Turkey's role in the international aid community has fundamentally changed, reflecting the transformations in Turkey's foreign policy orientation. The reason behind this new orientation can be attributed to the foreign policy priorities of the Turgut Özal government of the 1980s, which involved the promotion of Turkey's positive image worldwide, its integration into the world economy, and the use of aid as an effective instrument to enhance Turkey's trade relations with developing countries, especially the less-developed African countries. Indeed, the favourable economic environment that Turkey benefited from after 1984 may have encouraged the government to initiate aid programmes. The period between 1984 and 1989 witnessed the expansion of the Turkish economy, owing to the export-oriented growth strategy pursued by Turkey. During this period, the upward trend of the Western economy overlapped with Turkey's new strategy, resulting in the expansion of the volume of Turkish exports towards Western markets. Emboldened by such a favourable economic climate and in search of new markets in the developing world for its products, Turkish decision makers decided to use all tools available, within the context of aid for trade, including ODA. In addition, the improvement in Turkish living standards may have also encouraged the Özal government to consider tackling some global issues, which included poverty reduction through aid disbursement. This type of initiative served to promote Turkey's visibility in the international arena. Therefore, as a corollary to Turkey's efforts in exploring markets to export its goods, it considered all tools available, including the ODA.

## Key Agencies/Mechanism of Turkish Aid Programmes

As Turkey was exploring ways to reap the advantages of this new geopolitical reality in the Eurasian region and develop closer ties with these newly independent countries, it employed ODA as a powerful instrument to promote its presence. Based on its own previous experience as an aid recipient from important donor countries, Turkish leaders were convinced that effective ODA to these countries would only be possible through the establishment of a full-fledged official aid agency and other important mechanisms. Thus, the Turkish International Cooperation and Development Agency (TIKA) was created in 1992 to meet the immediate aid needs of Eurasian countries.[2]

### *Turkish International Cooperation and Development Agency (TIKA)*

The Turkish International Cooperation and Development Agency (or with its Turkish acronym TIKA) is the Turkish Government's Development Cooperation Agency and falls under the auspices of the Ministry of Foreign Affairs. It was set up by law under Act 480, based on a Cabinet decision in January 1992. TIKA is assigned the following duties and responsibilities by law:

- Defining development needs and targets as well as possible areas of cooperation and assistance while taking into consideration Turkey's priorities;
- Preparing required programmes and projects or facilitating preparation by private sector organisations;
- Improving economic, commercial, technical, social, cultural and educational cooperation through projects and programmes;
- Strengthening independent government bodies;
- Supporting efforts for transition to a market economy;

- Coordinating development cooperation activities of Turkish government institutions.

TIKA has 22 Project Coordination Offices in 20 countries in Africa, Asia and Europe, facilitating the coordination and implementation of its projects and programmes. Aid activities in countries where TIKA does not have an office are managed by the nearest office in the region or by Turkish Embassies and Consulates.

***Ministry of Foreign Affairs***

The Ministry of Foreign Affairs of the Turkish Government performs a guiding function for all public agencies and institutions in terms of development policy priorities. It also handles contributions and membership fee payments to some international organisations.

***Turkish Treasury***

Turkish ODA mainly consists of grants. Grants can be delivered cash or in-kind. Preparations, contacts and negotiations relating to cash grants are executed by the Under-secretariat of the Turkish Treasury in collaboration with the Ministry of Foreign Affairs. It also handles contributions and membership fee payments to some international organisations. On top of that, all development assistance endeavours by Turkish government institutions have to pass via the Under-secretariat of the Turkish Treasury to ensure financial viability of the consolidated Turkish budget.

***Türk EXIM Bank***

Whilst not directly implementing development projects, Turkey's Export-Import Bank and Turkey's Development Bank are involved in the financial and investment dimensions of Turkey's aid programmes. Türk EXIM Bank's annual report gives a good overview of its activities.

***Prime Ministry Emergency Administration***

Involvement of Government institutions (including the armed forces) in Emergency aid is coordinated by the Prime Ministry Emergency Administration.

## Turkish Development Assistance Statistics

Over the past decade the Government of Turkey has significantly increased its international assistance, alongside an expanding geopolitical role in the world. According to statistics collected by the Organisation for Economic Cooperation and Development (OECD), Development Assistance Committee (DAC), Turkey's Official Development Assistance in 2012 reached \$2.5 billion, up from \$600 million in 2005; a four-fold expansion in a mere seven years. The government has committed to reaching \$5 billion by 2015 and \$10 billion by 2020.2 While remaining a non-DAC donor, achieving the 2015 target would rank Turkey the ninth largest donor among the DAC donors, just behind Canada, and the 2020 target would bring this ranking up to sixth position.[3]

### *Turkish Foreign Aid Programmes & Policy and its Foreign Policy Activism in Africa*

The concept of aid to Africa was invented as a strategic tool in the Cold War efforts to ensure that developed countries' industries get subsidised in Africa and to basically maintain dominance and influence.[4] After the collapse of the USSR, in the forming new world order Turkey also had to find its place among the other regional powers. As the result of this development, the Turkish Government issued an Africa plan, called "Opening Up to Africa" in 1998 as in the period from 1923 to 1998 Turkey–Africa relations were at their lowest level. The most important action points of the plan are the following:

- To improve political and economical relations.
- To open three new consulates as soon as possible.
- Turkey to support and initiate every investment, aid and programme that is highly important for Africa in the UN.
- High level cooperation in the field of trade, health care, agriculture.
- To improve the education related relationship.

Within its framework set by the plan, Turkey hoped to further develop its political, economic and cultural ties with African countries in the forthcoming period. However, Turkey's opening to Africa truly came into existence only in 2005 when Turkey's Justice and Development

Party (AKP) Government announced "The Year of Africa" and Turkish Prime Minister Recep Tayyip Erdogan visited Ethiopia and South Africa in March 2005, becoming the first Turkish Prime Minister to officially visit a country under the equator line.[5]

During this same year, Turkey also enhanced its relations with Africa on an institutional level. Turkey obtained "observer status" in the African Union on April 12, 2005, and accredited its embassy in Addis Ababa to the African Union on May 5, 2005. The last African Union Summit held in Addis Ababa in January 2008 declared Turkey as a "strategic partner." It is in this context that there has been a revivalism of the Turkey–Africa relation. However, historically, relations between Turks and Africa go back several centuries. Some African countries were totally or partially subject to Ottoman rule, such as Egypt, Libya, Algeria, Tunisia, the Sudan, Eritrea, Ethiopia, Djibouti, Somalia and even Niger and Chad. In the northern Sub-Sahara region, the Ottomans were part of the balance of powers system, enjoying friendship and alliance with the Kanem Burnu Empire that still prevails in today's Northern Nigeria, Niger and Chad.[6]

On the other hand, in the last decade, aid has been one of the stronger elements in Turkey's overall foreign policy in general and its Africa policy in particular. It has been part of a soft power strategy. Hence, Turkish foreign policy focussed on its aid programmes in order to enhance the relationship as well as preparing for the role of an emerging regional power; therefore, the official Turkish aid agency, the TIKA, which was initially established to help the transition of states in Central Asia, the Caucasus and the Balkans. After 2003, it was transformed into a more global aid agency and expanded its areas of operation and TIKA has opened three offices located in Addis Ababa, Khartoum and Dakar, as part of Turkey's development aid to Africa. Through offices in the continent, Turkey aims to widen cooperation with Africa, and currently its three regional offices implement projects in 37 African countries.[7] Turkey has also promised to provide technical assistance to African countries through TIKA and strives to open an affiliated office in other African countries to further cement cooperation with Africa on the basis of several priorities. Besides the activities of TIKA, Turkey has also utilised international organisations to provide aid to Africa. For example, through the World Health Organization (WHO), World Food Programme (WFP) and the Red Crescent, Turkey has donated 7.5 million dollars to various African countries in the last 5 years (2005–07), to assist them in coping with the negative effects of drought and other natural disasters. In 2008, Turkey allocated 3.5 million dollars of humanitarian aid through the WFP, while in 2009 it made a modest donation of 0.5 million dollars to the African Union budget. In a similar step, in 2007 Turkey hosted for the first time a summit of the Least Developed Countries in Istanbul; 33 out of 49 of which are located in Africa. In this summit, Turkey committed 20 million dollars of development aid for these countries' use. Turkey also hosted the fourth conference on Least Developed Countries in the first half of 2011.[8]

In the last several years, Africa has forged new partnerships and renewed existing ones with several countries, as part of a conglomerate of economic and political entities or even on a bilateral basis. The Turkey–Africa partnership may be seen as the latest strategic link. The first Turkey–Africa Cooperation summit was held under the theme "Solidarity and Partnership for a Common Future" from August 18–August 21, 2008, in Istanbul. The summit is considered by many as a success, in terms of Turkish–African economic relations. It achieved several concrete results, including a decision that the next summit was to be held in an African country in 2013.[9]

In August 2008, TIKA initiated an African Agricultural Development Program in order to help develop agriculture in Africa. This project lasted for two years (2008–10) and was implemented in thirteen African countries—namely Burkina Faso, Djibouti, Ethiopia, Guinea, Guinea Bissau, Mali, Senegal, Comoros, Madagascar, Tanzania, Kenya, Rwanda and Uganda.[10] Politically, Africa expects Turkey's support through its membership in several international organisations. For example, Turkey promised that if it gets elected as a non-permanent member of the UN Security Council for the period of 2009–2010, it will pay special attention to African issues. Given that the Organization of the Islamic Conference and the UNDP have been headed by Turkish citizens, African countries also expect these forums to pay special attention to African issues and see its budding relations with Turkey in this light as an advantage for them.

TIKA has strong relations to all kinds of strategic institutions in Turkey, international organisations like UNIDO, UNDP, OECD, and it has operational units mainly in the countries where humanitarian camps were established. The key regions of its activity are the following: Near East, Balkans, Eastern Europe, Caucasus, Middle Asia, Far-East and Africa of course. However, in 2002 the organisation has only spent $85 million on humanitarian campaigns; this amount reached $780 million by the end of 2008. In Africa, only 6.6% of the total amount— $51.73 million—has been spent in 2008, but in two years it exceeded $967 million. Among the supported countries, Sudan has a special role. The country earned $13.21 million and with that result, on the list of the most supported TIKA countries, Khartoum is on the 13th position. At the moment TIKA has 26 offices in 23 countries all over the world, from which three can be found on the African continent: Ethiopia (2005), Sudan (2006) and Senegal (2007). The African programmes of TIKA mainly concentrated on agriculture, healthcare, supplying drinking water and in other humanitarian fields.[11]

Turkey also attaches great importance to capacity-building projects in African countries. To this end, vocational training courses are organised in Turkey or in partner countries in specific sectors depending on the priorities of partner countries. Besides capacity-building activities, Turkey, through TIKA, undertakes many projects in building physical infrastructures for the provision of social services such as the construction of schools and hospitals.[12] In addition to assisting African countries, Turkey is also actively engaged in international humanitarian efforts to ameliorate the conditions in fragile environments and post-conflict situations.[13]

## Turkish Foreign Policy Activism in Somalia

Turkey's foreign policy activism towards Somalia produced some positive image as over twenty years, many states and entities have tried to bring relief and secure peace in Somalia; often leaving behind a situation messier than that which they found. Hence, Prime Minister Recep Tayyip Erdoğan's courageous visit to Mogadishu in August 2011 at the height of famine and his decision to open an embassy gave fresh impetus to the efforts for establishing lasting peace. Therefore, Turkish Red Crescent, the most active organisation, arrived in August 2011 and made arrangements for various camps for 15,000 internally displaced people (IDPs), with a health facility, mosque and soccer field.

The Turkish government also tries to coordinate aid through the TIKA. It also implements a bilateral development agreement between the Somali and Turkish governments. TIKA's financed projects in Mogadishu include: drilling twenty boreholes, fencing and rehabilitating parts of Mogadishu airport, and restoring some government buildings. It also started rehabilitating Digfer Hospital and 33 km of roads in Mogadishu.[14]

Other Turkish government agencies providing humanitarian assistance include the Health Ministry and the Religious Affairs Directorate in the Prime Minister's Office (known as Diyanet). Since August 2011, the Health Ministry has sent seven teams each comprising some 40 volunteer doctors and medical practitioners, operating in three field hospitals. Diyanet, which has ten staff in Somalia, provided scholarships to 615 students and sent 300 tonnes of food to Somalia. It also distributed copies of the Quran and sent 40 Imams and twenty teachers to Turkey for training and seminars.[15]

## Turkish CSOs and their Activism in Africa

Turkey has had a vibrant, diverse and active civil society working in many areas of social development. It has a long history of private aid and philanthropic charities, including many rights-based NGOs, professional associations, community-based associations, human right associations and faith-based organisations, which form a highly diverse civil society. Turkish CSOs have been involved in international development cooperation at least since the early 1990s in parallel with the Turkish government assistance for Bosnia and Chechnya, working with victims of war. Turkish Civil Society Organisations such as IHH or the Humanitarian Relief Foundation, Turkish Confederation of Businessmen and Industrialists (TUSKON), Deniz Feneri Association, Doctors Worldwide, the Red Crescent, *Yardımeli* and *Kimse Yok Mu* (KYM) etc are the main examples of organisations involved in development cooperation.[16]

### *Foundation for Human Rights and Freedoms and Humanitarian Relief (IHH)*

The IHH is one of the leading humanitarian aid organisations in Turkey. It has been discharging the duty of a more complicated and extensive kind. Among their priorities are humanitarian campaigns, aids, and the aim of cultural and educational development. Emphasising the idea of voluntary, IHH officially tries to give support to anyone suffering from any kind of disease or even poverty. According to their slogan, 'despite the fast changing circumstances of today's world, the unchangeable, everlasting values must be maintained'. In their Africa related activities religion plays an outstanding role. Their aim is not only food distribution. Getting the Holy Quran available for the supported people and financial help with construction of mosques are also part of their activity. For instance during the period of Ramadan, Turkey has started to collect money and food aids for the thousands of suffering people all over the black continent. Along with its developmental work in 43 African countries, it has helped thousands of people to gain eyesight with its Cataract Project conducted in hospitals in Sudan and elsewhere. It also has well-drilling projects and supports technical and vocational education by setting up schools and hospitals.[17]

### *Turkish Confederation of Businessmen and Industrialists (TUSKON)*

It is the largest union of employers in Turkey. Ninety percent of the TUSKON members are Small or Medium Establishments with fewer than 50 employees. TUSKON is engaged in lobbying all decision-makers at the local, regional, national and global levels. It organises a number of delegations of Turkish business leaders with several projects to targeted countries, especially the underdeveloped and developing countries. Through the World Trade Bridge meetings and other means, TUSKON has pioneered the bringing of African businessmen to Turkey and encouraging Turkish businesses to expand to Africa. These meetings have taken place without interruption since 2006 with increasing participation each year. TUSKON also sends delegations to Africa to examine investment opportunities.[18]

## *Approaches to Turkish Foreign Aids Programmes & its Foreign Policy Activism in Africa*

Generally, the concept of foreign aid originated on humanitarian grounds with the purpose of alleviating poverty, hunger, improving health, fighting against disease, helping in crisis and encouraging progress in developing nations. But, aid has not always been given with humanitarian motives, but in some cases for a variety of political, strategic and economic reasons that benefit the donor countries in the long run. During the period of the Cold War up to the 1980s much ODA went to least developed countries (LDCs) for the purpose of maintaining politically acceptable governments and for the supply of natural resources that many LDCs produced. It is observed that the fear of LDCs becoming allies of the former Soviet Union motivated considerable foreign aid from the West. Likewise, the Soviet Union also provided development assistance to Eastern Bloc countries to maintain their allegiance.[19] Although, Turkish foreign policy activism and its aid programmes especially in Africa could be seen in a different perspective as other factors have also contributed to the Turkey–Africa relations.

### Humanitarian Perspective

There are more than a billion people—one in five of the world's population—still living in extreme poverty. Hence, concepts like the problems of nations are not only their own problems but the problems of the international community as well. In order to tackle these global problems, humanitarian feelings have driven world leaders to emphasise foreign aid programmes seriously in the 21st century. Therefore, Turkey also finds its place among the other leader donor countries through foreign policy activism as favourable economic environment encouraged a large expansion of Turkey's economy between 1984 and 1989. Hence, in the last decade, aid has been one of the stronger elements in Turkey's overall foreign policy in general and its Africa policy in particular—as Africa as a geographical area has always been considered a far away land full of problems, hunger, diseases and civil wars and its history has not called any attention in the academia or policy-making circles. The official Turkish aid agency, the TIKA, currently operates in Africa through three offices located in Addis Ababa, Khartoum and Dakar, as part of Turkey's development aid to Africa.

### Historical legacy

Historically, relations between Turks and Africa go back several centuries. North Africa and Sub Saharan Africa are the two main divisions on the geographical line in order of linkage in relation with Turks. Turkey has had relatively strong relations with North Africa, as it was totally or partially part of the Ottoman State dating back to 15$^{th}$ and 16$^{th}$ centuries, such as Egypt, Libya, Algeria, Tunisia, the Sudan, Eritrea, Ethiopia, Djibouti, Somalia and even Niger and Chad. On the other hand, relations with Sub-Saharan Africa are a more recent development, dating back to the 19th century. Hence, Turkey under the AK Party administration has brought a new vision to Turkey's Africa initiative, and certainly aims to fill the relations gap which emerged after nearly a century of negligence.[20]

### Religious Perspective (Islamic Solidarity)

Turkey, being a constitutionally secular state, had always maintained distance from participating in any Islamic or religious meetings, let alone organising such meetings domestically. This began to change after the Justice and Development Party (*Adalet ve Kalkınma Partisi*—AKP) assumed power in 2002 which showed a pro-Islamic approach. Turkey has since then actively participated in the activities of the Organisation of Islamic Cooperation (OIC). Turkey's hosting of African religious leaders in Istanbul relates directly to two paradigmatic shifts in Turkish foreign policy. First, Turkey softened its approach towards religious-based organisations and meetings, seeing these as opportunities to further Turkish national interests through soft power instruments. Secondly, Turkey understood that completing and sustaining its opening to Africa required a religious dimension. This also relates to Africa's Ottoman past, as evidenced by the fact that almost all religious leaders at the meeting positively emphasised their countries' Ottoman legacy and affirmed their wishes to restore it.[21] With the change towards a multidimensional approach to foreign policy, religion has become one of Turkey's soft power elements, and especially so in Africa.

## Economic Perspective

Self-interest is another driving force for donor communities to deliver foreign aid to partner countries.[22] Usually the recipients are required to purchase the exports of the donors. Hence, aid has not always been given with humanitarian motives, but in some cases for a variety of political, strategic and economic reasons that benefit the donor countries in the long run. Therefore, Turkey's Africa policy is driven by a long-term orientation of Turkey in international politics and can be understood within this context. Turkey's opening to Africa has gained more importance in terms of the opening up of new markets as a way to decrease the influence of the global economic meltdown.[23] Turkey´s growing involvement in Africa is also likely to continue in the near future, as it now has a solid economic and social base to support it at home. And Turkey has understood that the world has changed profoundly and new allies, strategic calculations and planning are a must in a rapidly shifting global economy.

## Turkey becoming an Emerging Multi-regional Power

In a broader perspective, Turkey's involvement in Africa has also caught the attention of international actors that have expressed an interest in cooperating with Turkey. The international dimension of Turkey's Africa opening has steadily developed as Turkey makes inroads into the continent. In 2012, Turkish leaders held political consultations with the leaders of US, Spain, UK, Sweden, Norway, Italy and the EU. Some countries like France have even suggested that Turkey and the EU should team up for joint trade missions to Africa in order to counter China's growing power in winning African contracts.[24]

## Conclusion

The evolution of Turkey's experience in foreign aid programmes has been reflective of the broader transformations in Turkey's economy and foreign policy orientation. Turkey has used its foreign aid programmes as a new instrument with the purpose of supporting its foreign policy activism, such as public diplomacy, peace operations, economic issues, mediation, and cultural diplomacy among others. On the other hand, Turkish involvement to Africa has served the best expression of peace globally as it did not experience any kind of disagreement between the state, civil society and the business sector. It has always been felt as a sort of satisfaction from various perspectives. Besides Turkey has a distinctive way of providing aid, as it has aimed to create long term and developmental projects ranging from infrastructure to education. Turkey's development aid has expanded in terms of numbers, content, and areas of operation, just as has been the case for Turkey's foreign policy in general; the challenge now is to ensure the sustainability of this activism, as Turkey as a new actor might trigger interesting reactions from other donors. So far, Turkey has managed to find a modus operandi with other players in Eurasia and the Balkans.

## Notes

1. Hakan Fidan and Rahmand Nurudun, "Turkey's Role in the Global Development Assistance Community: the Case of TIKA (Turkish International Cooperation and Development Agency)," *Journal of Southern Europe and the Balkans* (Online), vol. 10, no. 1, 2008, pp. 93-111.
2. Kulaklikaya Musa and Rahman Nurdun, "Turkey as a New Player in Development Cooperation," *Insight Turkey*, vol. 12, no. 4, 2010, pp. 131-145.
3. T. Daloglu, "Turkey Foreign-Aid Priority is Central Asia", *Al Monitor* (Turkey Pulse), 29 May 2013.
4. J. Gwartney and Robert Lawson (2006), *Economic Freedom of the World—2006 Annual Report*, The Fraser Institute: Vancouver.
5. Mehmet Özkan and Birol Akgün, "Turkey's Opening to Africa", *The Journal of Modern African Studies*, vol. 48, no.4, 2010, pp. 525-546.
6. Mehmet Özkan, "Turkey Discovers Africa: Implications and Prospects," *SETA Policy Brief*, no. 22, 2008.
7. Abdirahman Ali, 'Turkey's Foray into Africa: A New Humanitarian Power?" *Insight Turkey*, vol. 13, 2011, pp. 65-73.
8. Mehmet Özkan, "Turkey's Rising Role in Africa," *Turkish Policy Quarterly*, vol. 9, no. 4, Winter 2010.
9. Ibid.
10. Özkan, "Turkey Discovers Africa".
11. Besenyo János and Péter Oláh, "One of the New Competitors in Africa: Turkey", *AARMS*, vol. 11, no. 1, 2012, pp. 135–148.
12. Musa and Nurdun, "Turkey as a New Player in Development Cooperation," pp. 131-145.
13. Murphy Teri and Onur Sazak, "Turkey's Civilian Capacity in Post-Conflict Reconstruction", Istanbul Policy Center, Sabancı University, 2012.
14. International Crisis Group, "Assessing Turkey's Role in Somalia," *Policy Briefing*, no. 92, International Crisis Group, Brussels, 2012.
15. Ibid.
16. D. Kaya, "Opinion Piece: Implementation Paths and Challenges for CSOs in

Turkey," *Open Forum for CSO Development Effectiveness*, Brussels, 25 October 2012.

17. Ali, 'Turkey's Foray into Africa: A New Humanitarian Power?" pp. 65-73.
18. Mehmet Ozkan, "Turkey's Religious and Socio-Political Depth in Africa," Emerging Powers in Africa, LSE IDEAS Special Report 16, 2013, pp. 45-50.
19. Fidan and Nurudun, "Turkey's Role in the Global Development Assistance Community", pp. 93-111.
20. Mehmet Ozkan, "Turkey's Rising Role in Africa," *Turkish Policy Quarterly*, vol.9, no. 4. (n.d.).
21. Ozkan, "Turkey's Religious and Socio-Political Depth in Africa", pp. 45-50.
22. Fidan and Nurudun, "Turkey's Role in the Global Development Assistance Community", pp. 93-111.
23. Özkan and Akugn, 'Turkey's Opening to Africa'.
24. Ozkan, "Turkey's Religious and Socio-Political Depth in Africa", pp. 45-50.

# Index